INSIDE MANAGEMENT

A Selection of Readings from BUSINESS WEEK

INSIDE MANAGEMENT

A Selection of Readings from BUSINESS WEEK
Second Edition

David R. Hampton

Professor of Management
San Diego State University

McGraw-Hill Book Company

New York St. Louis San Francisco Auckland Bogotá Caracas Colorado Springs
Hamburg Lisbon London Madrid Mexico Milan Montreal New Delhi Oklahoma City
Panama Paris San Juan São Paulo Singapore Sydney Tokyo Toronto

INSIDE MANAGEMENT
A Selection of Readings from
BUSINESS WEEK

1 2 3 4 5 6 7 8 9 0 D O C D O C 8 9 2 1 0 9 8

ISBN 0-07-025954-2

The editors were Kathleen L. Loy and Joseph F. Murphy; the designer was Caliber Design Planning, Inc.; the production supervisor was Louise Karam. The drawings were done by Caliber Design Planning, Inc.
R. R. Donnelley & Sons Company was printer and binder.

Library of Congress Catalog Card Number: 88-60056

Contents

Preface

This second edition of *Inside Management*, like its predecessor, provides a remarkably convenient way to enrich the study of management with timely news and opinion from *Business Week*. Selected articles are organized by the basic topics of management textbooks and course designs. Typically, instructors pair the articles they choose with textbook reading assignments and lectures. The discussion questions at the end of every article invite deeper analysis of the practice of management with the theories and models of management. They also raise new issues and probe for personal opinions and values.

A few examples will suggest how the articles and discussion questions help students move between theory and practice and explore their views:

● Part 1's article "The Battle for Corporate Control" depicts top-level managers as besieged by conflicting demands from various corporate stakeholders. Executives argue that stockholders aren't the only ones with claims upon them, that they must respond to the interests of employees, customers, suppliers, and communities. Institutional investors, on the other hand, charge that managers sometimes hide behind the cloak of social responsibility to deflect criticism of their poor performance. Discussion questions call for identifying all the stakeholders mentioned in the article, and for exploring the implications for corporate success of weighting their importance differently—as do Japanese and American CEOs.

● Part 2's article "Glitzy Resorts and Suburban Hotels: Hyatt Breaks New Ground" reports on how this corporation seeks to expand by building two distinctly different types of hotels. Discussion questions call for analysis of Hyatt's plans using Michael Porter's generic, competitive strategies. They also require analysis of Hyatt's environment for threats and opportunities.

● Part 3's article "Who's Afraid of IBM?" is a richly detailed description of the activities of Compaq Computer Corporation. Its president poses the question: How can we continue to have good teamwork and fast responses and become a very large company? That and other discussion questions require students to ferret out Compaq's own attempts to solve the problem of finding an evolution of organization designs that fit the company's strategy.

● Part 4's article "The Billion-Dollar Whiz Kid" describes the miraculous success of Bill Gates, CEO of Microsoft Corporation. Discussion questions elicit evidence of his characteristics and skills and their role in his leadership of Microsoft. They also explore the reciprocal qualities required to be a successful subordinate under Gates's style. Finally, students are asked to describe the corporate culture at Microsoft and assess its fit with the company's strategy.

● Part 5's article "The Push for Quality" asserts that inferior quality of American products lies at the heart of weak competitiveness of U.S. business in world markets. Discussion questions explore that claim, the argument that scientific management is to blame, the concept of statistical quality control, and cultural differences that might be a factor in readiness to adopt practices that can boost quality.

● "Part 6's article "McWorld?" reports the success of McDonald's overseas. Discussion questions examine both the need for McDonald's to grow in this particular way and the combination of centralization and decentralization that appears central to its international success.

Instructors use the questions provided and original ones for stimulating discussion, for written assignments, and for examination questions. Whatever the variations, those of us who teach management generally welcome ways to help students cultivate skills to diagnose situations, to reason analytically making effective use of facts and concepts, and to express their thoughts. We welcome instructional materials that bring reality into the classroom and help us understand the deeper structure of events. *Inside Management* is offered to serve these purposes.

David R. Hampton

PART 1

MANAGERS AND MANAGING

Management courses and textbooks typically begin with a look at the processes of management and the roles and activities of managers. That organizations are systems alive in an aggressive and sensitive environment, a point also stressed early in the study of management, means that the population and work of managers change. The first two articles in Part 1 concretely illustrate two current changes of great importance. The first reports the progress of women in management; the second, the pressures on corporate executives from shareholders. A third article describes recent and faddish efforts at teaching practicing managers how best to cope with the evolving demands of their work.

Subsequent articles in Part 1 offer background information, exemplars, and advice to those who want to plan their education, job hunting, and on-the-job behavior to boost their careers in management. A final article reports the compensation of America's highest-paid executives in 1986. Lee Iacocca of Chrysler Corporation led the pack with $20.5 million, a fact that alone can start a remarkable class discussion of the role, power, and value of management in society.

CORPORATE WOMEN

THEY'RE ABOUT TO BREAK THROUGH TO THE TOP

JUNE 22, 1987, PP. 72-78

If you were searching the ranks of *RJR* Nabisco Inc. for a future chief executive, Ellen R. Marram would be an obvious candidate. As head of the $1.2 billion-a-year grocery products division, which sells 5 of Nabisco's 10 hottest brands, the 40-year-old Harvard *MBA* commands 4,000 employees and has earned a reputation as a persistent innovator. She has launched successful new lines and boosted market share for mature brands such as Fleischmann's margarine and Cream of Wheat.

Marram is one of the few women in America with wide-ranging, high-level line responsibilities at a major corporation. And it is from these tough, general management jobs that Corporate America generally selects the next generation of *CEO*s and other top managers.

Executives like Marram are thus in the vanguard of a new era for the corporate woman. About 37% of corporate managers now are women, compared with 24% a decade ago. And more than one-third of the 70,000 *MBA*s graduating each year are women, up from only 12% a decade ago and 2% in 1967.

More important than the numbers, female managers are finally moving beyond the mid-level and staff positions where they staked their claim in big corporations during the 1970s.

Women who are among the nation's highest-ranked female executives, selected from a survey of *BUSINESS WEEK* Top 1000 Companies, differ sharply from a group of successful businesswomen who appeared in a 1976 *BUSINESS WEEK* survey (page 6).

The new crop, which entered the work force in the late 1960s and 1970s, is better-educated, more determined to advance, and more apt to be "Organization Women," keeping mum on gender-related inequities. These women are more likely to be managers, and they hold far more senior positions. And because there are more of them, collectively they have a better shot at becoming chief executive officers.

Their odds of success are improving for other reasons, too. For one thing, the broad economic shift from manufacturing to services, a business sector that accepted women managers earlier, gives them a better chance of landing top jobs as opportunities expand. Second, many of the men working their way up in Corporate America are accustomed to having women as peers. They went to business school and lived in college dorms with women. They've worked with women as colleagues, subordinates, and superiors. None of this was true of the generation of men who now command most big U. S. companies.

PIVOTAL ROLE. Of course, women executives still face hurdles. At many companies, they encounter old-fashioned prejudice and resistance. On average, executive women still earn less than their male counterparts—42% less, according to a study by headhunters Heidrick & Struggles Inc. And finally, many women simply don't want to make the family sacrifices generally required in the highest ranks of Corporate America. It is no accident, for example, that of a group of 50 top women surveyed by *BUSINESS WEEK*, nearly half have never married or are divorced. Of those who married, almost one-third do not have children. Because women generally still bear the primary burden of child-rearing, many well-qualified professionals who are mothers just don't want high-pressure corporate jobs—or decide to drop out temporarily.

Some management experts predict it might take another generation before female *CEO*s are more than a rarity. "Quite a few companies and industries still haven't had their female pioneers," points out Elizabeth E. Bailey, dean of Carnegie-Mellon University's business school.

Yet other forces are at work that favor the continued progress of women in Corporate America. They are getting a boost from the wave of restructurings, spinoffs, and leveraged buyouts. These huge corporate reshufflings have broken up long-entrenched male cultures. Take International Harvester Co. (now Navistar International Corp.). Before it hit financial trouble in the late 1970s, female executives existed only in narrowly defined areas such as communications. But as Harvester peeled off division after division, a new culture was born. Now, one of Navistar's top officers is 34-year-old Roxanne J. Decyk, a senior vice-president for administration who plays a pivotal role in everything from strategic direction to labor relations.

Female executives are gaining ground for another reason, too. As it becomes more socially acceptable for women to focus single-mindedly on their careers, many are doing just that. Today's successful women contrast with their predecessors who more often tried to juggle the demands of home and office. Some of the jugglers, it now seems clear, never advanced as far as they might have.

"Women today feel free to express what we'd seen as male qualities: goal-orientation, competitiveness, the ability to conceptualize, the aggressive pursuit of responsibility," says Felice N. Schwartz, president of Catalyst, a New York research firm on corporate women. At the same time, women are being promoted because they bring new management styles to the corporation. Experts say that female personality traits, such as an ability to build consensus and encourage participation, are in demand today. Says Gerard R. Roche, chairman of Heidrick & Struggles: "Women typically show more warmth and concern about human relationships and human sensitivities."

Consider Nabisco's Marram. She is not an imposing figure. She's small and proper, wears her hair short, and prefers stylish dress to buttoned-down clothing. A 1968 graduate of Wellesley College and a 1970 Harvard *MBA*, she entered the

work force when women were just beginning to take jobs outside the teacher-nurse-secretary track. **DIRECT CHALLENGE.** Then, the number of executive women was infinitesimal. Women who tried to get jobs prior to the 1964 Civil Rights Act faced even bigger problems—outright rejection for positions and promotions. A typical experience: Zoe Coulson, 55, now vice-president for consumer issues at Campbell Soup Co., was a copywriter in the 1950s for a New York advertising agency. Coulson recalls her boss telling her: "You are a woman, so you aren't getting any other jobs here."

Marram began her career after the work environment had brightened. She joined Lever Brothers as a marketing assistant in 1970, jumping to Johnson & Johnson's Personal Products Co. two years later as a group products manager. In 1977, she took a similar job at Standard Brands Inc., which was acquired by Nabisco in 1981. Working her way through the product management and marketing side of the business, Marram took bold and innovative steps—using advertising, financing, distribution, and sales tactics—to fend off competitors on important product lines.

Her fourth promotion came in January, when she was named president of her division, a mini-conglomerate of eight product categories from cereal to margarine. "It was like becoming an orchestra conductor," Marram says. Her mission: to lead eight vice-presidents, for marketing, business development, finance, manufacturing, information systems, quality assurance, personnel, and research and development.

Last spring, Marram faced a test of her mettle from, ironically, her former employer, Lever Brothers. Its Promise margarine posed a direct threat to Fleischmann's, which was a 28-year-old, no-cholesterol, premium product that had been growing by a percentage point or two a year.

The task of launching a counterattack fell to Marram. First she decided she'd need a multi-million-dollar budget. But to get it, she would have to siphon money from other products. "It was a big risk," Marram says, "because we didn't know if our investment would pay off." She had to increase sales, and to do it she conceived a new ad campaign.

"We wanted to talk about heart disease," she

says. "But do you go all the way to someone who's had a heart attack or to someone who's worried about having one?" Marram took a stand, and the result was a powerful commercial: "I'm not an actor. I'm just a guy, 30 years old, who had a heart attack. . . . Fleischmann's margarine, ask your doctor."

She also shared Nabisco's sales analysis of margarine brands with supermarkets, winning the goodwill of grocers. They used the information to balance shelf supplies more efficiently. And Marram fine-tuned Fleischmann's promotional programs, tailoring them to regional markets. The result: Fleischmann's sales growth zipped up 15%, keeping the lead.

'FEROCIOUS.' Last fall, she scored another coup in the face of internal opposition. Her plan to increase the package size of Nabisco's instant Cream of Wheat meant raising the price. Some managers balked. "It was a huge debate," says Peter N. Rogers, president of Nabisco Brands *USA*. "John Murray [distribution and sales president] got ferocious. He said, 'That's stupid. The reason we've hung in there is we have a slightly smaller package and we're 10¢ below Quaker on the shelf.' Ellen said we should increase the package size so there'll be more servings per package."

Marram persisted until she prevailed. Nabisco's market share grew from 12% to 14% in six months, a $5 million gain. "It's ironic that she has such intuition about consumer behavior, because she doesn't shop much in grocery stores," Rogers says.

Like many of her successful counterparts in Corporate America, Marram plays down being a woman. She's not likely to lead a crusade for women's rights or blame a personal setback on discrimination—attitudes that have hindered women from progressing up the corporate ladder in the past. "I'm not sure anything I have to say has to do with being a woman," she says. "I suspect it doesn't."

Similarly, Ellen N. Monahan, 41, R. J. Reynolds Tobacco *USA*'s vice-president for planning, says: "I'm not a card-carrying feminist. The feminists got the revolution started in the 1970s. But the time when you were judged likely to fail before you had a chance is behind us."

One study found that women managers who were vocal about their gender were more likely to be derailed. "When you are a minority in a majority culture, there are taboos against speaking out," says Ellen Van Velsor, co-author of *Breaking the Glass Ceiling*. "They were seen as being too ambitious or too concerned about their status as a woman in the company."

That's one major difference between this new generation of women and the original female pioneers. "Five or 10 years ago," says Roche, "there was a defensiveness. They'd enter the room and say, 'I know you aren't going to like me.' They've matured and grown in many key jobs."

To understand successful corporate women such as Marram, you have to reach far back in their lives. As children, many of these women developed a strong bond, almost a mentor relationship, with one or both parents. Marram was close to her father, Stanley, a retired postman who owned a suburban Boston haberdashery. When Marram was only 3 years old, her father brought home Golden Books for her to read, and they would comb *The Boston Globe* for grammatical errors they could laugh at.

A former captain of the Boston University debate team, Stanley spent hours at the dinner table debating current politics and history with Ellen. "My father taught me not to take things at face value," says Marram, the older of two daughters by seven years. "There are a lot of sides to every issue and a number of solutions to each problem. That's something I think of every day in business." Her mother, Bertha, was employed as a social worker before her first daughter was born.

SATISFACTION. Like Marram, few of the most successful women had parents in the corporate world. Decyk's father worked in an outboard motor factory in Waukegan, Ill. An immigrant from the Ukraine who spoke seven languages, Walter Decyk had been a teacher and an artist. "I learned from him that you should not depend on your job alone to give you satisfaction," Decyk says. Her mother, Tillie, however, was her role model, because she worked outside the home as a hospital administrator and nursing instructor.

Many of these women cultivated basic values in their homes that they later drew on in corporate

WHERE ARE THEY NOW? BUSINESS WEEK'S LEADING CORPORATE WOMEN OF 1976

In 1962, when she was 30, Charlotte Schiff-Jones broke into the corporate ranks—as a secretary. Fourteen years later, she was one of the Top 100 corporate women featured in a 1976 *BUSINESS WEEK* cover story. Today she and many of her peers are frustrated with women's slow progress up the corporate ladder. Many are sticking it out, though, resigned to the idea that they may advance—but never to the highest corporate offices. Others have abandoned big companies to start their own businesses, new careers, or families.

The turning point for Schiff-Jones came in 1980, when *CBS* Inc. passed her over for the top job at its new, cultural cable-*TV* channel. She was shocked. She had suggested the project, spent five months on a task force planning it, and boasted 10 years of cable-*TV* experience. But a man without a cable-industry background was named general manager, while she was appointed marketing vice-president. When *CBS* later scuttled the venture, she left the corporate arena for good.

'DRIVEN OUT.' It was a painful bump against what has been dubbed the "glass ceiling"—a barrier that women often encounter in their corporate ascents. For Schiff-Jones, 55, whose life mirrored the changing role of women and work, the experience was especially frustrating. She left her suburban housewife's life in 1962 to become a secretary at a *TV* production company. But galvanized by *The Feminine Mystique*, she strived to attain higher positions. She worked in *TV* production and marketing and eventually was named executive vice-president of Manhattan Cable Television Inc., a Time Inc. subsidiary. She earned an *MBA* from Columbia University in 1977 and joined *CBS* in 1980.

Her career track was typical of the new opportunities for women in Corporate America. But now she must confront the limitations. "I'm one of the women driven out of corporate life," says Schiff-Jones, now a media consultant. "To put it simplistically, men don't like us there. There are more women battling men for jobs at the middle levels, but the real ceiling hasn't budged an inch."

A disturbing number of women who appeared in *BUSINESS WEEK*'s 1976 story echo that stark assessment. Those 100 women were bankers, lawyers, and managers, and they worked in industries as diverse as cosmetics andpetroleum. But their careers reflected a fundamental change in corporate culture. They were the vanguard, racking up many "firsts": the first woman vice-president, the first woman director, the first woman partner of a Big Eight accounting firm. In those heady days, anything seemed possible—including a shot at the chief executive's job.

Now, little more than a decade later, it is clear that the optimism was overblown. Of course there have been promotions. Patricia Wier moved from vice-president at Encyclopedia Britannica to president of the *USA* division of the company. Camron Cooper, formerly an investment officer with Atlantic Richfield Co., has become treasurer and vice-president. But not one of the women from the *BUSINESS WEEK* Class of '76 holds the top spot in a major public corporation, except for those who inherited positions or started their own businesses. And few seem likely to get there: Most hold staff jobs or appear stuck in middle management.

NO PLACE TO GO. *BUSINESS WEEK* tracked 46 women from the original list of 100. Of the 27 still working, 16 have stayed with the same companies. Three women have changed employers but remain in a corporate setting. Seven left the corporate world to start their own businesses or join professional firms. Only one left to start a family. The other 19 retired. In all, only five women are working in the kinds of line jobs considered crucial for a shot at senior executive positions.

What is more disturbing is that nearly one-third

of the women surveyed have left their corporate jobs. Why? Rarely because of the oft-cited conflict between work and family. Women such as Schiff-Jones quit because they felt there was no place left to go.

The fault may lie in a communication gap between a male-dominated corporate culture and the women themselves. Schiff-Jones says she would still be scaling corporate heights if not for a series of misunderstandings. After earning her *MBA*, she became associate publisher of Time's *People* magazine. She took the job producing a television version of *People*, not realizing it lacked the blessing of corporate brass. When the show was canceled, she couldn't get back on track at Time.

Taking the producer's spot was a mistake, she now realizes. Later she declined lateral moves Time offered, thinking she would wait for a promotion. None of her male managers advised her to make the sideways move as an interim step. She now thinks she missed some signals.

Faced with uncertainty about her career, Schiff-Jones approached *CBS* with the idea of starting a cable channel. Was she then passed over for the general-manager position because she was a woman or because the male *CBS* veteran who had no cable experience was legitimately more qualified? Thomas F. Leahy, president of *CBS* Television Network Inc., says the decision had nothing to do with Schiff-Jones's gender.

ON THE LINE. Another reason women became disenchanted is that they often were pigeonholed in staff jobs, such as public relations or personnel. Tina Santi Flaherty initiated several public-relations coups while she was vice-president at Col-

gate-Palmolive Co., including the Colgate-Dinah Shore Golf Championships. She became public affairs vice-president at *GTE* Corp. in 1984 but left last year to become a consultant. "I had thought I could make it to the top," she says. "To be fair, it's not likely that a man in a communications role would have been promoted to *CEO* either. The difference is that men in those jobs often get a chance to try a different arena."

The chance to try a new arena kept Mary Beth Crimmins moving through the corporate ranks at *ARA* Services Inc. After holding a variety of staff jobs, including vice-president of school services, she made the move in 1983 to regional vice-president. She is responsible for $60 million in sales in a 10-state Western area. "It was the only place for me to go," she says of her new job. "In order to progress in the company, I had to have some line experience."

Of course, some promising women managers leave the corporate rat race so they can devote more time to their families. J. Diane Folzenlogen Stanley held a high-profile position as treasurer of Electronic Data Systems Corp. in the 1976 survey. But she gave up 60-hour workweeks the following year to raise children and work in her husband's accounting firm. "I knew I had the ability, but I didn't want that kind of responsibility," she says of a potential top job. "I'm not saying most women can't do it, but most are not willing to make that sacrifice." Even for those in the 1976 group who were willing to make the sacrifice, however, it wasn't enough to carry them to the top.

By Gail DeGeorge in Miami

life. Diane C. Harris, who has risen to vice-president for corporate development after 20 years with Bausch & Lomb Inc., has a father who was a vice-president of a New York City carpenters' union when she was growing up on Long Island. "I got my negotiating skills from him," Harris says. "He taught me leadership and a sense of fair play."

To make progress in the corporate world, most successful women have sacrificed something, be it

marriage, family, or personal time. Says Navistar's Decyk, a veteran of two failed marriages: "I've concluded after some disappointment that if you're going to have successful relationships, you have to spend time working on them. I had gotten so thrilled with the demands of the job, I put family and friends in a distant second place."

Many successful women have nontraditional home lives—patterns that are becoming increasingly common. Marram, for example, married Manhattan lawyer David A. Ruttenberg, 50, last year after they'd known each other for six years. She works a 65-hour week, plus commuting an hour to Nabisco in Parsippany, N. J., from her co-op on Manhattan's Upper West Side. They spend weekends at their Westport (Conn.) home. Their lifestyle leaves little time for cooking or grocery shopping, much less children, none of which she is interested in. Marram checks for Nabisco products in New Jersey stores but rarely stops to make a purchase. Most nights, she and her husband eat take-out Japanese and Chinese meals.

Ellen M. Hancock, president of International Business Machines Corp.'s $5 billion communications products division, accepted three posts that required her to live away from her home and husband for extended periods. Those jobs were critical to her selection as the first woman division president at the company. "Those Friday night and Sunday night planes get to you," Hancock says. "But I got a good promotion out of it."

The Hancocks, both *IBM*ers, have devised an arrangement to fit the demands of their jobs. Most nights, W. Jason Hancock, a 54-year-old manager who develops software for *IBM*'s internal financial systems, arrives first at their Ridgefield (Conn.) home and does the cooking. Known for her limitless energy, Hancock has stayed at work until 2 a.m. when an important project is afoot. She also travels more than her husband and brings home a fatter paycheck. Does he mind? "I guess she'll take me to some nice places as a corporate husband," he jokes.

SORE POINT. Throughout their lives, such women have used their wits and persistence to turn critics into supporters. Hancock joined *IBM* as a programmer in 1966, after graduating from Fordham University with a masters' degree in math. Her presence in the male-dominated world of computer programming initially was a sore point, at least for her future husband. "I didn't like to work with girls, but my boss said, 'Take the girl along,'" recalls Jason. "I was impressed by how much she knew. I came back to my office and told my boss I was going to marry Ellen." They were married four years later.

Marram faced similar skepticism from classmates at Harvard business school in 1968. One of

three women in a section of 100, she sat quietly in the back of the classroom her first year. "She was so cute and attractive, initially I thought she would be the first to fall off the career ladder," says Lawrence Lovig, a Bain & Co. manager and former classmate. "But after you know her, you see a lot of intelligence and creativity and a core of steel guiding her." She had another obstacle to overcome. Marram hasn't had full use of her right arm since birth.

She is self-effacing about her success, attributing it to the efforts of "the team." When Marram speaks about her work at Nabisco, she says "we" more often than "I." "Nothing ever happens in a company because of one person," she says. "You have to work well with people and be a team player."

Marram wins praise from subordinates who say she doesn't hesitate to work alongside them. Preparing for a product test on a tight schedule, Marram once came onto the factory floor and started packing boxes of sanitary napkins.

The ability to motivate employees is a trait shared by many corporate women. When Hancock moved a group of 100 technical employees from a facility in Kingston, N. Y., to Raleigh, N. C., she sent a personalized welcome letter and flowers to all employees' hotel rooms on their first house-hunting trip. Donna R. Ecton, vice-president for administration at Campbell Soup, views her management style as a cross between "cheerleader and evangelist. If someone does something special, I will send flowers or balloons, whether they're male or female." When she ran Chemical Bank's midtown Manhattan branches in 1979, she went so far as to personally deliver boxes of candy to branch employees—and to hug them—the day they fought through a snowstorm to get to work.

'MAN'S WORLD.' Decyk was promoted at International Harvester specifically to bring a more participatory style to what had been an autocratic culture. Former Chairman Donald D. Lennox says he named her senior vice-president in 1984 after she had been with the company for three years over the protests of older male managers who objected to having a woman as a boss.

Will women like Decyk, Hancock, and Marram make it all the way to the top? They certainly have barriers to overcome. Marram, for one, has strong qualifications to put her in the running for *CEO*. But she still faces male bias. "She's female in what is essentially a man's world—sales," says Nabisco's Rogers. "She has to learn spontaneity. She thinks very well, but I'm trying to get her to be a little more risk-taking. It's not as easy to be a woman in that job."

Where success eventually takes Marram is not as important as the fact that she and her peers have cleared the way in upper management for generations of women to come.

By Laurie Baum in New York, with bureau reports

DISCUSSION QUESTIONS

1. What general trends and conditions bear upon the changing situation of women in management?
2. What specific obstacles and opportunities confront corporate women, and how do they differ from those which confront men?
3. What stereotypical views of women can you recognize in the article, and how can they affect thinking about women as managers?

THE BATTLE FOR CORPORATE CONTROL

MANAGEMENT IS BEING ASSAILED FROM ALL SIDES. WHO'S IN CHARGE HERE?

MAY 18, 1987, PP. 102-109

The setting is New York's Metropolitan Museum of Art. The date: Apr. 14. The occasion: International Paper Co.'s annual shareholder meeting. Corporate gadfly Lewis D. Gilbert stands up, his red patent-leather shoes sparkling, to remind directors that shareholders, not managers, own a company. Board members, sitting on a stage towering over the audience, smile benignly and agree wholeheartedly.

Then another shareholder rises. The smiles disappear. Richard M. Schlefer, investment manager of the $30 billion College Retirement Equities Fund *(CREF)*, proposes a resolution condemning management for adopting a poison pill to thwart hostile takeovers. He wants it put to a vote. Chairman John A. Georges stares down at Schlefer and defends the measure. "We wanted to protect the company against opportunists," he says. Schlefer is incensed. As he later puts it: "*CREF* owns 800,000 shares of International Paper stock, the bulk of it for 10 years. Who's the opportunist?"

Ten-weeks earlier, Roger B. Smith, chairman of General Motors Corp., is on an unexpected three-state odyssey to meet with some of *GM*'s biggest shareholders. Angered at his ousting last year of dissident director H. Ross Perot with $700 million in "hushmail," they berate Smith for *GM*'s meager profits, its falling market share, and its poor productivity despite $40 billion in new equipment since 1979. Why, they ask, is management paying itself big bonuses when much smaller Ford Motor Co. had overtaken *GM* in earnings? In a booming market, *GM*'s stock had moved mainly sideways. Unless Smith acts, some of them, members of the Council of Institutional Investors, threaten to introduce a proposal at this month's shareholder meeting critical of management.

Within weeks, *GM*'s management announces a series of major policy changes. The company says it will buy back stock, cut capital spending, trim production to reduce burgeoning inventories, and replace cash bonuses for managers with a stock-incentive compensation plan linked to long-term performance. The institutional shareholders withdraw their proposal.

If major earthquakes begin with minor tremors, then the events at *IP* and *GM* foretell traumatic times ahead in Corporate America. *CREF*'s proxy proposal against the poison pill at *IP* didn't win, but it got more support than anyone expected—28% of the votes cast. It was a direct challenge by big shareholders to the way corporations are actually governed. It won't be the last. Nor are Smith's efforts to mollify restive shareholders likely to be his last. The tight hold professional managers have on the corporation is slipping. Investors are no longer passive. Outside directors are asserting themselves. Other stakeholders—from employees (page 14) to communities—want a voice. The internal balance of power is beginning to shift.

At heart, the turmoil calls into question the very nature of the corporation. Traditionally, managers work for shareholders and are charged with maximizing the return to these owners of the corporation. But over the long term or the short term? And is this theory valid when institutional shareholders control so much stock and move big blocks at the drop of a computer program? "What right does someone who owns the stock for an hour have to decide a company's fate?" says Andrew C. Sigler, chairman of Champion International Corp. "That's the law, and it's wrong."

'HOGWASH'? Executives insist that they have duties beyond maximizing value for shareholders. "We have 40,000 employees and 1.3 million representatives around the world," says Hicks B. Waldron, chairman of Avon Products Inc. "We have a number of suppliers, institutions, customers, communities. None of them have the democratic freedom as shareholders do to buy or sell their shares. They have much deeper and much more important stakes in our company than our shareholders." Managers contend that only they can balance those conflicting claims—especially in today's mercurial markets.

"Hogwash," say institutional investors, who charge managers with hiding behind the cloak of social responsibility to entrench themselves in their jobs and deflect criticism of their poor performance. Many institutions insist that they don't fit the image, drawn by managers, of short-term investors allied with Wall Street arbitrageurs and the hated corporate raiders. They're interested in the long term, but they are also fed up with executives for mismanaging corporate assets, fending off raiders with greenmail, and, above all, evading market discipline with poison pills, staggered boards, and dual classes of stocks that stack voting power in friendly hands. "We view tender offers as a kind of free, competitive market for management," says Schlefer. "The best managers

will end up running a company."

It may be that the corporate raiders, in their quest to make a fast buck with underperforming companies, started this ruckus. But the questions they raised about managerial competence have found a receptive audience throughout the U. S.— not just among investors. Some government officials, citing "corpocracy," blame managers for the decline of global competitiveness and the gaping trade deficit. Employees criticize managers for making longtime workers pay for strategic errors with draconian layoffs, while they float to soft landings with lucrative golden parachutes.

By any measure, the current crop of corporate managers has reigned over an era of unprecedented American economic decline. For at least a decade, America's standard of living has been eroding, its share of the world export market shrinking, and its products retreating in the face of foreign competition. So it's no accident that the dominance of management is being challenged today.

FIRST STEP. "The system does not work the way it's supposed to," says Arthur R. Taylor, dean of the Fordham University graduate business school and former president of *CBS* Inc. "No one is happy. There's a sense that there's a kind of rot here." The increasingly powerful public institutional owners who banded together in the Council of Institutional Investors are spearheading a movement for change. With more than 50 pension fund members controlling $200 billion worth of investments, the *CII* is leading the proxy fight against antitakeover tactics in about 40 shareholder meetings this spring, from United Technologies to Control Data to J. C. Penney. Beyond that, some institutions are voicing complaints directly to management.

The *CII*'s campaign is only the first step in what promises to be a sustained drive by some institutions to chisel away at management control. It's easy to see why. Stock ownership today is in fewer hands than at any other time in the past 50 years. Institutional pools of money have grown so large that they can't easily be shifted from one stock to another.

More than ever, pension funds, pumped up to fulfill requirements of the Employee Retirement

Income Security Act *(ERISA)* of 1974, are the kingpins on Wall Street. Their assets have mushroomed from $548 billion in 1970 to more than $1.5 trillion now—and more than a third of that is invested in equities. In 1965, pension funds held only 6% of all corporate equity. They now own about a quarter of it. By the year 2000 that share could climb close to 50%, according to the Federal Reserve Board. And that doesn't count other institutions, which are also booming. Terrified of the new world of options, stock indexes, and program trading, individuals have been seeking the sanctuary of professional investment managers.

Together, the stock holdings of all institutions—pension funds, mutual funds, insurance companies, banks, brokers, and dealers—now add up to a third of all corporate stock, up from 25% in 1977. The figure is even higher at the big corporations that make up the Standard & Poor's 500-stock index. At Ford, institutions hold 63% of the stock; at Digital Equipment, they own 81%; K mart, 79%; and Citicorp, 72%.

The enormity of their holdings is leading to a major change in the way many institutions perceive entrenched management. The old "Wall Street Walk"—simply selling investments in a company whose performance is under par—doesn't work anymore. "We're not in a position to sell our stock. We own stock in 1,350 corporations," says Harrison J. Goldin, comptroller of New York City and co-chairman of the *CII.* "We could sell a given company here or there. But we've got to reinvest the money."

HUFFING AND PUFFING. That attitude is most common among Goldin's brethren at public pension funds. But lately some private money managers are coming around to that view—for pocketbook reasons. "The traditional institutional response is to vote with your feet," says John B. Neff, who manages $6 billion for Vanguard Group of Investment Cos. "But you can't do that anymore. The size of our position is such that it's hard to get out of some of our positions [without losing a lot of money]. The alternative of trying to alter management is sometimes necessary."

Neff is at the forefront of the professional money managers who may join the nascent institutional movement to invade the exclusive policy purview of management. Most professionals are still paid to beat the market—every quarter. They won't wait out changes in management policies. Huffing and puffing to try to outperform the *S&P* 500, they move in and out of stocks. Institutions make some 70% of the trades on the Big Board. "There's immense churning," says Champion's Sigler.

Mutual fund managers and investment advisers are guilty of much of that churning: They replace some 60% to 65% of their portfolios every year. That fickleness, executives claim, leaves their companies victim to raiders and thus forces managers to focus almost exclusively on short-term earnings to keep their stock prices up. As a result, companies are now managing their financial books—not their operations.

But Sigler and his colleagues must share the blame. Even while *CEO*s around the country complain about the short-term financial horizon of institutional investors, the worst offenders at churning are often corporate pension funds controlled by the same *CEO*s. The big public funds, such as the State of Wisconsin Investment Board and the California Public Employees' Retirement System, turn over about 20% of their portfolios a year. They tend to manage their portfolios inside and hold stocks for an average of about five years. Private pension funds, usually managed by professional advisers, churn much more. For example, Bell & Howell Co. turns over 40% a year. Avon uses three outside advisers who last year posted turnovers of 9%, 57%, and 75%.

'VICIOUS CIRCLE.' No one forces the corporate pension funds to move in and out of stocks so quickly. *ERISA* sets very broad investment parameters; investing for the long term would not violate fiduciary responsibilities. It is the *CEO*s themselves who control what performance targets are set and how their funds are managed. "We in the corporate world are our own worst enemy," concedes Avon's Waldron. "We call the money managers in here every quarter and we measure their performance, and if it's not better than the *S&P* 500, we fire them. It's a vicious circle."

Yet there is no evidence that playing the investment game for the short term makes any more profit than using long-term strategies. Most mon-

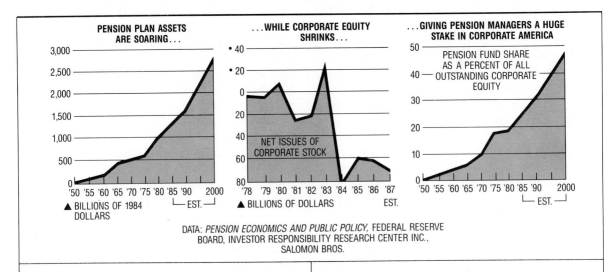

PENSION PLAN ASSETS ARE SOARING...

3,000
2,500
2,000
1,500
1,000
500
0

'50 '55 '60 '65 '70 '75 '80 '85 '90 2000
▲ BILLIONS OF 1984 DOLLARS
└─ EST. ─┘

...WHILE CORPORATE EQUITY SHRINKS...

• 40
• 20
0
20
40
60
80

NET ISSUES OF CORPORATE STOCK

'78 '79 '80 '81 '82 '83 '84 '85 '86 '87
▲ BILLIONS OF DOLLARS   EST.

...GIVING PENSION MANAGERS A HUGE STAKE IN CORPORATE AMERICA

50
40
30
20
10
0

PENSION FUND SHARE AS A PERCENT OF ALL OUTSTANDING CORPORATE EQUITY

'50 '55 '60 '65 '70 '75 '80 '85 '90 2000
└─ EST. ─┘

DATA: *PENSION ECONOMICS AND PUBLIC POLICY,* FEDERAL RESERVE BOARD, INVESTOR RESPONSIBILITY RESEARCH CENTER INC., SALOMON BROS.

ey managers have barely kept up with the *S&P* 500 in recent years. The evidence shows that those with a long view do better. In the past six years, *SEI* Corp. says, low-turnover portfolios averaged a 15.2% return, while high-turnover portfolios averaged only 13.5%. Even over a period of a decade, the low-turnover portfolios outperformed the churners.

But no group of money managers has consistently outperformed the *S&P*, up at a 20% annual rate in the past five years and 14% over the decade. Institutions, angered at this shortfall by their investment advisers, are stashing a growing portion of their cash in index funds. By simply putting billions into a weighted bundle of stocks that duplicates the *S&P* 500, they make sure they do at least as well as the overall stock market. Nearly $150 billion, 15% of all institutional equity holdings making up 7% of the entire stock market, is now indexed. *CREF*, which is a leader in the wave of proxy fights against poison pills, indexes about 80% of its $30 billion equity portfolio.

But even if institutions merely "buy the market" and not specific companies, indexing doesn't reduce their incentive to force changes in corporate control. Issues like poison pills or one share, one vote still matter a lot. In fact, they matter even more. Indexing depends on the smooth workings of the market, and anything that might interfere, such as poison pills or dual stock classes, hurts potential performance. "If you are indexed, you have a vested interest in increasing market

efficiency," says James E. Heard, corporate governance service director at the Investor Responsibility Research Center Inc. "The issue of one share, one vote has an important meaning for market efficiency."

If changes were made to reduce churning and to give managers longer-term planning horizons, everyone would be better off. Ironically—and management may not believe this—that appears to be what the market has been saying all along. Managers long have argued that it's the market that forces them to focus on the short term. But economists say there is no empirical evidence to support that. Just the opposite is true, says Kenneth M. Lehn, an economist formerly at the Securities & Exchange Commission and now at Washington University in St. Louis. Using spending on research and development as a proxy for investing for the long term, he found a direct relationship between large institutional shareholdings and bigger *R&D* expenditures.

NEW ACTIVISM. What's more, Lehn discovered that the market appears to reward companies that increase *R&D* expenditures: The stocks of these companies jump an average of about 1% on such announcements, he says. Indeed, it is the companies that don't invest in the future that are most vulnerable. Institutions dump these stocks, making them easy prey for corporate raiders. Surveying 217 companies taken over from 1980 to 1984, Lehn found that 160 of them did not list any material *R&D* expenditures in their financial reports. The remainder spent an average of 0.77% of revenues on *R&D*, less than half of that spent in those industries by companies that eluded the raiders. In sum, the market does seem to reward companies that invest in the long term.

But if managers can't blame the infamous corporate raiders for forcing them to focus on next quarter's earnings, they can accuse them of sparking the new activism among institutional investors. It all began about three years ago, when California State Treasurer Jesse M. Unruh, who ultimately oversees the state's pension funds, began to grow increasingly angry about greenmail payments and the losses they represented for shareholders. He and other officials from other state pension funds got together to form the *CII*. If the group had a motto, it might be what Oregon State Treasurer William D. Rutherford states flatly: "Institutional investors are not happy being treated like poor relations."

The group aims, in Goldin's words, to "assure that American public companies will be adequately responsive to shareholders, to consider them in the basic decisions in fundamental matters of policy." Above all, *CII* says it seeks a dialogue with managers. Members want to meet with management—as they did with *GM*—to make sure their opinions are considered and that management is accountable to someone. *GM* has, for example, agreed to set up a regular forum through which the institutions can be heard. *CII* members are also testifying at hearings in Washington and going public with some of their concerns. And they are likely to keep bringing up disputes with management through proxy resolutions. Eventually, the *CII* may orchestrate the voting of proxies in concert.

Not all big institutions are happy putting pressure on management. "That's not our role," says Martin Shea, senior vice-president at J. P. Morgan & Co. "Our role is to select the best-performing companies in the best industries with growth prospects." Shea has plenty of company among private money managers. So far, opinion on the role of the institutional shareholder generally splits along public-private lines. "The privates vote with management," says Heard.

But that statement is far too sweeping. Many money managers at mutual funds and even banks admit privately that they are voting against management—against poison pills—at some annual meetings this year. And cracks are beginning to fissure the ranks of private money managers. Some 34 institutions—including such big names as Citibank, First Boston, Bankers Trust, Alliance Capital Management, T. Rowe Price, and John Hancock Financial Services—have signed on as "sustaining members" of the *CII*. Eager to get private money managers into the fold, the *CII* wants them to help analyze corporate reorganizations and financings. Several attended *CII*'s annual meeting, held recently in Santa Monica, Calif. "They wanted to see how we function, how we thought, and that we're not hostile to business," Goldin declares.

Management seems terrified by the thought of having more diligent watchdogs on its trail. As Ira M. Millstein, counsel to the Business Roundtable, told *CII* members in Santa Monica: "Of course you are a threat to Corporate America. You represent change. Nobody likes change."

Indeed, corporate managers are fighting back. By the time this spring's proxy season drew near, many had appealed to their counterparts around the country for help in fighting the resolutions introduced by *CREF* and its fellow interventionists. Dozens of *CEO*s sent letters to their colleagues urging them to persuade their own pension fund managers to vote with management on antitakeover issues. They all said basically the same thing. As Theodore F. Brophy, chairman of *GTE* Corp., put it: "I would greatly appreciate your providing specific voting instructions to your money managers to vote for the proposals adopted by *GTE*'s board."

In a similar vein, Robert Anderson, chairman of Rockwell International Corp., wanted help to push through the setting up of two classes of stock at his company. "We are proposing this action in view of today's corporate takeover practices which frequently put companies 'into play,' often to the advantage of arbitrageurs and other short-term traders, but quite often to the detriment of long-term investors, employees, customers, and the communities in which businesses are located," Anderson wrote on Jan. 29, 1987. "I solicit your assistance in encouraging your pension fund managers who hold Rockwell stock to vote for the proposal."

A BIG WIN. Sigler, *IP*'s Georges, and Bell & Howell Chairman Donald N. Frey are among the *CEO*s who have sent similar missives. The letters are setting off a storm of protest from many of the big institutional investors, who claim the executives have no businesss influencing the proxy voting of their own pension funds. The funds, they say, have responsibility only to current and future pensioners, not to the corner office.

They are finding a receptive ear in Washington. "We are very concerned about the recent attempts to influence the votes of fiduciaries," says David M. Walker, Deputy Assistant Labor Secretary for pension and welfare benefit programs. "The area of corporate governance in proxy voting falls within the rubric of *ERISA*." Dallas L. Salisbury, president of the Employee Benefit Research Institute, a private think tank, goes further: "When a *CEO* starts calling like that, *ERISA* is why you have to

'WE'RE NOT GOING TO SIT AROUND AND ALLOW MANAGEMENT TO LOUSE THINGS UP'

Unions traditionally have accepted the idea that they should bargain for all they can get and allow management to run the business, however badly. But today unions are challenging management on a wider range of issues than ever before, using leverage gained from substantial stock ownership, board representation, and, in extreme cases, threatened worker buyouts. Management no longer can count on employees being silent partners in companies that they think are mismanaged.

The most dramatic union challenge to management is under way at Allegis Corp. (formerly *UAL* Inc.), where the Air Line Pilots Assn. is offering to buy the United Air Lines portion of the company for $4.5 billion. *ALPA*'s bid represents much more than a tactic in a labor-management battle. It is a broad-scale attack on Allegis Chairman Richard J. Ferris' strategy of trying to integrate the company's airline, hotel, and rental-car businesses. Although Allegis has rejected the offer, the pilots intend to press their case. "Our management has had the attitude for several years: 'We'll manage, and you fly the airplanes,'" says F. C. Dubinsky, *ALPA* chairman at United. "We've been flying the hell out of the airplanes, but they haven't been managing." Replies Ferris: "Our pilots are good people. I just wish they'd stick to flying."

ESOPs EVERYWHERE. The trend toward an expanded worker role in ownership and management is most widespread in airlines, trucking, and steel—industries that are being restructured because of deregulation and foreign competition. The growing number of companies wholly or partially owned by Employee Stock Ownership Plans (*ESOPs*) is also increasing the voice of labor—union and nonunion—at all levels of the corporation. Some 8 million workers belong to *ESOPs*, and the number of plans is rising at a 7% to 8% annual rate.

In the early postwar years, companies fiercely resisted attempts by the burgeoning labor movement to encroach on management's exclusive "right" to run the business. Unions accommodated to this definition of their role as long as management provided jobs and a rising standard of living. But this "social contract," says Joseph R. Blasi, a researcher on employee ownership at Harvard University, "has fallen apart in the era of shutdowns, mergers, the decline of the labor movement, and the rise of foreign competition." Now unions contend that employees have more at stake in a company—and suffer more when it is poorly managed—than shareholders, managers, and institutional investors. Therefore, labor wants to share power with owners and managers.

"We're not going to sit around and allow management to louse things up like they have in the past," says Lynn R. Williams, president of the

tell him to go to hell." If fund managers automatically vote for management without weighing the costs to plan members, it's illegal under *ERISA*. "If they know about all this stuff, they should be turning these people in," adds Salisbury.

While some in Washington may be balking at such corporate heavy-handedness, executives have found many friends there. In mid-April they won a major round when the U. S. Supreme Court upheld an Indiana law that allows management to wait 50 days before responding to a takeover bid and mandates a shareholder vote once a bidder buys 20% of a company's stock. The delay could easily up the financing ante for would-be acquirers. States around the country, including Delaware, where much of Corporate America is incorporated, are considering similar statutes.

'TROUBLEMAKERS.' These days executives are also getting more attention for their complaints on Capitol Hill. In early March, Senate Banking Committee Chairman William Proxmire (D-Wis.) allowed 16 *CEO*s to vent their spleen about corpo-

United Steelworkers. In return for wage concessions, *USW* members have won substantial stock ownership—and decision-making voice—in companies such as National Steel, Bethlehem, *LTV*, Wheeling Pittsburgh, McLouth Steel, Kaiser Aluminum, Colorado Fuel & Iron, and several smaller companies. Directors nominated by the *USW* now sit on the boards of *CF&I*, Kaiser, Wheeling Pittsburgh, Bliss-Salem, an Ohio manufacturing company, and Copper Range, a Michigan copper mine.

The intrusion into the managerial domain is part of Williams' strategy to play a central role in investment and labor decisions to preserve as much of the battered steel industry as possible. Like *ALPA*, the *USW* is willing to engage in leveraged buyouts, if necessary, to keep steelmakers out of the hands of raiders who have no interest in operating the companies. Indeed, the *USW* negotiated with Victor Posner for a possible stake in Sharon Steel Corp. before it recently went into Chapter 11.

Rail unions are offering to buy parts of railroads that are up for sale. At Pan American World Airways, four unions are seeking a merger partner. Through a combination of wage concessions and borrowing through an *ESOP*, the unions would throw in their lot with another company to get rid of Pan Am's present top management. The company rejected the unions' bid for increased stock ownership in return for concessions. "We're concerned about job security and the survivability of the carrier," says Margaret Brennan, president of the Pan Am Labor Council.

MORE CLOUT. Blasi believes that if American management doesn't improve its performance, co-alitions of employees and institutional shareholders eventually will form to challenge managers. One such case occurred in the mid-1970s when churches holding stock in J. P. Stevens Co. sponsored dissident shareholder resolutions calling for a change in the company's labor policy. This was one of many pressures that eventually caused Stevens to bargain with the Amalgamated Clothing & Textile Workers Union. A big barrier to this kind of movement, however, is that institutions such as pension and mutual funds still seem satisfied with short-term rewards, while employees stress such long-term goals as reinvestment for job security.

Meanwhile, employees are gaining influence over management decisions in thousands of privately held companies in which *ESOP*s hold a substantial amount of stock. The National Center for Employee Ownership estimates that nonmanagement employees sit on boards of directors at more than 300 of these companies, and employees can vote their *ESOP* stock for directors in many hundreds more. Until now, *ESOP*s have been established predominately in small to midsize private companies. But employees own at least 20% of nearly 30 publicly traded companies with more than 1,000 workers.

American labor has no intention of pressing for laws, like those in West Germany and Sweden, that mandate worker representation on corporate boards. But labor's aggressive use of the tools of ownership is fast eroding the old concept that only management has the right to run the business.

By John Hoerr, with Harris Collingwood, in New York

rate raiders and the need to reform securities laws. Said *USX* Corp. Chairman David M. Roderick: "Takeovers have become so abusive and so tilted in favor of the financial buccaneers that remedial action is required." Roderick may get help. Proxmire will soon introduce a bill designed to slow down substantially the hostile takeover game.

In the House, Representative John D. Dingell (D-Mich.) has already introduced a bill to rein in management by limiting greenmail and poison pills and tame raiders, too, with new provisions on disclosures for stock purchases, among other things. It also mandates one-share, one-vote stock. Says Dingell: "The one-share, one-vote provision, under which each share of common stock will carry one vote, will restore the traditional common-law approach under which shareholders are the true owners of corporations—notwithstanding the tendency of directors and managers to view them as 'dissidents' or troublemakers."

Dozens of similar bills have been introduced on the Hill. And, with the Democrats back in control of Congress, there's likely to be some action. The measures with the best chance of passing would extend the time period tender offers must remain open from the current 20 trading days and require that purchasers of 5% of a company's stock disclose their holdings faster than the currently required 10 days.

Meanwhile, the *SEC* is also taking up the one-share, one-vote question, which of late has acquired a mom-and-apple-pie flavor. Already, the New York Stock Exchange and the National Association of Securities Dealers, which oversees the over-the-counter market, have agreed to impose a one-share, one-vote rule for new listings on the three national exchanges, with limited exceptions. Only the American Stock Exchange has yet to go along, and it may discuss it at a May 14 board meeting. *SEC* Chairman John S. R. Shad, who has worked hard on this issue for a couple of years, appears to want an agreement before he becomes ambassador to the Netherlands.

All these measures may force managers to be more accountable to shareholders, while perhaps curbing the excesses of the raiders, too. Amid all the turmoil, however, one thing appears to be very clear. The battle between managers and shareholders for corporate control is only just beginning. The days when *CEO*s could neglect their big institutional owners and other corporate stakeholders are coming to an end. Where there has been little direct accountability, now managers will have to listen to—and learn from—other groups who are demanding a voice in the running of the corporation.

But there is some danger in owner activism, particularly as it spreads beyond the issue of anti-

SOME COMMONSENSE TINKERING MIGHT BE ALL THAT'S NEEDED

The corporation, perhaps more than most institutions, is based on a series of myths. Managers serve owners. One share of stock gets one vote. Shareholders elect representatives to the board of directors. The free market disciplines winners and losers. All the myths have a purpose: to make us believe the corporation is accountable and efficient.

The truth of the matter is that the public corporation has generally been a benevolent autocracy for decades. Managers have run the show. Shareholder meetings have been elaborate ceremonies. Proxy votes have been foreordained rituals. People

who have served as directors on boards have usually been friends of the boss.

For a long time, it didn't matter. As long as management delivered on economic growth, we shared in the myths and convinced ourselves of the international superiority of the American corporation. But in the early 1970s the U. S. economy started to run out of steam. At first we blamed the Vietnam War and the Great Society for our economic problems. Then we blamed *OPEC*. The real hammer on the economy, though, came from another source: foreign competition.

It forced us to face the truth. Once Europe and

Japan emerged from the shadow of World War II and began competing on world markets, we realized that American corporations had been playing, for 25 years, not on a level field but on an empty one. When other players showed up and challenged them to a game, they often crumbled.

The raiders, for all their greed, were the first to understand that many American corporations weren't measuring up. Their raids exploded the myths and revealed that the governing corporate elite was generally not managing economic assets very well. Worse, managers could do almost anything to keep their jobs—and usually get away with it.

It is no surprise that the issues of ownership, control, and accountability were first raised during an earlier time of tremendous economic strain. In 1932, Adolf A. Berle and Gardiner C. Means published *The Modern Corporation & Private Property*. In the corporation, they noted, shareholders surrender their wealth to outside management. The interests of those parties diverge. The problem gets worse as the number of shareholders increases and their influence grows even more diffuse. Management is often left to go its own way, accountable more in theory than in practice.

But today, owners are starting to act as if they really owned the companies once again. Only this time, the owners are not the Cornelius Vanderbilts and Andrew Carnegies but giant institutions. Their assertion of the rights of ownership is bringing howls of protest from entrenched management. Corporate managers, led by the Business Roundtable, are beseeching Congress to help them keep control.

They are proposing many silly, self-serving remedies. One oil company executive has suggested that raiders be required to write impact statements before being allowed to complete a deal. Management, meanwhile, would still be free to close plants, sell assets, or do whatever it wants without such constraints. Other managers want to make shareholders hold stock for six months before they're allowed to vote on proxy resolutions or bids, yet still feel free to lay off 20-year employees.

But these ideas don't address the nub of the problem. In the new battle for control, managers and institutional shareholders accuse each other of

SOME SUGGESTIONS FOR REFORM

MANAGEMENT SHOULD...

- Link operating managers' compensation to long-term performance.
- Give all employees a share in the improved performance of a company through incentive plans that reward increases in productivity, quality, or profits.
- Measure the performance of pension fund managers against long-term goals, not quarterly targets.

INDEPENDENT DIRECTORS SHOULD...

- Limit golden parachutes.
- Base executive compensation largely on long-term performance.
- Assert their independence on critical issues.

SHAREHOLDERS SHOULD...

- Always vote—and not automatically with management.
- Insist on quality outside directors.
- Buy stock in companies where management is investing for the long term.

GOVERNMENT SHOULD...

- Mandate one share, one vote for common stock, unless shareholders approve more than one class of stock.
- Require buyers of 5% of a company's stock to disclose within 24 hours, not 10 days.
- Ban two-tier tender offers. Require tender offers to remain open for 30 trading days, instead of 20 days.
- Require shareholder approval of poison pills and greenmail—including the payment of a raider's investment banking and legal fees.
- End "supermajorities," which require more than a simple majority to win proxy votes.
- Require independent firms to conduct proxy voting, thus allowing secret balloting and auditing of shareholder votes.
- Change securities regulations to give shareholders the same chance as management to get resolutions adopted.

precisely the same things—not being accountable and not focusing properly on long-term performance. There is an element of truth in what both groups are saying. That doesn't mean we need a raft of changes in corporate law. On the contrary, some commonsense tinkering is enough to allow markets to work the way they're supposed to. What can be done?

First, we need to recognize that takeover threats are generally good medicine for weak management. Neither Congress nor the U. S. Supreme Court, which recently upheld an Indiana law making mergers more difficult, should stand in the way of legitimate mergers and acquisitions. At the same time, no chop-shop raider should be able to grab a company overnight, with little investment of his own, for speculative purposes.

Between these two extremes lies reasonable compromise. A splash of cold water on some incendiary raider tactics would cool things down a bit. Coercing shareholders by paying those who tender quickly more than others could be ruled out-of-bounds. Requiring earlier disclosure of 5% stakes and preventing two-tier tender offers appear to be in order. To balance those moves, Washington could mandate one-share, one-vote common stock (table). And the government could tackle the problem of reforming antiquated proxy voting systems.

NO PARACHUTES. A number of securities regulations also need to be rewritten. Management rarely loses proxy battles, because the odds are stacked in its favor. Executives can use company funds to reach voters with all the arguments they want to offer. In contrast, shareholders are obliged to finance their own campaigns, can't solicit proxies from all shareholders, and have to confine their arguments to a limited number of words if they use the proxy published by the company.

Shareholders, outside directors, and managers have the most powerful levers to improve long-term performance and management accountability. Harried *CEO*s, striving to meet quarterly goals, could relax a bit if they told their own pension-fund managers, who do much of the stock-churning anyway, to forget quarterly earnings and look to long-term corporate performance.

Boards of directors could go a long way toward keeping management focused on the basic business of the company if they reminded themselves who elected them, if only in theory. Outside directors play a special role: They can make sure that compensation systems are fair and are geared to long-term performance. That probably means dumping golden parachutes for executives. After all, there aren't any for the 20-year employee forced to bail out. There aren't any parachutes for shareholders, either.

Managerial autocracy has not produced the kind of productivity and growth needed for America to succeed in the world. It's time for a change. The way corporations are governed is very much a competitiveness issue. Managing corporations for the short term is anticompetitive. And bad management is anticompetitive.

takeover measures. "If you've got all these institutional investors railing at corporate management, you put them off balance, and you may find yourself doing more damage than good," says Morgan's Shea. Agrees money manager Neff: "Institutional investors should be heard, but we can't manage companies."

Perhaps more worrisome, management may be hearing unrepresentative viewpoints. So far, the key activists are coming from the public pension funds, and these fund managers have their own constituencies to satisfy. Will a California fund manager be as eager to see a plant closed in Oakland as a plant in New Jersey—even if it's best for the company? Just as national politics has been splintered—and sometimes paralyzed—by the rise of special interest groups and political action funds, so, too, does the rise of activist shareholder groups pose the same risk for corporations. It may be only those who can organize and who have funds who can make their voices heard. The little guy may get lost in the shuffle.

Politics itself may be a problem. Many public fund managers already function partly in the political arena, and they could pervert the process to further political ambitions. At least one money manager believes that already happened at the *GM* meetings. "It seemed like a platform for [*CII* members] to get their names in the newspapers," he says.

Yet managers can't reverse what's happened any more than King Canute could turn back the tides. Owners who act like owners are here to stay. Once the activist institutions show some success, the other corporate stakeholders are sure to push harder for bigger voices, too. Employees and communities both have valid claims on a corporation and the way it's managed. From now on, executives will have to be much more accountable for their performance. For the foreseeable future, the corporate balance of power has changed.

By Bruce Nussbaum and Judith H. Dobrzynski in New York, with bureau reports

DISCUSSION QUESTIONS

1. Management textbooks typically picture an organization such as a corporation as the center of a constellation of claimants, interest groups, "stakeholders," and environmental factors. Implicitly, the top corporate managers are taken to be the principal contacts with these stakeholders. On the basis of this article, draw your own diagram with the corporation in the center and name all the stakeholders (of which shareholders are one) that circle and seek to influence the corporation.

2. When Japanese CEOs are asked to identify the stakeholder group to whom they feel most obligated, they say it is their employees; American CEOs say it is their shareholders. What implications, if any, do you think this difference would make in American and Japanese management and in their comparative corporate success?

BUSINESS FADS: WHAT'S IN—AND OUT

EXECUTIVES LATCH ON TO ANY MANAGEMENT IDEA
THAT LOOKS LIKE A QUICK FIX
JANUARY 20, 1986, PP. 52-55, 58-61

Allan A. Kennedy had just delivered his $5,000, 90-minute pep talk on corporate culture to a select group of top executives of an industrial-service corporation.

The show was slick. Kennedy, a former McKinsey & Co. consultant and co-author of *Corporate Cultures*, had run through his chat on company rituals some 200 times. "By now I've got an act that could play on Broadway," he says.

Yet even Kennedy was taken aback by the audience's enthusiasm when the curtain came down. "This corporate culture stuff is great," the chairman raved at dinner following the talk. Then, turning to his president, he demanded, "I want a culture by Monday."

Astonishing as it may seem, the executive was serious. There is, of course, merit in Kennedy's belief that a corporation's culture—its shared values, beliefs and rituals—strongly influence its success or failure. But it would seem obvious to most executives that a culture must be built over years, not ordained overnight.

Or would it? Like Kennedy's client, a lot of American executives these days seem eager to latch on to almost any new concept that promises a quick fix for their problems.

Having trouble developing new products? Try "intrapreneurship," the process for getting entrepreneurial juices flowing in a big company.

Having a tough time competing against the Japanese? Try "quality circles," the managerial export from Japan that has U. S. workers and managers sitting around tables finding ways to increase productivity and ensure quality.

Having problems with employee productivity? Try "wellness," the new buzzword for fitness programs that encourage managers to exercise, eat healthy foods, and stop smoking.

Facing the threat of a hostile takeover? Restructure your company by writing off a mature business and taking on a mountain of debt. Wall Street will almost surely respond by jacking up your stock price, and that should keep the raider at bay.

HOLLOW SYMBOLS. There's nothing inherently wrong with any of these ideas. What's wrong is that too many companies use them as gimmicks to evade the basic challenges they face. Unless such solutions are well thought out and supported by a sincere commitment from top management, they are doomed to fail. They quickly become meaningless buzzwords, hollow symbols, mere fads.

Even more disturbing is how these fads change, often by 180°. In the 1960s it seemed everyone wanted to diversify, to become a conglomerate. Today, an opposite trend has emerged under the fancy rubric of "asset redeployment." It's the term for conceding that a past diversification spree was a mistake, for spinning off businesses and getting back to the basics.

Or take strategic planning. In the late 1970s it was all the rage. Following the lead of General Electric Co., many companies hired planners at corporate headquarters to chart the future plans of their businesses. Today corporate planning staffs have been substantially reduced or eliminated, because it makes more sense for line managers, closer to the business, to plot strategy.

Business fads are something of a necessary evil and have always been with us. What's different—and alarming—today is the sudden rise and fall of so many conflicting fads and how they influence the modern manager.

What's hot right now? "Touchy-feely" managers who are "demassing." Translation: Nice-guy bosses are laying off still more workers. Other companies are forming "strategic alliances"—launching a joint venture with their No. 1 competitor, perhaps, to plug a product or technology void. The thoroughly modern corporation wants to turn its managers into "leaders" and "intrapreneurs" through "pay for performance." Those same managers flock to Outward Bound expeditions to learn survival skills.

On the other hand, autocratic bosses are out. So are the corporate planners and economists who not long ago pontificated on "reindustrialization," "synergy," and "management by objectives." On the way out: the hostile takeover wave that has dominated business for the past two years, the raiders who used junk bonds, and the golden parachutes that managers devised to protect themselves from the raiders.

And so it goes, to the consternation of those whose task it is to run a business. "Last year it was quality circles," says Harvey Gittler, a Borg-Warner Corp. manager in Elyria, Ohio. "This year it is zero inventories. The truth is, one more panacea and we will all go nuts."

'This corporate culture
stuff is great.
I want a culture by Monday'

He is not alone in this feeling. A marketing manager with a big Midwest equipment maker feels whipsawed. "In the past 18 months, we have heard that profit is more important than revenue, that quality is more important than profit, that people are more important than profit, that customers are more important than our people, that big customers are more important than small customers, and that growth is the key to our success," he recounts. "No wonder our performance is inconsistent."

One new fad seems to be an attempt to clear up some of this confusion. Some large companies, including General Motors Corp. and Ford Motor Co., have issued managers glossy, pocket-sized cards to remind them of their companies' guiding principles—a key ingredient of their changing corporate cultures. Ford's mission statement—handed out last March—was two years in the making, involved hundreds of employees, and was O. K.'d by its board of directors. Some *GM* managers have been issued as many as three reminders, each adorned with a mug shot or two of the top brass. Call it Management by Card.

Why the proliferation of business fads? And why have they become more ephemeral than ever? Perhaps it's because many managers are frustrated by their inability to compete in a world marketplace. Or perhaps it's because they are under intense pressure from Wall Street to perform short-term miracles. The result is a mad, almost aimless scramble for instant solutions. "We're all looking for magic," explains Thomas R. Horton, president of the American Management Assn. "If you tell me I can avoid a cold by taking half a pound of Vitamin C, I'll want to believe you even if it only gives me indigestion."

The search has fueled an industry of instant management gurus, new-idea consultants, and an endless stream of books promising the latest quick fix. Indeed, when it came time for Ralph H. Kilmann, a University of Pittsburgh business professor, to concoct a title for his new management book, he settled on *Beyond the Quick Fix*, in itself a reflection of how faddishness has come to dominate management thinking.

The book's point will probably be lost on many managers, however. A major corporation recently asked Kilmann if he could give its top 50 officers a seminar on his new book in only 15 minutes. "You mean you want me to do *Beyond the Quick Fix* quickly," he responded. The author declined the invitation.

TANGLED WEBS. It is not clear how big a threat this rash of palliative trends poses. Business fads have waxed and waned through the decades, yet corporations survive. Faddish ideas began to influence U. S. executives in a major way with the emergence of the professional manager in America after World War II. Seat-of-the-pants management was becoming old hat. Instead it became popular to follow the principles of Frederick Winslow Taylor, the inventor of time-and-motion studies 50 years earlier. He contended that running a company should be more a science than an art.

Managers rushed to try scientific methods, such as observation, experimentation, and reasoning. They immersed themselves in quantitative analysis. "Operations research" became the rallying cry. By itself, not a bad idea. But the success of operations research begat a series of unintelligible acronyms and buzzwords and an avalanche of charts, curves, and diagrams.

Remember *PERT*? Program Evaluation & Review Technique charts were spiderweb-like diagrams to ensure that projects would be completed on time. "We all did them," recalls Donald N. Frey, chief executive of Bell & Howell Co. "But it took so much effort to get the charts done, you might as well have spent the time getting the job done."

Frey, then a young manager at Ford, had a rude awakening about *PERT*'s pitfalls. "We went to Wright Patterson Air Force base, where they had *PERT* charting down to a science. They had more guys working on *PERT* charts than they had doing the job. It was an enormous overhead cost just to allow the generals to show visitors their *PERT* charts."

Executives also found that management by objectives, another 1950s invention, often tangled them in paper. "We got so balled up in the details that we spent more time on paperwork than the whole damn thing was worth," says George W. Baur, president of Hughes Tool Co.'s tool division.

MAINFRAME MONKEYS. When the mainframe computer came along in the 1950s, it contributed to the mounting pile of paper. Many companies installed computers in rooms with huge display windows to show them off. "A lot of people got computers because *GE* got them," says Ian Wilson, a 26-year *GE* veteran now with the Stanford Research Institute. "It was monkey see, monkey do."

When *GE* decentralized its operations in 1950, scores of companies followed, thinking that this was the antidote for corporate bureaucracies. Similar moves became so fashionable that almost no executive could be heard advocating centralized management. That is, until some companies discovered that decentralizing led to more vice-presidents who built up their own cumbersome fiefdoms and gave line managers even less autonomy.

Centralized companies decentralized, and then some decentralized corporations centralized. "It depended on which consultant you hired," remembers Donald P. Jacobs, dean of Northwestern's Kellogg School of Management.

In the 1960s a wave of "people-oriented" management thinkers gained prominence. Many of the fads they promoted mirrored social trends. T-Groups, group encounter sessions for executives, came into vogue as the Beatles and Bob Dylan sang to a new, less bridled generation. Their popularity heralded the start of the touchy-feely approach to business; "sensitive," participative managers started sharing the spotlight with the management-by-numbers conglomerateurs who dominated the times. The new managers espoused

Theory Y, a model for participative management created by a Massachusetts Institute of Technology management professor, Douglas McGregor, in the 1950s. It was the beginning of the end for Theory X, an authoritarian form of governance that grew out of managers' World War II military experiences.

Oh, how the times had changed. John Clemens, then a young, freshly scrubbed manager for Pillsbury and now a Hartwick College professor, remembers it well. Along with 20 or so colleagues, he was summoned to a country-club meeting room to face a bearded, rather hip, psychiatrist. The T-Group trainer, Clemens recalls, instructed them to take off their ties, shoes, and name tags. Then the lights went out.

"We began crawling on the floor in the dark when I bumped into our president," he says. "It was atrocious. We would have done better figuring out how to sell more brownie mix."

Tens of thousands of managers from such companies as *IBM*, *TRW*, Union Carbide, and Weyerhaeuser trekked to T-Group sessions in search of self-awareness and sensitivity. The concept, popularized by National Training Laboratories, was simple: Mix a dozen or more people together in a room without a leader or an agenda and see what happens. Often, delegates would hurl personal insults across a room. The resulting "feedback," it was hoped, would make Theory X managers less bossy and more participative.

PLOTTING PEOPLE. As the decade came to an

SEARCHING FOR EXCELLENCE AT $4,000 A CRACK

Senior Writer John W. Wilson recently sat in on a session of the Skunk Camp, one of the hottest executive seminars around. Here is his account:

We start the day by pulling on our bright red sweatshirts and stretching awkwardly in unison. When aerobics palls, we jog determinedly along a kelp-covered beach. We eat a quick, communal breakfast, and by 8:15 we are gathered attentively in the conference room waiting for enlightenment.

In walks our rumpled leader. Head down, hands in the pockets of his shapeless brown cords, he paces restlessly. His voice climbs to the treble clef as he runs through the litany: "De-humiliate-.... Get rid of your executive parking spots .... Listen to your customers.... Get everybody on the same team.... There are two ways to get rich: superior customer satisfaction and constant innovation."

It's a message that is familiar to anyone who has read *In Search of Excellence* or its sequel, *A Passion for Excellence*—and no wonder. The speaker is Thomas J. Peters, co-author of both best-sellers, and what he has to say draws heavily on his now-familiar prescriptions for

management success. But that doesn't trouble this audience of what one skeptic calls "Excellence groupies."

CLOSE TO MYSTICISM. These 40 managers come from companies that have accepted the books as gospel and have put up $4,000 to send each one of them to Skunk Camp—a four-day executive seminar that is essentially an immersion in Tom Peters' theories and personality. And they love it, almost to the point of mysticism. "Tom is a missionary," says John G. Alexander, a senior vice-president of Bank One in Columbus, Ohio. "He's an evangelist," chimes in Donald Dempsey, a Xerox Corp. vice-president.

I'm not convinced, but I have to admit it's an impressive performance. The trendy Skunk Camp show, orchestrated by Peters and co-director Robert Le Duc, goes on six times a year at the Pajaro Dunes vacation development on Monterey Bay, 70 mi. south of San Francisco. The name is derived from Lockheed Corp.'s legendary "Skunk Works," a cloistered research and development operation, which Peters holds up as a model of innovation. A skunk symbol decorates all the seminar literature, T-shirts, tote bags, coffee mugs, and other paraphernalia that the attendees carry away.

end, T-Groups gave way to Grid-Groups. And T-Grouped managers such as Clemens became G-Grouped quickly enough. Launched by Robert R. Blake and Jane S. Mouton's *The Managerial Grid* in 1964, the grid rated managers on two characteristics—concern for people vs. concern for production. "The beauty of it is that you could plot people all over the place," adds Clemens. "If you scored a high concern for people and a low concern for production, people would say, 'This guy's a wimp. He's a 1-9.' If you had a high concern for production (9-1), you were a dictator."

In the decade of the *MBA*, the 1970s, it was perhaps inevitable that the numbers-oriented students turned out by the B-schools would help to make strategic planning *de rigueur*. Another ap-proach pioneered by *GE*, it caught the fancy of many executives. "After we put in our strategic planning system in 1970, we were deluged with people from around the world wanting to talk to us about it," recalls *GE* alumnus Walker.

Some of these visitors failed to distinguish between form and substance. They became engrossed in the mechanics of setting up a planning system rather than focusing on finding the answers, says Harvard business school's Michael E. Porter. "Too often it became a function of shuffling papers with no underlying value."

DOG STARS. Porter was one of the many consultants who helped make strategic planning a buzzword. Consultants have always had a role in launching fads. They sold managers on psychologi-

There's even a skunk flashlight, helpful in negotiating the frosty boardwalks as you cross the sand dunes to predawn exercises or late-night bull sessions.

For their $4,000, Skunk Campers get four days of well-organized lectures, group discussions and brainstorming sessions on the excellence concepts espoused in Peters' books. Unlike many management seminars that stress broad concepts, this one is almost entirely devoted to practical applications and to persuading the participants to return home to implement what they've learned.

IDEA SCAVENGERS. In a typical session on customers, we're asked to work with five partners to fill out an "action sheet" that commits us to "develop and use hard-nosed, systematic customer-satisfaction measures." After initially letting us struggle on our own, Le Duc and Peters lead us in a brainstorming effort that elicits 45 ideas for measuring customer satisfaction. Most are obvious—such as counting canceled orders or complaints—but the level of enthusiasm is high. We watch a videotape on Stew Leonard's food stores—whose gimmicky promotions and consumer responsiveness made it a paragon of excellence in Peters' eyes—"the most amazing idea scavengers I've ever seen," he comments. Then we're asked to jot down ideas we can try at home, and a lot of scribbling ensues.

It all seems elementary to me. But my fellow Skunk Campers, who hail from midsize outfits such as Perdue Farms, Domino's Pizza, Patton Electric, and Buckman Laboratories, as well as Ford Motor, Crown Zellerbach, and American Telephone & Telegraph, find the exercises helpful.

Alexander of BankOne reports that he returned home with a dozen items on his action sheet and immediately accomplished one by enrolling himself in the next training class for the clerks who handle 80,000 customer calls monthly. He thinks that will help him stay close to his customers. Philip C. Lee, president of California Leisure Consultants Inc., took some underappreciated staffers to lunch and presented them with skunk pins. "Peters is a revolutionist who finds ways to get people back to being people-conscious," says Lee.

Could it be possible that Skunk Camp—and, indeed, the whole excellence phenomenon—is just a fad? "The people who come here are serious folks," claims Le Duc. "This is more than a fad."

Maybe. In fact, the excellence business may well become an industry. Robert H. Waterman Jr., the co-author of *In Search of Excellence*, is resigning from McKinsey & Co. to start his own consulting business and write two more books. Seminars? "We're not ruling them out," says Waterman. "We get a lot of requests, and the seminar market is so big that there is room for one more."

MANAGEMENT LINGO: HOW TO READ BETWEEN THE LINES

WHAT'S OUT

Centralization Father knows best.

Conglomerates Napoleon tried it, so did Harold Geneen. Enough said.

Consultants Company doctors. At least they still make house calls.

Corporate Planners Worrying about tomorrow's problems. It's more fun than worrying about today's.

Decentralization Then again, maybe Father doesn't know best.

Experience Curve Fight for market share. What you lose on each sale, you'll make up on volume.

Factory of the Future Robot heaven. Not yet available on earth.

Golden Parachutes The executive safety net. The problem is, not everybody's a highflier.

Management by Objectives Here an objective, there an objective, everywhere an objective.

Management by Walking Around The ultimate open-door policy. A few steps too far?

One-Minute Managing Balancing reward and punishment in managing your employees. The executive equivalent of paper-training your dog.

Quantitative Management The numbers tell it all. Except what to do next.

Raiders The thrill is gone. Ask Carl Icahn.

Reindustrialization The crusade to revive Smokestack America. Back to the future?

Synergy Genetic engineering for corporations. But don't forget, when you cross a horse with a donkey, the result is a mule.

T-Groups Building team spirit. "I am he. . .as you are me and we are all together." Oh well, at least the Beatles made millions.

Theory Y A form of participatory management. You really do have a say in how things are run. Sure you do.

Theory Z The art of Japanese management. For those who've forgotten the ABCs of American management.

WHAT'S IN

Asset Redeployment Divest losers; put your money where the growth is. Redeal. Pray for a better hand.

Back to Basics Where you go when your synergistic move into high tech flops.

Chapter 11 A new way to break labor contracts or to sidestep liability suits.

Corporate Culture Get everybody singing the same song and hope they're in key.

Demassing Slimming down at the top. The latest euphemism for firing people.

Intrapreneurship Discovering the entrepreneurs in your own ranks. That may be easier than keeping the bureaucracy at bay once you do.

Leveraged Buyouts Trading the short-term expectations of your stockholders for the short-term expectations of your bankers and bondholders.

Niches Markets your competitors haven't found. Yet.

Out-Sourcing When you can't afford to make it yourself.

Pay for Performance It used to be known as piecework.

Restructuring Writing down and leveraging up.

Skunk Camp Officially, a management seminar. Unofficially, it's a boot camp with Tom Peters.

Strategic Alliances Losing market share? Sign on with the competition.

Touchy-Feely Managers The boss is a really nice guy. He's also still the boss.

Wellness Part of the health craze. You'll know it's arrived when they stop serving lemon meringue pie in the company cafeteria.

By Stuart Jackson in New York

---

cal tools such as the Thematic Apperception Test in the 1950s. (Executives were told to conjure up stories based on series of pictures.) They also peddled sensitivity training in the 1960s. But consultants have been working overtime to roll out new fads since the 1970s.

One of the most rapidly spreading and widely used theories ever to emerge was the gospel ac-

cording to Bruce D. Henderson's Boston Consulting Group Inc. Henderson put cows, dogs, stars, and question marks on matrix charts in hundreds of executive suites. Businesses were put into such categories as cash cows (mature companies that could be milked) and dogs (marginal performers in a market with poor prospects).

Fads multiplied in the 1980s as U. S. executives

grappled for ways to contend with foreign competition—so much so that management by best-seller came into vogue (below). William Ouchi's *Theory Z* and Richard Pascale and Anthony Athos' *The Art of Japanese Management* were the first such best-sellers when published in 1981. Both books pushed U. S. companies to adopt such Japanese management techniques as quality circles and job enrichment.

Some wags wondered if U. S. managers would soon be issued kimonos and be required to eat with chopsticks. "There wasn't an American manager who wasn't talking about it four years ago," says James J. O'Toole, a management professor at the University of Southern California. But when O'Toole's *New Management* magazine recently asked readers to name the most influential management books in recent years, not a single reader mentioned *Theory Z*.

Theory Z is still having an impact, however. Quality circles, an updated version of the employ-ee suggestion programs and labor-management councils of the 1950s, are still in. In 1979, the International Association of Quality Circles had only 200 members. Now membership is almost 8,000.

IMMORTALITY. Why such mass popularity? Edward E. Lawler III, director of the University of Southern California's Center for Effective Organizations, says that *QC*s are partly a fad. "In a number of cases we studied," says Lawler, "the *CEO* of the company had seen a *TV* program or read a magazine article on *QC*s and decided to give them a try. Circles were simply something the top told the middle to do to the bottom."

Quality circles may be helping some companies improve productivity, though they have received mixed reviews. Koppers Co. installed *QC*s in 1981 at a plant in Follansbee, W. Va. They flopped when Koppers axed half the work force. Now it's trying a program called *PITCH*—for People Involved in Totally Changing History. The jury is

MANAGEMENT BY BEST-SELLER: A FIELD GUIDE TO TODAY'S GURUS

Gifford Pinchot III, the carrot-topped, boyish-looking author of *Intrapreneuring*, was feeling sorry for himself. The success of his book had put him on a whirlwind tour of lectures and consulting that kept him from his family for weeks.

"Why am I doing this?" he asked an executive over dinner in Minneapolis about six months ago. "I don't think I can go on with the schedule."

His dinner companion was aghast. "I understand what you're going through," Pinchot remembers him saying. "But you can't stop doing this. I don't care what it's doing to your life. You have to do what is right for the movement." It was enough to brighten the author's spirits once again.

Like Pinchot, today's management gurus are full of missionary zeal. Most of them ply the lecture circuit, proselytizing on corporate salva-tion for handsome fees. Their buzzwords, acronyms, clichés, and charts litter the corporate landscape. And they can trace much of their fame to the management-by-bestseller phenomenon.

Who's in and who's out? Pinchot, a former blacksmith and dairy farmer, is definitely in. He coined "intrapreneur"—one of the hottest '80s buzzwords. It refers to stirring entrepreneurial innovation in the corporation. This concept transformed Pinchot into an instant hero, and he became the spokesman for a new movement.

'SELFLESSLY HAPPY.' So have former McKinsey & Co. consultants Thomas J. Peters and Allan A. Kennedy. Peters has leveraged two books he co-authored, 1982's *In Search of Excellence* and last year's *A Passion for Excellence*, into a full-fledged business. Kennedy didn't achieve nearly half the acclaim. But his 1982 co-authored book, *Corporate Cultures*, was largely based on the same

McKinsey research as *In Search of Excellence* and won many fans.

The two gurus remain friends. When Peters received a $1.8 million royalty check on his first book, he called Kennedy at 3 a.m. to tell "someone" the news. Kennedy isn't hurting, either. "I'm selflessly happy to announce that the corporate-culture fad is alive and well," he reports from Boston, where he's president of the consulting firm Selkirk Associates Inc.

In a somewhat different category is John Naisbitt, the bearded 56-year-old author of *Megatrends*. Naisbitt claims he's a mere trend-spotter, not a management consultant. "Someone gave me some advice a long time ago," he says. "An *IBM* guy said, 'Don't be a consultant. They are like dentists. They only make money when they're on their feet.'"

Naisbitt listened. *Megatrends* has sold more than 6 million copies since its 1983 publication. Sales of *Reinventing the Corporation*, a 1985 sequel coauthored with his wife, Patricia Aburdene, have been somewhat disappointing. But Naisbitt is still in—and much in demand.

Of all the current management whizzes, no one has endured as well as Peter F. Drucker, who has been described as the antithesis of faddishness. The Vienna-born consultant invented management by objectives. He has weighed in with such mighty contributions as *Concept of the Corporation,* his best-seller about General Motors, in 1946, *Practice of Management*, 1954, and his 22nd book, *Innovation and Entrepreneurship*, last year.

NICE-GUY APPROACH. "I've never indulged in fads," Drucker, 76, says proudly. "I promote the simple and fundamental things and leave the ornamentation to others." Drucker isn't taken as seriously as he should be in today's fad-conscious era.

More trendy than Drucker is consultant and Professor Kenneth Blanchard. The co-author of 1982's best-selling *The One Minute Manager*, Blanchard's executive training guide sold 3 million copies by advocating a nice-guy approach to managing.

His first success spawned two other One-Minute business books, and this spring will see yet another: *The One Minute Manager Gets Fit*, which seeks to exploit the wellness fad. That's not all.

Blanchard and Norman Vincent Peale have teamed up for a hardcover on ethical management. A possible title: *One Minute Manager Gets Ethics*? In short, the One-Minute formula seems to be wearing thin.

Also less than popular these days is University of California Professor William G. Ouchi, whose 1981 *Theory Z* was the first of the business books in the 1980s to hit the best-seller list, staying there nearly six months. The book advocated Japanese management techniques, from lifetime employment to job rotation. Many U.S. managers quickly adopted some of them with little thought about the vast cultural differences between the two nations.

Ouchi was no Peters. "I never attempted to income-maximize the book," Ouchi says. And in retrospect, he thinks that many U.S. managers failed to grasp his central belief that participation works just as well in the U.S. as in Japan. "It makes me sad that people didn't get this message," he says. "A lot of companies have done things with little commitment or thought and described it as Theory Z."

In the same boat is Harvard business school strategic planner Michael E. Porter. He helped to make planning one of the hottest management tools of the early 1980s with his 1980 book, *Competitive Strategy,* followed by last year's *Competitive Advantage.*

SINGER'S COMEBACK. Porter, who once used his strategic planning skills to help folksinger Tom Rush stage a comeback, is still in great demand, even though corporate planners are out. Yet although he gets 15 requests to speak weekly, he accepts only six lectures a year—a pittance next to Naisbitt's 100-plus annual appearances, at $15,000 a pop.

Of course, almost all of these gurus potentially face the same fate as the fads they promote: They could disappear without a trace. "There are some people," says Pinchot, "who think intrapreneuring is the flavor of the month. If so, give me a few years off, and I'll come back with something else. Or I can always go back to blacksmithing."

By John A. Byrne in New York, with bureau reports

still out on *PITCH*, but outsiders wonder how seriously employees will take a program that seems to promise immortality for working at a plant that makes creosote roofing tar.

Taking the best-seller even further were consultants Thomas J. Peters and Robert H. Waterman Jr. Their *In Search of Excellence*, published in 1982, added Skunk Works, Management By Walking Around, and Stick to Your Knitting to the manager's vocabulary.

One *Excellence*-type slogan caught on more widely than any other: "People are our most important asset." But how seriously did executives take it? One major property and casualty insurer adopted this motto two years ago, promoting it in its annual report and in management memos. Yet as one divisional manager grouses, there was no real commitment. "Since the introduction of that campaign, our training budget has been cut in half and our employee profit-sharing plan has been eliminated," he says. "We've laid off 1,000 staff members. Our tuition reimbursement program has been dissolved, and the athletic center has been closed. A lot of those important assets are looking for new jobs."

PIES AND SALADS. Some of the folks who promote new management ideas will even call a fad a fad. Take wellness, fitness programs that attempt to get employees to eat salads instead of hamburgers. "We feel it probably has a two- to three-year life cycle," figures Robert G. Cox, president of *PA* Executive Search Group. Cox's consulting outfit tells potential clients that managers who smoke cost them $4,000 annually in lower productivity and higher absenteeism.

On a recent engagement, *PA*'s consultants stood duty in a corporation's cafeteria. "We noticed they picked up a lot of desserts when they went through the cafeteria line," relates Cox. "We also noticed that the lemon meringue pie was at the beginning of the line and the salads were in the back." The consultants' solution: switching the pies and the salads.

In many cases, a fad lasts as long as the boss is interested. "Our *CEO* got very excited about wellness two years ago," confides a personnel manager for a major transportation company. "We all went through stress-management programs, got reward-ed for stopping smoking, and had to read *Fit or Fat*. But last year wasn't profitable, and now all of that has stopped."

And today there is intense competition for the executive's attention. A slew of instant gurus have emerged to spread the differing gospels, each with a proprietary lexicon of his own. Gifford Pinchot talks of intrapreneurship. Allan Kennedy talks of corporate culture. Ichak Adizes, a self-styled "organizational therapist" based in Santa Monica, Calif., advocates consensus-building meetings and brainstorming sessions.

DIRTY HANDS. Adizes has the ear of Bank-America President Samuel H. Armacost. The banker was introduced to the Yugoslavia-born consultant by board director Charles R. Schwab in 1983 via cassette tape. Armacost, says Adizes, listened to his "Adizes Method Audio Series" until 2 a.m. one night and was so impressed that he arranged a retreat with the consulting whiz for top management at the posh Silverado Country Club in Napa County.

The upshot? The Adizes method cost BofA an estimated $3 million. Top managers, figures one BofA officer, spent much of their time trying to build consensus under the method. "Several senior guys were spending half their time in these meetings for months on end," says one insider. Adds a consultant who worked with the bank: "The real fix would have been to fire five levels of management so the top guys could get their hands dirty." A bank spokesman says Adizes helped reorganize the bank into two divisions.

The impact goes well beyond the waste of time and resources. Companies risk losing the support and confidence of their people. "The people below are often laughing at the senior management," says consultant Kilmann. "They are saying, 'How stupid can you be?'"

A little faddishness may be helpful because it makes managers think about new ways to do their jobs better. In earlier decades, fads appear to have had that effect. They tended to be in fashion for years, if not decades, and did less harm. They seemed less goofy, too.

Today, the bewildering array of fads pose far more serious diversions and distractions from the complex task of running a company. Too many modern managers are like compulsive dieters: trying the latest craze for a few days, then moving restlessly on.

By John A. Byrne in New York, with bureau reports

DISCUSSION QUESTIONS

1. My own consulting experience in high-tech organizations with highly educated scientists and engineers as managers—experience that included evaluating various consultants and training seminars the organizations had retained—left me with the strong impression that sometimes these managers were naive consumers of a sort of junk food of management education. They were suckers for highly energetic presentations of simplistic "quick fixes" that didn't actually work. Why would intelligent, educated managers be so disposed to spend large sums on a succession of pop management fads?

2. Which of the concepts in the article seem to have particular merit and which do you judge less likely to be useful? Why?

INTERVIEWS:
THE BEST FACE IS YOUR OWN

FEBRUARY 16, 1987, P. 122

You have landed the interview. Now you want to make the best possible impression and land the job. Should you seize the initiative and do most of the talking? Embellish your achievements? Or coolly sit back and let them court you?

Do any of the above and you'll be making a mistake. The National Association of Corporate & Professional Recruiters asked human resource officials and executive headhunters to pinpoint the major turnoffs that disqualify candidates in job interviews. They quickly came up with five common mistakes that can outweigh a long list of qualifications. Here's how, says the *NACPR*, candidates often shoot themselves in the foot:

■ **Playing games.** You are wrong if you think that playing hard to get will squeeze a higher bid from a company. Acting nonchalant usually will be taken at face value: You aren't interested enough.

■ **Talking too much.** Even nervousness, if you feel it, isn't a legitimate excuse for rambling on or trying to entertain the interviewer with chitchat about the Super Bowl. Stick to the subject at hand.

■ **Boasting.** Selling yourself is the objective, but interviewers who face large numbers of applicants can tell if you are embellishing responsibilities at previous jobs, exaggerating past accomplishments, covering up shortcomings, or simply bragging too much.

■ **Not listening.** You may be so anxious to prove yourself that you don't keep an ear tuned to the interviewer's questions. And, not surprisingly, you give wandering or incomplete answers.

■ **Being unprepared.** If you haven't done some homework to learn about the company and its culture, you can't ask the right questions.

"People sometimes blow the 'I' out of proportion," says John Johnson, president of Lamalie Associates, an executive search firm based in Tampa, Fla. "They say, 'I did this, I did that, I was in charge of, and I accomplished.' It's 'we' that we listen for. 'I' tells you to be careful of the candidate."

Overall, warns Johnson, never show the interviewer a face that's different from the one you normally wear. "If you go in and try to be someone you're not, you may sell the deal," he says. "But when you go on board," your bosses soon see the real you. If there's a big difference from the person the interviewer saw, "it won't be a good match."

John A. Byrne

DISCUSSION QUESTIONS
1. What mistakes have you made in your job interviewing experience?
2. What have you done well?

MBAs ARE
HOTTER THAN EVER

ANOTHER BOOM YEAR FOR B-SCHOOLS
MARCH 9, 1987, PP. 46-48

For years, they said the boom wouldn't last. But the obituary for *MBA*-mania apparently has been written prematurely.

Now in the midst of the application season, the nation's top business schools are being flooded by unprecedented numbers of would-be whiz kids. Many schools report that applications are up 20% to 30% from last year.

No less significant, greater numbers of people

are taking the Graduate Management Admissions Test *(GMAT)*, which schools use to help qualify *MBA* applicants. This year, in fact, test takers are expected to exceed the record 252,531 who took the exam in 1980-81.

SECOND PRINTING. In some cases, admissions officials are struggling to cope with the deluge. "We're going nuts here, we have so many applicants to deal with," says Eric Mokover, admissions director at the University of California at Los Angeles' B-school. Last year, 3,487 hopefuls rushed to apply for *UCLA*'s 370 openings. So far this year, the school's applications are up by 28%. Interest has been so high that *UCLA* scrambled to reprint 15,000 extra catalogs when it ran out of its supply in December.

Why the upswing, when not long ago many college officials were saying the numbers couldn't possibly rise further? "Companies think they are getting bright, articulate, educated people," says Russell E. Palmer, dean of the University of Pennsylvania's Wharton School. "The market wants more of these people, and the market will continue to want them as long as we continue to get top people. It feeds off itself."

More young people, he says, are opting out of law and medical schools to pursue business careers. At the same time, more companies in a greater variety of industries, from health care to high technology, require the degree.

"Many firms won't hire you unless you've got an *MBA*," says Mike Jentis, 26, a Merrill Lynch financial analyst who is headed for *UCLA* B-school. Adds a Harvard-bound executive in a small West Coast business: "One company told me they only hire brand-name *MBA*s."

Young people are even being urged by peers to get the degree. "The pressure being brought to bear to go to business school is incredible," says Joan Ryan, a spokeswoman for Yale University's School of Organization & Management. Friends of her 25-year-old son, Stuart, who works at the Federal Home Loan Bank in Boston, keep asking him when he's going to apply. "Maybe it's because we live in an impersonal society where people are increasingly being presented on paper," she says. "The more credentials you have, the more likely you're looked at."

So intense is the race to capture a seat in a brand-name school that some applicants are turn-

A LITTLE FRIENDLY ADVICE— AT $100 AN HOUR

When Kathy Gwynn worked as admissions director for Stanford University's Graduate School of Business, she would turn down at least 12 applicants for every one that she admitted. "Sometimes I felt like the director of rejections," she jokes.

Not anymore. Since leaving Stanford in 1985 she has been counseling business school applicants as a $100-an-hour consultant. Gwynn, 32, advises candidates on the nitty-gritty of getting into a top school—such things as how to portray oneself, essay writing, and letters of recommendation.

Gwynn's biggest clients? Investment bankers, such as Goldman, Sachs & Co. and First Boston Corp., and management consultants McKinsey &

Co. and Bain & Co., which want their financial analysts and associate consultants to get into the best schools. This year, Gwynn is advising 250 company-sponsored people and 100 others.

Gwynn's company, *MBA*/Strategies, based in Mountain View, Calif., has passed muster with clients. "She helped me focus on things I wanted to say and saved me a lot of time," says Ron Mika, 26, a Bain consultant, who just got Harvard's O. K.

Not everyone is cheering. Stanford and the University of California at Los Angeles now require applicants to attest that they didn't receive coaching help to complete their applications. "We can't stop someone from cheating, but at least they'll have to live with whatever guilt they have," says *UCLA*'s Eric Mokover.

There are, of course, no guarantees. "I can't make a silk purse out of a sow's ear," says Gwynn. "But a majority of my people last year ended up at Stanford, Harvard, or the school that was their first choice."

ing to consultants who help them complete applications, write essay answers, and get the most polished letters of recommendation (box). "Many people feel their long-term success is dependent on the schools that accept them," says Kathy Gwynn, a $100-an-hour consultant to *MBA* applicants. "Getting into a major business school means an awful lot these days."

Many of the prestige schools report that the average *GMAT* scores of admitted candidates are drifting higher and higher. At Dartmouth University's Amos Tuck School, average *GMAT* scores have gone up 10 points a year for the past four years. "We're turning down 60% of the people with grades in the 99th percentile," says Colin C. Blaydon, dean of Amos Tuck.

50-POINT HIKE. It's the same story elsewhere. At Duke University's Fuqua School of Business, successful applicants are averaging scores of 645, a 50-point jump from two years ago. That compares with an average *GMAT* score of 475 for all test takers on an exam with a 200-to-800 point range.

What's making the competition even hotter is that most top schools have fixed or even reduced their class size to ensure a quality education. The University of Chicago cut its full-time enrollment to 480 last year from 553 in 1985. Columbia University is reducing its incoming class this year to 475 from 500 students. Yet both institutions expect applications to be up by 20% this year.

No one knows for sure if the latest upturn means another sustained boom in *MBA*s, but some think it's possible. "Even the negative press about the wheeling and dealing on Wall Street hasn't turned it off," says Amos Tuck's Blaydon. "That tells me the increased interest may be long-term."

By John A. Byrne in New York

DISCUSSION QUESTIONS

If you consider obtaining an MBA a possible goal, how will you prepare to gain admission to a program?

ONE KEY TO B-SCHOOL: YOUR ESSAY

MARCH 23, 1987, P. 168

To write a succinct description of how you handled a real-life ethical dilemma can be a real challenge. So can describing the details of a failure in your career.

But if you try to enroll as an *MBA* candidate at Harvard, Stanford, or any top B-school, you'll have to meet such challenges. Satisfying a school's academic criteria is just one hurdle. Another is impressing the admissions staff with written responses to a series of questions designed to reveal the real you. How can you create a good impression?

Admissions officers say that most applications sound monotonously alike. Your essays should show how different you are, not how great you are. To stand out among countless applicants who all work capably at their jobs, tell how you have tutored underprivileged children. Discuss your Uncle Scrooge comics collection or your role as a guitarist in a rock band or cellist in a classical quartet.

"We pay a lot of attention to what people say about their lives outside the classroom or office," says Alice Brookner, associate director of admissions for the University of Chicago's B-school.

Accomplishments count, but schools also want to assess your values. So discuss an accomplishment in terms of the obstacles you overcame to achieve it.

NO RAMBLING. Don't plan to knock off the essays in an evening. Completing a set will take 20 to 40 hours. On each one, stick to the point you want to make. For an idea of what to emphasize, look over the school's brochures: They often contain clues about what kinds of students are wanted. Those with managerial potential? Diversified skills? Play up how well you fit their bill.

"Most candidates tend to use a grab-bag approach, hoping they'll hit on something that clicks with us," complains Stephen Christakos, Wharton's director of admissions. "We don't want people to ramble on."

Honesty is vital. "Don't play games," advises Karen Page, who runs a Learning Annex seminar for *MBA* applicants in New York. "Play up everything you've done for what it's worth, but don't cross the line to lie or cheat."

If you know a graduate of the school, ask him or her to read your essays before you turn them in. What about attention-getting ploys like writing in crayon or sending a videotape? Some applicants are bold enough to try them. But, as a rule, "we really don't like gimmicks," says Bruce Paton, director of admissions at Stanford.   *John A. Byrne*

DISCUSSION QUESTIONS

Write a draft essay of how you handled a
   real-life ethical dilemma.

FAST-TRACK KIDS

THEY'RE SMART,
IMPATIENT FOR AUTHORITY,
AND WILLING TO TAKE RISKS
NOVEMBER 10, 1986, PP. 91-94, 96

Wall Street. Consulting. Entrepreneurial ventures. They spell big money and instant power to most of the hot *MBA*s hitting the job market these days. But not all of them. Some of the best and brightest young people are choosing the conventional route to business success: scaling the hierarchical summit in a major corporation.

Call these corporate climbers the fast-track kids. And though many of them are sons and daughters of the Organization Men who built today's corporate giants, the new generation bears little resemblance to the fast-trackers of the past. The new breed is better-educated, more self-confident, and less fearful of challenging the status quo or taking big risks. U. S. corporations sorely need executives with these qualities if they are to do a better job of competing in the future.

CULTURAL CHANGES. But there is a darker side, too. Many of the rising stars are clearly part of the "Me Generation." They are impatient for raw management authority, they develop little loyalty to the institutions they work for, and they're often charged with lacking the sensitivity and people skills that typify today's most successful executives. These traits could also result in dramatic cultural changes in big corporations as the fast-track kids become the chief executives of the 21st century.

Who are these young comers who will have tremendous influence on the direction of U. S. business? What makes them tick? What impact will they have on the big companies they work for? To find out, *BUSINESS WEEK* correspondents conducted over a hundred interviews with business schools, executive recruiters, and executives to establish a profile of the fast-track kids and to identify 50 who are among the most promising of this 35-and-under group.

The emerging leaders are little like the homogeneous group of white, male, middle-aged executives who have ruled Corporate America as we

TOMORROW'S EXECUTIVES: HOW THEY MAY BE DIFFERENT

Generalizations are difficult to make. But according to management experts interviewed by BUSINESS WEEK, some broad differences do exist between today's executives and tomorrow's.

THE OLD GENERATION	THE NEW GENERATION
Cautious	Eager to take risks
Insecure	Optimistic
Resistant to change	Flexible
Loyal to company	Willing to job-hop
Value job security	Want to make impact
Male	Male or female
White	Ethnically diverse
A good day's work	Workaholic
Comfortable in bureaucracies	Crave autonomy, power
Conservative Republican	Independent
People-oriented	Numbers-oriented
Slide rules, legal pads	Computers, data nets
College degree	Advanced degrees
25-year career plan	Instant gratification

ORGANIZATION MAN: 'VERY MUCH ALIVE'

When William H. Whyte's *The Organization Man* was published in 1956, it quickly became a controversial bestseller. Sociologists said the book was evidence of the dangers of Big Business. Many executives disagreed, and Du Pont Co. even ran ads challenging the book's conclusions.

Whyte argued that the Protestant ethic was being supplanted by a new social ethic in which people were, in effect, selling their souls to the corporation. In his book, he painted a less-than-flattering portrait of a generation of Big Business executives. The author warned that men who surrendered their lives to the corporation would face powerful pressure to become conformists and that creativity and innovation would suffer.

These days, Whyte's thesis is unfashionable, largely because the recent entrepreneurial revolution proved that the Protestant ethic is alive and well. But Whyte, now 69, demurs. "Despite the current mythology of the entrepreneur, most people still work in organizations," he says. "When I wrote the book, we were a nation run by organization people, and they still are dominant. I don't see the Organization Man's death. He's very much alive."

NONTOPIC. Whyte pooh-poohs the notion that a new breed of executive is rising. "I keep hearing this about every 10 years," he says. Sure, concedes Whyte, there are changes. Women, for example, appeared in Whyte's book only as suburban housewives. And today's young managers, says Whyte, "are not necessarily bound to one firm anymore. The musical-chair phenomenon is a by-product of prosperity."

In 1949 "everybody was talking depression, saying, 'Boy, I'm going to join a big company to be safe.' When I bring up the question today, [young people] are not interested. It's a non-topic. They are extraordinarily optimistic. I think it's a little unsettling."

know it. Born of the Depression and World War II, the old guard was preoccupied with security. In exchange for that security, they took a pledge of loyalty to the corporation. They accepted with equanimity corporate control of their destiny. The essence of this contract was captured in William H. Whyte's *The Organization Man*, the 1956 management book that forewarned that this Faustian bargain could exact conformity and dullness.

The new generation grew up in a different world. Post-war affluence gave them a feeling of entitlement. Television, air travel, and the sexual revolution accustomed them to instant gratification. Moreover, they arrived in the corporate world at a time of unprecedented upheaval—restructurings, mergers, takeovers, spinoffs. The result: Younger managers generally don't subscribe to a code of loyalty. Neither do they demand it from employees. James T. Hackett, 32, marketing vice-president for Meridian Oil Inc., has worked for four companies and knows firsthand the volatility of bankruptcy and merger. "The social contract [between employer and employee] is no longer valid," he says. "There needs to be some allegiance to the company, but you can't forget the company is an economic being."

POWER AND AUTONOMY. If the previous generation so willingly embraced the corporation ethic, their children have adopted what some sociologists call the enterprise ethic. Whatever their commitment, it isn't being made in return for security or mere pay. "This newer group is trading off that commitment for power and autonomy," says Paul Leinberger, an industrial psychologist who is researching a book on the up-and-comers. "They want to control their own destiny. That's something the Organization Man was willing to give up for security."

Lacking memories of a depression, young corporate climbers boast unusual optimism and unquestioning faith in corporate capitalism—to the point that many of them seem brash. "I feel almost predestined to run General Electric," says Deborah A. Coleman, who at 33 is vice-president of operations for Apple Computer Inc. "I know it's partly irrational, but it's like training for the Olym-

A CHANCE TO SHAPE ONE COMPANY'S FUTURE

Michael D. White, 34, was very much the typical bright graduate of the mid-1970s—the kind who proved increasingly elusive to Corporate America.

A Phi Beta Kappa graduate of Boston College, White was chosen as a Ford Foundation Fellow at Leningrad State University. Astute and aggressive, he headed for the lucrative management-consulting business after picking up a master's degree in international economics from Johns Hopkins' prestigious School of Advanced International Studies in 1976.

But after a decade-long stint in consulting for Arthur Andersen & Co. and Bain & Co., White recently tossed it in for Corporate America. Too many airplane trips and too many dust-gathering studies made him jump at the opportunity last March to become vice-president for strategic planning at Avon Products Inc.'s $1.1 billion beauty division in New York City.

"I wanted to be part of building an organization as opposed to constantly whispering in someone's ear," he says. "It was a chance to be a small part of a team to shape the future of a major corporation. That's more than what a consultant can ever hope to do."

MISSED BIRTHDAYS. A decade ago, says White, it would not have been possible for an outsider to arrive at such a senior position at Avon. He believes that more corporations must undergo a similar cultural change if they hope to attract the best of his generation, a group less likely to spend a career at a single company.

From White's perspective, that's only part of the strategy for winning the recruiting wars with investment banks and consulting firms. "It requires the willingness of the large corporation to go outside, to empower people with responsibility, to provide a mentor to help them in the organization, and to keep throwing challenges at them," he says.

The corporation, as White sees it, also offered him a greater chance for a more balanced lifestyle, something most young married people are demanding. "I was missing too many birthdays, soccer games, and school plays," says White, who is married and has three children, aged 13, 9, and 7. "As a consultant, you're on a plane two to three nights a week, 52 weeks a year."

As one of the youngest vice-presidents at Avon, White has been handed a tough challenge. He and his group of 12 professionals must develop a broad-ranging plan to enhance the profitability of Avon's fragrance and cosmetics business, which has been hurt by demographic trends.

"Avon reflects what a lot of companies are going through," says White, whose sparsely decorated New York office overlooks Central Park. "American industry is changing, and it has to change. There aren't any easy businesses anymore. You've got to fight for what you've got."

His challenge to plot a new course for Avon's most important business is critical to his personal goals and ambitions. "There's no doubt that my generation is more impatient than any other," says White, who aims "to run a business someday," perhaps as president of a division. "Young people want to feel they make a difference."

By John A. Byrne in New York

---

pics. You may never make it, but you want to aspire to something."

Coleman and many of her peers tend to be nearly incurable workaholics—particularly if they are single or childless. Coleman, who is unmarried, routinely puts in 70- to 80-hour weeks. "If I work less than 60 hours a week, I have a twinge of guilt," she says.

These young executives, many of them members of two-career couples, have new ideas about the way companies should operate. "Our leaders feel some challenges from us in new-wave thinking, particularly in personnel," says Mark H. Dutell, 33, employee-relations manager for Gates Rubber Co. in Denver. "We push for child care and other things, which the generation currently leading Gates probably wouldn't think about otherwise."

Instead of being fearful of change, the fast-trackers seem to thrive on it. "This generation doesn't expect tomorrow to be a lot like yesterday," says ReBecca K. Roloff, who at 32 is Pillsbury Co.'s first female marketing director (page 37). "It doesn't hold the view that change is unfair."

It's a trait that the current generation of corporate executives often admires. "They're more able to cope with change and complexities," says L. M. Cook, chief executive officer of Arco. "They're at home with computers. I still use my slide rule." Burnell R. Roberts, chairman of Mead Corp., in Dayton, Ohio, agrees that the younger group is "more fluid, more flexible . . . more willing to try new things."

He might very well add impatience to the mix. "We are less willing to put in time in the ranks," admits Barbara L. Behrman, a product manager at H. J. Heinz Co. "My generation wants to jump right in and do."

Slow-moving organizations quickly frustrate the young stars. "We do not have time to wait," says Sharon Y. Reed, 35, corporate planning manager at Scott Paper Co. "We see opportunities loom on the horizon and disappear. We're more action-oriented." Adds Michael K. Lorelli, 35, a PepsiCo Inc. senior vice-president: "The new generation is less accepting of the status quo. They will challenge everything."

LOTS OF TIME. That willingness to challenge authority is causing generational clashes to erupt at many companies. Zara F. Rolfes, at 29 the manager of General Motors Corp.'s 1990 Corvette airbag program, is typical of her generation. Boasting advanced degrees in mechanical engineering and business, she is bold, bright, and outspoken.

Rolfes thinks that many of *GM*'s older manag-

BREATHING NEW LIFE INTO A FAILED S&L

When Mellon Bank Corp. needed a top manager to head its new Maryland banking subsidiary last May, it turned to Barrie G. Christman, 34, a loan vice-president in its Pittsburgh headquarters. Since arriving at Mellon as a management trainee 12 years ago, she has moved steadily up the ladder. The jump to chief executive of Mellon Bank (Md.), with $220 million in assets, made her the highest-ranking woman in the bank holding company.

Christman's assignment isn't easy. Racking up 12-hour days at her Bethesda (Md.) office, she is plotting long-term strategy to turn the subsidiary—previously a failed savings and loan—into a profitable full-service bank. She has been put on the spot in a whirlwind of meetings and appearances designed to placate 20,000 customers whose deposits were frozen for nearly a year.

BIG SACRIFICES. Christman got where she is by demonstrating unusual drive and initiative. After joining Mellon with a degree in math and economics, she found that her peers had *MBA*s. Soon she was hitting the books at night at the University of Pittsburgh's Graduate School of Business, earning an *MBA* in three years. "I don't like operating at a disadvantage," she says. After serving as a credit analyst and a loan officer, she was picked in 1981 to help head a pilot program to break into the lucrative market of lending to midsize companies. A year later she opened up the program's Chicago office and in 1984 moved to headquarters to oversee several of the program's offices.

There have been big sacrifices, however. Christman has moved five times in 12 years. Her hectic schedule forced her to forgo playing the violin in amateur symphonies. Having held off marriage until two years ago, there's a wisp of regret at not having had time yet to have children. Her husband, Douglas, has followed her last two moves and even changed careers from commercial banking to investment banking as a result. Says Christman: "We felt strongly about marrying a peer who understands the pressure."

Christman doesn't doubt for a minute that it's been worth the trouble—and admits that she is impatient to get ahead. "The *CEO*s of today found their way through the ranks, plodding along and paying their dues," she says. Her credo: "Get the biggest breadth of experience at a fairly rapid pace."

By Matt Rothman in Pittsburgh

TRADING A DESK JOB FOR THE FACTORY FLOOR

Thomas W. Gorman never even dreamed of the corporate world when he was studying to be a Jesuit priest in the 1970s. He was too busy building a church in Alaska, working with paraplegics in Pontiac, Mich., and teaching English in Spain.

But like many students of the early 1970s, Gorman's idealism wore off, and he decided not to become a priest in 1978, when he was 26. "I started to wonder if I could spend my life in a 15-by-20-ft. room with a bed, desk, and bookcase," Gorman says. "I realized I wouldn't be able to have a family giving up what I did." Gorman married a registered nurse from Cleveland in 1980 and a year later went to the University of Michigan for his *MBA*.

Today, Gorman is one month into a job as area production manager in Dana Corp.'s automotive-gasket division. His new manufacturing position comes after three years at a desk job—he was a divisional marketing manager. His superiors say his willingness to get his hands dirty and learn the guts of the company makes him an even more attractive candidate for senior management.

Unlike many young comers today, Gorman, 34, insists his career plans include remaining at one company. So he welcomes the chance to learn more about manufacturing. "I'm not vain enough to believe I can manage the whole company until I get down to the bottom level," he says.

WORK VS. FAMILY. Yet unlike many of his older predecessors, Gorman is not afraid to make waves. Already he is moving to raise product quality by giving assembly-line workers more responsibility. Gorman also balances work and family obligations: He sets aside time every day to help his wife raise their two young daughters. To work with both assembly-line shifts at Dana's Chicago plant, Gorman rises at 4:30 a.m. and returns home at 7 p.m.

Before he went to Dana, he shopped for a corporate culture that agreed with his values rather than one that provided high visibility, prestige, or pay. Dana's record in promoting from within and its flexibility in allowing employees to spend time with their families appealed to Gorman. He also sought a mainstream manufacturing company. "I grew up in the Rust Belt," he says. "I wanted to be part of mature American industry and make a difference." His superiors don't doubt that he will.

By Laurie Baum in New York

---

ers are mainly interested in "cranking out cars. They put people down as line items, like a roll of steel," she says. During the company's new Camaro launch in 1982, for example, she tackled production problems by exploring new ways to work with the rank and file, although she had been advised to steer clear of assembly workers by "more tenured" managers. "They had never gotten anywhere with hourly workers in the past because they probably had been dealing in a confrontational environment with them for 20 years," says Rolfes. To the managers' chagrin, she ignored their advice and was able quickly to solve some production-line problems.

"It's kind of like the best of times and the worst of times," observes Roger H. Ballou, 35, an American Express Co. executive vice-president. "At times it's nice being my age and knowing that I have time on my side. On the flip side, I have to be sensitive to people's feelings because many of the people I work with are older than me."

Peers of Rolfes and Ballou, though, are often knocked for being overly pragmatic when sensitivity is called for. Indeed, a survey by executive search firm Korn/Ferry International shows that only 14% of corporate executives under 39 think "concern for people" is important to success, while 35% of executives over 50 think it is important. "People don't fail due to lack of technical skills and energy," contends R. Peter Mercer, a human resources executive at General Electric Co. "They are most often derailed because of people problems."

The older generation also worries about the

SHE WORKED MAGIC IN A DEAD-END JOB

Pillsbury Co. executives used to refer sneeringly to the distribution department as an "elephant's graveyard." It was tantamount to corporate oblivion, involving little more than taking orders and shuffling invoices. But that was before Becky Roloff, 32, came along.

In her two years as distribution director, Roloff took 450 mostly uninspired employees and transformed them into a gung-ho group by rewarding them with recognition and reconceiving what was a bureaucratic task into a focused strategic mission. Now, when a job in distribution opens up, 30 or 40 people apply.

CORPORATE HUMANIST. After brief stints as a Cargill Inc. grain trader and in purchasing at Pillsbury, Roloff set out for Harvard business school. She rejoined Pillsbury in 1982 after graduating in the top 10% of her class. In 1984, Roloff headed a task force to deal with the pesticide-contamination crisis that engulfed the food industry. Last May she became Pillsbury's first female marketing director. Besides all that, she's a wife and a mother of an 18-month-old son.

ReBecca K. Roloff insists that she's unlike the "numbers jocks" with whom she trained at Harvard. She sees herself as a corporate humanist, an outgrowth perhaps of the prairie populism and strong, family-oriented German Catholic moralism of her upbringing in a small North Dakota town. Ask about the corporation's responsibilities, and she says: "How do you make money today and tomorrow so your employees can pay for the 30-year mortgages they have?"

Roloff credits her success to intuitive "people" skills—something that sets her apart from many contemporaries. "She believes that if you take care of people first, then you'll be taken care of, too," says her husband, Mark. Adds Warren G. Malkerson, a Pillsbury vice-president: "Becky has the ability to make people more productive than they

would ever expect themselves to be."

She proved that during her stint in distribution. There, she launched a program under which employees attempt to "catch each other in the act" of excellence. Those so caught are nominated for a

> ## Roloff can 'make people more productive than they would ever expect themselves to be'

special recognition. Just being nominated gets an employee a plaque. Big winners are brought to company headquarters to be feted, Roloff says, "as king or queen for a day."

Roloff was willing to break out of old molds. She defined distribution not merely as freight expediting but as a sales-support function for stores and distributors. She found that some 25% of sales could be tied to decisions by customers based on such things as timely and correct shipments. So she formulated new objectives that emphasized service and led to sales gains.

Outside of her 60-hour workweek, she juggles the demands of marriage and motherhood. It helps that her husband has quit the business world to help take care of their son, Luke, and to pursue a theology degree part-time. "Mark is an anchor in our home life, and I'm the anchor in our financial life," she says. "It's a balance that works pretty well."

Still, she acknowledges that trade-offs are sometimes necessary. After all, she says, "there are glass balls and rubber balls in life." The trick is knowing which is which. "Family, friends, and health are glass balls," she says. "Those you just can't drop."

By Patrick Houston in Minneapolis

impatience of their young managers. At Wichita-based Coleman Co., for example, Thomas W. Talbott is known as a whiz kid. Brought from Harvard business school in 1980 to the maker of

recreation equipment by former Coleman President Larry Jones, Talbott, 32, heads the company's acquisition efforts. "He's better at taking complex problems and coming to a reasonable

AN OIL-PATCH MANAGER WHO PUTS PEOPLE FIRST

Colleagues often ask Ronald J. Burns if he ever has a bad day. His answer: "I do, but I don't let people know." The ruddy-faced president of Enron Gas Transportation Co., a division of $10 billion Enron Corp., is known around Houston headquarters for his sunny disposition and high energy.

Burns realizes his demeanor is no small factor in his swift move up the ranks. At 34, he is responsible for managing the flow of natural gas through the country's largest pipeline system. "I've always felt the most important ingredient is knowing how to get along with people," says Burns.

With the once-staid pipeline industry gearing up under deregulation, managers like Burns are held at a premium. "Ron has the qualities you'd expect," says Dan L. Dienstbier, group president. "He's bright, aggressive, and articulate. But what separates Ron is his maturity of judgment." When Houston Natural Gas Corp. and InterNorth Inc. merged last year to create Enron, Burns was responsible for creating a new 150-member transportation department. He had to deal with such sticky issues as conflicting corporate cultures, turf fights, and job consolidations.

NO HINDRANCE. After a year as an accounting trainee with InterNorth, Burns shifted into regulatory affairs and marketing. Frequent travel to Washington for rate cases stopped him from getting an *MBA*, but that proved no hindrance.

Although his exuberance comes naturally, Burns says his management style is the result of careful study. He has written detailed critiques of each of his managers. "I find their strengths and weaknesses and determine which I want to emulate and which I want to avoid," he says. Some of his conclusions: Too many managers in high-stress environments lose respect for people; managers who dwell on details lose the big picture.

Burns believes that future chief executives will have to be more flexible. With fast-changing markets and a global economy, decisions that used to be black or white are now gray.

To compete, Burns predicts the bosses of tomorrow will have to abandon some of the trappings of success. "Older executives even differ from younger managers in the way they use their secretar-

conclusion than I was at that age," says Jones, 55. "But he tends to want to see things happen immediately. He may want to stop, abort, or change when the real need is to persevere."

LOOKING SMALL. What kind of corporation will emerge when the next generation takes charge? The old hierarchical model of the American corporation evolved from two structured institutions—the military and the church. Companies in the future will reflect younger managers' desire to cut through unwieldy bureaucracy. "People won't stand to work in multilevel, highly centralized companies," says George C. Greer, 53, a vice-president at Heinz. "That doesn't work with the younger people."

The new leaders will demand that their organizations create personal opportunities, rewards, and challenges for employees. They will try to forge a sense of esprit in small teams or around products. The new managers will have a "looser, more informal, less military, more professional style," says Harvard business school Professor D. Quinn Mills, who is writing a book on young managers called *Not Like Our Fathers*. "A lot will change in the way these young executives manage the corporation."

Increasingly, top-level corporate positions will have to become more accessible to outsiders—not only to recruit fast-trackers, but, as many young people maintain, to empower them with authority to make a difference. In the future, successful corporations may have to organize their businesses into small, independent units, in effect creating entrepreneurial enclaves for young managers bent on gaining the control necessary to have an impact.

ies," he observes. "They don't answer their own phones or place their own calls." He doesn't believe executives need personal secretaries. Burns, attuned to the criticism that younger managers are overly oriented to the short term, sets aside about 30% of his week for brainstorming with his staff.

Like many in his generation, Burns has rewritten the contract with the corporation. His commitment, he feels, is based not on lifetime security but on personal fulfillment. "I need three things: to be stimulated, challenged, and rewarded," he says. If personal goals were stifled, he wouldn't hesitate to explore outside options. Someday he'd like to run a major corporation.

For now, Burns appears content. He is making fewer business trips these days and has more time with his wife and three children, ages 10, 8, and 5. While the two oldest were toddlers, he was on the road four weeks out of five.

Besides his family, Burns's greatest passion is sports. He's willing to cut back to six hours of sleep a night to fit in weekly games of golf, basketball, and racquetball. And he's managed to apply tenets of sportsmanship to his management philosophy. His rule: "Play hard—but when it's over, it's over." He adds with a smile: "Of course, I prefer win-win situations."

By Jo Ellen Davis in Houston

Some of the biggest changes are expected to occur in human-resource departments. "There's going to be a revolution in corporate personnel policies in the next 10 years to meet the demand of young people to be continually challenged," predicts author Leinberger. Big corporations will have to look and act like smaller entrepreneurial companies to get the best from the new generation, he believes.

Young managers' dislike of bureaucracies should lead to leaner corporate staffs. Tomorrow's chief executive may be quicker to jettison an operation that isn't profitable even though it may be a traditional business for the company. Says Harvard's Mills: "They are more likely to abandon an old business if the economics of it don't look good."

Large companies are likely to face increased pressure from fast-trackers to redesign jobs to address the special needs of today's workers. For some, those changes may come in the form of flexible work schedules, shared jobs, and company-sponsored child care that allow working spouses to balance professional and personal lives.

Corporations already are straining to attract and keep these bright young executives. And they are struggling to hit on the best ways to inspire and direct them. "It is imperative we learn how to manage them so the organization doesn't stifle this aggressiveness," says Irving Margol, executive vice-president of Security Pacific Corp.

SOFT SKILLS. Most corporations seem to try to strike a balance: using training programs and mentors to polish young executives' rough edges while leaving their ambition intact. *GE* has a two-week off-site training program to inculcate young hires with its corporate culture. The company also provides "special events" for young managers to meet with group executives to give them greater visibility. "It gives these young people some strokes that are very important to them," says *GE*'s Mercer.

Companies also try to help the younger managers develop strategic vision and hone other skills in different functional disciplines. Some have training courses that emphasize "soft" skills, such as how to motivate people, that are ignored by many *MBA* programs.

The fast-track kids are profoundly altering the shape of mainstream corporate life as they move through the ranks of management. Despite some negatives, their overall contribution should bode well for the competitiveness of U.S. industry. Fast-trackers are already starting to push American companies to be more flexible, innovative, and aggressive. And that's no small feat.

By Teresa Carson in Los Angeles, with John A. Byrne in New York and bureau reports

DISCUSSION QUESTIONS

1. The article tells you what characteristics its author thinks distinguish the old from the new generation. What qualities do you think distinguish today's fast-track kids from today's slow-track kids?
2. What is your own profile of career-related qualities?

HOW TO BE SMARTER THAN THE BOSS AND KEEP YOUR JOB

JUNE 29, 1987, P. 112

Your boss stares blankly as you finish explaining your brilliant idea. He doesn't understand. Obviously, he's not as smart as you are.

It's frustrating, but don't rush to your desk to write a memo saying, "Dear Dimwit, I quit." There's a good chance that the boss is brighter than you think. "Absolute smarts aren't always called for," advises Allan Cohen, a business professor who is co-authoring a book on how to influence people over whom you have no control. "Raw intelligence isn't rewarded in organizations." Your boss may be politically wise—something you're not if you try to show him that you're more intelligent.

Again, your boss simply may be uninformed. "Any subordinate who's assigned a task will become more expert in that particular area than the boss," says Jeffrey Edwards, a professor at the Colgate Darden Graduate School of Business. "Having expertise gives the subordinate a sense of power," which can disrupt the formal reporting relationship.

MARTYRDOM. How to manage the tension? First try to understand the pressures the boss works under. Perhaps that seemingly "stupid" reaction stems from a lack of concentration in view of other pressing problems.

Make sure, too, that you communicate with your boss in his or her own lingo—talking out your idea with a verbal boss, putting it on paper for one who prefers words and diagrams.

Try, too, to put some "sell" into the idea. Tell your boss how it can make him or her look good. Or present your data sequentially and let the boss arrive at the conclusion you've already reached. Don't play the martyr too often, though: "If he always thinks it's his idea, then you never get credit and you lose your motivation," says Patricia King, author of Never Work for a Jerk (Franklin Watts, $16.95).

The boss still won't buy your idea? Try an end-run. Discuss it with other staff members and peers who could provide support. Perhaps you could bring it up with a more receptive superior in another area. A last—and risky—resort is to take your idea to your boss's boss. But before doing that, double-check the reasons your boss looks dimly on the idea. It's just possible that it's not as brilliant as you think.

Laurie Baum

DISCUSSION QUESTION
Describe and critique your own experience in handling tensions with any boss you have had.

Executive Compensation

EXECUTIVE PAY: WHO GOT WHAT IN '86

CEOs TOOK HOME 18% MORE LAST YEAR—ONE OF THE BIGGEST GAINS EVER

MAY 4, 1987, PP. 50-54, 58

"I didn't take $1 a year to be a martyr. . . . I did it for good, cold, pragmatic reasons. I wanted our employees and our suppliers to be thinking: 'I can follow a guy who sets that kind of example.'"
—Chrysler Corp. Chairman
Lee A. Iacocca

No one could ever have imagined the lucrative potential of taking a pay cut to a mere $1 a year. But now everybody knows. By forgoing hard cash in 1980 for mountains of stock options, Iacocca was gambling that he would someday benefit handsomely from a stunning turnaround at Chrysler.

The bet is paying off beyond his wildest dreams. After $11.4 million in compensation pushed him into the No. 2 spot in *BUSINESS WEEK*'s 1985 survey of executive pay, Iacocca landed first place in 1986. His thumping $20.5 million in compensation from salary, bonuses, and stock options was $8 million higher than second-place finisher Paul Fireman, chairman of Reebok International Ltd. In the past, only founder-entrepreneurs or corporate raiders could boast higher earnings than Iacocca in a single year.

Iacocca wasn't the only boss who pocketed a fat paycheck in 1986. Among the 317 companies in *BW*'s 37th Annual Executive Compensation Scoreboard, compiled with Standard & Poor's Compustat Services Inc., chief executives did remarkably well. While most managers and run-of-the-mill executives had to settle for raises of less than 6%, the average chief executive's salary and bonus jumped 17.9%, to $829,887, in 1986. That's nearly double 1985's 9% rise even after excluding a total of $22 million in one-year bonus payments to Iacocca and Reebok's Fireman. Along with a

56% rise in long-term incentive compensation, the *CEO*s' total pay increased 29%, to an average $1.2 million.

This is the largest single increase in years, far outstripping 1986's inflation rate of less than 2% and nudging out the 16% increase in pay for labor leaders. Some 220 executives out of the 634 surveyed made $1 million or more last year in total compensation. In 1981 only four executives did as well.

"It's a healthy jump, but profits have been up," says David N. Swinford, who heads the executive pay practice at consultant Towers, Perrin, Forster & Crosby. "Bonuses jumped strongly, and people were cashing out a lot of options."

Nearly half of the chief executives in the survey enjoyed salary and bonus increases of 20% or more, while only 42 of the top officers saw their salaries and bonuses decrease in 1986. All told, the companies in *BW*'s survey boosted their top two executives' pay and bonuses by an average 17%, to $703,096. The average pay increased 12.7% in 1984 and only 9% in 1985. If you add in long-term compensation, the annual increase for all executives bumps up to 26%. The combined average compensation is $1,019,226.

Iacocca is in elite company among the best-paid executives in *BW*'s sample, which comes from companies at the top of the *BUSINESS WEEK* 1000 rankings. Of the 25 highest-paid executives in the survey, a number hail from well-paying Wall Street firms such as Salomon, Bear Stearns, and First Boston. In fact, Bear, Stearns & Co. Chairman Alan C. Greenberg made the top 10 on only 6 months' pay—$4.1 million—which the company reported after going public last year.
SAFE LANDINGS. Victor Posner, the Miami

THE 25 HIGHEST-PAID EXECUTIVES

	Company	1986 salary and bonus	Long-term compensation	Total pay
		Thousands of dollars		
1. LEE A. IACOCCA, Chmn.	Chrysler	$10984	$9558	**$20542**
2. PAUL FIREMAN, Chmn.	Reebok Intl.	13063	—	**13063**
3. VICTOR POSNER, Chmn.	DWG	8400	—	**8400**
4. JOHN J. NEVIN, Chmn.	Firestone	785	5570	**6355**
5. CHARLES E. EXLEY JR., Chmn.	NCR	938	5357	**6295**
6. SIDNEY J. SHEINBERG, Pres.	MCA	559	5520	**6079**
7. MAURICE R. GREENBERG, Pres.	American Intl. Group	823	3780	**4603**
8. DONALD E. PETERSEN, Chmn.	Ford	1961	2375	**4336**
9. RAND V. ARASKOG, Chmn.	ITT	1665	2590	**4255**
10. ALAN C. GREENBERG, Chmn.	Bear Stearns	4078	—	**4078***
11. THOMAS S. MURPHY, Chmn.	Cap Cities/ABC	734	3342	**4076**
12. JOHN M. RICHMAN, Chmn.	Kraft	1037	2945	**3982**
13. RICHARD J. SCHMEELK, Exec. V-P	Salomon	3391	479	**3870**
14. JOHN F. WELCH JR., Chmn.	General Electric	1688	2179	**3867**
15. THOMAS SPIEGEL, Pres.	Columbia S & L	3860	—	**3860**
16. FREDERICK J. MANCHESKI, Chmn.	Echlin	799	3040	**3839**
17. DANIEL B. BURKE, Pres.	Cap Cities/ABC	697	3084	**3781**
18. JOHN N. GUTFREUND, Chmn.	Salomon	3114	523	**3637**
19. CHARLES F. KNIGHT, Chmn.	Emerson Electric	1279	2266	**3545**
20. MICHAEL D. EISNER, Chmn.	Walt Disney	3378	—	**3378**
21. DOUGLAS D. DANFORTH, Chmn.	Westinghouse	1245	2058	**3303**
22. ROBERT E. MERCER, Chmn.	Goodyear	557	2744	**3301**
23. PETER T. BUCHANAN, Pres.	First Boston	3000	218	**3218**
24. WILLIAM M. McCORMICK, Pres.	Fireman's Fund	707	2464	**3171**
25. ROBERTO C. GOIZUETA, Chmn.	Coca-Cola	1920	1195	**3115**

*Compensation for six months only; data for full year unavailable.

DATA: STANDARD & POOR'S COMPUSTAT SERVICES INC.

Beach financier who led last year's compensation derby, didn't do poorly in 1986 either. He comes in third at $8.4 million on the basis of his pay from *DWG* Corp., a holding company, which lost $8.4 million on $1.1 billion in revenues.

In a new, revised analysis comparing executive pay to corporate performance, the *BW* scoreboard evaluates compensation two ways. It measures how much executives were paid relative to the return their shareholders received in the last three years. It also measures executive pay relative to the profitability of their companies and the improvement or decline in profitability over three years.

The winners and losers: Crown Cork & Seal Co. Chairman John F. Connelly and Price Co.

Chairman Robert E. Price gave shareholders the best performance relative to the money they earned. In contrast, Humana Inc. Chairman David A. Jones and Panhandle Eastern Corp. Chief Executive Robert D. Hunsucker delivered the least, relative to their pay over the past three years (page 48).

Some of the biggest stars in compensation last year were executives who lost their jobs and took advantage of so-called golden parachutes. Indeed, 4 of the top 10 parachutes opened had nothing to do with takeovers but were triggered when executives either resigned or took early retirement. Two of the biggest of those packages went to executives who were ousted from their positions by boardroom votes: former *CBS* Inc. Chairman Thomas

THE 10 LARGEST GOLDEN PARACHUTES

	Company	What led to payment	Total package* Thousands of dollars
1. **THOMAS M. MACIOCE**, Chmn.	Allied Dept. Stores	Campeau takeover	$13600
2. **THOMAS H. WYMAN**, Chmn.	CBS	Ousted by board	11439
3. **GERALD S. OFFICE JR.**, Chmn.	Ponderosa	Asher Edelman takeover	8300
4. **GERALD G. PROBST**, CEO	Sperry	Burroughs merger	6670
5. **MICHEL VAILLAUD**, Chmn.	Schlumberger	Ousted by board	6200
6. **JOHN R. MILLER**, Pres.	Standard Oil	Resigned under pressure	5623
7. **JOSEPH H. JOHNSON**, Chmn.	Assoc. Dry Goods	May Dept. Stores takeover	4900
8. **ANTHONY LUISO**, Exec. V-P	Beatrice	Leveraged buyout	4557
9. **JOHN D. MACOMBER**, Chmn.	Celanese	Hoechst takeover	4514
10 **RALPH P. DAVIDSON**, Chmn.**	Time	Early retirement	4029

*Includes final salary, bonus, long-term compensation, certain retirement benefits, and estimated future annuity payments as well as parachute **Executive Committee

DATA: COMPANY REPORTS, BUSINESS WEEK ESTIMATES

H. Wyman, who is collecting an $11.4 million bundle, and former Schlumberger Ltd. Chief Executive Michel Vaillaud, who was awarded $6.2 million.

OPTIONS ROLE. This marks the third consecutive year Iacocca was among the top five corporate wage earners. In the past three years he has pulled down $37.5 million—more than twice as much as the next highest-paid chief executive, Humana's Jones. That's why Iacocca ranks poorly in *BW*'s pay-for-performance category (page 46)—despite the dynamic turnaround at Chrysler, whose aggregate market value has risen 25 times in the past five years.

Stock options played a big role in both Iacocca's and Jones's hefty compensation. By exercising options granted over many years, executives often end up with a huge gain in a single year. *BW* attempts to treat them fairly by comparing executive pay and performance over three years. But there are problems: Some executives can look bad because they collect a fat bonus for good performance in earlier years; others can look good because they have yet to cash in their option shares.

Scorekeeping will not get any easier in the future. An increasing number of companies have moved to long-term incentive plans that cause one-year spikes in pay. Many corporations, for example, handed out stock to their senior executives in lieu of short-term bonuses or salary increases in the early 1980s. Some of these plans are now paying off. The result: "Swings in pay are going to look wilder and wilder," says Robin A. Ferracone, vice-president at Management Compensation Group Inc.

Of course, no one can complain about Chrysler's performance under Iacocca. For every $100 shareholders invested in Chrysler three years ago, they had $214, counting stock appreciation and dividends, by last year's end. Given Iacocca's huge compensation totals, though, shareholders also paid him extremely well for that performance.

STYMIED SHAREHOLDERS. Predictably, some observers think he was paid far too handsomely. "No one individual can possibly be worth that much money to a corporation," says Owen F. Bieber, president of the United Auto Workers. "Compensation like this sends the wrong message, a message of greed and complacency in an industry that can't afford that kind of thinking."

Iacocca is virtually assured a spot among the top 10 next year, too, because he is entitled to another outright stock grant of 112,500 shares this year if he remains chairman of Chrysler. At the current price of $58 a share, that bonus alone would total $6.5 million.

Posner, however, isn't likely to come out of 1987 with quite such a huge take from *DWG*. One of the terms of a $55 million bailout last year by financier Carl H. Lindner was that *DWG* would

THESE PENNY-PINCHERS DELIVER A BIG BANG FOR THEIR BUCKS

Don't look for personalized stationery on the chief executive's desk at Price Co. Robert E. Price pens his notes on torn sheets of paper. And don't imagine that you've reached a male secretary when you call Crown Cork & Seal Co.'s executive offices. Chairman John F. Connelly is probably on the other end of the telephone line.

Their bare-bones approach has paid off handsomely. According to *BUSINESS WEEK*'s pay-performance analysis (page 46), Connelly, the 82-year-old chief executive of the Philadelphia-based can manufacturer, garnered shareholders the best returns for the least pay in the last three years. And Price, 45, who heads the nation's largest retail warehouse club, steered the San Diego-based company to the best profits relative to the chief executive's pay, on average, for the past three years.

The two executives are a nation apart geographically, but their operating philosophies are resoundingly similar. Both are hands-on operators who pay close attention to details, emphasize cost-cutting, and prefer to pay themselves meager salaries in an age when corporate compensation continues to skyrocket.

TIES THAT BIND. Connelly, for example, earned a total of only $663,000 in the past three years—less than the *CEO* average in 1986 alone. Yet Crown shareholders saw the value of their shares nearly triple in the same period. Price picked up even less pay—$655,000—while maintaining an enviable 25% return on equity since 1984. Both executives, however, closely tie their personal fortunes to the company's stock: Connelly owns $17.2 million worth of Crown and controls another $182 million through a charitable foundation he set up. Price owns a $58.1 million stake in his company.

As might be expected, Connelly and Price aren't typical buttoned-down corporate chieftains. Connelly believes workers should travel on their own time for company business. He sometimes

not pay Posner more than $3 million in salary and $600,000 in bonus. But the agreement didn't affect his fiscal 1986 pay, nor did a shareholders' suit that alleged his high salary and corporate perks were a "waste of corporate assets."

Despite the continued climb in executive pay, mounting public criticism of how much executives make is forcing a reevaluation in some circles. General Motors Corp. has decided to end its often-criticized bonus plan. The plan came under attack earlier this year when *GM* set aside $169 million for executive bonuses while deciding to omit profit-sharing payments to 500,000 workers.

Columbia Savings & Loan Assn. paid President Thomas Spiegel a smaller bonus in 1986 than it thought was "justified and deserved" because of pressure from the Federal Home Loan Bank Board. The board had asked Columbia to recover all but Spiegel's $960,000 salary after it announced he got almost $9 million in total pay in 1985. Even so, Spiegel made nearly $3.9 million last year, enough to rank him as the 15th highest-paid executive in the country.

PRIME PARACHUTES. Paying executives who leave is another controversial area. The latest wrinkle in these golden parachute severance and benefits packages significantly broadens their use. Many such plans now have what consultants call a "double trigger"—they're unfurled not only after a change in a company's control but also when an executive is fired or is required to relocate.

As golden parachutes become easier to open, however, they are getting smaller. This year's largest package—a $13.6 million deal for former Allied Dept. Stores Chairman Thomas M. Macioce—is only a third of the record $35 million taken away by former Revlon Chairman Michel Bergerac in 1985. Many companies are limiting

instructs managers on such small matters as moving their phones to the other side of their desks. Similarly, Price will unload merchandise from a truck or stock an empty shelf. He sits at a desk made of particleboard and Formica, and stacks his books on shelves made of cinder blocks and wood planks.

That penny-pinching shows up on the bottom line: Crown spent just 2.8% of sales on general and administrative costs last year—well below the industry average. Connelly intends to push these expenses even lower. He already has corporate headquarters on the second floor of a Philadelphia can plant that gives executives only glass-partitioned cubicles to call their own. "It's a no-nonsense, back-to-basics strategy—except they never left the basics," says Merrill Lynch & Co. analyst Richard Palm.

The son of a blacksmith, Connelly founded his company as Connelly Containers Inc. four decades ago, and in 1957 merged the $40 million business with Crown. The company last year sold $1.6 billion in cans and can machinery, mostly for the beverage industry.

NO RAISE, PLEASE. Price, son of the founder of Price Co., is as parsimonious as Connelly, and that has paid off in average store sales of $108,000 a year—among the highest in the industry. To keep merchandise markups slim, Price tries to hold down salaries, including his own. Price refused a suggestion from the board several months ago that he accept a big raise. Price's father, Sol, 70, draws no salary at all but owns $217.5 million in stock. "Robert's just trying to remind people of the value of a dollar," says Richard M. Libenson, executive vice-president. "It's easy to lose sight of that when a company grows big and profitable."

A former Peace Corps volunteer and a law-school dropout, Price joined FedMart, his father's discount chain, as a manager in the mid-1960s. In 1976, a year after they sold FedMart to German retailer Hugo Mann, Robert and his father opened their first Price Club, a members-only, no-frills, cash-and-carry warehouse store selling everything from televisions to peanut butter.

For an encore, Connelly intends to expand his overseas canmaking operations. Price plans to add 11 stores on both coasts to his 28-store base. But does either one plan any perks for senior executives? No way.

By Christopher S. Eklund in Philadelphia and Julie Flynn in Los Angeles, with Laurie Baum in New York

such packages to three times an executive's annual compensation. Still, parachute-type contracts are being granted to executives farther down the corporate ladder. One recent study by Gilbert Dwyer & Co. found the average estimated cost of these arrangements is more than $4 million per company, with the highest near $60 million.

Generally, though, even if shareholders are up in arms over the big numbers, there is little they can do about them. "There's a lot of back-scratching going on, and there are a lot of sweetheart deals being made," says Roland M. Machold, co-chairman of the Council of Institutional Investors, a group of state government and labor pension funds. "But it's hard to come to grips with this issue, because shareholders don't have the right to approve personnel issues."

Some experts, by contrast, believe corporate executives are far from overpaid—especially in comparison with what blue-chip investment bankers, attorneys, and consultants are pulling down. Take Firestone Tire & Rubber Co. Chairman John J. Nevin, who landed among the top 10 best-paid executives by earning $6.4 million in 1986. Most of the money came by way of an incentive clause that put a $5.6 million bonus in his pocket last year for boosting the tire company's earnings to a preset level over a period of six years. "There are guys on Wall Street who made as much in two days of speculating," says Nevin.

JUST SAYING 'NO.' At least one executive thought his performance didn't measure up to his compensation, however. Kenneth L. Lay, chairman of Houston-based Enron Corp., declined a $187,500 bonus to which he was entitled under his company's plan. Why? The natural gas pipeline company's net income rebounded to $57.7 million last year from a $54.7 million loss a year earlier

PAY FOR PERFORMANCE: WHO MEASURES UP...AND WHO DOESN'T

There is no perfect way to compare corporate compensation, but BUSINESS WEEK's two measurement systems offer useful benchmarks. One relates executive pay to total shareholder return. The other relates pay to an index that includes return on equity and change in return on equity. All data are for the three-year period that ended Dec. 31, 1986. Here are the chief executives who come off best and worst according to both measures:

EXECUTIVES WHO GAVE SHAREHOLDERS THE MOST FOR THEIR PAY...

		1984-86		
		Total pay* ($000)	Shareholder return**	Index
1. JOHN F. CONNELLY	Crown Cork & Seal	$663	176%	416
2. HAROLD V. MAVERTY	Deluxe Check Printers	981	268	376
3. ROBERT E. PRICE	Price	655	102	309
4. BERT BALLENGEE	Southwestern Public Service	651	86	286
5. ROBERT K. CAMPBELL	Pa. Power & Light	819	114	261

...AND THOSE WHO GAVE SHAREHOLDERS THE LEAST

1. DAVID A. JONES	Humana	17731	−3	5
2. LEE A. IACOCCA	Chrysler	37479	114	6
3. AN WANG	Wang Laboratories	5230	−66	6
4. EDSON D. DECASTRO	Data General	10099	−21	8
5. RICHARD K. EAMER	Natl. Medical	9854	5	11

EXECUTIVES WHOSE COMPANIES DID THE BEST RELATIVE TO THEIR PAY...

		1984-86			
		Total pay*	Avg. return on equity	Change in ROE***	Index
1. ROBERT E. PRICE	Price	655	25%	−2	182
2. SAMUEL J. HEYMAN	GAF	1717	17	42	172
3. HAROLD V. MAVERTY	Deluxe Check Printers	981	30	3	164
4. JOHN F. CONNELLY	Crown Cork & Seal	663	13	4	131
5. BERT BALLENGEE	Southwestern PS	651	18	−3	111

...AND THOSE WHOSE COMPANIES DID THE WORST

1. R. D. HUNSUCKER	Panhandle Eastern	1955	−8	−46	−138
2. DAVID S. TAPPAN JR.	Fluor	1447	−21	−11	−111
3. ROBERT A. HANSON	Deere	1206	−5	−21	−104
4. ROBERT M. PRICE	Control Data	2654	−22	−29	−97
5. GORDON E. MOORE	Intel	1160	0	−22	−96

*Salary, bonus, and long-term compensation paid for entire three-year period   **Stock price at the end of 1986 plus dividends for three years divided by stock price at the end of 1983   ***Change in index expressed in percentage points

DATA: STANDARD & POOR'S COMPUSTAT SERVICES INC.

but largely because of a gain from Enron's sale of its petrochemicals business. "I know our financial performance in 1986 was not what we would have liked it to be," concedes Lay, who merely collected his base pay of $650,973 last year.

Increasingly, boards are tying incentive clauses directly to a company's earnings. Reebok Chairman Fireman gets 5% of any pretax corporate profits exceeding $20 million. That clause—toned down from 10% before the company went public—provided Fireman with a $12.7 million bonus last year on top of his $363,931 in base pay.

Similarly, Walt Disney Co. Chief Executive Michael D. Eisner last year received a $2.6 million cash bonus on top of his $750,000 salary because an incentive clause in his contract provides for an annual bonus of 2% of the company's net income over a 9% return on equity. Disney's *ROE* rose to 19% last year from 8% in 1984. No one's griping. "If a guy ends up giving you a home run with the bases loaded, why complain?" says Lee S. Isgur, a PaineWebber Inc. analyst.

Some compensation specialists are applauding such plans because they provide for relatively low to moderate salaries and leave a greater proportion of pay at risk—and particularly because they seem to link executive pay to performance more closely. Still, not all evidence supports such a relationship. One new study of executive pay shows virtually no correlation between what executives get paid and how their companies perform. The report, by professors Michael C. Jensen and Kevin J. Murphy of the University of Rochester, examined the pay of nearly 2,000 executives in 1,200 companies from 1974 to 1984. On average, the study showed, chief executives received raises of less than 6¢ for each $1,000 of increased shareholder wealth. They also got pay cuts of less than 6¢ when shareholders lost $1,000.

"We've got a pay system that is out of whack," says Jensen, director of the school's Managerial Economics Research Center. "It looks like it was designed for bureaucrats, and that's what it's creating. It provides them with little incentive to take major risks. Executives tend to be overpaid for bad performance and underpaid for good performance."

While executive paychecks in the seven digits often prompt the public to wonder how anyone can be worth that much, a few compensation gurus believe that stellar performing chief executives deserve even far greater rewards. "*CEO* compensation is but a tiny fraction of total human

'If a guy ends up giving you a home run with the bases loaded, why complain?'

resources costs for large companies and an even smaller fraction of a major corporation's total worth," says Lance Berger, executive vice-president of consultants Hay Group Inc. "With the stakes so high, a million or multimillion-dollar compensation arrangement is no longer outrageous."

Some cite far more lucrative compensation contracts in other fields that compete with the corporate sector for the most talented individuals. Jensen and Murphy, for instance, maintain that the lack of heftier incentives in executive pay is partly behind the increasing number of leveraged buyouts by management teams as well as the reduced numbers of top business school graduates who enter the corporate sector.

*MBA*s from the Harvard business school who enter the investment banking and consulting fields boast salary premiums of more than 26% over their colleagues who enter corporate life. In 1976-77 the premium was less than 11%.

Prestige law firms, such as Wachtell, Lipton, Rosen & Katz, pay their many partners average annual incomes well exceeding half a million dollars. Indeed, the law firm of Skadden, Arps, Slate, Meagher & Flom was estimated to have paid its nearly 110 partners average incomes of $540,000 in 1984. The researchers point out that not a single U. S. corporation similarly rewards its senior executive team with such generosity.

"The system is pushing the most talented potential managers off into becoming entrepreneurs, investment bankers, attorneys, and consultants,"

THE PERFORMANCE TOOK A BEATING, THE PAYCHECKS DIDN'T

Neither David A. Jones, chairman of Humana Inc., nor Robert D. Hunsucker, chief executive of Panhandle Eastern Corp., has had it easy in the past few years. Jones's 86-hospital chain, based in Louisville, has faced unprecedented rivalry for patients. Hunsucker's Houston pipeline company has been hit by tumbling gas prices and a costly legal settlement with an Algerian supplier.

These problems have levied a heavy toll on both Jones's and Hunsucker's companies—but not on their own paychecks. *BUSINESS WEEK*'s pay-performance analysis flags the two out of some 317 corporate leaders. Jones's pay was the highest relative to a company's return to shareholders over the last three years. Hunsucker earned the most relative to his company's financial performance.

TIMELY PLAY. Jones, 55, raked in an estimated $17.7 million—most of it by exercising stock options in 1984. Over the same three-year period, Humana shareholders lost 3% on their investment. Hunsucker, 62, earned $2 million in the past three years, while Panhandle was falling deeply into the red.

The problems that have plagued both executives in recent years contrast with impressive pasts. Jones's foray into health care began in 1961 when he co-founded Humana. He had remarkable success, building a profitable billion-dollar sales giant by 1980.

In recent years, though, a crackdown by government and employers on insurance payments has left Humana—and the hospital industry—with a lot of unused capacity. Jones responded by moving Humana into health insurance and walk-in doctors' offices. Both ventures put pressure on Humana's results in fiscal 1986, when earnings plummeted 74.8%, to $54.4 million, on gross revenues of $3.4 billion.

Like many successful corporate builders, Jones was granted generous stock options when Humana was a growth star. In exercising some of them in early 1984, he realized a $15.8 million gain, just prior to the downturn of the entire hospital industry.

Humana says Jones's compensation is justified. Charles E. Teeple, Humana's vice-president for investor relations, points out that the company's stock has soared 8,315% since its original offering in 1968. "The performance of the company under Mr. Jones's leadership has been excellent," he says.

Humana, like many other companies, insists that it is unfair to compare income from options granted over many years with a company's performance over fewer years. But the government considers gains on stock options to be income in the year they are taken, even though they may have accumulated over many years. To minimize the impact of single-year windfalls, *BUSINESS WEEK* bases its compensation analysis on three-year periods.

At Panhandle Eastern, it was the company's severe financial problems—not sizable stock options—that made Hunsucker's compensation seem generous. Panhandle lost $542 million on revenues of $2.2 billion last year, the worst performance in its 58-year history.

Hunsucker makes no attempt to sugarcoat his company's performance. "We did have some serious problems," he admits. But he says he's made progress in the past year by getting Panhandle out of the money-losing oil-field-service business and writing down assets in a coal-mining unit. Last October he spun off Anadarko Petroleum Corp. to shareholders. Now, the two stocks together are trading around 56, up 65% from a year ago. Hunsucker's glad that he stood firm against an unsolicited $50-a-share takeover bid last June.

HIGH MARKS. Jones still gets high marks from analysts because Humana was a stellar performer for so many years. They also applaud his recent efforts to boost earnings. He plans to sell part of

MedFirst, the doctors' office venture. And he has installed more rigorous reviews of customers who bought Humana's health insurance. That product backfired when many of its members shunned Humana facilities in favor of more expensive hospitals, raising insurance payments beyond expectations.

Whether Jones and Hunsucker can bring performance more closely in line with their paychecks remains to be seen. Both men, at least, are working hard to fix what ails their companies.

By Jo Ellen Davis in Houston and Kathleen Deveny in Chicago, with Laurie Baum in New York

says Jensen. "In the long run, we'll end up starving our corporations of the talent they need at the helm."

With the kinds of numbers being posted by Iacocca and others this year, that may sound like an exaggeration. Still, the executives who run America's largest companies bear the most responsibility for keeping the economy productive—and

they clearly aren't making the most money.

By John A. Byrne in New York, with bureau reports

DISCUSSION QUESTIONS

1. What is the relationship between top executive pay and corporate performance?
2. What are some of the criticisms of executive compensation?

PART 2

PLANNING

Planning, the first of the conventional management processes, follows the introductory exploration of managers and organizations in the management course. The planning component of a typical introductory course includes such topics as corporate mission and objectives, strategy, and decision making. These topics would be treated in various ways by diverse instructors and textbook authors, but they are core topics in planning.

An intent shared by instructors is that students progress in their ability to apply these planning concepts to management practice. The articles in Part 2 help by describing the activities of several diverse corporations and, through discussion questions, asking the student to identify and analyze issues of planning in these cases.

The questions invite application of models and ideas such as Michael Porter's generic strategies, the BCG (Boston Consulting Group) matrix, and Miles and Snow's adaptive cycle model. Questions ask for recognition of missions and objectives, for evaluation of strategies, and for discussion of decision processes.

WILL ALL THAT RESTRUCTURING EVER PAY OFF FOR ED HENNESSY'S ALLIED?

THE CEO HAS BEEN SO WRAPPED UP IN DEALMAKING, IT'S HARD TO TELL WHERE THE COMPANY IS GOING

FEBRUARY 2, 1987, PP. 78-80

'There was a blinding snow storm," says Edward L. Hennessy Jr., recounting a treacherous flight to Springfield, Mass., in early January. The runway was nowhere to be seen. But the chairman of Allied-Signal Inc., sitting in the cockpit of his corporate jet, could see the landing strip as an image on the screen of the Falcon 50's instrument system—which just happens to be made by Allied's Bendix aerospace unit. "As we broke through the storm, we [could] see the runway for the first time. We were right on target," he beams, gliding his right hand in for a landing on his desk. "I had great faith."

Hennessy, a onetime pilot, is convinced he has landed Allied right on target, too. Since becoming chief executive in 1979, the 58-year-old Hennessy has made Allied one of the most restructured companies in America. He has spent more than $8 billion on acquisitions and sold operations with sales of more than $7 billion. He's moved into health care, information systems, and electronics businesses, then backed right out of them. He has hired and fired and slashed corporate staff. He engineered a stock split, then doubled the number of shares via a merger deal, only to embark on a stock buyback. Little of what he started with—the old Allied Chemical Corp., a stodgy $3.3 billion commodity chemicals and oil company—remains.

Today, Allied's sales run close to $12 billion annually. It trades in aerospace, automotive components, advanced materials, and electronics (charts)—though the electronics sector will soon be gone.

'A LOT OF CHURNING.' Unfortunately for Hennessy, many outsiders don't share his faith. To them, Allied hasn't crashed, but it hasn't soared either. In price-earnings ratios, Allied trails the Standard & Poor's 500 by more today than it did when Hennessy joined the company. In 1985, Allied posted a loss after a huge write-off. Earnings per share for 1986 will be off more than 20% from 1984, and profits will be flat in 1987. "There's been a lot of churning and not much to show for it," says Howard A. Rubel, an analyst at Cyrus J. Lawrence Inc.

The wheeling and dealing itself raises questions. At a time when experts are praising focused companies, Allied is viewed as a hodgepodge. It has sold units outside the aerospace, automotive, and materials businesses, but "it's really not a focused company," says one consultant. He calls Allied a "dinosaur" and derides its attempts to look high tech by renaming its chemicals sector "engineered materials." Indeed, much of Allied's business is decidedly middle-tech. And despite Hennessy's claims of synergy among his three businesses, managers can cite few such examples. At issue, too, is Hennessy's credibility. He has changed plans so many times, often reversing an earlier pronouncement, that it's hard to know what to expect.

A tough, impatient man, Hennessy is the Boston-born son of a salesman. He once intended to become a Catholic priest but left the seminary after three years. He worked in accounting while attending Fairleigh Dickinson University at night. After getting a *BS* in finance at 27, he began a series of jobs before signing on as a controller at *ITT* Corp. under Harold S. Geneen, the master conglomerateur. Four years later he went to Heublein Inc., rising to senior vice-president for administration and finance.

After seven years, Hennessy jumped to the same post at United Technologies Corp., run by Harry J. Gray, another grand acquisitor. There, Hennessy kept honing his skills as a dealmaker, not an operations man. But strains between the two men, both with strong egos, grew.

When the chance to run an entire corporation arose, Hennessy was ready to leap. But Allied was a mess. It drew nearly 80% of its income from oil and gas. Its 1978 financial statements had been qualified by accountants, pending the outcome of several lawsuits. "When I got here," he concedes, "I couldn't figure out where I wanted to go."

He began spending money. He talked up the buoyant prospects of health care and electronics, as he paid out more than $1.2 billion for Eltra Corp., a maker of typesetting equipment and other electronic equipment; Bunker Ramo Corp., an information services company; and Fisher Scientific Co., a laboratory equipment maker.

Everything began to change, however, in 1983. In the most celebrated takeover battle of its time, Bendix Corp. Chairman William M. Agee had lunged at Martin Marietta Co. Marietta fought back, and each company bought a stake in the other. *UTC* joined the fray, as did Allied. When the dust cleared, Hennessy had snapped up Bendix for $1.8 billion.

'MORE GLOBAL.' Bendix put Allied into the aerospace and automotive businesses, and Hennessy began to recast Allied around them. In 1985 his pace quickened: He sold 50% of Allied's last energy business, Union Texas Petroleum. Then he bolstered both the aerospace and automotive businesses by buying Signal Cos. Last year he spun off most of Allied's remaining troubles into the Henley Group Inc. (page 56).

Reviewing his record, Hennessy pronounces it good. "We have done a tremendous transformation, faster than I thought was possible when I was evaluating whether I wanted to work here," he says. He likes his idea of a technology-based company in huge, fairly stable businesses. Every Allied operation, except for those in development, is making money, he notes. Asked about the fu-

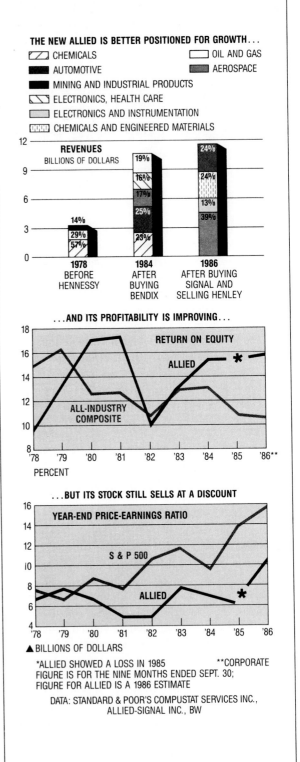

THE NEW ALLIED IS BETTER POSITIONED FOR GROWTH...

CHEMICALS   OIL AND GAS
AUTOMOTIVE   AEROSPACE
MINING AND INDUSTRIAL PRODUCTS
ELECTRONICS, HEALTH CARE
ELECTRONICS AND INSTRUMENTATION
CHEMICALS AND ENGINEERED MATERIALS

REVENUES
BILLIONS OF DOLLARS

1978 BEFORE HENNESSY — 14%, 29%, 57%
1984 AFTER BUYING BENDIX — 19%, 16%, 17%, 25%, 23%
1986 AFTER BUYING SIGNAL AND SELLING HENLEY — 24%, 24%, 13%, 39%

...AND ITS PROFITABILITY IS IMPROVING...

RETURN ON EQUITY
ALLIED
ALL-INDUSTRY COMPOSITE

'78 '79 '80 '81 '82 '83 '84 '85 '86**
PERCENT

...BUT ITS STOCK STILL SELLS AT A DISCOUNT

YEAR-END PRICE-EARNINGS RATIO
S & P 500
ALLIED

'78 '79 '80 '81 '82 '83 '84 '85 '86
▲ BILLIONS OF DOLLARS

*ALLIED SHOWED A LOSS IN 1985   **CORPORATE
FIGURE IS FOR THE NINE MONTHS ENDED SEPT. 30;
FIGURE FOR ALLIED IS A 1986 ESTIMATE

DATA: STANDARD & POOR'S COMPUSTAT SERVICES INC.,
ALLIED-SIGNAL INC., BW

ture, Hennessy slips into a 1992 forecast: "Our goals are to have a pretty well-focused business in the businesses we're in today." Allied will have more advanced technology. "And we'll be more global." Allied will grow internally and through acquisitions, he adds.

To some Wall Streeters, Hennessy's moves make him a hero. Others believe, in the words of one, that "the stock will go up the day he leaves." Allied's fate on Wall Street, more than that of most companies, turns on the personality of its hard-charging *CEO*. Doubters wonder if he has a clear vision of Allied's future—and if he'll stick with it.

Certainly, Hennessy has had some very public changes of mind—even recently. A year ago he said he'd finished remodeling Allied. But in December he said he'd sell the company's so-called electronics sector—businesses such as connectors, video tape, and typesetting equipment—which have sales of $1.5 billion a year. In fact, by mid-1987, Hennessy will have sold or closed virtually everything he bought before Bendix.

POOR CREDIBILITY. The rapid-fire changes in strategy have been disorienting, to say the least. Says one former Allied executive who continues to talk with his former colleagues: "There's a sense of 'We know what we're doing today, but we're not sure what we're doing tomorrow.' "

Hennessy's other erratic moments haven't helped. He used to say Allied would get new businesses from its own research efforts. Now spending on research continues to grow, but the new ventures group he started—intended to nurture new technologies and businesses with no direct connection to Allied's existing businesses—has been disbanded. And when he bought Signal, Hennessy promised Allied's *CEO* slot to Signal President Michael D. Dingman in 1990—a deal that ended when Hennessy asked Dingman to head Henley.

Hennessy also lost credibility by promising in 1985 to buy back up to 25 million of Allied's 174 million shares then outstanding. So far, Allied has repurchased some 8 million shares. But it has also called its preferred stock, most of which was converted into common. So Allied has only reduced its shares to 173 million. Wall Street, meanwhile, wants Hennessy to buy back about 40 million shares to raise earnings per share.

Hennessy professes to be unperturbed by the negative reviews. "We don't play to Wall Street, because it's pretty fickle," he says. An example: In 1979, "they were telling us to sell everything and invest in oil and gas.... If I listened to Wall Street, we wouldn't be here today."

Still, the stock market is on Hennessy's mind. Leaving his office, which is perched several steps above the rest of the second floor at Allied's Morristown (N. J.) headquarters, Hennessy regularly stops at a Bunker Ramo machine to check Allied's stock price. Pressed, he admits "I often sit back and look at the multiple of General Electric and say 'Why can't we be where they are?' I look at Teledyne, Litton, United Technologies, *TRW*...." He trails off. Those stocks sell for at least 15 times earnings. Allied trades at about 11.5. "But as Harold Geneen once said to me, 'You've got to be patient,' " he says.

Hennessy measures his progress in other ways. "Geneen taught me asset management," he explains. "I have a hobby of looking at the return on assets of the Dow companies. In 1978, Allied was at the bottom, 30 out of 30. Now we're in the upper 20%."

Hennessy has progressed on other fronts, too. Allied, now out of commodities and into industrial products, some proprietary, has improved growth prospects. Hennessy has hired new talent where necessary—most recently, Robert L. Kirk, a 30-year veteran of the aerospace business, to lead Allied's charge in aerospace. Debt, at about 40% of capital, is not uncomfortable.

Hennessy's defenders say his whirlwind moves show nimbleness. "He does change his mind," says Gerard R. Roche, chairman of Heidrick & Struggles Inc., who recruited Hennessy for Allied eight years ago. "But it's a credit to him. He doesn't get hung up on one concept." Agrees Kirk, who also worked for Geneen: "I regard ability to change as an asset. He has an architecture over everything he does, as did Geneen. That's what allows you to be opportunistic."

But where will it all end?

TRYING TO TURN HENLEY INTO MORE THAN 'ASSETS AND A DREAM'

Michael D. Dingman took over Henley Group Inc., spun off from Allied-Signal Inc., just eight months ago. But already he's turned Henley topsy-turvy, as befits an Allied offspring. Henley's chairman is plotting a $3 billion-to-$10 billion acquisition, a partial spinoff of a lab-equipment business, and the sale of refuse-to-energy plants. Add to that the recent sale of a $100 million stake in a Green River (Wyo.) soda-ash plant to a glassmaker.

It's vintage Dingman—and Wall Street is betting he can parlay the underperforming assets of the 35 mostly unprofitable chemical and engineering companies shed by Allied into value for shareholders. "All Henley has today is assets and a dream," says Thomas G. Burns Jr. of Goldman, Sachs & Co. Henley shares are poised around 24, about 3 points more than the initial offering price. They could soar above 30, analysts say, based on underlying asset values, once the brokering of Henley's parts revs up.

STANDARD TOOLS. Henley has yet to earn a penny on its $5 billion in assets, though. In fact, it will report an estimated $350 million loss for 1986, mostly from write-offs. Some analysts question Dingman's tendency to deal-making rather than to managing existing businesses. Dingman, 55, agrees he is more portfolio manager than hands-on operator. He's never even visited the Green River soda-ash plant. Given that bent, Dingman says he surrounds himself with strong managers, such as President Paul M. Montrone, whom he met in 1970 at Wheelabrator-Frye Inc.

Dingman is using his standard tools to boost Henley's stock price: spinoffs, share buybacks, cost-cutting, and management incentives. One of his first moves is a 20% spinoff of Fisher Scientific Group Inc., the $543 million biotechnology and laboratory equipment maker. His next sale targets: Wheelabrator Technologies Inc.'s engineering companies and refuse-to-energy plants and General Chemical Corp.

Dingman has used other tactics to boost Henley's stock price. The company has bought back 1.3 million odd-lot shares and is authorized to repurchase up to 10 million shares—management thinks its stock is undervalued. Dingman and his top executives have a lot to gain if his overall strategy translates into share price gains. Dingman owns 1.5 million of Henley's 129 million outstanding shares, while the others bought shares at 21¼ with 10% down and a 90% loan from the company. The plan is the target of a lawsuit by a dissident shareholder.

Analysts say Dingman is waiting to wrap up talks to get back Allied's 15% share of Henley before making his next move, most likely that big acquisition of all or part of an undervalued "basic industrial company." That includes health care but excludes high-tech. Dingman denies rumors that he is looking at Owens-Illinois Inc. He may opt for partial ownership to avoid a market premium, he says, and he thinks his contribution to the new company's management will buoy the share price. If history is any guide, Dingman will make money for himself and the shareholders.

By Laurie Baum in New York

Hennessy insists his current business plan is the definitive one. He aims to fortify Allied's position in aerospace, mainly by selling larger subsystems than it does now and venturing further into missiles, antisubmarine warfare, and command and control systems. In the automotive area, Hennessy plans to capitalize on carmakers' desire to buy more goods from fewer suppliers. In materials, he'll move deeper into specialty products for high-growth industries, such as lightweight aluminum for aerospace. Innovation should play a role in all three areas. In 1992, Allied's revenues are projected to reach $19 billion.

MORE SELL-OFFS. Those moves may win Allied the recognition it feels it deserves. "Wall Street isn't exactly certain what Allied is," explains Vice-Chairman Forrest N. Shumway. "That will straighten out as people realize how strong we are in our three businesses."

But there will undoubtedly be more sell-offs—probably in aerospace and materials. Hennessy insists they'll be small units that mean little to the company, but some insiders and outsiders say he has considered selling larger items, too.

With the coming sales of its 15% stake in Henley, its 50% of Union Texas, and its electronics sector, Allied will raise some $2 billion—enough to burn a big hole in Hennessy's pocket. Nonetheless, he claims to have no plans for a major acquisition, though he admits to having designs on aerospace companies at the right price. John W. Barter, senior vice-president for planning, says there are a dozen sizable companies on Allied's acquisition watch list, not all in aerospace.

In the meantime, Hennessy's reputation hinges on what happens now that his key businesses are in place. The glory days of the defense industry are over, and pricing in automotives is very competitive. Allied has already cut a lot of fat in its businesses, so profit gains won't come easily without growth.

All Hennessy will say is: "We've been trying to create value for shareholders, and I think we can do a better job." Yet only when he finally settles down to managing, rather than constantly restructuring, will anyone know whether he has the right flight plan for Allied.

By Judith H. Dobrzynski, with Laurie Baum, in Morristown

DISCUSSION QUESTIONS

1. Why is a "focused" company thought to have an advantage?
2. Describe as clearly as you can, on the basis of the article, what Allied-Signal's corporate mission and objectives are?
3. What difficulty did you have in answering question 2, and what might your difficulty reveal about the management of Allied-Signal?

SONY'S CHALLENGE

THE MIGHTY YEN AND FIERCE COMPETITION ARE FORCING IT INTO NEW MARKETS

JUNE 1, 1987, PP. 64-69

There he is, sitting on the floor of his office with three remote controls in his hand, listening to a Beethoven symphony at high volume. He recorded the symphony from a broadcast of a recent Vienna Philharmonic concert in Tokyo, and now he's putting the tape to good use. As much as he likes music, Akio Morita likes trying out new stereo gear even better.

Morita is 66, and the last flecks of black long ago vanished from his silver hair. Although he's spending less time these days in his cluttered, wood-paneled chairman's office at Sony Corp., it's clear that Morita still provides much of the spark that has made the company synonymous with the success of postwar Japan: innovation, shrewd marketing, and quality. As executives repeatedly dash in for consultations, Morita patiently explains why one set of speakers he's checking out doesn't quite have the Sony sound.

Sony. The very name speaks volumes about the company. It comes not from a Japanese word that foreigners might find difficult to pronounce, but from *sonus*, the Latin word for sound, fine-tuned for Japanese tongues. The name symbolizes the company's origins in its pioneering tape recorders and transistor radios. It also has come to signify the international orientation among so many mightily successful Japanese companies. Some 70% of Sony's sales come from outside Japan.

UPSIDE DOWN. Recently, though, Sony has become one of the most visible symbols of trouble in Japan. Like other Japanese companies in businesses ranging from autos and steel to electronics and computers, Sony's world has been turned upside down. The dramatic rise of the yen has cramped its ability to compete in export markets. Protectionist sentiment is growing in the U.S. and Europe. And foreign rivals are fighting back like never before. Far East competitors, such as Taiwan and South Korea, are exploiting their lower costs, and U. S. and European companies are achieving efficiency gains and improvements in quality.

The high yen—*endaka* in Japanese— is slamming the nation's exporters two ways. Foreign competitors with costs denominated in dollars or French francs have more room to undercut Japanese companies on prices, and a dollar's worth of sales is worth less in yen. Measured in dollars, Sony's U. S. sales rose 24% last year. Measured in yen, they were down 11%. "The falling dollar has produced a nearly 50% tax on us," complains Morita.

Overall, the numbers tell a disappointing story. Worldwide sales slipped 7%, to $8.2 billion, in the fiscal year that ended last October, while earnings from operations fell a stunning 75%. Earnings declined another 56% for the five months ended in March from a year earlier. Archrival Matsushita Electric Industrial Co., by contrast, endured a more manageable 44% drop in operating earnings last year.

For Sony, *endaka* is like a drought that follows a plague of locusts. The challenges facing Morita and his hand-picked president, former opera singer Norio Ohga, have become even more daunting than they already were.

BETA BLOCK. Competition in consumer electronics is brutal. After coming up with such hits as Trinitron *TV*s and Walkman tape players, Sony watched the hottest market of the 1980s pass it by. The company clung to its Betamax videorecorder format while the rest of the world switched to *VHS*. That setback was costly, and the experience helped embolden competitors. They no longer wait to see whether Sony's innovative products succeed. Rivals that took about two years to come up with their own U. S. versions of the Walkman now respond to new Sony products in months. And the rising quality of competitors' products has narrowed the advantage that once permitted the company to build a successful advertising campaign around the simple phrase: "It's a Sony." To make matters worse, some of the most troublesome competitors are in South Korea or other Asian countries where costs are lower.

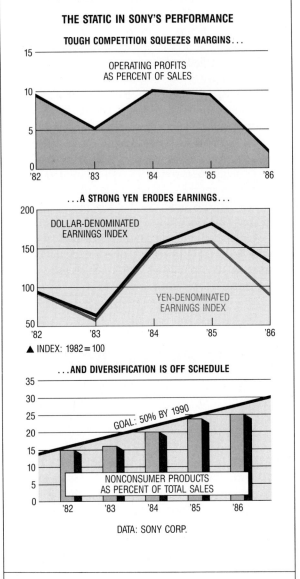

THE STATIC IN SONY'S PERFORMANCE

TOUGH COMPETITION SQUEEZES MARGINS...

OPERATING PROFITS AS PERCENT OF SALES

...A STRONG YEN ERODES EARNINGS...

DOLLAR-DENOMINATED EARNINGS INDEX

YEN-DENOMINATED EARNINGS INDEX

▲ INDEX: 1982 = 100

...AND DIVERSIFICATION IS OFF SCHEDULE

GOAL: 50% BY 1990

NONCONSUMER PRODUCTS AS PERCENT OF TOTAL SALES

DATA: SONY CORP.

Sony has fought back. Shortly after becoming president in 1982, Ohga set a goal of reducing Sony's dependence on consumer electronics by getting 50% of sales from nonconsumer products by 1990, compared with 15% at the time. Ohga has also served notice that executives at Sony factories must cut manufacturing costs beyond the 10% annual reductions of recent years. "We need quantum leaps in cost reduction," he says. To reduce its vulnerability to fluctuations in the yen and to become more responsive to its customers, Sony is expanding its substantial manufacturing operations overseas. And Sony clings almost defiantly to one of the company's most distinguishing characteristics: a research and development budget that amounts to about 9% of sales. Rival Matsushita spends only 4%.

Even for a company as innovative as Sony, the changes are not coming easily. "Our people are working very hard," says Morita. And all that hard work is carrying Sony into some unfamiliar territory, where the risk of missteps is high. The company's push into nonconsumer areas, such as computers and image processing, has been such tough going that Sony will not meet its timetable for diversification.

Other changes could be even more traumatic. In some areas, Sony is abandoning its time-honored, go-it-alone philosophy. It is sharing its technology with other companies, for example, in an effort to create industry standards for new products and to avoid another Betamax. Sony is also becoming more of a street fighter. It is pushing harder for larger shares of the markets for products, even if it means paring profit margins to compete head-to-head on price.

As if that's not turmoil enough, Sony must now sweat out a trade skirmish that could escalate into a war. So far, the company has avoided any serious damage from the cross-fire between Tokyo and Washington. Its semiconductors are not widely used in the computers covered by the tariff imposed by President Reagan recently, and all of the Sony television models that would have been covered by the tariff are made in San Diego. But the longer the U.S. trade account remains deeply in deficit, the greater the likelihood that Sony could get pinched in the U.S. market, which accounts for a third of its sales.

MAKING MISCHIEF? The opportunities for a retaliation-bent Congress to make mischief are legion. Even though Congress in April rejected a one-year ban on the ultrahigh-fidelity digital tape recorders recently introduced in Japan, legislators are likely to accomplish the same objective by other means. Congress is dawdling over legislation to require that the new products be equipped with devices that prevent them from duplicating tapes or re-

cords, a provision sought by the recording industry. Richard L. Sharp, president of Circuit City Stores Inc., isn't expecting digital tape machines to be in his stores for at least a year, as Sony and other manufacturers await a clear reading on the legislation.

Despite Sony's woes, Morita is as eager and enthusiastic as ever. He manages to sound upbeat about both the company's functional-looking, high-performance Profeel Pro *TV*, which is selling well, and the 8mm handheld video camera, which is struggling. "This year we will recover our profits, and next year will be a much better year," he says. Most analysts agree that Sony has at least halted the slide that has dragged its stock down to a recent five-year low in Tokyo and has kept its U.S.-traded shares essentially unchanged at about 20 for the past year. But analyst Eugene G. Glazer of Dean Witter Reynolds Inc. says it could be 1989 before Sony surpasses even last year's meager level of earnings.

Sony's struggle to recapture its glory will depend more and more on Ohga, since Morita is gradually diminishing his role in handling the company's day-to-day affairs. "As far as basic policy is concerned, I'm still in charge," Morita says. "But Ohga's running the company." The pair make a close-knit team. Ohga, 57, first met Morita more than 35 years ago, when he was studying opera at Tokyo University of the Arts. At that time, Ohga began writing letters to Sony in which he criticized the quality of the sound from the company's tape recorders, and by the time he left for Berlin to study voice, Morita signed him on as a consultant. After rebuffing several entreaties by Morita to forsake his opera career for a full-time position at Sony, Ohga finally relented in 1959. Before being named president, however, he served a 23-year apprenticeship that included running Sony's tape recorder division and a record company joint venture with *CBS* Inc.

ON THE STUMP. Ohga's growing authority allows Morita more freedom for the ambassadorial role he loves so much. He spends about a third of his time at Sony these days. The rest is devoted to trips overseas for such things as speechmaking or promoting his book, *Made in Japan,* and to his ceremonial functions in Japan. Last year he be-

THE SAGA OF SONY ALL STARTED WITH *SAKE*

Sony Corp. has built its reputation by staying up-to-date in the consumer electronics business. But the company might not be around today without help from a 300-year-old enterprise that is the single largest shareholder in Sony.

Sony's benefactor is Morita & Co., a family-owned business that has been brewing *sake*, the traditional Japanese rice-wine, under the brand name Nenohimatsu since the late 1600s. The company, which has 701 employees, is one among a host of small regional *sake* brewers in Japan. Morita & Co. also makes *miso*, a fermented soybean paste used in soups and sauces, and *shoyu*, or soy sauce. Under the management of Kyuzaemon Morita, the business provided a comfortable life for his son Akio and three other children in Nagoya, an industrial city 220 mi. southwest of Tokyo.

As the eldest son, Akio was expected to take over Morita & Co. Instead, after World War II, Morita, then 25, threw in his lot with business novices Masaru Ibuka and Tamon Maeda to start Tokyo Tsushin Kogyo, or Tokyo Telecommunications Engineering Co. Unable to get a bank loan for their struggling company, the trio turned to Akio's father, who repeatedly provided money through Morita & Co. in return for stock in the new venture.

AT HOME ABROAD. *TTK* evolved into Sony. And Morita & Co., with Akio's brother Kuzuaki at the helm, has seen some modest transformations of its own. Besides selling $40 million worth of *sake*, *shoyu*, and *miso* annually, the business now also includes food distributors, supermarkets, and a vineyard. Its boldest diversification so far, however, is Raykay Inc., an assortment of services that are aimed at Tokyo's foreign executives and their spouses. The venture offers a Japanese cooking school, interpreter services, and a language school.

Raykay is largely the brainchild of Hideo Morita, 35, Akio's eldest son. "I want people who come to Japan to know about my country, the differences between the cultures and how we really feel," he says. He plans to add courses in such Japanese arts as flower arranging and to help foreign companies set up in Japan, whether finding office space or renting furniture for executives' homes.

came a vice-chairman of Keidanren, the Japanese federation of economic organizations.

For all his outside activities, Morita still makes sure he gets involved in the crucial decisions at Sony. When it came time to price the portable compact disk player, for example, Morita decreed that it be priced at less than 50,000 yen, about $200 at the time. Even though the player cost more than that to make then, Morita correctly anticipated that the low price eventually would generate enough sales to provide the volume production that would trigger economies of scale—and profits. The episode shows how Sony is now pursuing market share more diligently. It is also an example of how Sony is responding to its experience with Betamax, the world's first home videorecorder. This high-profile product laid bare the company's strengths and its weaknesses.

As conceived, Betamax was a classic illustration of Sony's founding philosophy of looking for new markets where bigger, well-established companies were not a threat. The company correctly foresaw the immense latent demand for a machine that could make and play back home videotapes. But then it ceded the market to others by refusing to yield when the *VHS* format, first developed by Victor Co. of Japan, provided longer recording times and gradually became the industry standard. Sony still insists that its Beta recorders provide a superior picture. But a shrinking number of customers—currently about 5% of all buyers—are buying Beta.

MIDLIFE CRISIS? Some analysts think Betamax goes a long way toward explaining the new directions at Sony. "The Beta experience was so searing, so threatening, that it forced a major revision in the way the company positions itself," says James C. Abegglen, a Tokyo-based management consultant. One example: Sony has relaxed its tradition of sticking to the expensive, high-profit

Raykay was inspired by Hideo's own experiences overseas, particularly while studying at the University of California at Davis. He remembers vividly the trouble he had finding and furnishing an apartment. "The first night, I slept on an empty bed with no pillow or blanket. I had to sleep with my coat over me."

Hideo, who does not drink, always expected to work in the family *sake* business. In keeping with tradition, he will become president of Morita & Co. when Uncle Kuzuaki retires. He joined the company two years ago after stints in Sony's accounting and treasury departments and in the company's Japanese record venture with *CBS* Inc. At the artists and repertory department of *CBS/Sony Group Inc.*, he accompanied Julio Iglesias, Men at Work, Heart, and other performers on their tours of Japan.

Despite his diversification moves, Hideo says Morita's traditional products will always come first. "For my family, the Morita history has always been *miso*, *sake*, and *shoyu*," he says. Even Sony "is only a venture business for the Morita family." Some venture. Morita & Co. owns 9.4% of Sony. The initial $500 investment is now worth about $430 million.

By Amy Borrus in Tokyo

end of the market by coming out with a relatively cheap $32 Walkman just for the U. S. market.

Betamax is also one of the reasons Sony is showing more willingness to cooperate with competitors. In developing the technology for compact disks and players, Ohga forged an alliance with Dutch electronics giant Philips. Sony has since become the world's largest supplier of CD players, with 35% of the U.S. market, and is one of the largest producers of the disks themselves.

STUBBORNNESS. Sony has even started assembling products for its competitors. In an effort to win wider acceptance for its 8mm camcorder, which is incompatible with VHS video players, it has agreed with 127 manufacturers on standards for 8mm gear. Sony makes the 8mm equipment marketed by Pioneer, Fuji, and others.

Ultimately, the Betamax experience was "a blessing in disguise," says Yoshi Tsurumi, a professor of international business at the City University of New York and a friend of Morita. "Mr. Morita has become more receptive to other ideas and has been listening better." Tsurumi says he wouldn't be surprised to see Sony make an aquisition to strengthen its nonconsumer businesses.

It's not clear just how deep the new attitudes go, however. Sony's commitment to the VHS-incompatible 8mm camcorder resembles its stubbornness with Betamax. But this time, Sony executives say, the format could pay off in different products, such as individual movie players that could be rented on airplanes. More puzzling is Sony's unwillingness to give up on Betamax, which Morita still insists has technological advantages that can be exploited. Says one competitor: "If Sony switched to VHS format in their products, they would be No. 3 after one year." This summer, VHS makers plan to unveil an improved version in the U.S. that could make life even more difficult for both Betamax and the 8mm camcorder.

Sony's boldest move for dealing with a cutthroat consumer electronics market is its diversification into nonconsumer businesses. There, the theory goes, the company will be less dependent on coming up with a steady stream of relatively short-lived hit products—and able to use its unique talents in video and semiconductor technology to create its version of the office of the future. Sony engineers envision an office where they can "call up" their colleagues around the world by speaking their names to a video console on their desks. They could dictate memos to the same screen and send them with a voice command. They might carry a Walkman-size version with a tiny screen so they can review documents from the office files while entertaining clients on the golf course.

Sony's U.S. operation, which already gets 35% of its sales from nonconsumer products, is on the cutting edge of the diversification strategy. "We have approximately 20 new business areas just in Sony America where we are investing," says Neil Vander Dussen, president of Sony Corp. of America.

The efforts in the U.S. and around the world are producing some pieces of Sony's vision of the future. Sony was the first Japanese company with a powerful 32-bit desktop computer, which is the heart of its engineering workstation. It has quickly become a major producer of full-feature telephones in Japan. Sony also has taken the lead with the 3½-in. floppy disks and drives that are bidding to replace 5¼-in. disks as standard equipment on computers.

HOW SONY KEEPS THE COPYCATS SCAMPERING

Of all the problems besetting Sony, the two most frustrating are how to deal with copycat competitors and how to mute the impact of the rising yen on manufacturing costs. But Sony has shown it can rise to the challenge. Its experience with the Walkman is proof of that.

After Walkman's debut in July, 1979, Sony was not about to bask in the new product's almost instant success. Within months, Sony audio engineer Kozo Ohsone was heading a team trying to come up with a better Walkman. Ohsone carved a block of wood that was 25% smaller than the original design and gave it to his engineers as a model. The engineers grumbled, but they buckled down. By February, 1981, Sony was shipping thousands of Walkmans that were smaller, sounded better, and had nearly 50% fewer parts than Walkman I.

Sony continues to dominate the $1.3 billion business with a 30% share of personal tape players sold worldwide. The reason: "It has been more inventive than the others," says stock analyst Alan Bell of Salomon Brothers Asia Ltd. Walkman firsts include Dolby noise reduction in 1982 and a rechargeable battery in 1985.

Sony's inventiveness shows in more than technology. To keep Walkman fresh and to make it appealing to more customers, Sony churns out new models to suit virtually every taste and wallet. So far it has introduced about 100. Headed for the beach? Take the solar-powered, waterproof Walkman. Tennis, anyone? Here's an ultralight radio-only model that attaches to a sweatband. Want concert-hall sound? Slip on the oversize headphones of a deluxe Boodo Khan. In the U. S., where Sony has sold more than 13 million of the 27 million Walkmans it has made, prices run from a plain-vanilla playback-only model for $32 to a souped-up $449.95 version that boasts tape-deck-quality sound and records as well as plays.

Sony has used its image as a technology leader to gain a hammerlock on the lucrative premium end of the market. Walkman is the only portable stereo offered by the tony L. L. Bean catalog. Emphasizing that it is "made by Sony in Japan, like 'Mercedes Benz, made in Germany' " gives Walkman "intangible added value," says Ohsone, now audio group director.

PLAYING FOR KEEPS. All Walkman products are manufactured in Japan. And despite the soaring yen, Walkman production is the exception to Sony's strategy to move more production overseas. Even though the soaring yen squeezed profits, Sony says it still made money on the $432 million worth of Walkmans it sold last year. One reason: a decision four years ago to create a low-price model specifically for the U. S. That forced Sony to automate production drastically and design a new model that cut more than 30% off production costs partly by integrating the playing mechanism onto the printed circuit board. The basic $32 Walkman has become Sony's best-selling model in the U. S.

Analysts think Walkman's go-go years are coming to an end. But Sony disagrees. "Of the 4 billion people in the world, we estimate we could reach 600 million," says Ohsone. That may be an overstatement. But then, as long as Sony keeps grinding out new versions, there seems to be no shortage of people eager to tune in.

By Amy Borrus in Tokyo

Perhaps the most impressive marriage of video with the computer is what Sony calls interactive video. Sterling Drug Inc.'s Winthrop Pharmaceuticals unit uses a van with a custom-crafted version to provide simulated demonstrations of how its products work. The system lets a doctor "treat" a patient with heart failure. The doctor sees his patient going to the emergency room, while the system provides the patient's case history and vital signs. The patient's recovery depends on the doctor's response to onscreen questions and choices.

'GOOD DREAM.' Even though Sony has managed to raise sales of such nonconsumer products to 25% of worldwide sales, executives now concede their timetable for hitting 50% has been thrown off. "It was a good dream, and I think it is still a good target," says Shiro Koriyama, who heads Sony's Communication Products Marketing Group. "Unfortunately, we won't be there by 1990."

> ## The Betamax debacle taught Sony the value of sharing technology and not going it alone

The main problem has been coming up with enough distinctive products to make strong headway in an already competitive market, particularly computers. Sony has "a number of good engineers and marketing guys, but unfortunately almost none of the top guys understand the PC or computer market," says a former Sony executive. And Sony has discovered in its non-consumer business, just as it has in consumer goods, that its vaunted performance advantage is narrowing. Last year, NBC Inc. tapped Matsushita for a $50 million, five-year contract to supply videotape equipment. "Sony was comparable but not as good," says Steven Bonica, vice-president for engineering at NBC. Sony has since countered with a new system that recently won a contract at Capital Cities/ABC Inc., but it is clear that the company no longer has the market to itself.

Where Sony has earned almost universal respect is in its effort to become a more global company, which will go a long way toward softening the impact of a strong yen. Even though having large overseas sales makes Sony more vulnerable than most Japanese industrials, it is already among the most international of companies. Foreigners own 23% of its stock, which is traded on 23 exchanges around the world. Sony also moved early and fast into local manufacturing. It makes TV sets in Bridgend, Wales, as well as in San Diego. It makes compact disks in Terre Haute, Ind., and in Salzburg, Austria. All told, 20% of Sony's manufacturing is overseas. It aims to increase that to 35% by 1990. Such globalization will help Sony earn its revenues and pay its bills in the same currency, rather than paying workers in yen and logging sales in a depreciating dollar. While the yen was appreciating 50% against the dollar since September, 1985, Sony was able to raise prices only about 15% in the U.S.

Moving plants overseas is only the first step. The more difficult task will be to integrate planning and research and design internationally, too. But if an international staff is any measure, Sony is well along in the integration process. Of 7,000 employees in the U.S., for example, only 150 are Japanese. Sony, virtually alone among Japanese companies, has stuck to a policy of giving the top job in its foreign operations to a local national. Before long, it may become the first major Japanese company to name a foreigner as a director. A leading candidate is Jack Schmuckli, the head of Sony's European operations.

Such a move would send a strong signal that Sony has reached a new, more mature phase of development after riding the crest of Japan's postwar economic miracle. In essence, Sony's tradition of searching for gaps is another way of seeking market niches—a classic approach for young companies. To keep growing, bigger companies must also learn to defend their existing markets while broadening their product line. Mastering new skills is never easy. But Morita, now an inveterate skier, didn't even try the slopes until he was 60. There's no reason Sony can't accomplish a similar feat in the business world.

By Larry Armstrong in Tokyo, with Christopher Power and G. David Wallace in New York

DISCUSSION QUESTIONS
1. What are some of the goals that Sony has set, and how do they fit its adaptation to the challenges it faces?
2. How is Sony's definition of its basic purposes and modes of operation changing?

GLITZY RESORTS AND SUBURBAN HOTELS: HYATT BREAKS NEW GROUND

WITH BIG CITIES ALREADY SATURATED, THE PRITZKERS HAVE TO LOOK ELSEWHERE FOR GROWTH

MAY 4, 1987, PP. 100-101

To hear Jay A. Pritzker tell it, Hyatt Corp.'s success in the hotel business owes more to good fortune than to a grand design. The dealmaker extraordinaire stumbled into the hotel business in 1957, buying the small Hyatt House motel at Los Angeles International Airport on a dare from a boyhood chum. A decade later, his family picked up what became the Hyatt Regency Atlanta when the original developers ran into financial problems. It was only after acquiring the Atlanta hotel, as a matter of fact, that Pritzker finally took a crash course in managing convention hotels. "I guess you could say that we didn't have the greatest planning around here," Pritzker says sheepishly.

Pritzker, 64, and his family are placing a higher value on planning these days. Hyatt Hotels Corp. may have been born of the same opportunistic fervor that has allowed the Chicago-based family to assemble a diverse empire ranging from the $2.8 billion rail-car lessor Marmon Group Inc. to smokeless-tobacco giant Conwood Corp. But the hotel chain is running out of cities to dazzle with the dramatic, atrium-centered structures it pioneered. With estimated annual revenues of $1.7 billion, Hyatt Hotels owns or operates 84 hotels in North America. Hyatt International Corp. manages an additional 42 foreign properties. "The volume of large downtown hotels is behind us, so we've got to be flexible enough to seize new opportunities," explains Jay's cousin, Nicholas J. Pritzker, president of Hyatt Development Corp.

For Hyatt, only finding new sites for hotels can provide new opportunities. Analyst Richard P. Simon of Goldman Sachs & Co. explains: "In the hotel business, you don't drive earnings through an increase in room occupancies or through rate increases in a time of low inflation. You grow through expansion."

FANTASY ISLAND. The Pritzkers are seeking expansion in two seemingly disparate places: posh resorts and suburban hotels. Hyatt will spend $1.5 billion over the next five years on at least 12 luxury resorts, including the Hyatt Regency Waikoloa, which, at $360 million, will be one of the most expensive hotels ever built. The Pritzkers also have embarked on a $750 million building spree to construct 40 small, 200-to-300-room Hyatts in suburbs and smaller cities by 1991.

In keeping with Hyatt's flashy architectural tradition, the Pritzkers hope to outclass ordinary resorts by including distinctive—and sometimes outrageous—features. The new Hyatt Regency Scottsdale, for example, is a' water wonderland patterned after the hanging gardens of Babylon, complete with 10 pools, 28 fountains, 47 waterfalls, a man-made sand beach, and a Roman-style aqueduct. The pool system alone cost $3.8 million. And at the Hyatt Regency Cerromar Beach in Puerto Rico, it takes a full 15 minutes to float from one end of the 600-yd.-long river pool to the other—not counting time out for a drink at a swim-up bar or water volleyball at an adjoining court.

But Waikoloa, due to open next year on the island of Hawaii, will be Hyatt's showpiece. A partnership among the Pritzkers, the Bass brothers, and several Japanese investors, the 1,244-

AT BRANIFF, NO FRILLS AND FEW THRILLS

These days Braniff Inc. is about as far from the glitzy Hyatt empire as you can get. While Hyatt Corp. boasts fresh flowers and fine dining, Braniff has no first-class section and serves cold snacks. Concedes Pat Foley, Braniff's vice-chairman as well as Hyatt's chairman: "They're not exactly after the same customer."

Instead, the airline that once featured planes decorated by Alexander Calder now sells itself on price, not pizzazz. Braniff has gradually managed to attract more passengers since the Pritzker dynasty bought control in 1983, shortly after the airline escaped from Chapter 11 bankruptcy proceedings. But Braniff has yet to prove that it can yield strong, sustainable returns in an industry beset by consolidation and fare wars. Even with a 17% increase in passengers last year, the carrier showed an operating loss of $13.5 million on flat revenues of $239.5 million.

That's not an intolerable amount of red ink for the Pritzkers, who own 69% of the airline's common stock and hold 94% voting control. The family's empire is valued at more than $2 billion, after all. But few believe the family has developed an enduring fondness for Braniff. Says a top officer at one competitor: "If the Pritzkers could find a buyer for it, they'd sell it today."

K.C. BLUES. Braniff hasn't failed for lack of effort. Following an infusion of Pritzker cash and a $21.4 million stock offering, in May, 1984, the airline started targeting the same business travelers that Hyatt woos, with fine food, leather seats, and full fares. Braniff soon began losing money, so five months later it became a no-frills carrier offering unrestricted fares up to 60% below competitors' normal prices. Braniff also shifted many of its flights from Dallas, where American Airlines Inc. and Delta Air Lines Inc. are dominant, to Kansas City, which was then the new Midwest hub for ailing Eastern Air Lines Inc. "Our strategy saw a struggling Eastern eventually out of that market, leaving us there alone," recalls Foley.

Wrong. Braniff did attract hordes of passengers at first, and Eastern's financial position did worsen. But last year Eastern sold out to Texas Air Corp., another low-fare specialist. Since then, Eastern has been one of the industry's most aggressive sellers of discount seats, shrinking profits on flights through Kansas City.

Discounting by other carriers also has hurt. So to boost traffic recently, Braniff gave away two free tickets and discount certificates on each of its flights for two months. It also eased restrictions on some cheap fares. But the 16.5% growth in traffic at Braniff in March has not kept up with rising capacity. That means more empty seats.

Ultimately, Braniff must wait for competitors to raise fares so it can again become a low-cost alternative on its routes. But Patrick J. O'Shea, the former marketing chief at Air Florida System Inc. and now president of *ATN* Inc., a consortium of travel agents, wonders if Braniff's strategy will doom it to being a perennial also-ran to larger, more profitable airlines. "The question is: At what time do they get large enough to be a thorn in the side of those others, just like Frontier became a problem for United and Continental?" he asks.

Frontier Airlines Inc. was acquired in bankruptcy by People Express Airlines Inc., which then hit troubles that led to its takeover by Texas Air. That's not the sort of example apt to make the Pritzkers more patient.

By James E. Ellis in Chicago

room megaresort will feature a $1 million art collection and a seven-acre swimming lagoon stocked with porpoises and sea turtles. Guests will be able to choose between overhead trams or canal-faring gondolas to get to their rooms. "For a brief period each year, people today want to be removed from their ordinary lives," explains Hyatt Hotels President Darryl Hartley-Leonard.

"They want Fantasy Island, and we will provide it."

And even though the $200,000 per room Hyatt spends on resorts is almost 50% higher than the cost of a room for a downtown hotel, the investment seems to be worth it. Daily rates at upscale resorts were about 65% higher than average hotel rates last year. And resort occupancy rates last year ran at about 78%, some 12 percentage points higher than the hotel industry average.

'INSATIABLE' DEMAND. What's more, the current transformation of many resorts from playgrounds for the rich into meeting centers for corporations gives big hoteliers such as Hyatt a decided advantage in keeping resorts occupied. Notes Gary Hedges, a partner and resorts expert at Laventhol & Horwath: "At the bigger resorts, 60% to 70% of the business is from groups and small meetings, and the national chains have the marketing forces to sell those groups."

Accordingly, few in the hotel business see Hyatt's heavy investment in costly resorts as unduly risky—even in Hawaii, where Allegis Corp.'s Westin Hotel Co. unit is constructing two large super-resorts. "The demand for this type of thing is insatiable," says Westin Chief Executive Harry Mullikin. Besides, figures Ronald A. Nykiel, senior vice-president of marketing at Stouffer Hotel Management Corp., "with the Japanese eager to buy U. S. [hotel] real estate, you can probably always find somebody to buy it for more than you put in it."

Hyatt's move into small hotels involves more risk. By concentrating primarily on downtown and convention-center hotels for more than a decade, Hyatt missed out on the mushrooming of deluxe suburban office parks. Chasing suburban leader Marriott Corp., Hyatt now has designed prototypes for 300-room and 200-room hotels that can be built for $70,000 to $85,000 per room. A downtown Regency hotel can cost up to $150,000 per room. Hyatt is cutting costs by slashing costly ballroom and meeting space and even leaving out atriums.

The mass-production approach to hotels has traditionally been anathema at Hyatt, but executives think they can vary the basic designs enough to maintain the Hyatt image. Explains Laurence Geller, executive vice-president at Hyatt Development Corp.: "We've got to keep the allure that makes it a Hyatt and makes people say 'Gosh!' We're not using a cookie cutter—it's more like a giant Lego set."

Marriott's big headstart in the suburbs means Hyatt will need more than distinctive hotels to catch up. So the Pritzkers are getting Hyatt in on

the ground floor in some new office developments by providing equity money when developments include a Hyatt hotel. Small Hyatts in suburban Chicago and near Washington's Dulles International Airport are being constructed under such arrangements.

Unlike rivals Marriott and Holiday Corp., however, Hyatt won't seek growth in medium- and economy-priced hotels. Says Jay's son, Thomas, who is president of Hyatt Corp.: "The problem we have is that if we downscale, we risk bastardizing that Hyatt name." Some 30 years after buying Hyatt on a whim, the Pritzkers have too much invested in the name to let that happen.

By James E. Ellis in Chicago

DISCUSSION QUESTIONS

1. Discuss Hyatt's plans in terms of Michael Porter's three generic, competitive strategies: cost leadership, differentiation, and focus.
2. What threats and opportunities can you recognize in Hyatt's environment?

WHY KODAK IS STARTING TO CLICK AGAIN

NEW PRODUCTS AND LOWER OVERHEAD ARE PAYING OFF AT HOME AND ABROAD
FEBRUARY 23, 1987, PP. 134-135, 138

It's early morning in the Tokyo fish market. Amid the steaming bulks of tuna and the tumult of buying and selling, a fumbling photographer catches the eye of a visiting American. The photographer is struggling to pry open a film container while holding his camera. Finally, the photographer holds the container in one hand and pulls the top off with his teeth. The American makes a mental note to himself.

Containers of Kodak film can be opened with

one hand now, thanks to that trip to the fish market by Raymond H. DeMoulin, general manager of the professional photography division at Eastman Kodak Co. A small thing, a film container. But that was before five years of sagging profits at Kodak. Today, containers made with more flexible lids are only one of the ways DeMoulin and Kodak are combating the inroads made by Japan's Fuji Photo Film Co. Robb Kendrick, a professional photographer in Houston, is one customer who welcomes the competition. "It has gotten Kodak off their rear end," he says.

Kodak is up and at 'em in more arenas than just professional photography. The century-old company introduced 100 new products last year—the most ever. New automatic 35mm cameras and new films inside the ubiquitous yellow boxes were just the beginning: Kodak is pursuing broader horizons in the batteries, electronic publishing systems, blood-analysis tests, and optical-disk data-storage systems it has also introduced.

'A POWERHOUSE.' No one is prouder of Kodak's proliferating line of products than Colby H. Chandler, 61, who has directed a far-reaching overhaul at Kodak since becoming chief executive officer in 1983. "We have such a powerhouse of new products," says Chandler, "it is like a rubber band that's been stretched. We will get unusual growth for several years."

This outpouring of new products is particularly promising because more of the money they bring in will go to the bottom line. Kodak, whose virtually guaranteed lifetime-employment policies earned it the nickname "Great Yellow Father" in its hometown of Rochester, N. Y., has drastically cut overhead. The employee bowling alleys are closed, and employment has been pared to 121,500, nearly 25,000 less than three years ago. Even the ranks of top management have been thinned by 25%.

After absorbing what should be the last of the costs from those layoffs, Kodak will post a 14% or so increase in earnings for 1986, to roughly $380 million on sales of $11.5 billion. Chandler expects to increase earnings more than twofold this year, surpassing Kodak's 1981 record of $5.11 a share. Wall Street believes him: Kodak stock, at 76 recently, has risen 52% during the past year,

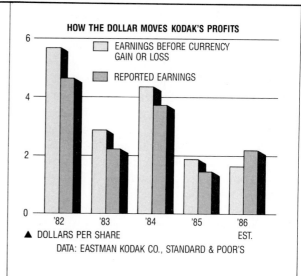

HOW THE DOLLAR MOVES KODAK'S PROFITS

- EARNINGS BEFORE CURRENCY GAIN OR LOSS
- REPORTED EARNINGS

▲ DOLLARS PER SHARE   EST.
DATA: EASTMAN KODAK CO., STANDARD & POOR'S

almost double the rise in the Standard & Poor's 500-stock index.

Chandler doesn't deserve all the credit for Kodak's turnaround. The declining dollar has sharply boosted profits. The company depends on foreign operations for nearly 40% of its sales. And like many U. S. companies with large overseas sales and fierce competition from foreigners at home, the strong dollar was a spur to become more efficient and more competitive. In the early 1980s it meant Kodak's products were relatively more expensive at home and earnings in foreign currency were diluted. What a difference now. Fluctuations in the dollar, which in 1985 took a 40¢ bite out of earnings per share, padded earnings by 60¢ a share last year (chart).

THINKING SMALL. In effect, Kodak and companies like it are getting something of a reprieve from foreign competition. Kodak is raising film prices, and it has managed to blunt the growth in imported photographic paper. The challenge for Chandler is to use Kodak's surging profits to recapture positions in its traditional, slower-growing businesses while making solid headway in new, faster-growing ones. And he must do this before competitors—domestic and foreign—can adjust. As far as Chandler is concerned, the task boils down to this: "How do you make a big company act like a small company?"

KODAK FIGHTS FUJI WITH 'ME-TOO' TACTICS

A large photograph of majestic, snow-laden Mt. Fuji hangs in the office of William F. Fowble, Kodak's general manager of manufacturing. "It's a constant reminder of the competition," says Fowble. After decades of belittling the company that takes its name from that sacred Japanese mountain, Kodak is now offering Fuji Photo Film Co. the highest form of flattery—its undivided attention.

In the Kodak laboratories where modern photography was born, researchers now methodically analyze Fuji films to uncover their magic. "It's me-too technology," says one researcher distastefully. "We do what Fuji does. We're obsessed with Fuji." For years, Fuji sold film with brighter colors. Kodak researchers thought the colors looked unrealistic, but they soon discovered customers liked Fuji film. Last year, Kodak came out with its series of *VR-G* films that feature the same vibrant colors found in Fuji. More realistic color reproduction "is not what people prefer," concludes Judith A. Schwan, director of Kodak's Photographic Research laboratories.

BLIMP WARS. The concern with Fuji's products pales, however, in comparison with the effort to match Fuji's productivity. Fuji's sales per employee last year were about $370,000, nearly four times Kodak's. To close the gap, Kodak studies every aspect of its rival's performance. "We as Americans tend to look for home runs. We don't pay attention to the singles," says Fowbles.

In one case, going for a single resulted in a home run. In the photo paper coating plant, where a defect one-tenth the width of a human hair can lead to huge rolls of paper being wasted, Kodak brought in specialists to train the workers in Japanese-style quality control. Employees were taught to isolate problems and find solutions on their own. The result: Last year the factory increased productivity by 20%. "Now," says factory superintendent Robert M. Ward, "we are ahead of Fuji." Kodak is trying to extend that experience to other factories.

Productivity gains are widespread. Ronald L. Heidke, vice-president for manufacturing in Kodak's film products area, has one wall covered with line graphs charting the progress. Until 1985 about 32% of all photo products coming off the production line were defective. The number was down to 26% at the end of last year, and Heidke is shooting for 10% this year.

Kodak is making even faster headway against Fuji in marketing. After watching the green Fuji blimp attract the eyes of millions of spectators at sports events in Europe and the U. S., Kodak decided to use the same tactic in Japan. Last

Colleagues say Chandler's ability to make the wrenching changes at Kodak is attributable to a tough-mindedness at the core of a placid exterior. After growing up on a farm in Maine, Chandler went off to serve as a Marine sergeant in the Pacific during World War II. He also boxed in his spare time. After the war, he earned a degree in engineering physics at the University of Maine before joining Kodak's quality-control division in 1950. In the early 1970s he distinguished himself as project manager for Kodak's first successful major effort at diversification: office copiers. By 1977, he was president of the company.

When Chandler took over in 1983, Kodak was already headed for serious trouble. Its nemesis, Fuji (above), was armed with new products, a weak yen, and a willingness to cut prices to win market share. Kodak was in retreat. Its cameras lost out to higher-quality 35mm models from overseas, and it had to retreat from instant photography after losing a patent battle to Polaroid Corp.

Chandler was hardly idle. He cut 11,000 jobs in his first year and streamlined management by breaking the company up into 17 small, autonomous business units. He sought overseas suppliers to fill gaps in Kodak's product line, including cameras. To expand Kodak's reach more quickly, he embarked on the company's first acquisition binge.

BRANCHING OUT. Chandler bolstered Kodak's

August, Kodak leased the only available blimp in Japan and now floats supreme above Fuji's home turf. To rub it in, Kodak's customary New Year's greeting cards in Japan showed the Kodak blimp with Mt. Fuji in the background.

OLYMPIC GRIP. The blimp will be plugging Kodak film in Seoul during the 1988 summer Olympics. After its embarrassing loss of the 1984 Los Angeles Olympics sponsorship to Fuji, Kodak plunked down about $8 million to get an early grip on the rights to use the five-ring emblem. Kodak hopes to use the Olympic sponsorship to rout Fuji's aggressive moves into such fast-growing markets as Taiwan, India, and China.

Back in Rochester, Fuji's emergence as a strong challenger and a focus of Kodak's attention as a common enemy has helped overcome internal bickering. Employees still talk of a "silver curtain" around the film emulsion laboratory because of its unwillingness to cooperate with other parts of the company. But a decades-long rift between the film and paper divisions, which used to lead to redundant research and petty rivalries, is now gone. And while some employees grumble about Kodak's obsession, it is clearly making things tougher on Fuji. "I'd just as soon they go back to not paying attention to us," says Carl Chapman, vice-president at Fuji Photo Film *USA*. "I don't need that kind of flattery."

By Leslie Helm in Rochester, with Barbara Buell in Tokyo

photography business last November, buying film processor Fox Photo Inc. for $96 million. That was just part of the money he has poured into photography. To stanch the flow of business to 1-hr. minilabs, Kodak is selling a faster minilab that uses only Kodak paper and chemicals. It has introduced more than a dozen new films in the past year. And this spring it will launch a multi-million-dollar advertising campaign featuring Bill Cosby.

Despite its push in the field, however, Kodak realizes it cannot be just a photography company. Sales in the U. S. market grow only 5% a year. And with 80% of the market, Kodak has scant room to expand. Says Leo J. Thomas, who heads

Kodak's effort in drugs and health care technology: "We need to broaden our base of business to where growth potential will carry us into the next century."

FOOT IN THE DOOR. Part of that effort means trying to start a drug business almost from scratch. Kodak sees drugs as an outgrowth of its expertise in plastics and chemicals, a $2 billion business for the company. So far, however, Kodak has no products to sell. It has set up a laboratory near Philadelphia and hopes to come up with drugs to fight cancer and age-related diseases—on its own or by making acquisitions.

Kodak is further along in its return to instant photography. This time, though, it's counting on electronic images. On Feb. 17 it plans to announce a system that thermally prints a color photo on identity cards, such as driver's licenses. Kodak sees the new system as a foot in the door of a market that could one day replace conventional photography.

Data storage, an estimated $10 billion market, is another area where Kodak has high hopes. With the purchase of Verbatim Corp. in 1985, Kodak became one of the top three U. S. makers of floppy magnetic disks. This year Kodak will begin selling a 14-in. optical-storage system that has some 1,000 times the capacity of floppy disks. But some analysts say Kodak is fighting in vain against a trend toward 12-in. systems. Scott C. McCleary, an analyst at Yankee Group Inc. of Boston, calls Kodak's 14-in. system "a white elephant."

MOONLIGHTING. Clearly there is no shortage of ideas at Kodak these days. Its foray into batteries last year, for example, was the result of an employee's proposal to begin making a 9-volt lithium battery that would last twice as long as existing batteries. Kodak figured that as long as it was going to sell batteries, it might as well go all out, introducing a full line of gold-topped alkaline batteries. Kodak's market share so far is only 5%, but executives see the main function of the new batteries as cementing a distribution system until the lithium battery is ready, probably this spring.

Kodak executives are encouraged by the new ideas bubbling up through the company. "The thrill of the hunt is beginning to permeate the ranks," says Vice-Chairman J. Phillip Samper. "It's enthusiasm driven by success."

Kodak is hardly home free. For one thing, there's a different kind of hunt going on among demoralized workers, who fear that they will be next to feel the ax. "People are really nervous," says a Kodak veteran of more than 20 years. The worker has started a business on the side just in case, and he says many others have done the same.

Another danger facing the company is that innovation and product development could wither if Kodak doesn't make more of its own products. Its batteries and cameras, for example, are made in Japan. Dependence on outside sources could bring on a repeat of its 1984 failure in the 8mm video-camera market, which many analysts blame on the outdated design of the cameras supplied by Matsushita Electric Industrial Co.

Chandler, a part-time farmer, is accustomed to the task of nurturing. At Kodak, he'll have to cultivate greater strengths in production and innovation if he is to see new businesses take root.

By Leslie Helm in Rochester, with bureau reports

DISCUSSION QUESTION
Discuss Kodak's strategy utilizing any
  theoretical models of strategy you select.

THE NEXT ACT AT CHRYSLER
ITS COMEBACK IS HISTORY—NOW IT HAS A NEW STRATEGY
NOVEMBER 3, 1986, PP. 66-69, 72

For a revealing look at the new Chrysler Corp., stop by Kenosha, Wis., one of these crisp fall mornings and visit one of the world's oldest automobile factories. Sure, the sign on the gate says American Motors Corp. But inside, the production line that workers are setting up will turn out cars with the familiar Chrysler Pentastar insignia. You see, Chrysler has hired American Motors, which has plenty of excess capacity, to build the highly profitable Fifth Avenue, Diplomat, and Gran Fury cars. Meanwhile, Chrysler is using the St. Louis plant that usually builds those cars to begin making longer versions of its popular minivans, the Plymouth Voyager and Dodge Caravan. When you've been through what Chrysler has been through the past few years, you're nothing if not resourceful.

These days, Chrysler is pursuing a unique notion of what an American car company should be. It's offering buyers fewer nameplates, farming out work where it can, and resisting the seemingly immutable inclination of a business to grow for growth's sake. Lounging back on his office couch and waving one of his trademark big cigars, Chairman Lee A. Iacocca sums up his vision: "We can be a first-rate company as long as we respect our size and don't try to have any delusions of grandeur."

That may sound like uncharacteristic modesty from a man who skewered his antagonists in a freewheeling autobiography, hired Texas Stadium in Dallas to launch 1987 models as "America's Team," and cannot seem to shake speculation that he may become a Presidential candidate. But modesty has nothing to do with it. Iacocca has a compelling reason for refusing to get into a growth race with General Motors Corp. and Ford Motor Co., each of which sells two to four times as many cars as Chrysler. In its present configuration, Chrysler can build cars in its U. S. plants more cheaply than its bigger rivals—for $500 less per vehicle, according to one estimate. Having achieved that position after evading creditors who were snapping at his heels every inch of the way, Iacocca is not about to risk squandering it in an expensive expansion binge. Rather than build his own shiny new plant and see it sit idle in the next slump, he'd prefer to rent a competitor's factory, put up the money to retool the production line, and pay another company to have its workers assemble the cars.

In many ways, Chrysler couldn't be more different from what it was just six years ago. Then, reeling after three years of losses that totaled $3 billion, it symbolized everything that was wrong with the U. S. auto industry. Costs were out of control. Its products were out of touch with the market. Inefficiency was rampant. Since then, Chrysler has repaid $1.2 billion in government-backed loans, piled up $5.6 billion in profits, beefed up its cash hoard, and reclaimed a big piece of lost market share, mostly at *GM*'s expense. Clearly, Iacocca is moving beyond mere survival to secure a profitable niche in an industry where the competition comes at you from every corner of the globe.

He isn't there yet. Chrysler's turnaround shows what adept crisis management and government help can do—as long as people are buying cars in droves. But what happens now that the crisis is over? Can the company remain profitable when sales slump again? Most experts are optimistic. "In this more competitive market, small is beautiful," says Scott F. Merlis, an auto analyst at Morgan Stanley & Co. "Chrysler can react faster and redeploy its assets faster." Still, when it comes to putting their money on the line, investors are skeptical. Despite the breathtaking 13-fold rise in Chrysler stock in the past five years, its recent price of 37 is only five times this year's expected earnings. The Standard & Poor's index of 400 industrial companies, by contrast, is at 15 times earnings.

Chrysler must cope with one imposing obstacle. Much more than either *GM* or Ford, it is at the mercy of the North American car buyer, counting on revenues from the U. S. and Canada for some 97% of its sales (chart). Chrysler lacks the worldwide cushions of Ford and *GM*, although it has increased its stake in Mitsubishi Motors Corp. from 15% to 24% and expects to acquire Maserati by 1995. Iacocca does not plan to alter Chrysler's dependence on the domestic market anytime soon, in spite of his interest in diversifying modest-ly into high tech. "We're not going to play conglomerate," he says, "and we're not going to be a big global company."

Nevertheless, Iacocca is ready to dabble again in the European market, from which Chrysler withdrew in its retrenchment phase. Yet even here his approach is distinctive—even audacious. He wants to skirt the costs of reestablishing a manufacturing base in Europe, either by shipping U. S.-built vehicles or by working out a deal to use someone else's plant in Europe. Chrysler feels it has already pulled ahead of European makers by cutting 25 hours out of the time it needed to build a car. That means Chrysler has cut in half the advantage once enjoyed by Japanese car makers, and Iacocca hopes to have his costs on a par with Japan's by 1990.

A more immediate goal is exploiting Chrysler's hard-won position in the U. S. Fierce price-cutting has already helped drive down the company's earnings in the first half of this year by 23% from 1985, when it had record profits of $1.6 billion on sales of $21.3 billion for the year. So a key strategy is to sell more expensive cars, which carry fatter profits. The 1987 models, for example, include sporty Sundance and Shadow subcompacts, a midsize Dakota pickup truck, a midsize LeBaron sports coupe and convertible, and "stretched" minivans. In 12 months Chrysler will reenter the full-size car market it abandoned in 1981, and it expects to introduce a $30,000 sports car built by Maserati.

'INSURANCE POLICIES.' To focus the attack, Chrysler recently realigned its product development and marketing staffs. Now each staff is divided into four groups, one for each of the company's brands. Their mandate is to develop and market vehicles around key themes for each line: Plymouth for value and integrity, Dodge for performance, Chrysler for luxury and comfort, and Dodge trucks for quality and toughness.

Given its plans for the domestic market, where it sold 1.8 million cars and trucks last year, Chrysler's immediate hopes for Europe are conservative. Executives speak of selling perhaps 10,000 sporty cars or minivans there. "There's no compelling strategic or tactical necessity for Chrysler to broaden its base beyond the U. S.," says Robert A.

Lutz, former chairman of Ford of Europe Inc., who joined Chrysler in June as executive vice-president, "but it would be like having insurance policies to cover all eventualities."

As his company gets into fighting trim, Iacocca is determined not to let the fast-moving auto market leave Chrysler in the dust. He has had more time to plot long-term strategy since spring, when his company formally reorganized as a holding company. Now Chrysler's businesses are divided into three operating subsidiaries: automotive, financial, and aerospace. Analysts expect the company will eventually issue special stock pegged to the performance of each group, much as *GM* did with its acquisitions of Electronic Data Systems Corp. and Hughes Aircraft Co. Iacocca isn't tipping his hand.

ONE STRIKEOUT. The new structure reflects some discernible differences at Chrysler. In the early 1980s, when the company was desperate for appealing products, Iacocca took things in hand personally, deciding, for example, to resurrect convertible models and to bring in ex-racer Carroll Shelby to build special editions of sporty cars. Now, his lieutenants are more involved. Gerald Greenwald and Harold K. Sperlich, members of the six-man executive committee (page 74), came up with the idea for the popular "America" versions of the subcompacts Omni and Horizon.

Iacocca, 62, is clearly grooming his potential successors. But he shows no sign of leaving soon. "We feel more accountable, and we feel responsible, but the big guy hasn't gone away," says Sperlich, president of Chrysler Motors Corp. "We still check the major decisions with Lee." Iacocca also has a strong financial incentive to stay for at least another year or so. He took the No. 2 spot on *BUSINESS WEEK*'s executive pay survey for 1985, earning $11.4 million—$9.8 million of which came from stock options granted him by the board in 1982 to encourage him to stay on. At current stock prices, he stands to pick up an additional $8.3 million from stock options this year and $2.8 million next year. He could wind up holding $85.1 million worth of stock at today's prices.

Much of Iacocca's time recently has gone into looking for acquisitions with which to form a fourth unit, already named Chrysler Technologies Corp. Iacocca is shopping primarily for defense companies costing $1 billion or less, and he insists that any takeovers be friendly. "It's time-consuming as hell," Iacocca confesses. "We've been at it

---

Chrysler makes cars more cheaply than GM or Ford —but matching Japanese costs is the problem

---

18 months, and we've virtually struck out. I thought it would be somewhat easier."

The search is continuing, but a frustrated Iacocca is taking a new tack. Now he wants to create Chrysler Technologies out of existing high-tech operations within the company, provide the new organization with a budget of as much as $1 billion, and then let it develop its own strategy and takeover candidates. Likely components of the new company include Chrysler's own data systems group and its electronics complex in Huntsville, Ala. Iacocca would also add portions of Gulfstream Aerospace Corp., the executive aircraft producer that Chrysler bought 14 months ago for $642 million.

CHEAP MONEY. Chrysler has had better luck strengthening its financial company. Three years ago, Chrysler Financial Corp. was a $5 billion subsidiary wholly dedicated to financing cars and trucks. Now it is four times that size and offers much broader commercial and retail services. It acquired E. F. Hutton Credit Corp. for $125 million in mid-1985. A few months later it added FinanceAmerica and *BA* Financial Services from BankAmerica for $405 million. This year it bought the inventory financing division of Westinghouse Credit Corp.

No other big financial acquisitions are likely. But Chrysler Financial Chairman Robert S. Miller Jr. believes he can expand his company by a further 50%, to $30 billion in assets, by 1990. Virtually all that expansion, he says, will be nonautomotive business. Miller figures Chrysler Finan-

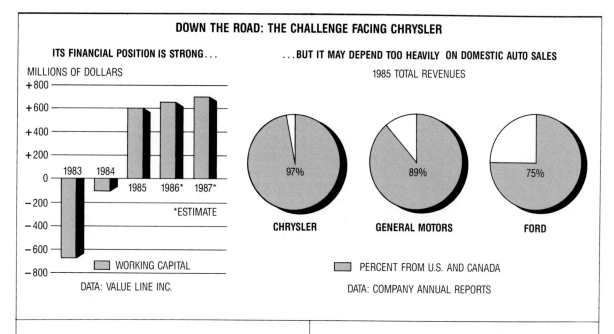

DOWN THE ROAD: THE CHALLENGE FACING CHRYSLER

ITS FINANCIAL POSITION IS STRONG...

MILLIONS OF DOLLARS

1983 1984 1985 1986 1987*

*ESTIMATE

WORKING CAPITAL

DATA: VALUE LINE INC.

...BUT IT MAY DEPEND TOO HEAVILY ON DOMESTIC AUTO SALES

1985 TOTAL REVENUES

97% — CHRYSLER

89% — GENERAL MOTORS

75% — FORD

PERCENT FROM U.S. AND CANADA

DATA: COMPANY ANNUAL REPORTS

cial's performance should result in better ratings on Wall Street and ensure a source of cheap money for automotive operations.

Keeping Chrysler's future car and truck programs well-watered with funds is critical. Chrysler plans to spend $12.5 billion developing new vehicles and overhauling plants from now to 1990. It intends to bankroll the effort without borrowing, despite the industrywide sales slump analysts expect in late 1988 or 1989. Miller, who doubles as Chrysler vice-chairman and chief financial officer, vows to maintain "considerable liquidity" to avoid trouble. "Historically," he acknowledges, "this company committed the sin of jerking its product development people around, depending on what the cash balance was in the treasurer's office."

Merely getting products to market on time won't be enough to guarantee Chrysler's future. The company must also learn to match Japanese production costs—regardless of whether the dollar is strong or weak against the yen. A crucial element in cutting costs is keeping factories running as close to capacity as possible. "Their goal isn't necessarily to have the best products on the market, but to have products that will sell out the factory's production," says Ronald A. Glantz, auto analyst at Montgomery Securities in San Francisco.

Chrysler cut back enough in 1980 to break even on sales of only 1.1 million vehicles, compared with about 2.3 million previously. Its breakeven point has crept up to about 1.25 million units, but executives say it is a Chrysler commandment to prevent the level from climbing further. As production rises from the breakeven point to full capacity, Chrysler earns a profit of more than $2,500 per vehicle.

His desire to keep the breakeven point low explains why Iacocca shuns building new plants. He figures that increasing foreign competition, coupled with new Japanese auto plants under construction in the U. S., will soon leave the American market with the equivalent of about six assembly plants too many. *GM* is already hinting that it may mothball several factories soon. Iacocca says that Chrysler will be able to build 300,000 more cars and trucks by 1988 anyway, pointing to his company's *AMC* deal as an example of new capacity.

Iacocca has also combined with Mitsubishi Motors in a joint venture called Diamond-Star Motors Corp., which is scheduled to begin building cars in Illinois by 1988. And Iacocca announced on Oct. 20 a $1.2 billion plan to rebuild Chrysler's aging Jefferson Avenue plant—the birthplace of the K-cars that were crucial in restoring Chrysler

THE MEN WHO MAKE CHRYSLER WORK

There's never any question of who's in the limelight at Chrysler Corp. To many outsiders, Chairman Lee A. Iacocca is the company. But Iacocca, who turned 62 on Oct. 15, relies on the five other members of his executive committee to help him run the show. In contrast to the pre-Iacocca era, when some outside directors were included, the committee now consists solely of the company's own top operations executives. Like Iacocca himself, all five are former employees of Ford Motor Co.

With Chrysler's recent reorganization, they will take on heavier day-to-day responsibilities. Iacocca discourages speculation that he might leave before reaching retirement age—if then. But with a man who's so involved in so many outside activities and is still mentioned as a Presidential prospect, anything can happen. Whenever the Iacocca era ends, his successor most likely will be chosen from the executive committee.

■ **Gerald Greenwald.** An impeccable dresser who favors conservative suits with double-breasted jackets, Greenwald, 51, is the front-runner to succeed Iacocca. As chairman of the auto subsidiary, Chrysler Motors Corp., he holds the single most powerful position in the company after Iacocca. Greenwald is also the executive most often called upon to represent the company at public appearances when Iacocca isn't available.

Greenwald, the son of a chicken farmer, grew up in St. Louis and went on to graduate from Princeton University with a *BA* in economics. He quickly joined Ford to pursue a career in finance, spending considerable time in South America and Europe in the 1960s and 1970s. His last post at Ford was president of its manufacturing and sales operations in Venezuela, where one of his accomplishments was to carve out the biggest market share of any Ford subsidiary.

When Iacocca arrived at Chrysler in November, 1978, he was appalled at the haphazard financial controls. Six months later, he brought on Greenwald as controller. Greenwald quickly became Iacocca's right-hand man in mapping out the company's survival strategy. How is life on the executive committee under the new corporate structure? "It's the same old democratic process that it's always been," says Greenwald, setting up a familiar joke among Chrysler executives. "Everybody gets a vote. Lee gets six."

■ **Robert A. Lutz.** The latest refugee from Ford, Lutz joined Iacocca's team last June after a career that included positions at General Motors Corp. and *BMW*. As chairman of Ford of Europe Inc., Lutz, 54, implemented tough cost controls and demonstrated his willingness to sacrifice market share to get higher prices and improved profits. Describing Lutz as "an entrepreneur," Iacocca hired him as executive vice-president to oversee the company's top three growth priorities: trucks, international development, and component operations. He has quickly become regarded as a contender to succeed Iacocca.

Lutz, who was born in Switzerland and main-

to good health. The facility will manufacture a truck to be phased in early in the next decade.

Meanwhile, a leaner production line is very much in vogue at Chrysler. The goal, dubbed the Liberty Project, is to slash manufacturing costs 30%, or $2,500 per car, by 1995. Only about $500 of the savings will result from cutting fixed costs. The rest, says Chrysler Motors Chairman Greenwald, must come from lower labor content, more efficient assembly methods, and a greater reliance on suppliers to "pre-assemble" such components as instrument panels and cooling systems. Greenwald says Chrysler has already identified and scheduled changes that are worth about $1,200 per car.

Much of Chrysler's current cost advantage over other U. S. producers comes from shopping around for cheap sources of components, rather than making the parts itself. Chrysler gets 70% of its components from outside, including about 10% from overseas vendors. *GM* uses outside vendors for only 30% of its parts, and Ford for about

tains dual citizenship, is both aristocratic and folksy. When Chrysler introduced its 1987 cars in Dallas, Lutz readily doffed his tie to join more casually dressed participants in learning to rope cattle and dance the two-step.

■ **Bennett E. Bidwell.** The puckish Bidwell, 59, is arguably Detroit's most intuitive marketing expert. Disarmingly blunt and earthy, he is the glue that bonds Chrysler's dealers and Iacocca.

An Iacocca loyalist at Ford, Bidwell left there in 1981 to run Hertz Corp. but itched to return to the auto industry. He got his chance in 1983 when Iacocca recruited him as an executive vice-president to run Chrysler's sales and marketing operations. Without Iacocca's instinctive marketing skills, Bidwell's role at Chrysler would undoubtedly loom larger.

Bidwell became a vice-chairman of the parent company a year ago. He is responsible for Washington lobbying, personnel, public affairs, corporate planning, and marketing strategies. But marketing remains his first love. "I'm not a grand strategist," he says jokingly in a voice that reveals traces of his New Hampshire roots. "I've got a dart board here, and I hurl things at it. If they stick, I get up, go over, and look at it and say, 'Oh, yeah, okay, we'll do that today.'"

■ **Harold K. Sperlich.** Sperlich, 56, is as enthusiastic about product development and production as Bidwell is about selling. An astoundingly hard worker, his schedule as president of Chrysler Motors, say insiders, is even tighter than Iacocca's, a man for whom he holds unabashed admiration.

Sperlich orchestrated Chrysler's K-car program and fathered its enormously successful minivan—a concept he first pushed unsuccessfully at Ford back in the 1970s. Sperlich came to Chrysler in 1977 after being fired at Ford for pressing too hard to add a small, front-wheel-drive car to Ford's lineup.

Intense almost to a fault, Sperlich epitomizes the can-do attitude that Chrysler developed during its crisis years. "The competition is so tough, everybody has to give 150%," he says. "We're like a five-man traveling basketball squad. Everybody gets all the playing time he wants."

■ **Robert S. Miller Jr.** At 44, Steve Miller is the youngest member of Chrysler's top echelon. He also has the most formal education, with degrees in economics and business administration from Stanford University and a degree from Harvard Law School. Miller's rise at Chrysler has been meteoric since he signed on in 1979 as assistant controller. He was named treasurer a year later and is credited with patching together the company's complicated bailout loans. Miller was rewarded with a promotion to chief financial officer in 1981, and he took over as chairman of Chrysler Financial Corp. in 1985. Seven months later he got the additional duties of vice-chairman of the parent company.

Miller, who is remarkably soft-spoken compared with the rest of Iacocca's lieutenants, loves a practical joke. He once shocked a roomful of bankers, assembled to grant bailout loans to Chrysler, by announcing that the company had gone bankrupt and wouldn't need their money after all. It was April Fool's Day.

By William J. Hampton in Detroit

50%. "We're more the size and integration of a Japanese company than are [*GM* and Ford]," says Sperlich. "We have enough mass to be efficient, but we're small enough to be manageable."

HELPFUL IMAGE. Internally, Chrysler is streamlining production by shortening its list of equipment options. This year the company's new cars will average only 25 options, compared with about 60 five years ago. George F. Butts, vice-president for quality and productivity, says the simplification program has already reduced the number of parts most plants must handle from about 8,000 to fewer than 5,000.

Foreign-based auto makers, of course, have done the same thing for years. Chrysler tested the concept in April with its "America" subcompacts. The company added almost $700 in optional equipment to the cars, cut their price by $710, and offered shoppers a choice of only six colors, three trim packages, and two equipment options. The moves eliminated a total of 702 parts from the manufacturing process, helping Chrysler squeeze out a profit in spite of the cars' lower retail price. Concludes Greenwald: "You can cut way down on the options and still satisfy 99.5% of your customers."

Simplifying production also helps improve quality. Chrysler says its quality, as measured by war-

---

'We feel more accountable, and we feel responsible, but the big guy hasn't gone away'

---

ranty claims, is up 45% in seven years and now surpasses that of any other domestic producer. Ford disputes that claim, however, and Chrysler acknowledges that it must do more to satisfy the buyers who went to Chrysler because they admired its come-from-behind corporate image. "Today people like us before they buy our product because we survived, hung in, and seem to be innovating," says Vice-Chairman Bennett E. Bidwell. "Then they buy, and sometimes they don't like us as well. We've got to turn that around." That means bringing Chrysler's quality up to the level of Japanese cars, Bidwell says.

'BIG TROUBLE.' Improving customer satisfaction, observers say, could take years. In the meantime, Japanese producers are shifting toward the high end of the market at about the same pace as Chrysler. James P. Womack, research director for the International Motor Vehicle Program at Massachusetts Institute of Technology, predicts a collision in the late 1980s when Japan's U. S.-based auto plants begin cranking out more than 1 million upscale vehicles of their own each year. "*GM is in big trouble,*" he warns. "Ford and Chrysler are only in less big trouble."

Womack's point is that the ultimate strength of all Detroit auto makers rests on their ability to match Japan's costs, not just each other's. Certainly Chrysler has taken an early lead over its domestic competitors. Its long-run success will depend on whether Iacocca can execute every aspect of his new strategy, without losing the sense of urgency that took hold when the company was running for its life. *By William J. Hampton in Detroit*

DISCUSSION QUESTIONS

1. Conduct an "organizational diagnosis" of Chrysler. That is, discuss its strengths and weaknesses as a part of strategic planning.
2. The article mentions ". . . the seemingly immutable inclination of a business to grow for growth's sake" and Chrysler's apparent intent to resist mindless growth. Under what conditions might an antigrowth strategy be preferable? What conditions seem to figure in Chrysler's choice?
3. One model for analyzing strategy is the Miles and Snow "adaptive cycle model." Its application requires investigation of a company's integrated solutions to three kinds of problems: entrepreneurial, engineering, and administrative. Analyze Chrysler using this model.

CAN JIM OLSON'S GRAND DESIGN GET AT&T GOING?

HE'S TRIMMING JOBS, MODERNIZING, AND BETTING ON A NEW LONG-TERM STRATEGY
DECEMBER 22, 1986, PP. 48-49

Jim Olson, the new chairman of American Telephone & Telegraph Co., gets excited when he's talking about how he's going to invigorate his company. He leans forward in his chair and makes point after point—folksy, avuncular, but always in control.

No doubt about it, James E. Olson has a lot on his mind. Since *AT&T*'s breakup in January, 1984, the revenues of the $35 billion company have languished, with gains in long-distance phone service and sales of switching and transmission gear only partly offsetting declines or losses in business phone and computer systems. Profits are flat. Despite the strong stock market, *AT&T*'s shares have hovered in the mid-20s all year. Analysts are asking whether *AT&T* will ever become the information-age titan envisioned after the breakup—or remain little more than a huge phone company.

With only four years until retirement, the 61-year-old Olson will have to move fast if he is to get *AT&T* back on track. In a rare interview, Olson laid out his plan: He wants to use cost-cutting and other measures to strengthen the company's core businesses. And he is setting in motion· a long-term strategy he calls "data networking" (table).

FALLING SHORT. Until this year, *AT&T* has largely sold phone services, phone equipment, and computers separately. Starting now, Olson plans to package its products and services into "a total solution—everything from computers to multiplexers to enhanced long-distance service to *PBX*s." The idea is to tap the growing demand from customers for help in managing huge amounts of information. *AT&T* says that this market, now $135 billion, is growing by 15% a year.

The company won't say when it expects the long-term strategy to show results. Moreover, critics contend that Olson's idea isn't really new but rather an extension of a marketing approach, begun in the 1970s, that has never been very successful. Clearly, though, he has to do something. After subtracting a 33¢-per-share gain from changes in pension-fund accounting, *AT&T* earned 99¢ for the first nine months of 1986, down from $1.05 a year earlier. And this came after margins in *AT&T*'s backbone long-distance business rose from 11.9% to 16%. With *AT&T*'s computer business draining $500 million a year or more from profits, analysts say it could be at least 1988 before the company earns the $2.02 per share that it projected for 1984.

The toughest element in Olson's strategy is cutting *AT&T*'s $32 billion in operating costs. He concedes that he has fallen short of a goal he announced as vice-chairman two years ago to cut costs by 20%. He failed to first persuade managers of the need for such cuts. Now, he says, the managers have a plan. Interest expense is one target. Over a period he won't define, Olson wants to cut perhaps $2 billion out of the company's current $8.1 billion in total debt. This would come on top of a $980 million debt reduction in the first

JIM OLSON'S PLAN

CUT COSTS: His short-term cure for flagging earnings is to cut at least 20% out of AT&T's $32 billion in annual costs. Analysts expect that to eliminate up to 10% of AT&T's 330,000 jobs in the next year, bringing to 80,000 the number of positions cut since January, 1984.

STRENGTHEN CORE BUSINESSES: He plans to fortify AT&T's $17 billion long-distance business in 1987 by further modernizing its network and by lobbying regulators at the Federal Communications Commission for higher rates of return. AT&T Network Systems, whose $7 billion in sales makes it the world's largest supplier of switching and transmission equipment to phone companies, will improve its factory automation to keep costs in line with price pressures. Olson also plans to meld AT&T's separate sales and service forces for computer and phone equipment into one team that will push long-distance service as well, and he will try to increase the company's computer and PBX sales in Europe.

BOLSTER FUTURE GROWTH: Olson's biggest challenge is to get AT&T back to double-digit growth. He hopes to do this with a strategy called "data networking." Rather than limiting the company to stand-alone computer sales, he will push complete computer and communications systems, including long-distance network services, to U.S. and international customers. Olson figures that the world market for such systems is already nearing $135 billion, of which AT&T has about 9%.

DATA: BW, AMERICAN TELEPHONE & TELEGRAPH CO.

nine months of 1986. In addition, the merger of sales and support staffs in the company's information systems and long-distance units, announced last spring, should be completed in early 1987. Analysts expect this and other moves to eliminate up to 30,000 more jobs in a cost-cutting program that could mean a fourth-quarter write-down of more than $500 million.

'IN A DAZE.' The departure from a tradition of lifetime employment is traumatic for everyone. "People are walking around here in a daze," says one insider. Olson, who started at *AT&T* 43 years ago cleaning silt out of phone company manholes and later met his wife at the company, understands: "Do you know how tough it is asking people to support your strategy when you know you can't promise all of them jobs when this is over?" He recently took a nationwide tour of

AT&T facilities as a gesture to employees. "It's a lot better if the employee hears about what we're trying to do from the guy at the top," he says.

As a corollary to cost-cutting, Olson is trying to strengthen his core businesses: long-distance; network systems, which sells equipment to phone companies; and information systems, which sells computers and telecommunications equipment to offices and individuals. Although the first two are very profitable, equipment sales fell 12.7% in the quarter ended Sept. 30, as the industry took a downturn. And long-distance profits are being held in check by regulators. Competitors—including *MCI* Communications Corp. and U. S. Sprint Communications Co.—are still nipping at *AT&T*'s heels. And the seven regional Bell companies spun off from *AT&T* in the divestiture are lobbying hard to be allowed into long distance and manufacturing.

Olson isn't taking any chances. To protect his long-distance business, he plans to spend more than $2 billion on advanced digital switching and transmission equipment in 1987, including sophisticated undersea fiber-optic cable to make international communications faster and clearer. He's also fighting the regulators. The Federal Communications Commission's decision to lower *AT&T*'s long-distance rate of return to 12.2% in 1987 from 12.75% in 1986 has meant cutting rates by $1.2 billion. Olson, who says his goal is total deregulation of *AT&T*, is lobbying for relief. "If we've been successful in our marketing and operational efficiencies, we should keep the fruits of our labor," he declares.

Such relief may be long in coming. In the meantime, Olson is trying for inroads in foreign markets, which account for less than 10% of his overall revenues. Voice traffic is *AT&T*'s best shot overseas, says Jack B. Grubman, an analyst at PaineWebber Inc. Because of lower costs abroad, he adds, profit margins are "maybe 25%" vs. 16% for *AT&T*'s domestic and international long-distance traffic combined. Moreover, *AT&T*'s revenues from international traffic grew 20% this year vs. 10% for domestic traffic, he says.

Olson wants to sell more equipment overseas as well, and he's counting on joint ventures with Holland's Philips, which sells phone company equipment; with Italy's Olivetti, which sells computers; and with Spain's Compañía Telefónica Nacional de España, with which it plans to build integrated circuits. So far, success in equipment has been more elusive than in long distance.

> Olson's approach features 'data networking': selling products and services in one lucrative package

AT&T-Philips has landed three firm orders for multimillion-dollar digital switches in the past three years. The company hopes to land a key spot as France's second supplier of switching equipment, but that is by no means certain. The Third World, with its need for a communications infrastructure, may turn out to be the best market of all, says Olson. China and India in particular offer excellent sales opportunities, he says.

SURGERY. *AT&T* won't reap the full benefits of such moves without radical surgery at its information systems unit, which has lost more than $1 billion in the past two years. *AT&T*'s margins have shrunk in the competitive personal computer business, and its midrange computers have not caught on with big customers. One insider estimated recently that *AT&T* lost more than $400 million in information systems between January and August of this year vs. the $50 million the company hoped to earn there in 1986. Rentals of *PBX* switching equipment to businesses—nearly half the unit's revenues—may dip below $5 billion this year from $7.2 billion in 1984.

The good news is that Olson now has fewer restraints in managing information systems. Last spring federal rules that made him keep this unregulated business separate from the regulated long-distance business were relaxed, letting *AT&T* merge the two and cut overhead. Olson hopes to cut more costs in 1987, though he isn't even guessing when the unit will make money.

But his biggest challenge may be producing double-digit growth—the performance analysts expect of the new *AT&T*. Olson's theory is that *AT&T*'s vast experience in voice networks will give it an edge in data networks. Moreover, demand for such services is so strong that many huge customers, such as *GM*, *GE*, and Boeing, are setting up their own networks—all using *AT&T* equipment and support. Olson says he'll pursue both alliances and acquisitions to get more of this action. *AT&T* already has an alliance with General Motors Corp.'s Electronic Data Systems Corp. subsidiary, and on Dec. 9, *AT&T* teamed up with Boeing Computer Services Co. to bid on a $4.5 billion contract for a new federal voice-and-data network.

Olson has a long way to go, however. Since the early 1970s, *AT&T* has made at least three different attempts to sell data services—Bell Data Network, Advanced Communications Service, and Net 1000. All have flopped because of equipment failure or lack of customer interest. So far, *AT&T* executives refuse to talk about what new products will back up the new game plan. "It's great for the top guys to talk about data networking. But rolling out products is where rubber meets the road," says Grubman.

'INDIGESTION.' Moreover, linking data communications gear requires different expertise than integrating voice equipment—*AT&T*'s traditional stronghold. The company succeeded in voice largely because it owned more than 80% of the U. S. phone network and set most of the standards for the network's equipment. *AT&T* may never gain such dominance in computers, where standards that permit machines of different kinds and brands to "talk" have yet to fully evolve. Olson disagrees, but few experts believe *AT&T* is best-equipped to alleviate what he calls data "indigestion."

With *AT&T* at a major turning point, Jim Olson may be the company's most important leader since Theodore N. Vail. At the turn of the century, Vail set *AT&T*'s course for the next 75 years: providing universal phone service through a nationwide network of local phone companies. Olson is uncomfortable with such comparisons. He feels history will mark his predecessor, Charles L. Brown, as more important. Brown gave up *AT&T*'s local phone companies and saw *AT&T*

through the divestiture. He also moved *AT&T* into the Information Age.

But if Olson demurs, others do not: "Charlie Brown brought the ship out of the harbor," says Robert J. Casale, a partner at Kidder, Peabody & Co. and a former *AT&T* executive. "It's Jim Olson's job now to sail it."

By John J. Keller in New York

DISCUSSION QUESTIONS

1. Retrenchment is a strategy often applied by management. What are signs of its application at AT&T?
2. Apply the BCG (Boston Consulting Group) business portfolio matrix to analyzing AT&T. Assume its "core businesses" are SBUs (strategic business units).

DISNEY'S MAGIC
A TURNAROUND PROVES WISHES CAN COME TRUE
MARCH 9, 1987, PP. 62-65, 68-69

There's a new movie out that is fast becoming one of the season's biggest hits. The comedy stars Bette Midler as a blowsy sometime porno actress whose language would make a New York City cabdriver blanch. Attentive moviegoers might notice that *Outrageous Fortune*, which also stars Shelley Long, is released by Touchstone Pictures. But few would know that Touchstone is a unit of Walt Disney Co.

That's right—Walt Disney, as in Bambi and Thumper. The fantasy factory that gave America squeaky-clean dreams filled with cuddly creatures is now bringing you R-rated movies. Walt would be appalled. Or maybe not: "Walt would love what's going on with his company," says Roy E. Disney, vice-chairman of the board and nephew of the founder. "We've become an idea company again."

It wasn't long ago that Disney seemed to have run out of ideas. In the two decades following Walt's death in 1966, the company often stagnated. A revolution in the way Hollywood makes and sells movies had passed Disney by, leaving Mickey looking a bit moth-eaten and Sneezy a little shopworn. The movie studio seemed unable to do anything but turn out costly bombs, and Disney, once a staple of the small screen, had disappeared from *TV*. That left the company dangerously dependent on its theme parks. By 1984, after three successive years of declining earnings, the raiders were sharpening their knives.

TV STAR. But if frogs can turn into princes, the Disney kingdom can get its magic back. The turnaround began in late 1984, with the arrival of Michael D. Eisner as Disney's chairman and chief executive and Frank G. Wells as its president and chief operating officer. The two, already successful Hollywood executives, took on the formidable task of dragging Disney into the modern world of entertainment.

Signs of renewal are all around. In 1986, Disney, a perennial also-ran at the box office, was No. 3, thanks to such hits as *Down and Out in Beverly Hills* and *Ruthless People*. Only Paramount Pictures Corp. and Warner Brothers did better. Disney came roaring back to network *TV* with the nation's fifth-rated show, *Golden Girls*. Attendance at the theme parks rose 8%. And despite a flat cable-*TV* market, the Disney Channel's subscriber base grew 27% last year, to almost 3.2 million.

Net profits companywide have nearly tripled since 1983, to more than $247 million on $2.5 billion in revenues for the fiscal year ended Sept. 30. During the same period, the price of the company's stock has grown more than fivefold, to around 58 from a low of 11, adjusted for a 4-to-1 split.

Under Eisner and Wells, Disney has begun a two-pronged strategy of exploiting its existing assets to the fullest while creating new properties for the future. For Disney, assets mean its theme parks and hotels, of course, but also its characters such as Mickey, Goofy, and Dumbo and the vaults of movies and *TV* shows in which they star. Worldwide, the company is making the most of its menagerie with everything from videocassettes to product licensing to—maybe—a Disneyland in China.

ON THE PROWL. At the same time, with its newly sophisticated studios turning out hit movies for grownups, new cartoons for kids, and hit shows for *TV*, Disney is creating equities for the future. From rock concerts at Disneyland to *Captain EO*, a $17 million 3-D music video starring Michael Jackson, Disney is becoming hip. This is the same Disney whose board, only three years ago, berated previous managers for making the hit movie *Splash* because of its partial nudity and hints of premarital sex. "It was a true sleeping giant until these guys arrived," says Barry Diller, chairman of Twentieth Century-Fox Film Corp. "Now we'd all better watch out."

The company is also building new parks and hotels and is on the prowl for a major entertainment acquisition. To help pay for those plans, Disney has agreed to sell its Arvida Disney Corp. real estate unit to *JMB* Realty Trust for about $400 million in cash and notes. Disney bought Arvida in 1984 for about $200 million in stock. And later this year, Disney is expected to raise an additional $1.2 billion by selling its four-year-old Epcot Center in Orlando to a master limited partnership.

Some of that money will finance the continuing development of Disney's still-vast Florida holdings, including several new hotels and a $300 million combined movie studio and tour attraction. Roughly $150 million will buy a 17% stake in the new European Disneyland (page 84). But the rest, Disney officials say privately, is earmarked for at least one major entertainment investment by 1990.

The new Disney has its critics, of course. A source who knows the company well argues that Eisner and Wells have worked no fancier magic than to raise prices at Disney's theme parks. Admission prices had failed to keep pace with inflation, and the new management hiked them by 45% over two years. The higher prices alone accounted for 59% of the company's total revenue growth of $455 million last year and fully 94% of the earnings growth of $158 million. "It didn't take a lot of brains," this source says, "to see that the company's biggest asset was being incredibly underused."

DONALD DUCKED. Other doubters say that with

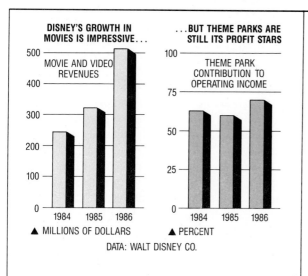

DISNEY'S GROWTH IN MOVIES IS IMPRESSIVE...

MOVIE AND VIDEO REVENUES

500
400
300
200
100
0

1984 1985 1986

▲ MILLIONS OF DOLLARS

...BUT THEME PARKS ARE STILL ITS PROFIT STARS

THEME PARK CONTRIBUTION TO OPERATING INCOME

100
75
50
25
0

1984 1985 1986

▲ PERCENT

DATA: WALT DISNEY CO.

its big push into *TV* and movies, Disney is trying to temper its dependence on the theme parks by increasing its reliance on an even more volatile business. Two of the studio's four prime-time *TV* shows have been received poorly—*The Ellen Burstyn Show*, which *ABC* has canceled, and *Sidekicks*, one of the lowest-rated shows of the year. A recent feature film from Disney, *The Color of Money*, has performed well below expectations, grossing $48 million to date. But that's not bad, considering that the movie, starring Tom Cruise and Paul Newman, cost only about $12 million to make.

The Disney board clearly approves of Eisner's moves. In 1986 he received bonuses of $2.6 million on top of his $750,000 salary. Even if Disney's critics are right, the company is in far better shape than it was in 1984, when its stock price was so low that Donald Duck came perilously close to ending up as *canard à l'orange* on some raider's plate. With Saul P. Steinberg and Irwin L. Jacobs about to breach the Magic Kingdom's gates, only a last-minute rescue by Texas' Bass brothers saved the company from possible dismemberment. But in return for buying a 25% stake, the Basses demanded a total management overhaul.

BOY LOSES GIRL. The Disney board chose Eisner partly on the recommendation of filmmakers Steven Spielberg and George Lucas (page 82). the 44-year-old Eisner is an unlikely movie mogul. Raised on New York's Upper East Side and educated in private schools, he was supposed to go to medical school after graduating from Denison University. But to impress a pretty drama major, Eisner took several theater courses. He lost the girl and nearly flunked makeup, but got hooked on entertainment.

After a brief stint at *CBS* Inc., Eisner spent 10 years at *ABC*, where he worked his way up to head of programming. During his tenure, the traditionally last-place network became No. 1. Then came Paramount Pictures, where Eisner was president for eight years. He helped make the studio one of Hollywood's top box-office earners with a run of hits such as *Saturday Night Fever* and *Raiders of the Lost Ark*.

"Every place he has ever been, Michael Eisner brings energy and creativity in high concentration," says Fox Chairman Diller, who was Eisner's boss at both *ABC* and Paramount. "And that's exactly the two ingredients that Disney needed to tap." Both Eisner and Diller moved from Paramount shortly after Martin S. Davis succeeded the late Charles Bluhdorn as chairman of Gulf & Western Industries Inc., Paramount's parent company.

Eisner's solid combination of network and studio experience made him the right executive to lead Disney's blitz into *TV* and movies. But Eisner is suited to Disney in other ways, too. Despite his long hours, he is a devoted father. He refuses to work late on the Tuesday evenings when he goes with his eight-year-old son to Indian Guide meetings. And he recently showed up late for a breakfast meeting because he had spent two hours helping his 17-year-old son cram for a Latin exam. "He's the epitome of what we were looking for to head this company," says Raymond L. Watson, head of Disney's executive committee and the company's chairman until Eisner arrived. "He has almost as many family values as Walt did himself."

IN SYNC. Indeed, Eisner's boosters make him sound almost like a reincarnation of Walt. "He's the perfect successor to Walt Disney, not only because he's a business genius but because he's someone who is in sync with his product," says

THE FORCE OF GEORGE LUCAS IS NOW WITH DISNEY

As a Modesto (Calif.) 11-year-old, George Lucas stood in line for opening day at Disneyland in 1955, and was captivated. Later he spent summer vacations at the park. To this day, says an associate, "George can discuss in depth all of Disney's characters. There's a natural affinity."

Lucas, of course, grew up to create his own legendary fantasies in *Star Wars* and *Raiders of the Lost Ark*, while Disney's monopoly on childhood imaginations waned. "Lucas' films are the films Disney should have been doing," says Sid R. Bass, a major Walt Disney Co. shareholder. It's no wonder, then, that Bass asked Lucas for recommendations when the company needed new management. Lucas' suggestions: Michael D. Eisner and Frank G. Wells, the current chairman and president. No wonder, either, that Eisner is bringing Lucas into the fold. "There are just so many true geniuses of this caliber," Eisner says. "After Walt Disney and George Lucas, who is there, really?"

STAR TOURS. Already, Lucas has produced *Captain EO*, a $17 million 3-D music video directed by Francis Ford Coppola and starring Michael Jackson. Lucas and his Industrial Light & Magic also came up with the story and special effects for Star Tours, a new $32 million spaceship ride at Disneyland. What's more, the park will soon carry *Star Wars* merchandise, marking only the second time—after Winnie the Pooh—that non-Disney characters have been allowed through its gates.

Production of a third attraction, based on the exploits of Indiana Jones, is expected to begin shortly. And a Disney insider says Lucas is toying with the idea of redoing virtually all of Disneyland's five-ride Tomorrowland complex. "He's not going to be finished until it's 'Lucasland,' " according to this source.

More important to Disney is possible collaboration on feature films. Eisner has charged Walt Disney Studios Chairman Jeffrey Katzenberg with signing Lucas to produce films for Disney, and talks are under way.

Lucas refuses to commit himself to a single studio. Lucasfilm Ltd. has no intention of becoming Disney's surrogate font of creativity. "That's not our purpose in life," says the president of Lucasfilm, R. Douglas Norby. Still, he declares: "We want to keep working with Disney." For a wide-eyed kid from Modesto, it's a childhood dream come true.

By Jonathan B. Levine in San Francisco and Todd Mason in Dallas

longtime friend Senator Bill Bradley (D-N. J.). Eisner introduces every episode of the *Disney Sunday Movie*—and works with a speech coach at each filming. He once fretted about his inept on-camera appearances to Bradley, who consoled Eisner with tales of his own *TV* commercials. "He turned out to be quite a performer," Bradley says.

Eisner also seems to be quite a headhunter. He has lured some of Hollywood's most talented people to Disney, including as many as 20 top executives from Paramount. Insiders attribute much of the studio's comeback to Paramount veteran Jeffrey Katzenberg, head of motion pictures and *TV*. Katzenberg is known as "the golden retriever" for his ability to sniff out just the right script or actor.

Disney needed such talent badly. At a time when other studios had already moved into *TV*, cable, and video, Eisner found himself atop a somnolent company best known for some fading animation classics and a few dimwitted films starring Fred MacMurray or Don Knotts. Theme parks and real estate still generated steady revenues, but one good gasoline-price shock could torpedo earnings. Worse, the Disney name was getting musty. "Disney was sitting on top of exceedingly valuable assets," says Alfred A. Checchi, a top aide to the Basses until 1986. "And they were being undermanaged."

Eisner and Wells moved quickly to make more of those assets. To tap the video market, Disney now releases at least one of its classics on cassette each year. In 1986 it sold 1 million copies of *Sleeping Beauty* and sold out its 25,000-unit supply of a special six-pack of Disney classics priced at $180.

> 'The theme parks may be the heart of this company, but the movie business is its soul'

A NATURAL. It sometimes seems as if Disney is marketing every character, story, and image in its archives. A Mickey Mouse blimp, dubbed Ear Force One, will visit all 50 states this year. Snow White kicked off a yearlong celebration of her 50th birthday by visiting the floor of the New York Stock Exchange with her seven dwarfs. And Disney produced the halftime show at Super Bowl XXI. Disney's ad budget has tripled in the past three years, to $90 million.

The company is also pushing into *TV* syndication. Almost overnight it has grabbed a large chunk of the market for syndicated programs, an area where other studios have been cleaning up for years. It's a natural: The company has more than 29 years of *Wonderful World of Disney TV* shows, hundreds of cartoons, and nearly 200 feature movies. The three separate packages that Disney has put up for sale in the past year have helped to double first-quarter film revenues to an estimated $262 million.

But Disney is starting to do more than just live off its inheritance. "There is virtually no limit to where Disney can go in television," says Ted Harbert, *ABC*'s vice-president for motion pictures. Besides the hit sitcom *Golden Girls*, the *Disney Sunday Movie* is back on network *TV* after a two-year hiatus. This month, *ABC* is adding another Disney show to its lineup, *Harry*, starring Alan Arkin in his first *TV* series. In off-network syndication, Disney is distributing *Siskel & Ebert & the Movies*

and, in September, its first game show. And it distributes *Today's Business*, a business news program featuring *BUSINESS WEEK* Editor William Wolman, which has been picked up by 133 stations. *BUSINESS WEEK* has no financial interest in the venture.

Disney is also vigorously expanding its foreign presence. Videocassette sales are soaring in Britain, Spain, and Israel, and Mickey and Donald are now prime-time stars on Chinese *TV*. Tokyo Disneyland is booming, and by 1992, millions of Europeans will probably be visiting a new French Disneyland.

The U. S. theme parks are growing, too. Besides the studio and tour at the Walt Disney World complex in Orlando, work will soon begin on Typhoon Lagoon, a 50-acre park with water slides and wave machines. Disney also plans to build as many as four new hotels in Orlando. The company is planning a new park in Southern California and considering several sites for its first regional entertainment center, combining restaurants, night spots, and shopping malls. In all, there may be no better comment on Disney's long-term prospects than this from 44-year-old Sid R. Bass: "I anticipate that the executor of my estate will end up handling my Disney shares."

HOLLYWOOD GAME. Disney has been frustrated, however, in one arena—acquisitions. Although the company won't talk about targets, it clearly wants to play the now-familiar Hollywood game of vertical integration by buying distribution outlets for the product of its studios. A staff of six strategic planners has spent a year poring over a list of targets. So far, though, other players have kept the prizes from Disney's grasp. It studied the 360-screen Mann Theater chain, bought by Gulf & Western in October for $220 million. It eyed the independent New York *TV* station *WOR-TV*, which *MCA* Inc. agreed to buy for $387 million in 1986.

Disney has also failed to buy its way to a bigger library of *TV* shows and movies for syndication, after looking at libraries owned by Viacom International and *MCA*. And it hasn't supplemented its $30 million children's record business with music for teens. It sounded out *CBS* about buying *CBS* Records but was spurned by the network's board.

DISNEYLAND ABROAD: TODAY TOKYO, TOMORROW THE WORLD

It's a bit unsettling, but there it is: Cinderella's Castle, rising out of land reclaimed from Tokyo Bay and looking spectacularly out of place against the dull Tokyo skyline. Disneyland, that peculiarly American institution, has become an institution in Japan as well.

Tokyo Disneyland opened nearly four years ago and lured more than 10 million visitors its first year—almost outdrawing the Anaheim original. The biggest single day was this past New Year's Eve, when 130,000 Japanese braved near-freezing temperatures for an all-night bash, complete with countdown, fireworks, and Minnie Mouse in a kimono. In 1987 the park should attract 11 million guests who will spend more than $500 million.

By design, the atmosphere is all-American. In the late 1970s the park's planners agonized over whether to add Japanese touches. "We finally decided that we wanted it to look and feel like an experience in the States," says Toshio Kagami, managing director of Oriental Land Co., the Japanese company that owns and operates the park. "Now we consider that the biggest factor in our success."

TRASH CANS. The result is a near-copy of Tokyo Disneyland's U. S. cousins, down to such details as the design of trash cans and the placement of drinking fountains. One change: A roof over Main Street, a concession to Tokyo's wet weather. "The first time I went, I was surprised," says 24-year-old Rie Fujioka, a three-time visitor. "There were so many things I'd never seen in Japanese amusement parks. I thought: 'So this is the American way.'"

In the past, outsiders often asked Disney about creating foreign parks. Until the Tokyo request, however, the company never seriously considered the offers. "But this was a market that understood Disney already," says Ronald D. Pogue, managing director of Disneyland International. "We had been successful for years in Japan with films and books and consumer products." Japan's 84-year-old Emperor sometimes sports a Mickey Mouse watch.

FRANCE IS NEXT. What's more, the project didn't cost Disney a cent. Oriental Land, a joint venture of Mitsui Real Estate Development Co. and Keisei Electric Ry. Co., financed and built the park for $750 million. Disney designed it, advises Oriental Land on operations, and receives royalties of 10% on admissions and 5% on sales.

The phenomenal success of Tokyo Disneyland

"We're going to be awfully conservative in what we go after," says Eisner. "But if there is something out there that could add immediate value to this company, we're going to go for it."

The search for new assets is another part of Eisner's strategy to reduce the company's heavy reliance on theme parks and hotels. Those operations contributed $403.7 million in operating income last year, about 70% of the company's total. Disney has been better diversified in the past: In 1974 theme parks and hotels contributed less than 40% of operating income.

When Eisner arrived at Disney, movies and *TV* accounted for only about 13% of company profits.

Disney officials would like to triple that proportion. Eisner has set an ambitious goal of releasing 15 to 18 films a year, up from 10 in 1986. A dozen will be pictures with adult themes, released under the Touchstone label. The rest will be either new children's movies or reissues of such classics as *Snow White and the Seven Dwarfs*. "The theme parks may be the heart of this company," Eisner says, "but the movie business is its soul."

This year the studio is likely to release 15 films, the highest total in its history. The goal is simple: to get as many movies as possible into the long entertainment pipeline, collecting not only box-office receipts but also added revenues from home-is prompting Disney to plan a European version. It's scheduled to open in 1992 on 4,500 acres near Paris. Disney will be a 17% owner of the private consortium developing the $1.7 billion park and will have control of the park's management.

To win the contract away from rival Spanish bidders, the French government had to add some expensive sweeteners, such as building subway extensions and highway interchanges and reducing its amusement taxes on the park's receipts. But it demanded that Disney give some attractions a European flavor and use French as the first language on signposts. Such a thought horrifies the Japanese: English is the first language at Tokyo Disneyland.

Tokyo Disneyland hopes to have 12 million visitors a year by 1990—a goal that it plans to meet by adding new attractions, developing the empty landfill surrounding the park, and advertising more. Now under construction is Big Thunder Mountain, a $50 million train ride. Further down the road could be a second attraction, perhaps something like the studio tour Disney is adding in Florida.

The future also includes a somewhat shorter Cinderella's Castle. The structure is slowly sinking back into the bay—a typical problem of building on landfill. But Cinderella won't have to move: The engineers anticipated that the castle would sink as much as 3 ft. over the next 25 years and designed it so that it would, at least, settle evenly.

By Larry Armstrong in Tokyo

video sales and contracts with pay and broadcast TV. The strategy is already paying off. Touchstone's *Ruthless People* and *Down and Out in Beverly Hills* were among the top 10 box-office hits of 1986, and *Down and Out* followed that up with record video rentals of more than $10 million. In addition, Disney signed a five-year, $200 million deal giving Showtime/The Movie Channel Inc. cable rights to as many as 50 Touchstone films.

HITTING SINGLES. Mining extra revenue from such sources is nothing new in Hollywood. But while other studios spend an average of nearly $16 million per movie, Disney spends about $11 mil-

lion. "Our movie philosophy is to go for singles and doubles when we make our films," says Eisner. "If you go for the home run all the time, you strike out a lot."

To keep costs down, the studio signs such stars as Midler, Newman, and Richard Dreyfuss to long-term commitments by dangling offers for them to direct or produce their own films. And the studio entices virtually all of its stars to take reduced salaries in return for a percentage of box-office receipts and other sales. Disney executives "know what they want and how to get it," says Midler, who has signed to do three more films for Disney. "Right now they want to make comedies, and they are making the best in town."

What's more, the movies are doing boffo business. *Outrageous Fortune* is expected to rival *Ruthless People*'s $72 million in box-office receipts. The studio has signed Ron Howard to direct a sequel to *Splash* and will soon release *Tin Men*, written by *Diner* director Barry Levinson.

Moviemaking is a risky business, of course. A series of punishments at the box office could stunt Disney's comeback. And even though the studios are revving up, much of the payoff is years away. But it wasn't long ago that critics were saying Disney was too cautious, paying its way by selling off the family heirlooms. Not so today. For now, and with luck for well into the future, the wearer of the Magic Kingdom's crown can enjoy a prosperous reign.

By Ronald Grover in Los Angeles, with Mark N. Vamos in New York, Todd Mason in Dallas, and bureau reports

DISCUSSION QUESTIONS

1. Describe Disney's strategy in your own terms and evaluate it against such standards as these:
   a. Is there a comprehensive, integrated plan?
   b. If so, is it consistent and appropriate considering objectives and environmental and internal conditions?
   c. Do Disney's plans seem workable?
2. Classify what you judge to be Disney's SBUs in a BCG matrix.

WHY RIVALS ARE QUAKING AS NORDSTROM HEADS EAST

THE DEPARTMENT-STORE CHAIN'S CUSTOMER SERVICE IS UNBEATABLE

JUNE 15, 1987, PP. 99-100

At many department stores these days, the customer isn't always right. In fact, the customer is barely tolerated. But Nordstrom Inc., a Seattle-based apparel, shoe, and soft-goods retailer since 1901, has become legendary for its good service. Sales clerks gift-wrap packages for no extra charge and drop off orders at customers' homes. Piano players serenade shoppers year-round. In Alaska, Nordstrom employees have been known to warm up cars while drivers spend a few more minutes shopping. There's even a story—which the company doesn't deny—about a customer who got his money back on a tire. Since Nordstrom doesn't sell tires, it was a testament to the store's no-questions-asked return policy.

Retailers on the West Coast, where Nordstrom's 46 stores are located, are all too familiar with these tales. But soon merchants east of the Rockies will experience what all the fuss is about. The company plans to open its first Washington (D. C.)-area store next March and its second in 1989. It will soon announce locations in Chicago and Minneapolis, and it is scouting sites in Boston, Atlanta, and New Jersey. To serve up to 15 new stores, Nordstrom broke ground in May for a distribution center in Maryland. "You could say we're poised, ready to pounce," said President James F. Nordstrom in a rare interview following the company's May 19 annual meeting in Portland, Ore. By 1992, he predicted, the new stores will help boost sales by $500 million.

CHEERFUL GROUP. The prospect of having Nordstrom as a neighbor rattles competitors, many of which have cut services to improve their profit margins. Nordstrom has proven that retailers can do well by treating customers well. That not only means assisting them whenever possible, but giving them attractive, well-stocked stores that sell better quality merchandise at prices comparable to those of other upscale retailers. Profits surged 46% to $72.9 million in 1986, while sales of stores open at least a year rose 14%. Revenues, projected to reach $1.9 billion this year, have grown at least 25% a year since 1984 and should continue at that pace through 1992. The company enjoys the highest sales per sq. ft. of any department store: $310. That's $160 more than the average and $55 more than No. 2 Parisian Inc., a Birmingham (Ala.)-based retailer that also has a reputation for outstanding service.

What is the secret of Nordstrom's success? "I have never met a more helpful, cheerful group of people," says Keri L. Christenfeld, a specialty retailing analyst for Cowen & Co. and a Nordstrom shopper. Nordstrom executives, every one of whom started on the selling floor, mean it when they say the sales clerks are their most important employees. Unlike many department stores, where sales is a low-paying, dead-end job, Nordstrom uses sales as a career track, attracting highly motivated people.

Nordstrom puts great effort into recruiting sales associates. It rewards them, through commissions and profit-sharing, with some of the highest salaries in the industry. College graduates start at $20,000, and a store manager can top $100,000 with bonuses. Once hired, "you prove yourself at every level, or you get fired," says Douglas J. Tigert, professor of marketing at Babson College in Wellesley, Mass.

Yet as simple as the formula might appear, it is

not easy to copy. Nordstrom can promote sales clerks into higher-level jobs because the company is growing and new positions keep opening up. Many other department stores are retrenching. Beyond that, experts speak of an attitude at Nordstrom that many retail companies have lost. "There is a very strong culture of what it means to represent Nordstrom," says Leonard L. Berry, director of the Center for Retailing Studies at Texas A&M University. Bill Baer, a men's-clothing salesman in the Palo Alto store, defines it this way: "Nordstrom tells me to do whatever I need to do to make you happy. Period."

'FEAR OF GOD.' Nordstrom's service record is having a profound effect on retailing. It has been eye-opening to department stores, whose declining service has cost them share in many markets. "Nordstrom is putting the fear of God into the competition," says John S. Tschohl, president of Better Than Money Corp., a Minneapolis service consulting firm. "I think they will raise the level of service everywhere they go."

That has happened in California, where Nordstrom competitors such as Macy's and The Broadway are paying sales commissions and offering personalized shopping services. But executives of those companies concede that change doesn't happen overnight. "Service is an attitude, a kind of caring on the part of everybody in the store. It takes a lot of coaching and leadership" to instill those qualities, says Philip M. Hawley, chairman of Los Angeles-based Carter Hawley Hale Stores Inc., which owns The Broadway and Emporium Capwell Co.

In Chicago, Marshall Field & Co. hopes to whip its service into shape before Nordstrom puts it to the test. The venerable 25-unit department-store chain is in the midst of a multimillion-dollar push to revive the founder's edict: "Give the lady what she wants." The task is formidable, because the company's "service standards have eroded throughout the years of real-estate ventures, draining of capital, less-than-terrific business, and corporate takeover activity," says Gary M. Witkin, Marshall Field's executive vice-president for stores.

FRANGLOONS. Marshall Field is making noticeable progress. When the company started its service-improvement campaign four years ago, it took a salesperson 10 minutes on average to approach a customer. Thanks to such changes as a computer scheduling program that puts salespeople where they're needed most, Field lopped eight

---

Says a clothing salesman: 'Nordstrom tells me to do whatever I need to do to make you happy. Period'

---

minutes off the average response time. To maintain such standards, the company developed an unusual incentive plan. Every time a manager observes a sales clerk being extra helpful to a customer, the employee receives a silver coin called a "Frangloon." Ten coins can be traded for a box of Field's Frango mint chocolates and 100 get an extra day of paid vacation.

Witkin says Field is looking at all phases of its operation. It is considering putting lights outside the dressing rooms that customers can turn on when they need help, much the way they would summon a flight attendant on a plane. Witkin sees two basic issues in upgrading service: "It doesn't come cheap, and it is an ongoing process requiring constant reinforcement."

That advice might serve some East Coast retailers well as they brace for the Nordstrom invasion. Co-Chairman Bruce A. Nordstrom, whose family owns about 45% of the stock, hinted at the unmet demand for his company's special brand of retailing by describing a recent San Jose store opening, when 2,000 customers lined up at the door. "They came rushing in with this glazed look in their eyes and their charge plates ready," he says. Perhaps their enthusiasm reflected one too many encounters with surly sales clerks at competing stores.

By Joan O'C. Hamilton in San Francisco, with Amy Dunkin in New York and bureau reports

DISCUSSION QUESTION
Analyze Nordstrom's strategy in terms of Porter's generic strategies.

IF YOU OWN A PORSCHE, DON'T BOTHER APPLYING

INSURER 20TH CENTURY MAKES
HIGH PROFITS FORM THE LOW END

AUGUST 10, 1987, P. 61

Louis W. Foster runs an insurance company—to be more precise, a property/casualty insurance company. But it won't touch his Mercedes or his Los Angeles home. They are simply too pricey and, therefore, too risky. "We don't insure Rolls-Royces or Porsches. We want the Chevy and Buick owner," Foster says. He prefers doing business with "the guy who has been with the phone company for 22 years. You just talk to him, and you can see his well-cared-for home."

That attitude has helped the 74-year-old chairman create one of the nation's fastest-growing and most successful insurance companies in the country. His formula is simple: Get business by offering rock-bottom prices. Keep risks down by avoiding the upscale market. And keep costs down by eschewing insurance agents and by selling policies directly to consumers.

MAIL BONDING. The plan has worked out well. Foster's 20th Century Industries, the holding company for 20th Century Insurance Co., which houses most of its operation in an unpretentious office building in the San Fernando Valley, has enjoyed an average 23% return on equity for the past five years. The Woodland Hills (Calif.) company's profits more than doubled, from $13.7 million in 1985 to $31.9 million in 1986. And first-quarter results this year were up 27% compared with 1986.

20th Century, with $538 million in assets, doesn't advertise in the media for auto insurance business. And it has only recently begun soliciting new business through direct-mail marketing—after a three-year hiatus. The company's main selling point: insurance premium rates that are among the cheapest in the huge Southern California market.

The company's telephone operators are besieged by some 2,500 callers a day seeking relief from Southern California's astronomical auto and home insurance rates. Yet only half the callers are sent applications, and 15% of those applicants are rejected. The company not only steers clear of insuring expensive cars, but also avoids drivers with poor records and even those who are shopping for auto insurance for the first time.

Still, 20th Century has had its share of problems. Some Wall Street analysts say that Foster kept prices too low for too long in the face of rising auto and bodily injury claims. They point to the company's dip in earnings in 1982 and 1983, which stemmed mainly from poor automobile underwriting results. Most competitors, however, suffered more than 20th Century during those years of fierce competitive battles for market share in the property and casualty business. Although the company raised rates 20% in 1986, the problem reappeared in this year's first quarter. Most of that period's fat gain in earnings came from investment income, while the company actually suffered a $1.4 million loss in underwriting. Foster is confident, however, that after an 11% premium hike the loss problem is ending.

Foster has also acted to shore up another potential trouble area: lack of management depth. Until recently he has been criticized for running a one-man show at the company he founded 30 years ago. But in past months he has hired and promoted several managers. The stronger management team is part of Foster's plan to double 20th Century's size by 1990.

BEYOND THE VALLEY. Yet getting bigger does not mean getting into different businesses. "We'll stay with what we know best," says President Neil H. Ashley, who worked for 25 years at Allstate Insurance Co.

Foster sees plenty of opportunity just in reaching out of the company's stronghold in the San Fernando Valley north of Los Angeles and expanding the homeowners' insurance business, which now accounts for about 9% of policies. "There's so much here, why would we want to go outside the state?" he says.

Foster has always been a go-getter. At 12, after his father died leaving 11 children, he hauled laundry in a wagon to help support the family. After graduating from Stanford University, he served in the Navy, then sold washing machines door-to-door. But insurance, it seems, was his true calling. Foster spent 20 years as an independent agent. Then, in 1958, armed with two decades' worth of insight, he started the company that evolved into 20th Century. His philosophy? That insurance agents are nothing more than unnecessary—and expensive—overhead.

Many insurance companies have expense ratios of 30% of premiums or more, most of it attributable to agents' commissions. Even *GEICO*, the big auto insurer that doesn't use agents but does advertise, has a 15% expense ratio. In 1986, 20th Century's ratio was a paltry 8.3%.

With Foster getting on in years, 20th Century could be a takeover candidate. "Those rumors are around all the time," says Ashley. There are no antitakeover measures in place. But there are some defenses nonetheless. Insiders own about 25% of the company's stock, which sells at 23 a share, a rich 17 times earnings. Any insurance company that relies on agents would be reluctant to buy it. Their agents would give management too much flak.

Foster says he is in no hurry to sell out or retire: "God will tell me when to leave." Foster wants to remain the king of bargain-basement insurance.

By Teresa Carson in Woodland Hills

DISCUSSION QUESTION
Analyze 20th Century Industries' strategy with the theoretical model or models you judge most applicable.

PART 3

ORGANIZING

Organizations are like those organisms whose structures change during their development. Caterpillars become butterflies; small entrepreneurial organizations turn into stolid bureaucracies. Unlike the organisms, however, the bureaucracies can go back. Managers design and redesign organizations.

In the articles in Part 3 students can locate examples of the types of structures described in their texts and lectures: functional, product, territorial, matrix, and so on. They can see managers switching from one to another, in pursuit of an adaptive design. A common thread through the articles is a favoring of movement back from bureaucracy to decentralized forms that can regain a lost nimbleness. On the other hand, students can find the occasional celebration of the virtues of centralization, Hewlett-Packard's experience being a case in point.

The last group of three articles stresses teamwork, a literally precise usage here that draws attention to the possibilities of organizing work by teams instead of the traditional design of work by individual jobs.

WHO'S AFRAID OF IBM?

NOT COMPAQ. THE FEISTY NO. 2 IN OFFICE PCs IS PICKING A FIGHT

JUNE 29, 1987, PP. 68-72, 74

On a morning in mid-May, 1,200 employees of Compaq Computer Corp. assembled at a modern Baptist church in northwest Houston. At the pulpit was Joseph R. "Rod" Canion, the president who for five years has led Compaq on an unerring path from obscure startup to International Business Machines Corp.'s No. 1 rival in office personal computers. Diligence, patience, teamwork, and humility—those had always been Canion's watchwords. This day, however, Canion was preaching the gospel of a bolder Compaq. He told his flock that they, not *IBM*, now lead the industry. "*IBM* is running behind and not catching up," he declared.

Canion, 42, a former Texas Instruments Inc. engineer who had to take public speaking lessons when he became Compaq's leader, is preaching the same sermon to customers, dealers, and investors: With *IBM*'s introduction of its Personal System/2 computers on Apr. 2, he says, the No. 1 computer maker deviated from the hardware and software standards that had developed around its original *PC*s. In their place, he argues, *IBM* substituted proprietary innovations that mainly serve to strengthen Big Blue's control over microcomputer customers—while providing few benefits. "Some people said they should have done it on April Fool's Day," he jokes. "They came as close as they could."

ON THE DEFENSIVE. Such rhetoric has "surprised a lot of people," says Compaq Chairman Benjamin M. Rosen. Until now, the company has largely avoided direct confrontation with *IBM*, often a losing strategy. "You don't fight *IBM*, you undermine it," says Seymour Merrin, a consultant who has advised Canion to button his lip and stick to the formula that has made Compaq a $625 million company with a market valuation of $1.6 billion. Canion did it by building *IBM*-compatible computers that cost about the same as Big Blue's but outperformed them or offered something extra. The paradigm is Compaq's first computer, the suitcase-sized portable model that inspired the company's name. It was a hit because *IBM* didn't have a comparable product.

So why change the formula now? Partly because *IBM* has put Canion on the defensive. In its efforts to sell PS/2 models, *IBM* is implying that in the future only they will perform such tasks as sharing complex software with *IBM* mainframes across companywide networks. If *IBM* persuades customers of this, it will hurt Compaq's following in large companies, whose purchases accounted for 45% of Compaq's sales last year. "Canion has to be vocal now," says David Carnevale, a vice-president at market researcher InfoCorp. "The worst thing that could happen is that people become confused and stop buying."

But Canion's aggressiveness also is aimed at cashing in on a golden opportunity. There are some 10 million *IBM PC*s and compatibles in businesses around the world. Getting their owners to trade up to the PS/2 line may not be easy—even given *IBM*'s marketing clout. The PS/2 computers use a different kind of floppy disk from the *PC*'s, making it difficult to transfer programs and files to the new machines. The new *IBM* machines can't use the add-in circuit cards designed for existing *PC*s. And although the new *IBM* machines are more powerful than their predecessors, the software that will let them use that power won't exist for another year. In the meantime, *IBM PC*s are in short supply because *IBM* has curtailed shipments of them in hopes of converting customers quickly to PS/2.

In Canion's view, that means the time is ripe to attack. In a recent International Data Corp. survey, 52% of corporate computer buyers indicated that the introduction of the PS/2 may cause them to delay major purchasing decisions in the next six months. That leaves 48% that won't wait. Canion figures that customers have sunk $80 billion into *IBM PCs*, *PC* clones, and the hardware options and software that work with them. He's betting that even *IBM* can't redirect that movement—at least not quickly. "*IBM* has a less dominant role in this market" than in mainframes, notes Rosen. "Customers have more choice."

MARKING TIME. If Canion can make fresh inroads as buyers ponder PS/2, he's likely to boost his market share again this year (chart at right). "The strategy is to slam the PS/2 now because Compaq doesn't have one to sell," says George Colony, president of Forrester Research. "Meanwhile, they are madly cloning PS/2 in their labs." Canion insists the company has no plans to clone the PS/2 unless it becomes a widely accepted standard. But the minute the tide turns toward PS/2, analysts think Canion will follow.

So far this strategy looks like the right one. In the first quarter of 1987, despite the specter of the PS/2 introduction, earnings soared 142%, to $20.2 million, as sales rose 46%, to $210.9 million. In April the company chalked up its largest backlog of orders ever for its desktop models, the computers that compete directly with *IBM*'s *PC/AT*. Analysts say that the backlog grew again in May. Demand for Compaq's newest portable, the Portable III, is so strong, the company says, that it will be unable to fill all the orders until fall.

"Is Compaq just a winner or a huge winner?" asks Michele Preston, an analyst at Salomon Brothers. She recently upped her estimate of 1987 earnings by 10%, to $98 million, or $2.50 per share on sales of $931 million. In 1986 Compaq earned $43 million on $625 million in sales. Estimates for 1988 earnings run from $3 to $3.50 a share, with analysts expecting revenues to reach $1.2 billion.

Even Wall Street, which for years worried that

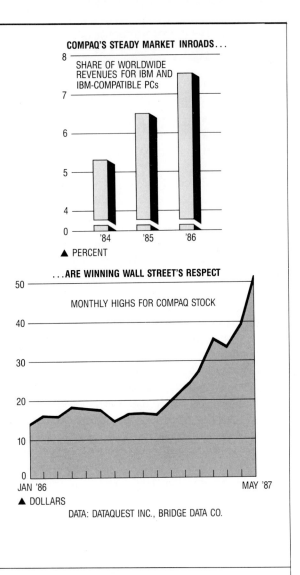

COMPAQ'S STEADY MARKET INROADS...

SHARE OF WORLDWIDE REVENUES FOR IBM AND IBM-COMPATIBLE PCs

▲ PERCENT

...ARE WINNING WALL STREET'S RESPECT

MONTHLY HIGHS FOR COMPAQ STOCK

JAN '86   MAY '87

▲ DOLLARS

DATA: DATAQUEST INC., BRIDGE DATA CO.

IBM would somehow hamstring the young company, is taking note. Though Chairman Rosen, the venture capitalist who first backed the company and a former Morgan Stanley & Co. analyst, listed Compaq's shares on the New York Stock Exchange to get better visibility, the stock languished in the teens until late 1986. It has since hit a record 50, buoyed by reports of a slow start for *IBM*'s new models and intensifying demand for machines that are compatible with the older *PC/AT* line. The stock has also made the most active list lately.

Some of the market share that Compaq grabs now could be difficult to hold, warns Wertheim & Co. analyst Harvey C. Allison. Because *IBM* products have been in short supply, he argues, Compaq got an artificial boost. Compaq's results may even be flat in the September quarter, he says, because of the company's increasing dependence on European sales, which usually slow in the summer. Still, Allison agrees that Compaq's overall outlook is positive for the next two years.

Oddly for a young company, Compaq's greatest strength appears to be good management. From the beginning it has relied on a tightly knit group of seasoned industry veterans to give it management depth. Of Compaq's 21 officers, 17 are Texas Instruments alumni who had as much as 21 years of experience. "We didn't always know what to do," admits Senior Vice-President B. Kevin Ellington, 49, "but we knew what not to do." Despite the urgings of critics, Compaq resisted the temptation to branch out too far from microcomputers. It also maintained strong relations with dealers by not setting up its own sales force. Canion's philosophy is the company's byword: Stick with what you know—and do it better than anyone else.

Experienced management helped Compaq sidestep the pitfalls that eliminated most of its original competitors. Those companies fell victim to a variety of marketing, distribution, and financing problems when the *PC* boom began slowing in late 1984. With its tight controls, Compaq sailed through the 1985-86 computer slump—without the kind of earnings drop that Apple Computer Inc. took as a result of inventory write-downs and layoffs. And as inexpensive clones sliced *IBM*'s share of the worldwide *PC* market from 52% to 32% last year, Compaq's share rose 15% to 7.5% (chart).

The key to Compaq's success seems to be the right blend of engineering and marketing savvy. It is the only major maker of *IBM*-compatible *PC*s that does all its own reverse engineering—the process of coming up with the electronic circuits and software that duplicate the functions of the *IBM PC*. "Their engineering is top-notch," says Jean-Claude Cornet, vice-president of Intel Corp.'s microcomputer group, the supplier of microchips for *IBM* and *IBM*-compatible personal computers. But the company also pays close attention to what the marketing folks say. "They haven't become so bureaucratic that they can't respond to customers," says Sherrie L. Burger, manager of office information systems at Blue Cross/Blue Shield in Chicago.

Maintaining that management style is the company's greatest worry as it passes the billion-dollar sales mark and extends its operations to new plants in Singapore and Scotland, says Ellington, who is in charge of corporate development. In the coming year, the company will be entering new overseas markets in an attempt to boost sales outside the U.S. from 19% to about 45% of revenues. In addition, Compaq has a backlog of new products to launch, including a widely expected portable using the advanced Intel 80386 microchip. "We have more products than we can introduce," says Canion. Ellington's concern: "How can we continue to have good teamwork and fast response and become a very large company?"

Canion might still be a nerdish engineer if he had found a topic for his PhD dissertation in electrical engineering. Frustrated, he left the University of Houston to try business. A lifelong Houstonian—the son of a Sears, Roebuck & Co. salesman and a schoolteacher—Canion joined *TI* in Houston, because "I liked its reputation and it was local." He climbed the ranks, becoming a business unit manager. Thomas Stringfellow, now a *TI* division manager, recalls him as a "very forward thinker" who was "soft-spoken but very effective."

'TOO EASY.' But after 13 years, Canion tired of *TI*'s bureaucratic style and its emphasis on technical excellence at the expense of marketing. The turning point came in 1980. After he set up a disk-drive manufacturing unit, Canion was abruptly transferred to another business unit because management considered his job finished. "The job just begins when you start selling product," he contends. "You need to continue the marketing focus." The last straw was his assignment to the group designing *TI*'s first office microcomputer. Canion quit within 18 months because he felt management misunderstood personal computers. His biggest gripe, ironic in light of Compaq's

A MACHINE THAT ONLY ITS MAKERS COULD LOVE

Compaq Computer Corp. may be batting 1,000 with its *PC* products, but it's hitting way below average in a related field: telecommunications. In 1984 it set up a subsidiary called Compaq Telecommunications Corp. to develop new products. Since then, the Dallas-based unit has soaked up investments of $20 million. Now, limping along, it's a reminder that even Compaq's much-praised management can take its eye off the ball.

On the surface, the company's interest in tele-communications made sense. The January, 1984, breakup of American Telephone & Telegraph Co. was spurring innovations in communications systems. Many companies, including giant Northern Telecom Ltd., believed that products combining phones and personal computers would be the next wave. Rival International Business Machines Corp. had already bought Rolm Corp., a leader in *PBX* systems that was also building *PC*/telephone products.

LINE ENGAGED. Compaq President Rod Canion moved quickly. In March, 1985, Compaq Telecommunications introduced six models of the Telecompaq *PC*/telephone. Compaq immediately sewed up deals with several phone companies to retail the machines for a hefty $4,194 to $6,395.

Unfortunately, Compaq overlooked one of its prime business tenets: Understand your custom-

present market battle: "*TI* wouldn't accept the importance of *IBM*'s products."

Canion and *TI* buddies William H. Murto and James M. Harris set up Compaq—and promptly got off to a slow start. Contrary to its early advertising, the company did not spring to life one afternoon when the founders sketched the idea for a portable *PC* on a napkin at a Houston pie shop. According to L. J. Sevin, Rosen's partner in Sevin Rosen Management, Canion called with a plan for building circuit cards to expand the storage capacity of *IBM PC*s. Sevin was underwhelmed. He felt that the product was "a little too easy to do. We made him go back to the drawing board."

Canion's fourth or fifth idea clicked. It was for an *IBM*-compatible portable. With $1.5 million in seed money, Canion and his crew began designing Compaq's first *PC* in February, 1982. By early 1983, when Compaq began shipping its portables, the company had raised $30 million. In late 1983 it raised $66 million more in a public offering, then finished the year with sales of $111 million.

By then, the experience the *TI* veterans had in running a big company had come into play. With scarcely enough sales to support the expenditure, Compaq had installed a Hewlett-Packard 3000 minicomputer system to manage inventories, finance, and forecasting. The company also institut-ed the type of formalized management reporting systems that many startups overlook.

GOOF-PROOF. But the last thing Canion wanted was another *TI*-style bureaucracy. Compaq's reporting lines are changed as needed. In early 1984, for example, when the original portable was still the only product, Canion felt the company had to develop more models in a hurry. He took three strong managers and gave each one a product area, complete with its own marketing, manufacturing, and engineering staff. Within a year "we went from one product to many," he says. Then the problem changed. How could the company introduce and build so many models when each product line was acting independently? Canion redrew the organization chart with four functional groups: marketing, engineering, sales, and manufacturing. By centralizing marketing, for instance, the company can make sure a new model does not prematurely kill off any of Compaq's current *PC*s.

Compaq managers boast that mistakes seldom get out the door. One perennial research project, a laptop computer dubbed "sleek and sexy" by insiders, has never advanced beyond the prototype stage because Canion feels the available technology requires too many compromises, such as crowded keyboards. In five years only one true flop has emerged: Telecompaq, a combination *PC*

ers. The buyers it had in mind—middle-level managers—saw no reason to shell out twice the cost of a regular personal computer for a Telecompaq. The machine "doesn't do anything more than what you could do separately," contends Kenneth G. Bosomworth, president of International Resource Development Inc., a Norwalk (Conn.) market researcher. Electronic mail and automatic telephone dialing, Telecompaq's most vaunted features, could be accomplished just as easily with a $500 terminal and an inexpensive speed dialer.

FEW CHAMPIONS. Compaq also failed to grasp the politics of corporate purchasing decisions. "Typically, telecommunications decision makers and computer decision makers don't get along terribly well," says Gary Hawthorne, director of business line management for data systems at Pac-Tel InfoSystems, which sold the Telecompaq for about 18 months. The mixed-breed machine required input from both, and frequently neither would champion it.

Finally, Telecompaqs often were hard to hook up, say dealers, because of differences in phone systems. And until new software came along this year, a Telecompaq could send electronic mail only to another Telecompaq. Worse, the machine still uses an 8086 chip, much slower than the ones now used in the most popular *PC*s.

Although Compaq is still filling orders, Canion concedes that the product has been "a failure from a revenue standpoint." Still, there's one bright spot. Compaq Telecommunications is credited with developing the internal modem that enables Compaq's successful Portable III to communicate with other computers via phone lines.

By Jo Ellen Davis in Houston

and telephone that was introduced in 1985 (box, page 96).

To make such errors rare, Canion says he has tried to create an egalitarian atmosphere that fosters teamwork and communication. There are no assigned parking spaces at Compaq's lush wooded campus, and all employees get stock options. In return, employees are fiercely loyal. Says Ross Cooley, vice-president of sales: "Another former *IBM*er told me that it's the solution to everything that was frustrating at *IBM*, and he was right." Still, life at Compaq is demanding. In April, cofounder Bill Murto dropped out to pursue a Master's degree in religious studies.

Indeed, by Silicon Valley standards, the Compaq culture might appear confining. Wingtips and pinstripes are the norm, not Reeboks and Hawaiian shirts. California-style Friday beer bashes are out—alcohol is *verboten* on Compaq property. When a trade magazine sent champagne to celebrate Compaq's winning a product award, it was locked away, and it still is. Instead, Compaq gives its 2,000 headquarters employees all the free soft drinks they can consume—about a million cans last year.

Managers have a Compaq type in mind when they recruit. Applicants must be smart and motivated, but above all easy to get along with. It is not unusual for a new hire to interview with 15 people who represent all departments of the company and a variety of seniority levels. Who is cut? Loners, plus anyone who wears his ego on his sleeve. "The No. 1 issue is whether they fit into the way we do our business," says Sales and Marketing Vice-President Michael S. Swavely, 33, a former marketing manager at Chrysler Corp. and the company's youngest top-level executive. "We can find lots of people who are competent."

Some former employees are critical of this homogeneous culture. "You need some wild ducks around," argues H. L. Sparks, former vice-president for sales and now president of Amdek Corp., a company that sells *PC* add-ons such as monitors. But wild ducks don't fit Compaq's consensus management style. Known simply as "the process," it involves informal team meetings where members discuss a problem or policy. Every department involved gives its view. Then the group attempts to separate fact from instinct, examines the trade-offs, and arrives at a decision. At a new-product meeting recently, representatives from Compaq's international group argued against the date the domestic division had chosen for a launch. And sales department staffers worried about the product's effect on dealer inventories. It is rare that a single member or group will dominate. "Most organizations have winners and losers," observes Canion, "but not at Compaq."

Top managers use the same process to fine-tune Compaq's strategy. And Compaq maintains close relationships with its customers, dealers, and suppliers, using them as a sounding board. "Some companies think they know the answers," says Jeffrey D. McKeever, president of MicroAge Inc., a 176-unit chain. "Compaq listens." McKeever suggested in 1984 that Compaq offer a built-in tape drive for duplicating the contents of a hard disk to protect against accidents. Compaq followed his advice, and the feature—not then available on *IBM PC*s—became a major selling point.

Compaq's meteoric rise has surprised even Canion, a down-to-earth type who passed up the big corner office designed for him in Compaq's headquarters. He claims he was always confident of Compaq's strategy but had no idea it would work so well. "My definition of success was nothing like what Compaq turned out to be," he says in his Texas drawl.

GADGET-HAPPY. Canion's personal gains have also exceeded his expectations. His compensation hit $550,000 last year and his approximately 1% chunk of Compaq stock is worth about $16 million. However, Canion has eschewed most of the trappings of wealth. Although an occasional drag racer in high school, he drives a Mitsubishi sports car rather than the flashier Porsches and Ferraris favored by other Compaq executives. He still flies coach, even cross-country. Though travel often keeps him away from Houston, Canion's one extravagance is a huge house facing a country club. He also loves to buy electronic toys—everything from laptop typewriters to cellular phones.

Lately he's been on the road more than ever, trying to keep Compaq's momentum going. And to do so, Compaq has started assuming the role of leader. That became clear last September when the company brought out the first *IBM*-compatible *PC* to use Intel's 80386, a microchip with more than twice the power of the chips then used in *IBM*'s most powerful model. Prior to that, Compaq had always taken its cues from *IBM*, following the introduction of new *IBM* computers with its own versions within a year. Compaq's machine beat *IBM*'s 80386-based models by nine months.

CAN IBM CONTINUE TO CALL THE TUNE?

There are two kinds of standards in the computer business: those that arise from concerted industry efforts and those that are established by the best-selling products from the most influential suppliers. The second type usually dominates, and there's no better example than the *IBM PC*. By last year, however, International Business Machines Corp. felt that things had gotten a bit out of hand: Copies of the *PC* were outselling the original by two to one. Even *IBM*'s best customers were wondering why they should buy the *IBM* version.

BIG QUESTION. So *IBM* brought out the Personal System/2 line in April and is trying to set a new standard. With its 32% share of the *PC* market, *IBM* is likely to succeed—eventually. But for now, it is in the odd position of promoting a new standard to replace the one it set five years ago. That has a lot of experts asking the question that Compaq Computer Corp. President Rod Canion has posed: What is the standard now: Compaq and the clones or *IBM*?

The new game plan worked better than expected. The company sold about 20,000 Deskpro 386s in the last quarter of 1986 and 25,000 in the first quarter of 1987, adding $225 million in revenues. More important, Compaq established itself as the technology leader and as a result, expanded its presence in large corporations. "We couldn't wait for *IBM*," says Fred Herpel, director of controller accounting systems at Primerica Inc., which has six Deskpro 386s.

The success of the Deskpro 386 may have helped give Canion the gumption to launch his campaign against the *IBM* PS/2. One of his big gripes is the PS/2's 3½-in. floppy disks. Although they hold more information and are sturdier than the current "industry standard" 5¼-in. floppies, Canion argues that "this advance in technology is not justified" because customers have a greater need for a standard disk that can be used to

The existing standard seems to be holding. Last month, PS/2 models accounted for a respectable 15% of the personal computers sold in U. S. computer stores, according to market researcher InfoCorp. But two-thirds were the PS/2 Model 30, which does not include the advanced PS/2 features. At the same time, *IBM PC*-compatible machines were up more than 10% in the first five months of 1987, suggesting that many customers aren't yet inclined to switch over to PS/2.

That's ammunition for Canion and other *IBM* competitors, who urge *PC* buyers not to follow *IBM* automatically. "Just because *IBM* comes out with something new doesn't mean that you goose-step in line with them," says Max Toy, a former Compaq and *IBM* executive and now senior vice-president of *ITT*'s Xtra Business Systems Div. "We're all saying the same thing," adds Phil White, president of Wyse Technology. These competitors concede that some aspects of the PS/2, such as better graphics, will benefit computer buyers. But they regard with suspicion other features, such as the new Micro Channel for connecting circuit cards. "The big question is 'What's it going to add?'" asks Tandy Corp. Chairman John V. Roach.

Not much, according to Neil Colvin, founder of Phoenix Technologies Ltd., a Norwood (Mass.) company that sells software needed for cloning *IBM PC*s. Micro Channel accepts only add-ons designed for it, making existing *PC* circuit cards obsolete. Colvin says the badly needed speed improvements of Micro Channel can be had with a design that also accommodates the older cards. Phoenix leads a group of computer companies that have proposed such a format as the standard to be sanctioned by a committee of the Institute of Electrical & Electronics Engineers.

While such a committee is bound to have less influence than *IBM* does, clonemakers are betting that it will make a difference. The most likely scenario, says William D. Kirwin, an analyst with market researcher Gartner Group Inc., is that the market will divide. *IBM*'s top 1,500 mainframe customers, the companies that will use the Micro Channel to connect personal computers to mainframes, will switch to PS/2. "*IBM* gets very, very territorial about these accounts," says Kirwin. But he thinks that much of the rest of the market may react like Robert G. Castellano, manager of office systems at Readers Digest Assn., who is still mulling over his decision. "I don't think any one company can set the standard any more," Castellano says. "*IBM* has tried to force our hand, but I have as much power—to buy or not to buy."

By Geoff Lewis in New York

exchange programs and data. He derides the PS/2 by comparing it to New Coke, Coca-Cola Co.'s ill-fated effort to move the market en masse to a new product.

But computers aren't cola, and plenty of customers welcome the improvements in *IBM*'s new machines, even if some of the benefits are still a year away. "If Rod Canion would just shut up, he'd be much better off," says Matt Fitzsimmons, president of ComputerLand of White Plains, N. Y. "When he talks about sticking with the old floppy disk, nobody's even listening." Jeffrey L. Ehrlich, manager of product technology for General Electric Corporate Information Technology in Bridgeport, Conn., agrees. "PS/2 is the future, the new direction," he says. The new machines will work intimately with *GE*'s mainframes in a way that Canion's "industry standard" *PC*s can't, he argues. By insisting that customers cling to standards that grew up around early 1980s technology, "Compaq is just posturing," Ehrlich says.

Compaq is likely to win the war of words, at least for awhile. It's using the confusion over PS/2 to strengthen its role, especially in companies that don't rely heavily on *IBM* mainframes. But as *IBM* starts to deliver on its promises for PS/2, Canion will have to make some of his most crucial decisions yet.

Should he continue insisting that Compaq and other imitators of *IBM PC*s have established their own market? The risk there is that by lumping itself with what has become an army of clonemakers, Compaq might lose its distinctive position as a strong No. 2 to *IBM*. Indeed, Apple already is challenging Compaq for that role. The alternative may be to revert to Compaq's original strategy and simply match *IBM* move for move. Canion says he hasn't decided yet which path to take—

and he won't until his customers tell him. "We're not arrogant or dumb," he says. "We're actively looking to see what the market wants." So far, he's shown a pretty good feel for that.

By Jo Ellen Davis in Houston, with Geoff Lewis in New York

DISCUSSION QUESTIONS

1. Compaq's President, Joseph R. "Rod" Canion, asks, "How can we continue to have good teamwork and fast responses and become a very large company?" How would you answer him?
2. Trace the evolution of Compaq's organization design, drawing charts and identifying structure types used at various stages.
3. Describe the atmosphere or culture at Compaq. How is it meant to facilitate coordination?

HOW IBM IS FIGHTING BACK

TO REIGNITE GROWTH,
IT'S UNDERGOING ITS TOUGHEST
SELF-SCRUTINY IN YEARS
NOVEMBER 17, 1986, PP. 152-157

There's one sure way to irritate John F. Akers. Once his layers of underlings have thoroughly dissected a problem, the chairman of International Business Machines Corp. gets exercised when a subordinate reacts to one of his suggestions with a promise to study it some more. "Study?" the former Yale hockey star and Navy pilot snaps. "We do, we make, we buy, we sell."

Such decisiveness has seemed to be in short supply at *IBM* for the past two years—or at least it hasn't helped much. The company has had seven straight quarters of slowing revenue growth and sagging earnings, capped most recently by a 27% drop in third-quarter profits. Analysts' earnings estimates for 1986 have declined steadily, to

roughly $9 per share, down from 1985's $10.67. While competitors such as Digital Equipment Corp. can seem to do no wrong, investors think that *IBM* may have lost its touch—for the time being, anyway. *IBM* stock, once the bluest chip of all, has dropped 25% since it hit a high of 161 six months ago. The company's total market value now stands at $75 billion, down from $97 billion back then. A decade ago return on equity was more than twice the average for the Standard & Poor's 500 index. Now it's 1.4 times as big.

But the signs are everywhere that Akers isn't going to take it anymore. For the first time, the company is saying publicly that *IBM* management is as responsible for the company's slump as the sluggish economy has been. "We are affected by the economy but also by a lot of other things, including our product cycles," says Frank A. Metz Jr., senior vice-president for finance and planning.

That said, Akers is celebrating his 20th month at the *IBM* helm by launching the most rigorous corporate self-scrutiny in recent memory. He has set up task forces to ask tough questions. Has *IBM* become too bureaucratic and slow? Is it too concerned with selling what it makes rather than making what customers want? Is its traditional view of the world computer market out of date? With an estimated $52 billion in 1986 revenues and $5.4 billion in profits, Big Blue is still healthy enough to turn most other companies green with envy. But the current downturn has proven that the company can't dawdle on the way to its ambitious goal of at least matching the growth of all segments of its industry. "*IBM* hasn't looked at itself this deeply in decades," observes D. Quinn Mills, professor of business administration at Harvard business school.

ADRENALINE. *IBM* may not have all the answers yet, but it has enough to start fighting back. In the short run it plans to cut costs to reverse the 36% decline in aftertax margins it has suffered in the past 21 months. The idea is to reduce 1987's expenses by about $2.25 billion from this year's $32 billion, analysts say (below). That could boost 1987 earnings by about $1, to more than $10 a share. By 1988, the plan goes, new products should let *IBM* revive margins the old-fashioned way: charging hefty prices for popular new machines (chart, page 102).

To ensure a lasting rebound, the company also plans to cut layers of management while redeploying many employees. It hopes that by eliminating bureaucracy, it can inject some adrenaline into its lumbering product-planning process. It's counting on a larger and more solicitous sales force to win new customers. And long term, *IBM* still plans to alter its sales mix. Software and computer services now account for 23% of revenues. By the 1990s, when all but the most complicated computers may be commodity items, Akers wants more than 30% of revenues to come from those two areas, where profit margins approach the company's 70% or more on mainframes.

Most investors are prepared to wait. Many big investment funds are so loaded with *IBM* stock that they can't afford to sell it now (BW—Oct. 10). Others have plenty of faith in the No. 1 computer maker. "I haven't felt the slightest need to dump my shares," says F. Warren McFarlan, a professor at Harvard's B-school. "They're living in a game where we keep score in decades."

Still, it will be tougher than in the past to get *IBM* back on course. The company is seven to eight times as big as it was during its last comparable catharsis, in 1970-71, and has 50% more employees. During the 1970 recession, *IBM*'s sales of computers dropped by 20%. But because about 60% of revenues then came from rental income, overall company revenues rose. Since then, *IBM* has completed a strategic shift away from rentals, which now account for 7% of revenues. So the company is more sensitive to market volatility. In 1971 vigorous foreign sales saved the day. Today,

IBM's overseas growth is moderating, with the computer slump about to engulf Europe (page 104). IBM also has to deal with a fundamental new challenge: Customers are moving away from big mainframe installations to decentralized computing built around smaller machines—particularly those made by minicomputer companies such as DEC.

Facing all this has been a chilly baptism for Akers. The 51-year-old former IBM salesman took over as chief executive in early 1985 on the crest of the company's best year ever. Internal predictions suggested that revenues, then $46 billion, could near $200 billion by 1995, fueling comparably higher profits along the way. The dream began fading when 1985 revenues rose only 9%, earnings flattened, and return on equity dropped from 27% to 22%. Says a former IBM scientist: "We simply read the market wrong." Because of the long lead time for new products, a disappointing 1986 was inevitable.

Some blame IBM's inbred corporate culture: The company has traditionally emphasized looking inside for both management talent and new ideas. "There are a lot of guys in IBM headquarters who have never even seen a Macintosh," says

Carl Ledbetter, who headed IBM's work in supercomputing before leaving in July to become a vice-president at Prime Computer Inc.

A ponderous planning process doesn't help. With multiple layers of management in each business sector, "you can't make a change in a year," says Phillip E. White, who once reported to Akers at IBM and is now president of Wyse Technology. "It takes more like three."

IBM is ruled by an eight-member management committee and a 19-member corporate management board. But Akers—who declined to be interviewed for this story—has lately asserted more control. He has replaced most of the top aides he inherited with contemporaries who worked with him in the 1970s. Among them: Edward E. Lucente, who heads IBM's marketing efforts; Jack D. Kuehler, who directs manufacturing; and Stephen B. Schwartz, George H. Conrades, and Terry R. Lautenbach, who manage major product lines. In one recent move, Akers replaced chief financial officer Allen J. Krowe with Metz, Akers' finance man when the chairman was a group executive in the early 1980s.

After spending much of this year trying to determine what went wrong and how to fix it,

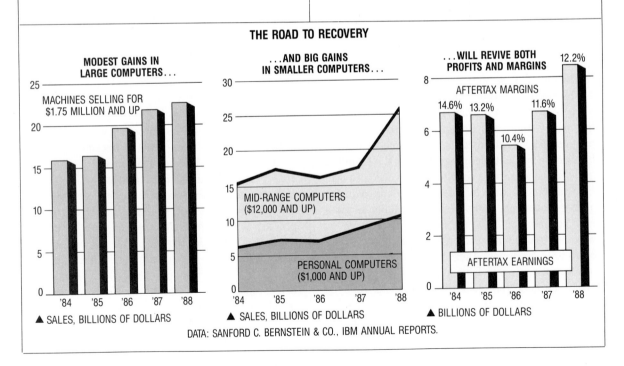

THE ROAD TO RECOVERY

MODEST GAINS IN LARGE COMPUTERS...

MACHINES SELLING FOR $1.75 MILLION AND UP

▲ SALES, BILLIONS OF DOLLARS

...AND BIG GAINS IN SMALLER COMPUTERS...

MID-RANGE COMPUTERS ($12,000 AND UP)

PERSONAL COMPUTERS ($1,000 AND UP)

▲ SALES, BILLIONS OF DOLLARS

...WILL REVIVE BOTH PROFITS AND MARGINS

AFTERTAX MARGINS

14.6% 13.2% 10.4% 11.6% 12.2%

AFTERTAX EARNINGS

▲ BILLIONS OF DOLLARS

DATA: SANFORD C. BERNSTEIN & CO., IBM ANNUAL REPORTS.

Akers' team has settled on first cutting roughly 7% out of current expenses. *IBM* expects to spend $1 billion less next year on capital investment. The slowdown will hardly hurt. If anything, critics say, *IBM*'s $28 billion investment in the past five years was excessive given the computer slump. Discretionary expenses are being cut by 50% in some divisions, with a goal of trimming $500 million next year to match this year's savings. "We weren't slovenly, but the realities of the revenue stream told us that we have to bring our costs into line," says Metz.

STAYING HOME. So it's farewell to sunny California conferences and "must" visits to *IBM*'s lab on the French Riviera. Says Tom Sissel, a manager in *IBM*'s Burlington (Vt.) plant: "While we used to send two people to examine a tool we were considering buying, now we'd probably send one." To trim travel, *IBM* has set up a closed-circuit television network both for internal use and press announcements, complete with a network-trained director. "It's like *Saturday Night Live*," says a 14-year veteran. "Even stiff *IBM*ers started getting hammy."

The company hopes to save another $500 million by leaving vacant jobs unfilled, offering early-retirement incentives, and asking employees to take accrued vacation that it carries on the books as a liability. Managers are even asking employees to pay for personal calls that appear on company bills.

Although *IBM*'s no-layoff practice will remain in effect, the early-retirement incentives should take more than 5,000 people off the 238,000-person U. S. payroll by July. Except for 1,500 outside hires to fill critical jobs and 1,000 college hires—down from a high of 6,000 three years ago—most empty positions are being filled from inside or eliminated.

Under a plan that Lucente's organization announced in September, many people in headquarters jobs are being asked to dust off their sales suits. By abolishing an entire division level in *IBM*'s Information Systems Group, 2,800 headquarters staffers will be shifted into 200 branch sales offices. Although executives insist these are voluntary moves, one ex-staffer calls the relocations "invisible layoffs." He adds: "You tell a guy

in White Plains who used to be a salesman that the opportunities available are in Des Moines or Fargo. Maybe he stays, maybe he leaves."

MAKING DO. One way or another, *IBM*'s 40,000-strong managerial force is being pared to remove layers of bureaucracy everywhere from labs to plants. Now, high-level managers in stripped-down divisions must compete to hold their jobs. An even broader restructuring is likely. Walton E. Burdick, vice-president for personnel, questions "whether we need all these managers." So for some, the future looks grim. "Many executives have reached their highest level," says one manager. "It's hard."

The disruption within *IBM*'s zealous army is selective. For Silicon Valley *IBM*ers, the September company picnic at Laguna Seca raceway was as festive as last year's, a staffer says. But some attendees won't be around for the next. The manager of Reuben's, a popular watering hole for *IBM*ers in San Jose, Calif., has hosted several recent farewell parties, including one in October for 25 regulars who soon will work at various far-flung *IBM* sites.

What *IBM*ers find especially worrisome is the company's near-freeze on outside hiring, which halts the influx of new blood—and new ideas—so crucial to moving ahead in the high-technology arena. "It's difficult to staff up new projects," complains a software design manager at *IBM*'s Santa Teresa (Calif.) lab. A Kingston (N. Y.) technical manager, deprived of a budget for personal computers and software, is more stoic: "We just learn how to make do with less."

But even deep cost-cutting is only a temporary measure. It will take a stream of new products to power *IBM* out of the doldrums. At headquarters, says a longtime *IBM* consultant, the pressure to come up with them is "intense." Timetables have been moved up. Although the company denies it, some insiders contend that the new 9370 minicomputer series was announced ahead of schedule: Unveiled in October, it won't be shipped in volume until late next year. To bring technology to market faster, *IBM* scientists and product developers are working together for the first time on projects as diverse as disk drives and silicon structures.

Though management won't say so, it's focusing more than ever on *DEC*, the minicomputer maker whose revenues, profits, and stock have all surged this year despite the industry slump. Akers insisted in April that *IBM* doesn't "deal with the ebb and flow of someone else's product line." But just a month later, the management committee approved plans for a so-called competitive-analysis task force that, according to a former *IBM* marketing strategist, targeted *DEC*. *IBM* even set up a "war room" at marketing headquarters, he says, with maps and lists of target areas. The management committee authorized a specially trained force of up to 1,300 salespeople, possibly including 500 new hires, to win the scientific and engineering accounts that favor midrange machines. "I'd never seen such paranoia in all my years there," the former *IBM*er says. "It's an *IBM SWAT* team going against *DEC*."

All this won't help much without more new products. About 40% of *IBM*'s current product line is less than 18 months old, vs. 85% of *DEC*'s, says Michael L. Geran, an analyst at E. F. Hutton & Co. And there's plenty of competition besides *DEC*. As clonemakers like Leading Edge Products Inc. and Epson America ship lower-cost imitations of the *IBM PC*, *IBM*'s unit share of the worldwide *IBM-PC* and *PC*-compatible market will slip to 34% this year from 65% in 1984, Dataquest Inc. estimates. In the first quarter, *IBM*-watchers say, look for new *IBM PC*s to replace most current models.

CLONE-KILLING. The scene-stealer, which may not appear before summer, should be *IBM*'s first *PC* to use Intel Corp.'s 80386 chip. The new machine may include features that will be hard for clonemakers to copy quickly. With a dozen rival 80386-based products due by yearend, there's mounting pressure on *IBM* to deliver its own version. Meanwhile, retailers are complaining that the company is getting tough on them. "*IBM* is pushing its weight around, trying to get retailers

IBM HAS TROUBLES ACROSS THE ATLANTIC, TOO

Jean-Serge Bertoncini won't be rushed by *IBM*. As director of information resources and technology for French carmaker Peugeot, he wants an $8 million *IBM* 3090 mainframe. But he's trying to make better use of the $145 million in computers that Peugeot already has, so he won't be buying until May. "*IBM* people tried to persuade us to move the date," he says. "We want to brake a little."

Some 3,600 mi. away, at its Armonk (N. Y.) headquarters, *IBM* feels the deceleration. The actions of Bertoncini and customers like him have led Chairman John F. Akers to warn that *IBM*'s growth abroad "has begun to moderate." The outlook is especially somber in Europe, the bright spot in *IBM* profits for the past two years. Last year, European sales accounted for 28% of its $50 billion in revenues and 32% of its $6.6 billion in profits. With a boost from currency translations, *IBM*'s European sales may have been up 20% in the first nine months, estimates Ulric Weil, an analyst at Gartner Group Inc. But had the dollar

not been sliding, he adds, European revenues would have shrunk 2%.

The decline may signal that the problems dogging the U. S. computer industry are moving abroad. Many European buyers have too much computing capacity—and they're pausing to reassess their needs. Declares René Aubron, chief executive of Promodata, a French computer-leasing company: "The slump has arrived in Europe."

SUFFERING. *IBM*, the biggest player in Europe's data processing equipment market, with an estimated 25% share of total sales, is getting hit first and hardest. Nearly all its key product lines are suffering. Its 3090 mainframe, better known as Sierra, has sold slowly because the machine doesn't deliver much more bang for the buck than its ancestor, the 308X series. "Some customers are saying the older system is good enough," says Jacques H. Vernier, president of the French division of National Advanced Systems, which sells Hitachi mainframes.

IBM's other products aren't picking up the

to drop the clones," says Matt Fitzsimmons, an ex-*IBM*er who owns a ComputerLand store in White Plains, N. Y. An *IBM* spokeswoman calls such reports "absolutely inaccurate."

In mainframe processors, which account for nearly a quarter of revenues, the company's toughest competitor has been itself. Many customers have stuck with *IBM*'s older 308X series instead of upgrading to the 3090 series, better known as Sierra. The reason: *IBM* hasn't delivered the full complement of software to match the high-performance hardware. Next year should see more of that software—plus more powerful versions of the 3090.

IBM's Achilles' heel, however, has been the midrange. Its System/36 and System/38 minicomputers can't "talk" as easily with other computers as customers want. So *DEC*, with a product line that adheres to one internal architecture called Vax, is making inroads into accounts that were once true blue to *IBM*.

IBM is striking back: The 9370 will bring the company's mainframe architecture down to its minis for the first time, allowing customers to avoid the expense and hassle of rewriting software when they want to move up or down the product line. "It is a watershed product," says Francis R. Gens, an analyst at market researcher International Data Corp. As *IBM* adds more powerful models in 1987, mid-range sales could help restore *IBM*'s sagging bottom line within two years.

The company is already lining up foot soldiers to sell the new machines once they're out. With all the transfers from headquarters, plants, and labs into revenue-generating sales and marketing jobs, the company's total marketing force will swell by 5,000, or 22%, by springtime. Included in the new total are 10,000 direct salespeople, more than twice the team fielded by No. 2 computer maker Burroughs-Sperry.

REPENTING. These people signal *IBM*'s desire to repent for what its executives concede were seri-

slack. The company's European share in minicomputers could drop to 26% next year, from 30% in 1985, while rival Digital Equipment Corp.'s share should climb to 13% from 11%, predicts market researcher *IDC* Europa. In microcomputers, *IDC* expects *IBM*'s share to slip to 25% this year, from 29% in 1985, despite prices that have been slashed about 40% this year.

Like the U. S. slump, Europe's slowdown is selective. Sperry, Tandem, Burroughs, Wang, and *NCR* are all doing well there. And *DEC*, having reported a 15% rise in European sales, to $2.3 billion for the year ended June 30, doesn't see "any change in the pattern of growth," says Jean-Claude Peterschmitt, chairman of its European operations. Even *IBM* should post strong showings this year in West Germany, Britain, Spain, and Denmark, analysts say. But French sales, accounting for 15% of the company's European business, are likely to be flat. And in Italy, where Olivetti is putting on intense pressure to take over as No. 1, analysts say *IBM* shipped only 17,000 of the 29,000 *PC*s it planned to distribute for the first half of this year.

CUTTING DEALS. To protect itself, *IBM* slashed

European Sierra prices by up to 20% in February, then up to an additional 9% in five countries in September. A competitor says he lost a British account that effectively got a Sierra at a 35% discount from list. *IBM* salespeople offered Danish Sugar Factories in Copenhagen an interest-free, six-month loan to buy a Sierra right away, says data processing manager Peter Timm. He isn't biting yet.

IBM Europe is also cutting overhead. In France it's pruning wage increases and slowing hiring. And it's shifting people around. On Oct. 29, C. Michael Armstrong, 48, became its director general. A 25-year *IBM*er who becomes the No. 2 man under 58-year-old *IBM* Europe President Kaspar V. Cassani, Armstrong "is seen as an up-and-coming guy who'll help fix up Europe," says Jonathan M. Fram, an analyst at Bear, Stearns & Co.

It will take more than new faces to turn the tide. But almost no one is counting *IBM* out. As a former *IBM*er puts it: "They've got some big problems right now, but they'll be back."

By Gordon Bock in New York and Thane Peterson in Paris, with Mark Maremont in London and bureau reports

ous lapses. "In the '70s we focused on the competitiveness of each individual computer and lost a little sight of the customer's needs," says Victor J. Goldberg, assistant group executive under Lucente. Akers' directive, according to Goldberg:

'There's much more responsiveness and much less trying to ram a product down your throat'

"Get inside the customer's head, focus on his problem, and solve it."

To that end, a new "customer sector" marketing team is charged with finding ways to help customers install computer and software systems—even if it means including non-*IBM* gear. Another wrinkle: sending technical experts at no extra charge to help customers plot computer strategy, as *IBM* did recently for Northwestern National Life Insurance Co. in Minneapolis. Says David W. Haskin, Northwestern's senior vice-president for corporate resources: "There's much more responsiveness and much less trying to ram a product down your throat."

IBM is also setting up separate sales offices organized along industry lines. There's one for selling to finance and brokerage customers in New York, another for General Motors Corp. in Detroit, and another for Ford Motor Co. in nearby Dearborn. Today's *IBM* salesperson is also rediscovering the art of creative sales calls. A senior sales manager recently booked a seat on a plane heading to Boston so he could sit next to a Harvard University professor in charge of a $2 million purchase of laptop computers. The *IBM*er did all the listening—and won the contract. "In the past, *IBM* salesmen had an attitude of 'take it or leave it,'" says John M. Hammitt, vice-president for information management at Pillsbury Co. "Now, they're willing to spend more time understanding our needs."

Masterminding the company's new sales thrust is marketing chief Lucente. Colleagues call him a hard-driving man well-suited for such a campaign, and they mention him along with Conrades as a candidate for a higher spot at *IBM*. An *IBM* marketer for 25 years, the poker-faced Lucente, 46, waxes eloquent about his favorite California chardonnay—1984 Sterling—but keeps his counsel when it comes to talking about *DEC*. "We wanted to get more aggressive" in the mid-range market is all he'll say.

IBM has plenty to think about beyond 1987. Faced with declining overall growth rates in hardware, Akers and his top executives are honing a long-term strategy that seeks to make software and computer services an ever-bigger chunk of the business. The strategy predated Akers and the computer slump, but the chairman is making it a reality. Earl Wheeler, who worked with Akers in the 1970s, now reports to him as corporate software chief. A software executive council meets every six weeks to coordinate the efforts of 24 development labs and to establish more coherence across product lines. Recently, Akers asked John E. Steuri, general manager of the Information Services unit, to form a single software strategy to improve *IBM*'s position in office systems.

With no inclination to acquire software houses, *IBM* has found a promising temporary solution for coming up with the right software fast: joint development and marketing ventures. It entered the first one last summer with a mainframe software and services company, Dallas-based Hogan Systems Inc., that specializes in banking systems.

Even more important, *IBM* must grapple with the paradoxes created by its own success. *IBM* still wants to be all things to all people, competing in its traditional mainframe, minicomputer, personal computer, and software markets—and expanding into robotics; value-added networks that connect companies, banks, and customers; and artificial intelligence that helps computers do everything from monitoring and repairing themselves to diagnosing human illnesses. Yet that very breadth "creates a defocusing of energy," says David N. Martin, president of National Advanced Systems, the National Semiconductor Corp. unit that sells mainframes.

The key to *IBM*'s future success, says *IDC*'s Gens, is to help customers create companywide information networks that pull together such scattered resources as customized data bases, telecommunications, and software applications. "Only when that connection is made and customers understand how critical this is to their profitability, will *IBM* see a return to robust sales," Gens says. "They're in the midst of a five-year change."

CATCH-22. Clearly, *IBM* is aware of the pressing need to make customers' equipment work together. The 9370 is the first big step. But as the company pares its product line down to three main architectures—370, System/36, and *PC*—it will have to work hard to retain the customers whose systems won't survive. There's another catch-22: By coming to market with its advanced *PC* line, as powerful as a mini at a micro's price, *IBM* could cannibalize its own minicomputer sales. Yet it has little choice: The alternative is to risk its position as a market leader.

The next few years will probably be tough for *IBM*. For example, when *DEC* chose its single-architecture Vax strategy from several competing systems five years ago, the infighting that surrounded the decision nearly tore *DEC* apart. There will no doubt be some of the same strife as *IBM* sorts out its product plans.

Still, *IBM* has repeatedly proven itself to be resilient—once it mobilizes all its resources. Japan, a market that appeared to be slipping away a few years ago, is today *IBM*'s showcase and one of the few regions where the company is hiring vigorously. This will be the fifth straight year of double-digit growth in Japanese sales, which hit $6 billion in 1985, says Richard T. Gerstner, group executive of the Asia/Pacific Group.

If *IBM* can continue shaving costs, trimming staff, and rethinking its business, it should cash in when its new products are ready. To sustain himself, *IBM* Chief Scientist Ralph E. Gomory likes to quote a line from Shakespeare's *As You Like It*: "Sweet are the uses of adversity." In an industry where intense competition has narrowed the margin for error, *IBM* has run smack into adversity. Now its management is scrambling to find the sweetness.

By Marilyn A. Harris in Armonk, with Gordon Bock, Anne R. Field, and Geoff Lewis in New York, and bureau reports

DISCUSSION QUESTIONS

1. In what ways is IBM's organization design alleged to have impeded the corporation's coping with its competition?
2. What design changes are being considered, and how would they enable IBM to cope more effectively?

THE LOOSE-REINS APPROACH PAYS OFF FOR KEMPER

SEPTEMBER 8, 1986, PP. 78-79

A quick look at Kemper Corp.'s organization chart could confuse even the sharpest Harvard *MBA*. At Kemper, 19 wildly overlapping companies sell everything from life insurance to stocks—successfully. In only six years, Chairman Joseph E. Luecke has transformed a staid insurer into a highly profitable conglomerate. "Kemper is further along than any other insurance company in financial services," contends David J. O'Leary, director of research for Fox-Pitt, Kelton Inc.

But this is no monument to the synergy of the financial supermarket. In fact, Kemper has taken the opposite tack, downplaying the ties between its businesses. Rather than a supermarket, Kemper is more like a wholesale co-op for grocers: Each store runs independently, but all hold down costs by sharing a single source of merchandise and back-office expertise.

MAKING A STIR. Kemper avoids, for example, tying the company name to its regional brokerage houses. In the past four years it has added Bateman Eichler, Hill Richards in Los Angeles, Boettcher in Denver, Blunt Ellis & Loewi in Milwaukee, and Prescott, Ball & Turben in Cleveland. It also owns nearly 50% of Lovett Mitchell Webb & Garrison in Houston. In late August, Kemper raised its stake in *ISFA* Corp., a Florida broker, from 27% to 40%. The brokers have kept their names and regional identities.

Although the parent company hovers in the background, Kemper is not completely publicity-shy. It has run commercials on network television and is grooming chief economist David D. Hale as one of the nation's most-quoted forecasters. There's also nothing anonymous about Kemper's earnings, which have been making a stir on Wall Street. Operating earnings increased 190%, to $64 million, during the first six months of 1986—on top of last year's 168% gain on revenues of $2.4 billion. Kemper's stock climbed from 73 at the start of this year to near 94 before a 3-for-1 split on June 21. It now trades at about 33 a share.

"You're starting to see all the cylinders in the Kemper engine firing at once," says Ernest G. Jacob, an analyst at Drexel Burnham Lambert Inc. In addition to the regional brokers, those cylinders include Kemper Financial Services Inc., which in four years has nearly doubled the mutual funds and other assets it manages to roughly $36 billion. The parent company also has large property-casualty and life insurance operations under its corporate umbrella. An expansion of its reinsurance business, which takes on part of another insurer's risk in return for premium income, has catapulted Kemper from 10th place to seventh among U. S. reinsurers in the past two years.

Now, in what's much more than a routine reshuffling, Kemper is about to create a new holding company, Kemper Financial Cos. It will house its investment-services firms and one life insurance company, which sells annuity and universal-life policies mainly through brokers. Kemper will sell 10% of the holding company's stock to more than 1,000 of the unit's officers. The parent company is keeping the rest. Wall Street believes the company will eventually sell part of its stake to the public to finance still more brokerage acquisitions. Company officials are noncommittal but stress that the new subsidiary will produce back-office efficiencies, while stock ownership will reinforce the company's entrepreneurial culture.

HANDS OFF. One advantage to Kemper's strategy of allowing operating companies autonomy, Luecke contends, is that it's easier for them to keep a watch on individual markets and respond with new products. In life insurance, for example, Kemper was one of the first to recognize public disenchantment with old-fashioned whole-life policies and to promote interest-rate-sensitive insurance products. Four years ago, Kemper sold a paltry $3.9 million in high-yielding life insurance. Last year such sales topped $327 million.

"We have a planning process—each entity plans for itself," says Luecke. Lumbermens Mutual Casualty Co., which owns 42% of Kemper, leaves him alone. Now 59, Luecke started with Kemper as an auditor in Philadelphia 35 years ago. He moved to headquarters in 1962 and quickly earned a reputation as a manager who knew how to keep costs down. Luecke also proved adept at reconciling differences between Kemper's strong-willed middle managers. He realized early on that Kemper employees won't stomach interference from a "big brother" corporate hierarchy. Kemper "has a bunch of mavericks who you can't tell too much or they'll leave and take their business with them," notes Robert W. Back, an analyst at Rodman & Renshaw Inc.

But Kemper's strategy is not without its risks. So far, "Kemper's managed to buy brokerage firms without scaring off wire houses or other regionals who sell their products," notes A. Michael Lipper, a mutual fund analyst. Kemper's own brokers sell only 22% of all its mutual funds. He cautions that any move to combine its firms into a "superbroker" could cost Kemper sales at other Wall Street houses. Kemper's response? "We have never been so imprudent that we did stupid things to get business," says Thomas R. Anderson, chairman and chief executive of Kemper Financial Services Inc.

"Management is trying to manage a little bit of incoherence coherently," quips one analyst, and Kemper's hands-off management approach has backfired at least once. Its Bateman Eichler subsidiary was the principal cause of the brokerage group's $15.3 million loss in 1984. Bateman specializes in energy and technology stocks, and the losses kept piling up as those markets went sour. Luecke also acknowledges that Bateman's expenses got out of hand. Now "we think we've got that ship turned around," says Anderson.

Kemper's fervent belief in decentralization extends even to such matters as where employees work. Money management staffers are located in the heart of Chicago's financial district—36 mi. from Kemper's plush, art-filled headquarters on 620 suburban acres. When Kemper erected a building near headquarters for its reinsurance operations, the facility was purposely not connected to existing structures. "That's a different corporate culture back there," Luecke murmurs.

So far, that willingness to tolerate difference, without the straining for synergy found at so many of its peers, seems to be giving Kemper an edge.   *By John N. Frank in Chicago*

DISCUSSION QUESTION
What are the reported strengths and weaknesses in Kemper's use of decentralization?

CAN HEWLETT-PACKARD PUT THE PIECES BACK TOGETHER?
ITS COMPUTER BUSINESS IN DISARRAY,
IT'S BETTING EVERYTHING ON A SINGLE TECHNOLOGY
MARCH 10, 1986, PP. 114-116

Almost from the day he took over as chief executive officer at Hewlett-Packard Co. in 1978, John A. Young realized he had a serious problem. The company was the world's largest maker of electronic instruments, but computers were about to take over as its main product. The trouble was that the company's efforts to develop new computers were badly fragmented, and HP was becoming a technological laggard in a highly competitive field.

HP needed a well-orchestrated line of machines for the 1980s. Instead, it had three separate computer divisions, all pumping out products that were incompatible. Watching the company fall dangerously behind archrivals Digital Equipment, Data General, and *IBM*, Young looked for a drastic remedy. "We had to do something, or we'd sink," he remembers.

BLAZING SPEEDS. He did something big. In a move that ran counter to *HP*'s tradition of autonomous, entrepreneurial divisions, the unflappable Young set out to centralize *HP*'s computer research efforts. The project—the biggest in the company's 47-year history—was called Spectrum, and it was risky. Young was putting all the company's eggs in one basket: He killed *HP*'s other computer design projects. If he didn't succeed in building a unified computer organization and creating a central technology that could be used in all the company's machines, *HP* would be consigned to the computer industry's backwaters.

On Feb. 25, after spending an estimated $200 million on Spectrum, Young introduced his first two machines, built around a new and largely unproven approach known as *RISC*, for Reduced-Instruction-Set Computer. Its more efficient design lets a computer gain blazing speed by drastically reducing the complexity of its central processor.

Many analysts and customers think Young is playing a winning hand. His first Spectrum machine, code-named Indigo during development and now called the *HP* 3000 Series 930, sounds impressive. It's supposed to perform better than competing $450,000 minicomputers from Digital Equipment Corp. and International Business Machines Corp.—for about half the price. That could help *HP* steal accounts from the two giants. With its new machines, notes Grant S. Bushee, executive vice-president of the market research firm InfoCorp, "*HP* can go after any market."

The company needs a boost. Its overall share of the worldwide minicomputer market slipped to 5% last year from 5.5% in 1983, according to InfoCorp (chart). In the $37 billion market for commercial minis, it dropped from a 4.2% share in 1983 to 3.9% last year, while *DEC* nudged up from 5% to 7%. In the $15 billion market for technical minis, *HP* sank to 7.8%, from more than 12% five years ago. *DEC*'s inroads mostly caused that, too, but so did competition from *IBM* and *AT&T*. Says George F. Colony, president of Forrester Research Inc. in Cambridge, Mass: "It's damage-control time for *HP* in the minicomputer market."

Not everyone is convinced that Young's *RISC* strategy will be a winning one. One critic is Stephen K. Smith, a PaineWebber Inc. computer analyst who warns that many claims about *RISC*'s advantages "have yet to be substantiated outside an academic environment."

Even if Spectrum does succeed, it will be a while before Young's moves bolster *HP*'s flagging computer profits or improve its overall bottom line. Spectrum "isn't going to show great payoffs in 1986 or 1987," says David C. Moschella, director of systems research for International Data Corp. That's bad news for investors, who bid up the company's shares from 29 in the fall to 44 recently in what analysts say was anticipation of the Spectrum line.

'BAD SMELL.' Spectrum's payoff will be slow because the Series 930 machine isn't scheduled for shipment until the end of this year, and its big brother, the powerful Series 950, code-named Cheetah, won't ship until 1987. *HP* is moving slowly to make sure the machines' software works. "*HP* was built on a reputation of quality and dependability, and they don't want to monkey with that," says William C. Rosser, a vice-president of Gartner Group Inc. "If it comes out, and somebody gets a bad smell, that would hurt them more than any delay."

Such thoroughness has been largely responsible for *HP*'s success in the past. But the delay could push away customers who have grown restless for more computing power. "We've been holding on by our toenails," says Wayne E. Holp, a Seattle-based consultant to *HP* customers. "The fingernails gave way a long time ago." Some of his clients are disappointed because *HP* has been using

---

With HP's share of the minicomputer market down and big profits some years off, 'it's damage-control time'

---

100 of its Spectrum-line machines internally for a year—and they expected to have at least a few by now.

This problem coincides with two others. Instrument sales, accounting for nearly half the Palo Alto (Calif.) company's revenues, dropped 3% last year, estimates Kidder, Peabody & Co. And there's the industrywide slump, which caused *HP*'s overall revenues to grow only a modest 8%, to $6.5 billion, in the fiscal year ended in October. That compares with a double-digit growth rate for most other computer makers. *HP*'s earnings in the same period fell for the first time since 1975, by 10%, to $489 million. In August, Young had to impose 10% salary cuts, since trimmed to 5% for everyone but top executives.

Although Spectrum's delay has created problems for Young, the project has given him a chance to put his stamp on a company molded by two of Silicon Valley's most revered figures. Before Spectrum, Young had the titles of president and *CEO*. But he still toiled in the shadows of William R. Hewlett and David Packard, who chaired the executive committee and board respectively.

The founders, now semiretired, were set in their ways, and *HP* needed dramatic change. The small, entrepreneurial divisions they had used so successfully to invent instruments were a big problem when it came to computers. Customers wanted products that could work together, and that made a unified, companywide approach essential. Young was reluctant to tamper with the founders' formula, and it was several years before he centralized product development, as *IBM* and *DEC* had done.

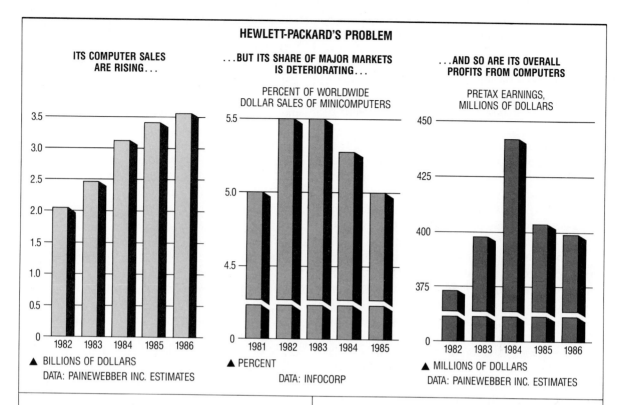

HEWLETT-PACKARD'S PROBLEM

ITS COMPUTER SALES ARE RISING...

BILLIONS OF DOLLARS
DATA: PAINEWEBBER INC. ESTIMATES

...BUT ITS SHARE OF MAJOR MARKETS IS DETERIORATING...

PERCENT OF WORLDWIDE DOLLAR SALES OF MINICOMPUTERS

PERCENT
DATA: INFOCORP

...AND SO ARE ITS OVERALL PROFITS FROM COMPUTERS

PRETAX EARNINGS, MILLIONS OF DOLLARS

MILLIONS OF DOLLARS
DATA: PAINEWEBBER INC. ESTIMATES

By finally conceiving a more coordinated approach and building a consensus among his computer division managers to go with Spectrum, Young put his imprint on *HP*.

In doing so, he radically reshaped a management system long held up as a paragon of excellence. Not only did he have to squelch at least four competing approaches to building high-powered computers, but he also had to sell the untried *RISC* technology to the losing divisions and then harness them to the task of making it work. Division managers, who once had a virtually free hand at *HP*, now spend much of their time coordinating their activities with counterparts in other units. Says a former manager: "*HP* is now organized as a John Young company."

While Hewlett and Packard both were decisive, creative entrepreneurs, Young, 53, is more a detail man who relies on committees and consensus-building before acting. Since getting his *MBA* from Stanford University, Young has spent his entire 28-year career with *HP*, mostly on the instruments side. "His style is to lead people where he wants them to go rather than tell them what to do," says

an insider. To some, that's a weakness. Complains a former *HP* manager: "I never saw him make a decision."

He did make a key one in 1980. One of *HP*'s weaknesses was that Young and fellow officers had little experience with computers. "People at the decision-making level didn't have a good gut feel for what made sense technically," says a former employee. "So they tended not to make decisions." To beef up research and development, which was then still focused on test-and-measurement technology, Young launched a recruiting campaign. His prize catch: Joel S. Birnbaum, who was for five years the head of computer sciences at *IBM*'s Thomas J. Watson Research Center (page 112). Taking over as *HP*'s director of computer research, Birnbaum quickly proposed a program to bring order out of the divisional chaos. "I felt it was hopeless unless we could do this," he recalls.

MISTRUST. Loquacious, quick-witted, and sociable, the new research chief was a veteran of *IBM*'s early work on *RISC* designs. He felt that *HP* should be making simpler computers, not the more complex ones many divisions were design-

JOEL BIRNBAUM, THE ODD MAN IN AT HEWLETT-PACKARD

Joel S. Birnbaum may be the closest thing to a Renaissance man at Hewlett-Packard Co. An amateur photographer, nuclear physicist, computer visionary, and former Ivy League baseball pitcher, he is an anomaly in a California company run largely by an ingrown crowd of test-and-measurement engineers.

It might seem that an Easterner with Birnbaum's varied credentials would have trouble fitting in at a place like *HP*. But Birnbaum, 48, won a heated intramural battle to switch the company's minicomputers to a drastically simplified architecture known as *RISC* (page 109). In doing so, he has emerged as a corporate vice-president and director of *HP* Laboratories, which he is rapidly turning into one of the computer industry's hottest research facilities.

KINDRED SPIRITS. After attending Cornell on a baseball scholarship and picking up a physics PhD at Yale, Birnbaum spent 15 years at International Business Machines Corp. But as director of computer research there, he became frustrated by the difficulty of getting ideas to market. "I had the feeling I didn't make a difference," he says. When a recruiter for *HP* called in 1980, Birnbaum found: "I could talk to the *HP* guys in a different way.

The top guys at *IBM* were not technical people."

It was at *IBM*, however, that Birnbaum ran across *RISC* technology—during a mid-1970s research project for a digital phone switch that could route a million calls an hour. John Cocke, another *IBM* researcher, came up with an idea for special software, plus a simplified processor that eliminated the circuitry needed to decode seldom-used instructions. It could thus run much faster than existing processors. The phone switch was dropped, but Birnbaum built a model processor. Although crude, it worked—and became the basis for the *RT PC* technical workstation, a *RISC* machine that *IBM* introduced in January.

The prototype for Spectrum, the machine designed for *HP* by Birnbaum and William S. Worley Jr., another ex-*IBM* researcher, fell short of pure *RISC* technology. *HP* wanted to minimize risks, so it used well-proven chips instead of the hottest ones available. That limits the speed of its new machines. But they're still faster than most conventional ones, and Birnbaum plans to soup them up. That might make it possible to "domesticate" computers by building in artificial intelligence that makes them much easier to use.

His work at *HP* Labs leaves Birnbaum with little time for athletics or his darkroom, where he develops his own portrait and landscape shots. But his real love, he says, is ideas. And tossing those around isn't a bad occupation for an ex-pitcher.

By John W. Wilson in Palo Alto, with Marilyn A. Harris in Stamford, Conn.

---

ing. Realizing that *HP* was run by engineers, not the marketing specialists who dominate *IBM*, he set out to discover what customers wanted *HP*'s computers to do. His research created the impetus for a prototype *RISC* machine he called *LESS*, for Low-End Spectrum System. "Our motto was: *LESS* is more," Birnbaum says. "And even that little machine was much faster than what was then our top of the line." *RISC* design strips away from a computer's central processor all but its essential functions, so it can process information faster.

Once Young developed the consensus he wanted to give Spectrum a final go-ahead in February,

1983, he needed someone who could make sure that all the divisions agreed on the details of how the project should proceed. That job fell to Douglas C. Chance, general manager of *HP*'s Information Systems Group. Young saw Chance as a strong strategist who could build a team and develop confidence. This was crucial because many technical decisions had to be made quickly before the machine could be handed over to a development team.

Chance set up a committee of top officers and division managers that met monthly over dinner. As often as not, Chance learned, the issues that worried them most weren't technical. "The real concerns had to do with whether they could trust the others to do what we had all agreed to do," he recalls. Such fears "typically surfaced late at night after several bottles of wine."

Eventually, as Spectrum grew, *HP*'s divisions learned to cooperate under a new umbrella called the Information Technology Group. At its helm was veteran engineer George E. Bodway, a hearty, rumpled man with a knack for administration. "Nothing escapes him," an admirer says. Formed in May, 1984, *ITG* quickly built a staff of 1,000 and for the first time brought into one group the people who develop such key elements of computers as operating systems, programming languages, and integrated-circuit designs. Some 20 divisions chipped in specialized software, peripheral devices, and other elements of Spectrum, with disagreements arbitrated by Bodway and a series of specialized councils.

LOSING VERVE? Young is keeping the centralization in place and shifting the role of the once-autonomous divisions dramatically. The divisions continue as marketing arms for specific groups of customers. But when it comes to product development, they can no longer "do any damn thing they want," he says. Young hopes new reporting and performance-measuring systems will help develop links among divisions "without getting swamped in a lot of bureaucracy."

Some former employees fear that *HP* is in danger of losing its entrepreneurial verve. Now, "*HP* looks a lot more like *DEC* or *IBM*," says one. "That creates a different work environment." But it is clear to Young that the company's old environment didn't work well in the high-stakes computer game. The combination of new technology and a new corporate structure looks like his only bet.

By John W. Wilson in Palo Alto and Catherine L. Harris in New York, with Gordon Bock in New York

DISCUSSION QUESTIONS
1. What prompted Hewlett-Packard to centralize its computer research and development efforts?
2. What mechanisms is HP using to achieve coordination across divisions and avoid excessive bureaucracy?

AND NOW, THE POST-INDUSTRIAL CORPORATION

IT COULD FARM OUT EVERYTHING FROM MANUFACTURING TO BILLING

MARCH 3, 1986, PP. 64-66, 71

Lewis Galoob Toys Inc. is obviously a successful company. It sold $58 million worth of its sword-wielding Golden Girls "action figures" and other trendy toys last year—10 times the 1981 total. Its stock, issued in 1984 at 10, has soared as high as 15 and now sells for 13½. Yet by traditional standards of structure, strategy, and management practice, Galoob is hardly a company at all.

A mere 115 employees run the entire operation. Independent inventors and entertainment companies dream up most of Galoob's products, while outside specialists do most of the design and engineering. Galoob farms out manufacturing and packaging to a dozen or so contractors in Hong Kong, and they, in turn, pass on the most labor-intensive work to factories in China. When the toys land in the U. S., they're distributed by commissioned manufacturers' representatives. Galoob doesn't even collect its accounts. It sells its receivables to Commercial Credit Corp., a factoring company that also sets Galoob's credit policy. In short, says Executive Vice-President Robert Galoob, "our business is one of relationships." Galoob and his brother, David, the company's president, spend their time making all the pieces of the toy company fit together, with their phones, facsimile machines, and telexes working overtime.

'DYNAMIC NETWORKS.' Galoob is just one of a crowd of companies emerging in toys, garments, electronics, sporting goods, and other industries that are as different from today's industrial giants as early mammals were from dinosaurs (table, page 116). In management jargon, these new corporations are "vertically disaggregated," relying on other companies for manufacturing and many crucial business functions. They are industrial companies without industrial production. And they just may be the organizational model for businesses in the post-industrial era. As the U. S. increasingly exports the production of commodity goods, these companies will become more and more common, says Raymond E. Miles, dean of the School of Business Administration at the University of California at Berkeley. "What you'll have is a switchboard instead of a corporation," Miles predicts.

That may be overstating things. But there are strong forces pushing U. S. companies in this direction. These new corporations—Miles calls them "dynamic networks"—can take advantage of low-cost foreign labor and foreign technology. They can pounce more quickly on new markets or new technologies. With less bureaucracy, they are well-suited to an era in which managers and workers are demanding a bigger say in their jobs. At a time when U. S. companies find it harder and harder to earn a living manufacturing domestically, these corporations offer a way to exploit some of the same advantages foreign companies have.

In a 1984 book, *The Second Industrial Divide*, economist Michael J. Piore and political scientist Charles F. Sabel come to similar conclusions. The Massachusetts Institute of Technology professors forecast a new international economy in which mass production shifts to the Third World, while developed countries turn increasingly to "flexible specialization." Piore and Sabel believe "solar-system organizations," with external suppliers orbiting small central headquarters, will be prominent players in this scheme of things.

STAGE THREE. In such a universe, vertically integrated companies won't disappear altogether. Few large corporations, so far, have turned completely into network organizations. But even many big companies that continue, for now, to do most of their own manufacturing are edging toward disaggregation. Forced by the high cost of developing products and penetrating world markets, many are turning to foreign sources for finished products. Others are forming joint ventures and temporary alliances overseas. General Motors Corp., a prototypical vertically integrated company, does all of the above. Industrial giants such as Firestone, 3M, and General Electric all sell finished products bought from foreign companies. Says

Henry Wendt, president of SmithKline Beckman Corp.: "We'll see more collaborative arrangements rather than less."

The network model, if it is broadly adopted, would be only the third real organizational innova-

---

A network corporation is vulnerable to cruel blows—competition from its own suppliers

---

tion since the corporation evolved in the mid-19th century. Around 1850, as industrial processes grew more complex and as national markets developed, businesses grew larger. They took on more managers—each assigned to oversee a phase in the commercial chain from raw material to finished product—and the vertically integrated industrial company was born.

The first important change came in the 1920s: *GM* pioneered the divisional structure still typical of U. S. industry, where vertical chains of command for each operating division exist in parallel. Then, after World War II, aerospace companies started the trend toward the "matrix" system. Matrices, with workers reporting to various supervisors depending on the task they performed, make it easier to assemble temporary teams for big projects.

Now network companies may have their day. They are not entirely new—publishers, garment makers, and construction companies have contracted out work for years. But the network structure is spreading, pushed in part by communication breakthroughs that make it easy to coordinate suppliers and customers around the world.

Academics and consultants are divided about the future of disaggregated companies. They are only now beginning to study the impact on corporate structure of recent changes in technology, work force, and competition. *MIT*'s Sloan School of Management, for example, has launched a multidisciplinary research program on management in the 1990s. Michael Scott-Morton, the professor who heads the program, says it's too early to draw conclusions—but he adds that the trend toward increased flexibility and away from vertical hierarchies is clear. Others doubt that networks will be the wave of the future. "It may be a transitory stage," says Robert J. Cardinal, director of *SRI* International's Manufacturing Consulting Practice.

Indeed, no one knows whether disaggregation is a brave new world or a blind alley, leading U. S. companies further astray from improving their competitiveness. Because network companies typically ride waves of fashion or technology, their earnings can be extremely volatile—and their existence precarious. Nike Inc., the sports-shoe giant that has used offshore contract manufacturers since it started in 1964, lost money for two quarters last year when its designers guessed wrong, and 22 million pairs of shoes went unsold. Galoob, too, dipped into the red in the fourth quarter of 1985 when it failed to meet sales projections.

TURNCOATS. Network companies may be more vulnerable to attack from integrated companies, from new network companies that need to put up very little capital to join the competitive fray, and—cruelest of all—from their manufacturing suppliers. Several U. S. sporting-goods companies, for example, turned to Taiwan's Kunnan Enterprises to make rackets. Now, Kunnan is invading the U. S. market with its own rackets. Japan's Seiko Instruments & Electronics Ltd., which makes a 20-in. color-graphics display terminal for Tektronix Inc., now offers its own comparable model priced 20% below the Tektronix unit. At one recent trade show, Seiko salespeople were sniping at the Tektronix model, trying to woo buyers to Seiko.

Diversified and integrated companies, meanwhile, tend to have more staying power in the marketplace: With a broader base, they can better afford to subsidize unprofitable parts of their operations. "I question whether in the long run [network companies] will be competitive against integrated Japanese and European operations," says *SRI*'s Cardinal. Japanese companies would seem to agree. In fact, some of Japan's big, traditional trading companies—in some ways similar to the new network companies—are moving into manufacturing.

Longer-term, there's an even bigger worry. Without the ability to manufacture, companies can lose the capacity to design innovative products, some experts say. Others, however, downplay this as a drawback. They counter that technological advances usually come from outside established companies, which have a vested interest in extending the life of their products. What's more, they note that network companies are flourishing in areas such as toys and garments, where fashion is more important than innovation.

FIXED-ASSET FREEDOM. In any case, many U. S. companies are convinced that a network structure works best for them. Nike thinks of itself not as a manufacturer but as a research, development, and marketing corporation that, like other companies in labor-intensive industries, probably could not compete any other way. A pair of shoes that it buys in Korea and sells in the U. S. for $45 would have to be priced at $65 or more if manufactured at home.

Pitney Bowes Inc. had other reasons for going overseas when its Dictaphone Corp. subsidiary

HOW THE CORPORATION HAS EVOLVED

1800 **Owner-managed**—Small companies, generally making one product for a regional market, are controlled by one person who performs many administrative tasks

1850 **Vertical**—Companies grow larger and hire more managers, each to oversee a stage of the chain from raw material to finished product

1900 **Divisional**—Large companies organize around a series of vertical chains of command to manage each product, or group of related products, that the company makes

1950 **Matrix**—Large companies with vertical structures add a second, informal reporting chain that links managers with allied responsibilities or managers working together on temporary projects

2000 **Network**—Small central organizations rely on other companies and suppliers to perform manufacturing, distribution, marketing, or other crucial business functions on a contract basis

discovered demand for a super-small dictating unit. Dictaphone could design it, but it had little experience making very small components in high volume. Recalls President James L. Bast: "That said we've got to find a competent vendor who

> 'The manufacturer's mind-set is sell what he can make. We're market-driven now'

has worked with small components. It was a technology decision." Dictaphone chose Victor Co. of Japan as its supplier.

Emerson Radio Corp. designs and engineers its *TV*s, stereos, and other consumer electronics items, but it contracts out production to Asian suppliers, largely for cost reasons. Now, Emerson cities other advantages to the arrangement: Besides having greater flexibility, the company can spend more money on research and advertising than it otherwise might since there is less need to invest in fixed assets. In fact, President Stephen L. Lane cannot think of a single disadvantage Emerson has compared with an integrated company. "Reliability of supply is a fear, but it has never worked out as a problem," he says.

Even International Business Machines Corp., which used to pride itself on making virtually everything it sold, adopted a disaggregated format when it decided in 1981 to enter the personal computer market. In Boca Raton, Fla.—far from its Armonk (N. Y.) headquarters—*IBM* set up its Entry Systems Div., which relied heavily on off-the-shelf components and contract manufacturers to get its popular *PC* to market quickly and keep costs down. *ESD* provided another plus, too: It fostered the entrepreneurial spirit so prized but so hard to cultivate at large corporations.

General Electric has followed suit. To stay in the cutthroat consumer-electronics market, it is buying *TV*s and videocassette recorders, based on its own designs, from the Far East. By mid-1986,

only 10% of the employees in *GE*'s consumer-electronics unit will be engaged in manufacturing vs. 60% in mid-1984. "The value added [in consumer electronics] is in marketing, sales, and distribution—not manufacturing," argues Vice-President Jacques A. Robinson. He concedes that return on sales will decline, but he says investment declines faster. "You're working your capital much harder," so return on investment goes up "most noticeably."

All in all, the network structure allows companies to zero in on what they do best and leave the rest to other experts. U. S. companies most often focus on design or marketing—but not always. A cadre of American specialists has sprung up to do manufacturing for electronics companies. California's Flextronics Inc., for example, counts only 50 or so of its 1,400 employees in sales, marketing, administration, or finance jobs. "Everybody else is in manufacturing, purchasing, and customer service," says President Robert G. Todd Jr. "We are dedicated to doing one thing and doing it well."

LOSS OF CONTROL. Schwinn Bicycle Co. is more typical. It decided that it was really a design, distribution, and merchandising company, not a

A GALLERY OF COMPANIES THAT ARE ALREADY 'NETWORKS'

Company	Products	Revenues* (millions)	Total employees/ manufacturing employees
NIKE	Athletic shoes	$1,000	3,500/100
ESPRIT	Apparel	800	3,000/500
LIZ CLAIBORNE	Apparel	570	2,000/250
EMERSON RADIO	Consumer electronics	500	700/150
TIE	Telecommunications	500	2,100/900
SCHWINN BICYCLE	Bicycles	150	NA/NA
SUN MICROSYSTEMS	Computers	150	1,400/200
LEWIS GALOOB	Toys	58	115/0
ELECTRONIC ARTS	Software	20	75/0
OCEAN PACIFIC SUNWEAR	Apparel	15	67/0

*Estimated 1985   DATA: BW   NA = Not available

manufacturer. "The leverage of the business was no longer in manufacturing," explains President Edward R. Schwinn Jr. Now Schwinn imports most of its bikes from Asia. "When you are a manufacturing company, your mind-set tends to be to sell what you can make," says Jay Townley, a Schwinn vice-president. "We're market-driven now."

Ocean Pacific Sunwear Ltd., meanwhile, is thriving by licensing the Op name to other companies, who also do much of the design work. Chairman Larry Ornitz sees his mission as cultivating the Op mystique. He does that by fielding a common sales force, advertising, and sponsoring special events such as surfing contests and Beach Boys concerts. Sales of Op clothing have bloomed from $7 million to $270 million in 10 years. Yet Ocean Pacific has only its name at risk: If a line of shorts or shirts bombs, the licensees swallow the losses.

If there is one managerial drawback to the network organization, it's the lack of close control over operations. George Morrow's San Leandro (Calif.) company, Morrow Designs Inc., relies heavily on outsiders to develop and manufacture its microcomputers, and he recalls the frustration of watching 5,000 unneeded machines pour in from contractors in the Far East. "We tried to turn the spigot off," he says, "but it kept running."

SUPPLIER SYMBIOSIS. Even slight misunderstandings can be expensive, as Caterpillar Tractor Co. learned when it transferred manufacturing of some undercarriage parts to a supplier in Scotland. "We assumed when they machined the product, they'd use essentially the same [machining] location points as we used," recalls Robert E. Ranney, Cat's product-availability manager. "It didn't turn out that way. We ended up with more than $100,000 worth of a product that wouldn't work." And *IBM* restructured *ESD* along traditional lines when the unit rushed ill-conceived, low-cost, and portable versions of the *PC* to market.

Information technology solves only part of the control problem. Nike product managers still fly the Pacific on occasion with a pair of hot prototype shoes to rush a product change or to press for a tricky manufacturing detail. Designers at

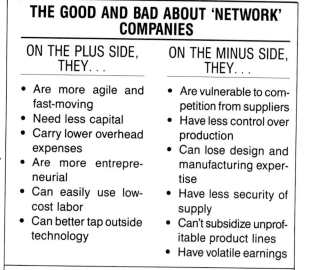

THE GOOD AND BAD ABOUT 'NETWORK' COMPANIES

ON THE PLUS SIDE, THEY...	ON THE MINUS SIDE, THEY...
• Are more agile and fast-moving	• Are vulnerable to competition from suppliers
• Need less capital	• Have less control over production
• Carry lower overhead expenses	• Can lose design and manufacturing expertise
• Are more entrepreneurial	• Have less security of supply
• Can easily use low-cost labor	• Can't subsidize unprofitable product lines
• Can better tap outside technology	• Have volatile earnings

San Francisco's Esprit de Corp, a fast-growing apparel company with ties to more than 150 outside factories around the world, spend six months a year on the road. "No matter how great your specification is, it will be changed by the manufacturer if you aren't standing there," says Roger Kase, president of the Esprit Div.

Often, relationships with suppliers grow to be almost as close as internal corporate ties. *TIE* Communications Inc. relies on Japan's Nitsuko Ltd. for most of the telephone equipment it sells, and the two companies' engineers work side-by-side to develop products. Isamu Watanabe, president of Nitsuko America Corp., whose factory is just down the street from *TIE*'s Shelton (Conn.) headquarters, sometimes wanders the halls at *TIE*. Emerson Radio once had to help pay a supplier's payroll. When price competition heats up, Emerson's management quickly teams up with its Asian suppliers. "We help them find ways to reduce the cost of products," says Lane. Such symbiotic relationships do much to reduce the risk of having a supplier turn into a rival.

These situations demand management skills far different from those commonly valued today. At network companies, strong financial, operations, or legal skills may well take a back seat to the ability to spot trends quickly, to set an entrepreneurial example, and to develop strong outside relationships. Says *GE*'s Robinson: "It's partnership management, not the classic pyramid where you issue orders every day."

As a result, different kinds of executives are likely to rise to the top. Doug Tompkins, a prep-school dropout and avid outdoorsman who cofounded Esprit, considers himself a corporate "image director." The Galoob brothers, who hold degrees in cinematography and psychology, pride themselves on the strength of their relationships with outside manufacturers. Scott McNealy, president of Sun Microsystems Inc., has presided over a meteoric rise in computer workstations though he barely comprehends the work of his systems and software designers. He feels that a central part of his role is setting a tone and sense of urgency for Sun. "Companies take on the character of their top managers," he says. These ebullient managers probably wouldn't function well in traditional corporations.

Some large companies are, however, finding that they may have to function as networks. Disaggregation helped save a big chunk of business for Sulzer Brothers Ltd., a Swiss company that once was a world leader in manufacturing big, low-speed marine diesel engines. Years ago, Sulzer turned to licensing its designs and servicing engines made by licensees. Otherwise, says President Pierre Borgeaud, Sulzer would have been squeezed out of the market entirely by low-cost Asian rivals and by developing countries intent on building their own manufacturing base. These days, Sulzer still claims 45% of its market.

ONSHORE REMEDY. In other mature businesses, too, the network structure might help keep some of the action—and the jobs—onshore. Some experts argue that America's big steel companies, which control steelmaking from the coal and iron mines to finished slab steel, could have stemmed their decline by disaggregating. Rival "minimills," which make their raw steel from cheap steel scrap, have grabbed nearly 20% of the U. S. steel market, and they're still gaining. But for big producers to disaggregate now, by using more scrap, would mean huge write-offs of investments in integrated mills. And, having lobbied for stiff import quotas, they have reduced their chances to buy a lot of cheaper foreign slab, at least until 1989, when current restraints end.

Some companies that still have the network option are turning to outsiders to fill out their product lines, to stanch losses in tough markets without giving up a brand franchise, or to focus on more profitable products. New companies may want to organize as networks to gain agility and cost advantages. What's good for them, however, may not be good for the economy as a whole. If it goes too far, the U. S. could be left without a vibrant manufacturing base. That would leave the nation more dependent than ever on the fewer and lower-paying jobs in the service economy.

By John W. Wilson in San Francisco, with Judith H. Dobrzynski in New York and bureau reports

DISCUSSION QUESTIONS
1. How does the network model of organization design differ from its predecessors?
2. What risks are involved in vertical disaggregation?

MANAGEMENT DISCOVERS THE HUMAN SIDE OF AUTOMATION

COMPANIES ARE FINDING THAT WORKERS
ARE THE KEY TO MAKING TECHNOLOGY PAY OFF

SEPTEMBER 29, 1986, PP. 70-74, 79

Like thousands of companies in the early 1980s, Shenandoah Life Insurance Co. marched eagerly into the world of high technology. It installed a $2 million system to computerize processing and claims operations at its Roanoke (Va.) headquarters. But the results were disappointing. It still took 27 working days—and handling by 32 clerks in three departments—to process a typical application for a policy conversion.

Shenandoah's problem stemmed from its bureaucratic maze, not from defects in the technology. Only by radically reorganizing its work system could it reap the benefits of automation. The company grouped the clerks in "semiautonomous" teams of five to seven members. Each team now performs all the functions that once were spread over three departments. Team members learned new skills, bringing them greater job satisfaction—and better pay. As a result, the typical case-handling time dropped to two days, and service complaints were practically eliminated. By 1986, Shenandoah was processing 50% more applications and queries with 10% fewer employees than it did in 1980.

The productivity gains at Shenandoah Life are part of a powerful synergism taking root in the U. S.—the pairing of people with automation. American managers are finally learning what the Japanese discovered years ago: The solution to fading competitive ability, sluggish productivity growth, and poor quality cannot be found in the mythical black box of a miraculous technology. To realize the full potential of automation, lead-

ing-edge companies are integrating workers and technology in "sociotechnical" systems that revolutionize the way work is organized and managed.

This is an immensely important trend, one that is producing a new model of job design and work relations that will shape the workplace well into the 21st century. Nevertheless, the changeover isn't occurring fast enough. The great wave of automation that has swept through offices and factories since 1980 is losing momentum, largely because not enough companies are adopting the innovative work practices that get the most out of automation. Many managers are reluctant to "run the kind of social revolution at work that is needed to make technology pay for itself," says productivity expert George H. Kuper, who heads the Manufacturing Studies Board, a research arm of the National Academy of Sciences.

PEOPLE PROBLEMS. With or without work reforms, computer-based technology is having an enormous impact on workers. In one way or another, it has changed the jobs of 40 million to 50 million people, almost half of the U. S. work force. It has made some jobs more challenging and "deskilled" others. It has caused severe dislocations at specific work sites by eliminating jobs, raising a fundamental question of whether government and business are investing enough money and expertise in retraining displaced workers (page 122). For the entire nonfarm economy, however, technological change helped produce a 10.4 million increase in jobs between 1979 and this year.

But contrary to the engineers' vision of factories

THE CHANGING APPROACH TO ORGANIZING WORK

WHAT MANAGEMENT ASSUMES ABOUT WORKERS

OLD WAY Worker wants nothing from the job except pay, avoids responsibility, and must be controlled and coerced

NEW WAY Worker desires challenging job and will seek responsibility and autonomy if management permits

HOW THE JOB IS DESIGNED

OLD WAY Work is fragmented and deskilled. Worker is confined to narrow job. Doing and thinking are separated

NEW WAY Work is multi-skilled and performed by teamwork where possible. Worker can upgrade whole system. Doing and thinking are combined

MANAGEMENT'S ORGANIZATION AND STYLE

OLD WAY Top-down military command with worker at bottom of many supervisory layers; worker is expected to obey orders and has no power

NEW WAY Relatively flat structure with few layers; worker makes suggestions and has power to implement changes

JOB TRAINING AND SECURITY

OLD WAY Worker is regarded as a replaceable part and is given little initial training or retraining for new jobs. Layoffs are routine when business declines

NEW WAY Worker is considered a valuable resource and is constantly retrained in new skills. Layoffs are avoided if possible in a downturn

HOW WAGES ARE DETERMINED

OLD WAY Pay is geared to the job, not the person, and is determined by evaluation and job classification systems

NEW WAY Pay is linked to skills acquired. Group incentive and profit-sharing plans are used to enhance commitment

LABOR RELATIONS

OLD WAY Labor and management interests are considered incompatible. Conflict arises on the shop floor and in bargaining

NEW WAY Mutual interests are emphasized. Management shares information about the business. Labor shares responsibility for making it succeed

DATA: RICHARD E. WALTON, HARVARD UNIVERSITY; BW

---

run by robots, the high-tech workplace depends more than ever on people. "There will be fewer of them, but the ones who are there will be critical," says Gerald I. Susman, an expert on work and technology at Pennsylvania State University. Mistakes by poorly trained, poorly motivated workers can cause enormous damage, as demonstrated by the nuclear accidents at Three Mile Island and Chernobyl. Says Lyman D. Ketchum, a pioneering consultant on teamwork: "We're moving increasingly into dangerous, unforgiving technologies that can't be operated safely with uncommitted people."

Most important, it is becoming evident that advanced computer technology calls for a radical change in traditional work practices. The old "scientific management" method of dividing work into discrete tasks that require little skill or training becomes obsolete in a computerized workplace where many functions—including materials handling, assembly, inventory control, and testing—are integrated by computer. "The integration no longer makes it possible to define jobs individually or measure individual performance," says Richard E. Walton of Harvard University. "It requires a collection of people to manage a segment of technology and perform as a team."

GLOBAL COMPETITION. For these reasons, more companies are installing work systems that emphasize broader-based jobs, teamwork, participative managers, and multiskilled workers. The innovations include a range of other labor policies aimed at developing "committed" workers, including enhanced job security, continuous training programs, and compensation schemes that reward group performance (table). Industries such as autos, steel, and communications have been moving slowly in this direction with the cooperation of their unions since the beginning of the "quality-of-work-life" movement in the 1970s.

But the new innovations go far beyond *QWL* reforms that involve workers in problem-solving groups or otherwise aim at making jobs more satisfying. Now the movement is being fueled by global competition and the need for a high rate of product innovation. The average life cycle of an electronics product, for example, is only three to five years. Experts say that while the U. S. may not be able to compete with countries that turn out standardized products and parts at low wages, it can create new market niches for customized products. But manufacturers must be able to switch quickly from one product line to another, and flexible work systems—when combined with computer-based technology—give them that ability.

The new "paradigm," as organizational behavior specialists call it, will gradually replace the old system characterized by authoritarian management and an extreme division of labor epitomized by the assembly line. The new approach often entails sociotechnical planning—that is, integrating the psychological and social needs of workers with technological requirements in designing a new plant or redesigning an old one. Harvard's Walton contrasts the old "control" paradigm with the new model of "commitment."

The payoff can be significant. Many plants that were designed with sociotechnical methods and use the most radical innovation, semiautonomous teams, are 30% to 50% more productive than their conventional counterparts. In most plants, these teams manage themselves without first-line supervisors, determine their own work pace within parameters set by management, schedule their own vacations, and have a voice in hiring and firing team members and deciding when they qualify for raises. This is a relatively new creature on the U. S. industrial scene, and both managers and workers give it high praise.

Ten years ago, fewer than two dozen manufacturing plants in the U. S. organized work on a team basis. Today teamwork is used in several hundred offices and factories, especially new, highly automated plants with small work forces of 25 to 500 people. One example is a diesel engine plant jointly owned by Cummins Engine Co. and J. I. Case Co. in Whittakers, N. C. Teamwork, says plant manager John C. Read, brings out "an entrepreneurial cowboy spirit" in American workers. "When this spirit gets wrapped into team efforts to figure out why a machine went down— and if management gets out of the way—it's a tremendously powerful tool."

Many workers like teamwork for its greater variety of tasks, compared with repetitive jobs on a conventional assembly line. That's true of Randy Gilbert, a 10-year veteran at General Motors Corp. who now is an elected team coordinator in Buick City, GM's showcase plant that combines high technology and Japanese management meth-

---

Managers are being taught not to control employees but to encourage them to use their own initiative

---

ods. "Once in a while I get bored and switch jobs with someone just to relieve the tedium," he says. That wasn't possible before.

NOT FAST ENOUGH? But technology experts say teamwork and other innovative practices are not spreading fast enough. Although the sociotechnical revolution is here to stay, plants that use teamwork still constitute only a small minority of U. S. workplaces.

If teamwork produces such good results, why haven't more companies tried it? For one thing, it requires a drastic change in management style and methods. The old idea that a manager's main function is to control workers is replaced with the concept that a manager should encourage employees to use initiative. This goes against the grain of everything managers have been taught since the early years of the century, says Lyman Ketchum, who helped design one of the first sociotechnical plants in the U. S., a Gaines Foods Inc. plant that opened in Topeka, Kan., in 1971. To accept the commitment model of work, he says, managers have to go through a "personal paradigm shift, which is a deep psychological process."

John B. Myers, vice-president for human resources at Shenandoah Life, adds that most managers are comfortable with old-style bureaucracies in which orders are passed from top to bottom. "Bureaucratic organizations become habit-forming, just like cigarettes," he says. "That's why they don't change."

The slowness to change may have implications

BUSINESS IS DRAGGING ITS FEET ON RETRAINING

In Americus, Ga., robots are writing the script for a tragedy. Michigan-based Ex-Cell-O Corp. employs 400 hourly workers in this hamlet of 17,000 people to make plastic car parts, including brightly colored urethane shells for masking auto bumpers. But now robots are taking over the spray-painting of the shells. The resulting gains in quality and productivity will help secure the jobs of most Ex-Cell-O employees. But that isn't any consolation to as many as 100 workers who will be replaced by the robots.

Only a handful of the painters qualify for the highly skilled and technical job of servicing the robots. Others may be able to transfer to lower-skilled slots at Ex-Cell-O, but that would displace workers with less seniority. The remainder may have to job-hunt elsewhere. "These people may have heard that there will be new jobs for them in plants that manufacture robots," says a company executive. "But that won't be in Americus."

The Ex-Cell-O example illustrates an important public-policy issue raised by automation: Who is responsible for retraining workers who are thrown into the labor market by new technology? Traditionally, most companies have left this role to government. But public concern may force them to reassess this position—or face greater pressure from Washington to act.

PAINFUL PREDICAMENT. More and more workers across the nation are finding themselves in the painters' predicament. From insurance companies to machine shops, new technology is altering work radically. Many of the technologically unemployed will drop into relatively unskilled service-industry jobs. But occupational experts say the demand is rising for workers in new, more technically oriented jobs being created by automation. If displaced workers are to get these jobs, however, they will have to be retrained.

"The new jobs require much greater literacy and skill," says Roger D. Semerad, Assistant Labor Secretary for employment and training, who worries that displaced workers may not be equipped to fill the new high-tech slots. "There could hardly be any more significant issue with respect to employment policy than this one," adds Harvard business school Professor D. Quinn Mills, a member of the National Commission on Employment Policy, an independent group that reports to the President.

Dislocation is not the only serious problem caused by technology. Some workers complain about being deskilled; others say their employers use the computer as a control device. For example, reservations clerk Toni M. Watson works at a computer terminal in the San Diego office of a regional airline. Her performance, including how many minutes she devotes to each incoming call, is continuously monitored by computer. Three years ago she suffered a nervous breakdown, largely because of job pressures, and entered eight months of therapy. Management, she says, is acting as if "I am supposed to have a digital clock in my head. I'm not a machine."

Government policy, of course, can't solve these kinds of problems. But retraining dislocated workers is another matter. Currently, as many as 2 million jobs are thought to be vanishing each year in the U. S. Most economists believe that foreign competition is more to blame for this than automation, and in any case the economy is generating more jobs overall than are being lost.

LAST-MINUTE LOBBYING. Nevertheless, the National Commission on Employment Policy estimates that through the rest of this decade 400,000 workers a year may need extensive retraining to find new jobs. This includes people who must acquire higher technical skills, as well as those who will need remedial training in basic English and mathematics, whether they are active employees or just entering the work force. The federal government's primary jobs program, the Job Training Partnership Act of 1982, serves less than 200,000 dislocated workers, and its budget is being halved to $100 million a year.

Labor experts and union leaders contend that the government should spend far more on retraining. But the Reagan Administration's opposition to big domestic spending makes the White House unlikely to support such an idea. With unemployment edging downward to 6.8% in August and federal deficits headed in the opposite direction, even Congress would look askance at new spending programs.

Some legislation to limit dislocation by restricting plant shutdowns is gaining momentum, however. In mid-1985, for instance, support was strong for plant-closing legislation because of a widespread perception in Washington that plant shutdowns were on the rise. A bill requiring employers to notify workers well in advance of shutdowns was voted down in the House only after an intense, last-ditch lobbying effort by business. Warns Randolph M. Hale, a vice-president of the National Association of Manufacturers: "If employers expect to have the flexibility to close plants when they want, they are going to have to do a better job at retraining and placing workers where there are jobs."

Hale and other business lobbyists are urging companies not to wait for Washington to act. They point out that retraining workers with obsolete skills and keeping them at work fosters corporate loyalty. By giving workers the knowledge to perform several jobs, companies also would benefit from a more flexible and adaptable work force. A few companies go even further and retrain workers for jobs outside the company if none is available inside. Ford Motor Co., for example, runs a joint training program with the United Auto Workers and has retrained some 1,700 displaced Ford workers for other jobs since 1982.

A more visible effort by companies to beef up training and improve the quality of work life would reduce the political heat being generated by the issue. In the long run, that could help industry considerably. For if employers ignore the problem and dislocations increase substantially, the federal government will step in sooner or later—with results that business may not like.

By Michael A. Pollock

---

for productivity growth. The rise in output per man-hour in the U. S. has lagged behind that of Japan and European nations for more than a decade. Bureau of Labor Statistics economists estimate that productivity will increase at an average annual rate of 1.7% through the mid-1990s, about double the rate of the past 10 years, largely because of new technology.

This projection, however, is based on a continuing high rate of technological innovation that may not happen. The 1980s started with glowing predictions of pushbutton factories linked to executive suites in vast computer networks. And the "paperless" electronic office was said to be just around the corner.

But the unmanned factory has not arrived. Computer-integrated manufacturing *(CIM)*, in which shop-floor machines are operated by a central computer, is a reality in only a few plants. And offices are still struggling with primitive computer networks.

PULLING BACK. Investment in new technology is not increasing nearly as fast as was predicted in the early 1980s. In early September, Dataquest Inc., a San Jose (Calif.) market research firm, lowered its projection of industrial automation sales in 1990 by 13%, to $34 billion. Robot sales are also slowing down. "I'm very discouraged," says Richard M. Cyert, president of Carnegie-Mellon University. "For the future of manufacturing in this country, we have to find a way to move automation ahead at a faster pace."

Many companies are pulling back from overambitious automation projects. In its blueprint to convert seven plants to produce a new midsize car, *GM* had intended to install more than 1,000 robots and replace conventional car assembly lines with the automatic guided vehicle *(AGV)*, a moving "island" of car parts. Now, however, only three plants will be converted. In addition to financial and marketing reasons, *GM* has had problems integrating technology with its management systems, observers say.

The complexities involved in making *CIM* work are stymieing automation efforts at many companies. Few have managed to tie the major management functions of engineering, production, and marketing into a single, computerized information system. This kind of linking is necessary for companies to gain one of the larger benefits of computer technology—eliminating layers of middle managers and technicians who now do this work. In addition, computerizing new techniques such as just-in-time inventory control may have as much impact in cutting production costs as eliminating direct labor and managers, says Penn State's Susman. "But reducing inventory tightens the couplings between parts of an organization," he adds, "and this requires workers who know what they're doing."

GM is going ahead with other projects, including a highly automated front-axle plant in Saginaw, Mich. When this plant reaches full production in late 1987, it will be run entirely by robots part of each working day. This plant illustrates the new U. S. emphasis on human skills. It will be operated by 38 hourly employees, all members of the United Auto Workers, who survived a stringent selection process. They are now being schooled in electronic, mechanical, and problem-solving skills and will have more than a year of training before the plant begins making axles.

This amount of training is new in the U. S., although the Japanese have routinely engaged in such comprehensive programs for years. It is one of the ways Japan invests in human resources so that automation will "make people more productive," says Thomas J. Gallogly, a metalworking expert in the Commerce Dept.'s International Trade Administration. The Japanese also enlist workers in "quality circles" to solve production and quality problems. Lifetime job security is emphasized in Japan as well, although for limited numbers of workers in the larger companies.

WIDER SCOPE. When American managers began touring Japanese plants in the mid-1970s, the Japanese stressed the importance of these human factors, recalls Kuper of the Manufacturing Studies Board, who led some of those tours. "Our managers kept looking for the technological solution to the growing Japanese success," he says. "The Japanese were trying to be honest with us, but we were too stupid to listen."

Now, U. S. employers are belatedly turning to the human side of technology, partly by borrowing the Japanese techniques but also by using other methods. For example, Japanese companies do not emphasize a fundamental redesign of jobs to make them more appealing to workers. Furthermore, when the Japanese use production teams, they usually keep them under the control of first-line foremen.

Indeed, the semiautonomous team idea originated in experiments at British coal mines in the late 1940s. Behavioral scientists at London's Tavistock Institute of Human Relations, led by Eric Trist—now professor emeritus at the Wharton School—concluded that industry needed a new paradigm of work organization. By stressing autonomous work groups, jobs of wider scope, and worker involvement in decision-making, Trist and his colleagues said, companies could adjust much more easily to fast-changing market and political conditions.

Trist and others developed the "sociotechnical systems" concept of work design. STS calls for involving workers whenever possible in planning a new or redesigned plant, as auto workers have been involved in GM's Saturn project. Usually, the technical design came first, and work flow and the placement of work stations followed. In designing an auto plant, for example, engineers would specify a conventional assembly line that allows only one social system: Workers must stay at fixed stations along the line, performing the same task every 30 seconds or so.

"Traditionally, jobs were designed with no capacity for people to initiate anything," says Harvey F. Kolodny, a professor at the University of Toronto. "If things went wrong, you'd get an inflexible response. We should design jobs so that workers can be more than a pair of hands behaving in a mechanical way."

To give workers a greater variety of duties, a sociotechnical auto-plant design would call for teams to assemble entire subunits of a car from parts moved through the plant on AGVs. Team members would be free to move around, rotate jobs, pace themselves within a much longer work cycle of perhaps five minutes or more, and have more control over product quality. Studies show that group assembly not only makes workers feel better but also produces higher quality.

The STS concept moved from Britain to Norway and Sweden, where Volvo used it in designing its plant at Kalmar, Sweden, which opened in

1974. Kalmar's work force is divided into about 20 production teams; each assembles a major unit of a car in an average of 20 minutes to 40 minutes. Production costs at Kalmar are 25% lower than at Volvo's conventional plants, and the com-

---

> 'Once in a while I get
> bored and switch jobs
> with someone just
> to relieve the tedium'

---

pany is building a new plant at Uddevalla based on the Kalmar experience.

Teamwork also began to appear in the U. S. in the 1960s. But for years it was confined to a handful of pioneering companies, including Procter & Gamble, Cummins Engine, Gaines Foods, Sherwin-Williams, the Packard Electric Div. of *GM*, Hewlett-Packard, *TRW*, and Best Food, a unit of *CPC* International.

In the past few years, scores of companies that traditionally set the patterns in industrial relations have adopted the concept. Among them are General Electric, Ford, most *GM* divisions, and Westinghouse, as well as Xerox, Honeywell, Digital Equipment, and other high-tech companies. Shell Canada Ltd. runs four chemical and refinery plants with sociotechnical principles. Even the financial services industry is picking up the concept. In addition to Shenandoah Life, Lincoln National Life and American Transtech have reorganized their paper-processing operations into teams, and one giant insurance company, Aetna, is on the verge of doing so.

For the most part, the teamwork movement has been a quiet revolution. Many of the leading companies have not trumpeted their findings, partly because they believed their innovations provided a competitive edge. Now some of the pioneers are opening up a bit, and their evidence of superior performance in teamwork is impressive.

Procter & Gamble Co., which established its first team-based plants in the 1960s and now has 18 such sites, has always refused to comment publicly on the matter. However, it confirms remarks made in late 1984 by Senior Vice-President David Swanson in a closed meeting at Harvard. Swanson said *P&G*'s teamwork plants were "30% to 40% more productive than their traditional counterparts and significantly more able to adapt quickly to the changing needs of the business."

PERSON TO PERSON. Cummins Engine has three teamwork plants, including the North Carolina site, and has used elements of the team approach at its older plants in Columbus, Ind. Cummins also has been reticent about the new-style plants. But in a recent interview with *BUSINESS WEEK*, Vice-President Ted L. Marsten said that Cummins is convinced that "this is the most cost-effective way to run plants. In traditional plants, work was broken down to the lowest common denominator, and there was not a lot of flexibility. We created teams to get the work to flow in the most productive way. The people felt a lot better about the work they did, and we got a much higher-quality product."

In Oregon, Tektronix Inc. converted a few years ago from assembly-line manufacturing in its metals group to teams. Each "cell" of 6 to 12 workers turns out a product that can be manufactured in relatively few steps. One particular cell now turns out as many defect-free products in three days as an entire assembly line did in 14 days with twice as many people. Xerox Corp. began using teams in some of its operations a few years ago and has found them to be "at least 30% more productive" than conventionally organized operations, says Dominick R. Argona, manager of employee involvement.

The Gaines Foods plant in Topeka, which received heavy publicity in the early 1970s for its new style of management, has proved that teamwork there was not a passing fad. Fifteen years after it started production, the plant still uses teamwork—both in the office and on the shop floor. Plant manager Herman R. Simon says Topeka produces the same pet foods as a sister plant in Kankakee, Ill., at 7% lower labor costs. Once a unit of General Foods Corp., Gaines is now a wholly owned subsidiary of Anderson, Clayton & Co.

Shenandoah Life's decision to embrace teamwork is a classic illustration of why technology can't solve all problems. Even after installing an automated system, the company found that processing clerks were still, in effect, "passing papers from person to person electronically," says Myers. "It made no sense to have a new technology and yet operate the old social system."

Since experimenting with one clerical team in 1983, Shenandoah has formed nine teams of employees who before worked in separate departments. Former first-line supervisors belong to a team that "advises" the processing groups. Shenandoah has never laid off employees, but the team system has enabled it to reduce the work force by 14%, down to 229, over the past year and a half.

'TURF ISSUES.' The team approach also can help shape the kinds of goods and services a company produces. Shenandoah's disability income team—which includes an actuary, an underwriter, and a marketing specialist—took only six months to develop and market a policy amendment designed to attract new business. If all the skills needed to design a new product are contained in one team, Myers says, product development doesn't get hung up on the "turf issues" that arise when several departments are involved in planning a new product.

Because of the difficulty in changing the culture and management style in existing plants, most teamwork plants are "greenfield" sites, and most are nonunion. Indeed, the sociotechnical trend can present a problem for unions. Where employees have been allowed a strong voice in decision-making and largely manage themselves in teams, organizers have had a tough time presenting a case for unionization.

A number of unions, however, have worked jointly with management to convert existing plants to the team concept. These include the Auto Workers, Electronic Workers, Clothing & Textile Workers, and Steelworkers. One successful example involves the Aluminum Workers and a Rohm & Haas Co. plexiglass plant in Knoxville, Tenn. Within four years after the plant began changing to team organization, productivity—measured as square feet of plexiglass produced per worker-hour—had risen some 60%.

But resistance to the concept remains fairly strong in these and other unions because it requires changes in many traditional union-management relations. Instead of multiple job classifica-

> 'Bureaucratic organizations become habit-forming, just like cigarettes. That's why they don't change.'

tions, for example, a teamwork plant usually has only one or two. Production and maintenance work, traditionally separated under the scientific management organization of work, tend to merge into one fluid work system.

HIGH ANXIETY. For all its productiveness, teamwork is very difficult to implement and keep working successfully. Changes in plant and corporate management, from participative to old-style managers, have doomed many a promising teamwork experiment. Personality conflicts in teams also cause problems. Indeed, says Cummins' John Read, tension levels in sociotechnical plants tend to be higher than in conventional workplaces. "It's wrong to think of teamwork plants as merely happy places," he says. "But the tensions tend to be constructive, and they produce high performance."

High performance is what U. S. industry needs if it is to make the most of computer-based automation, say technology experts. While the U. S. is still behind Japan in matching workers and new manufacturing techniques, it is trying to catch up. "We need work environments that produce continuous innovation in a highly competitive global economy," says Eric Trist. The new model of work relations is not yet the dominant one, he adds, but "I'd be sad if we weren't getting close to that point by the end of the century."

By John Hoerr in New York and Michael A. Pollock in Washington, with David E. Whiteside in Detroit and bureau reports

STEELMAKERS WANT TO MAKE TEAMWORK AN INSTITUTION

SEVEN COMPANIES UNITE ON WORKER-MANAGEMENT COOPERATION

MAY 11, 1987, P. 84

Cooperation has been a buzzword in the U. S. steel industry since 1980, when the United Steelworkers and big steelmakers agreed to form "labor-management participation teams." *LMPT*s have spread to many steel plants since then, but only piecemeal: Not all local union and management officials have been interested in the idea. This has dissatisfied *LMPT* backers, who believe that the teams can improve efficiency as well as working conditions in troubled U. S. mills. So now eight companies have begun an unusual joint effort with the *USW* to institutionalize *LMPT*s throughout the industry.

The idea of a coordinated approach to worker participation developed last November after several companies and the *USW* got a $25,000 training grant from the Labor Dept. to teach participation techniques to their staffs. The pilot project went so well that the group formed a joint planning committee to continue the process. The seven companies involved are Inland, *LTV*, Bethlehem, Wheeling-Pittsburgh, Armco, Acme, and Cleveland-Cliffs. Several other companies haven't joined the planning committee but will participate in the training, including industry leader *USX*, which has long had a combative relationship with the *USW*. Officials from all the companies will join high-level union officers in a two-week training session starting on May 18 at a union education center in Dawson, Pa.

NO SWEEPING CHANGES. "I think both sides feel that *LMPT*s can improve the industry," Sam Camens, a staff official who has spearheaded partici-

pation efforts for the *USW*, told union and company officials at an Apr. 24 meeting in Princeton, N. J. "But," he added, "there's a feeling that we haven't given it the total support that the idea needs for local union and management to go ahead with it."

The main function of *LMPT*s is to tap steelworkers' knowledge of their jobs. The idea is that because workers are intimately acquainted with the shop floor, they should have good notions about how to do things more safely and efficiently. Participation teams in steel are similar to so-called quality circles that have been tried in other industries. Usually they consist of 10 to 15 workers who meet every week or so to consider how their jobs might be done better. Because the bene-

ONE APPROACH TO WORKER PARTICIPATION

Level	Members	Function
POLICY COMMITTEE	Senior corporate, plant, and union leaders	Set long-term policy, plan alternatives to layoffs
ADVISORY COMMITTEE	Middle-management and local union leaders	Develop and co-ordinate teams, help implement team suggestions
TEAMS	10-15 workers and a leader in different plant departments	Identify and analyze problems and implement solutions

DATA: PARTICIPATIVE SYSTEMS INC.

fits derived from workers' suggestions often are small and incremental, they can be difficult to quantify. But the *USW* and many steel companies are convinced that they can help make a difference in the ailing industry's fortunes.

National Steel Corp., a joint venture of National Intergroup Inc. and Nippon Kokan, a Japanese steel producer, has been one of the most enthusiastic endorsers of *LMPT*s. Richard P. Coffee, National's vice-president for human affairs, says that 1,200 of the company's 8,225 union workers participate. He's sure the teams save money as well as improve life in the mills, and he points to a National plant in Portage, Ind., as an example. On a tin-plating line there, steel is bathed in an extremely caustic cleaning solution that used to be transported to the mill in tank trucks, transferred to a hopper, and then taken by forklift to the bath. "It was a very dangerous operation," says Coffee.

About six months ago, an *LMPT* devised a system in which the truck was driven directly to the bath, eliminating the messy transfer step. "It did away with 90% of the potential for burns," says Coffee. In addition, an automatic feed system was created that shuts off the cleaning solution's flow at the proper time. This reduced the waste that had occurred when too much fluid entered the bath. Coffee estimates that the combined changes save about $40,000 a month. "*LMPT*s have been a great success at National," agrees Buddy W. Davis, a *USW* Midwest district director.

SURVIVAL INSTINCTS. Executives at A. O. Smith Corp., which uses steel to make components for the auto industry, go even further. They say *LMPT*s are crucial to their company's survival. Together with its independent Smith Steel Workers Union, the company has been using a system devised by Participative Systems Inc. in Princeton (table, page 127), one of several consultants that have been helping set up *LMPT*s. Smith says that the participation efforts, in conjunction with other moves such as big cuts in white-collar employment, will help it reduce its prices drastically in the next several years. "Our customers wanted huge price cuts, and we either have to reduce prices or lose

volume," says Terrence J. Baudhuin, a Smith senior vice-president.

*LMPT*s won't become a routine part of steelmaking overnight. Union and management officials at the companies involved in the latest joint effort will receive the same training in participation and problem-solving techniques. But each company, and even each plant, probably will continue to implement the process in a somewhat different way.

In addition, some union members fear that *LMPT*s are just another management method for squeezing more work out of them. And although the *USW*'s contracts typically provide job protection for work that is eliminated after *LMPT* suggestions, some workers still feel that they are undercutting their long-term livelihood. "Workers are reluctant to come up with good ideas that will eliminate jobs," says the *USW*'s Davis. Still, the beleaguered steel industry can't pass up any opportunity to compete, and the survival instincts of workers and managers alike should give *LMPT*s a good chance to spread through much of the U. S. steel business.

By Aaron Bernstein in Princeton and Matt Rothman in Pittsburgh

DISCUSSION QUESTIONS

1. It is often suggested that whereas Japan has seen cooperation between labor and management increase, the United States has had adversarial labor-management relations. What role do you think this difference plays in productivity?

2. Robert Howard's book *Brave New Workplace* reports instances in which workers in groups such as quality circles have raised concerns about workplace health and safety conditions and been told such topics are outside the scope of their committees. Does this experience validate worker's concerns that such participative arrangements are more like exploitation than workplace democracy? Discuss.

3. Is an industry-wide approach to teamwork more promising than one developed on a company-by-company basis?

DETROIT VS. THE UAW: AT ODDS OVER TEAMWORK

EVEN THE UNION IS SPLIT OVER A MOVE FOR JAPAN-STYLE PRODUCTION

AUGUST 24, 1987, PP. 54-55

It sounded like a reasonable request last fall when General Motors Corp. asked the 9,000 workers at its Pontiac (Mich.) truck and bus plant to accept a production system based on Japanese-style teams. GM wanted a new local contract easing union work rules that impede such changes. In return, it promised to consider giving Pontiac a new truck to build. Local leaders of the United Auto Workers say that after they rejected GM's proposal, the company went ahead with teams anyway. GM also announced that it would build the new truck at another plant that has agreed to work rule changes. This and other issues boiled over into a four-day strike last March that blocked teams at Pontiac. Declares Local 594 President Donny G. Douglas: "The traditional system can work."

The dispute highlights what is fast becoming a central issue in current negotiations at GM and Ford Motor Co., whose labor pacts expire on Sept. 14. GM, Ford, and Chrysler have toyed for years with the team concept. Now, based in part on the astonishing productivity achieved at a Toyota-GM joint venture in Fremont, Calif., Detroit has settled on teams as a key way to compete with imports and new U. S. factories owned by Japanese carmakers. GM wants UAW President Owen F. Bieber to make a commitment to teams in the national contract—paving the way for GM in negotiations at local plants where work-rule changes are decided.

STEEP PRICE. This prospect is causing turmoil in the union. Donald F. Ephlin, the UAW's chief negotiator at GM, believes that teams can make work more fulfilling and save jobs by making the industry more competitive. His position has provoked a severe attack from UAW dissidents who blame union leaders for letting GM pit one plant against another. The split ensures that the companies will have to pay dearly to win an endorsement in the national contracts.

In early August the UAW added a dramatic new job security proposal to its demands. Going beyond its traditional goal of protecting current workers, the union said it wants to guarantee a specific number of jobs—an idea long rejected by Detroit as too risky. Surprisingly, GM responded Aug. 12 by offering some job guarantees for a UAW commitment to plant-level efficiency gains—most of which would come from teams.

Teams really are just one element of a more efficient alternative to the mass production system popularized by Frederick Winslow Taylor 85 years ago. He argued that work should be chopped into small, repetitive tasks simple enough to be done by "a child or a gorilla." As unions organized, their contracts codified work rules governing these employer-designed job classifications. This produced a rigid system that employers have been trying to change for several decades.

By contrast, worker participation and flexibility are bywords of the team philosophy. At its heart is the idea of training workers to perform several jobs instead of just one, so that they'll be less bored and more motivated. Management also hands over some control of production on the theory that employees will design a workplace more efficiently than management can. Coupled with this is a range of new manufacturing methods such as just-in-time inventory control. A key ingredient is the guarantee that if an employee finds a more efficient way to work, he won't be laid off.

A number of U. S. manufacturers have experimented with teams recently, including General Electric, Goodyear, and Procter & Gamble. De-

THE LURE OF TEAM PRODUCTION

1   A MORE FLEXIBLE ORGANIZATION—A components or assembly plant is divided into teams composed of as few as 5 or as many as 20 employees who already work next to one another. Unlike the procedure in a traditional plant where each worker does one specific job, team members learn several jobs. Work can thus be reorganized as needed.

2   HIGHER PRODUCTIVITY—Because so many workers are trained in more than one job, classifications are reduced from as many as 100 to as few as 2, and union work rules are loosened. As a result, output jumps by 20% to 40%. A major union objection: Some members feel that without work rules, management will overwork them.

3   MORE WORKER SATISFACTION—Teams give employees more control over their jobs and a greater variety of work. A team might come up with a better way to install windshields, for example, traditionally a responsibility of industrial engineers. The team also decides who does what—decisions previously made by foremen and governed by seniority.

4   AND BETTER PRODUCT QUALITY—The traditional approach in American industry has been to emphasize speed of production and to fix whatever mistakes were made later. By contrast, the team concept encourages employees to solve quality problems as they occur. That way quality can approach levels achieved in Japanese plants.

DATA: BW

troit started in 1973, when the *UAW* suggested giving workers more control through a process known as quality of work life. But companies remained cool to such approaches until they realized that giving workers more control would improve productivity.

This, indeed, has happened. The *GM*-Toyota venture, New United Motor Manufacturing Inc. *(NUMMI)*, makes fewer models and less complex cars than when it was just a *GM* plant. But most experts say teams are a main reason *NUMMI* makes about the same number of units with about half the workers. Mark Hogan, *NUMMI*'s general manager, says his plant is some 20% less productive in man-hours per vehicle than Toyota, which may be the world's most efficient carmaker. But

that's 10 points better than a year ago, and Hogan expects to catch up in time. More important, the consensus is that *NUMMI* is 20% to 40% more efficient than most *GM* plants.

Actually, *GM* learned about teams before *NUMMI*. The going was bumpy after the company opened its Shreveport (La.) light-truck assembly plant with teams in 1981. But by 1984 management and the union agreed to persuade, rather than force, workers to learn multiple jobs with an approach called pay-for-knowledge. As workers learn more jobs, their hourly pay goes up, to a maximum of 50¢ over the base wage of $12.82 an hour. The flexibility this creates makes it easy to operate more efficiently.

JOB-SWAPPING. Recently, management wanted to cut a job from the team of Dave Smith, who installs rear bumpers. "The team experimented with different ways to get rid of the work," says Smith, who came to Shreveport in 1984 from *GM*'s Tonawanda (N. Y.) plant. "We all switched jobs and came up with four or five different plans for cutting a job." The team is still deciding which of the two best schemes to adopt, and whoever's job goes will move to another part of the plant. "But at my old plant, management would just have told us to do it their way," says Smith.

The flexibility of teams also holds down the need for relief workers, and it reduces boredom. Earnest Hilliard, who's been at Shreveport since 1981, says that it's easy to cover for an absent comrade—or just switch jobs for a while—as long as some team members know several jobs. "I used to switch jobs for half a day with one of my buddies just because we were bored," he says. "It makes the day go by faster."

Today, Shreveport is one of *GM*'s best plants. *GM*'s weekly internal Labor Performance Report rates each plant according to its overall labor efficiency. "We're not first every week, but on average we are," says Thomas Dennig, the plant's production manager. The report also measures the number of hours needed to build a vehicle. In the week ended Aug. 2, Shreveport's hourly and salaried work forces averaged 23.2 hours—the lowest in *GM* and the same as *NUMMI*'s.

Coming off such successes, "*GM* has decided to spread teams to all its 175 plants," says *NUMMI*'s

Hogan. *GM* has started teams in a dozen or more components plants. Since January, 30-odd assembly plants have sent groups of managers and *UAW* officers to study *NUMMI*. *GM* also set up an executive task force headed by Richard M. Donnelly, to develop a "common" *GM* production system involving everything from materials handling to teams. *GM* already has decided to use *NUMMI*'s five-member teams as its model instead of those in Shreveport, which average 15 people.

Though many *UAW* members welcome teams as a way to achieve industrial democracy, *GM*'s impatience has provoked mounting resistance. Some workers feel teams are a company trick to get them to work harder. A vocal minority has railed at *UAW* conventions against what it calls "whipsawing," or management playing one local against another, as the union claims occurred at Pontiac.

The dissidents point to *GM*'s decision to close its Norwood (Ohio) assembly plant as another example. Both Norwood and *GM*'s Van Nuys (Calif.) plant made the same car, but Norwood made them for about $600 a car cheaper. Nonetheless, last year, *GM* decided to shut down its Norwood plant and keep Van Nuys open, largely because Van Nuys has agreed to switch to teams. Alfred S. Warren Jr., *GM*'s vice-president of labor relations, denies that this constitutes whipsawing. A longtime supporter of teams, he insists that worker cooperation can't be forced. But, he adds, "if I have to put a new product somewhere, I'm going to put it where the attitude is most cooperative."

Resistance also stems from lower-level managers' reluctance to give up power. Most team systems replace foremen with team leaders, who are union members. Remaining managers must suggest and discuss rather than issue orders, which is a major cultural change for many. Says Ken Norden, a manager "at an old-style, dog-eat-dog *GM* plant in Baltimore" before he moved to Shreveport: "The adjustment was a little hard for me at first. It's difficult to share respect with others. I got used to it, but many managers can't who grew up in the old, dictatorial role."

The bigger problem is *GM*'s need to move fast

as its profits sink—which creates something of a catch-22. Management is growing more desperate to get productivity gains from teams. But by pushing too hard for the union to accept them, *GM* risks causing so much worker resentment that much of the new system's motivational benefits could be lost.

BIG RISKS. The Japanese avoid this problem by exchanging job security for worker cooperation—and that may be what's in the works in current auto talks. *NUMMI* managers reduced the *UAW*'s fear of job losses by promising that they would bring work now subcontracted to outside companies back into the plant and even to take pay cuts themselves before laying off workers. Both *GM* and Ford could bring in subcontracted work if their plants were more productive.

The big question is how far they'll go to meet the union's demand for a guaranteed number of jobs. The *UAW* may be content to establish that principle without insisting on the 370,000 jobs Ephlin has mentioned—the *UAW* employment at *GM* before it recently idled 41,000 workers indefinitely. But the risks are large. With a high guarantee, an economic downturn could leave the companies paying many employees for whom there was no work. Detroit's willingness even to discuss such a deal is one indication of the promise of teams.

"We see domestic and foreign manufacturers making significant quality and productivity improvements by adopting more flexible systems," says Stanley J. Surma, Ford's chief labor negotiator. "We think this notion needs to be discussed at the national level."

By Aaron Bernstein in Shreveport, La., and Wendy Zellner in Pontiac, Mich.

DISCUSSION QUESTIONS

1. Discuss the underlying issue of trust as a prerequisite for labor-management cooperation.
2. How do the proposals discussed in the article reveal problems of mistrust and attempt to promote trust?
3. What advantages would you expect teamwork to offer?

PART 4

LEADING

Part 4's articles report on issues of leadership, corporate culture, change, conflict, and human resources management. The first five articles depict the successes and troubles of five CEOs. The next four focus on culture, change, and conflict in various organizations.

How corporate leaders embed their values in the culture of organizations is perhaps at the heart of leading. The constant need to change and the conflict that changing conditions and multiple objectives foster challenge leaders. All of these articles show how managers on the firing line respond to these challenges.

The final seven articles describe corporate practices, developments in the law, and issues in the crucial area of human resources management. Rapid and important change in this area necessitates increased vigilance and flexibility in leadership to keep organizations competitive and to enhance the quality of life at work. As the articles make clear, today's challenges call for the best leadership skills.

THE BILLION-DOLLAR WHIZ KID

AT 31, BILL GATES HAS BUILT MICROSOFT INTO A SOFTWARE POWERHOUSE

APRIL 13, 1987, PP. 68-72, 76

On a spring day nearly a year ago, after an all-night flight from Seattle, Bill Gates arrived for a meeting at *IBM*'s suburban New York offices. He hardly expected the bad news that awaited him. Four years earlier, the boyish chairman of Microsoft Corp. had dreamed up a piece of software, called Windows, that he hoped would push his company to the top of the personal-computer software industry. Gates was betting that International Business Machines Corp., already his prime customer, would eventually use the product in its personal computers, guaranteeing that the program would sell millions of copies. He was so sure of it that he had built much of Microsoft's long-term growth strategy around that one product. Now *IBM* was saying no—it would design its own program.

For a moment, Gates seemed destined to join the dozens of entrepreneurs who over the years had hitched their stars to *IBM*, then faltered when the No. 1 computer maker switched gears. But he hadn't built 12-year-old Microsoft from a startup to the No. 2 personal-computer software company by being meek. Nose-to-nose with William C. Lowe, the executive in charge of *IBM*'s personal-computer business, Gates argued Microsoft's case.

Windows had a two-year headstart over *IBM*'s product, Gates insists. Lowe countered that Gates didn't understand complicated communications between computers. Gates rebutted that he understood personal computer customers better than *IBM*. In two hours Gates had won a reprieve. He would work with *IBM*'s engineers to modify Windows to their liking. And *IBM* would see if it could do business that way. It could.

A VISION. On Apr. 2, *IBM* chose Windows officially as a key piece of software for the new generation of machines it's counting on to regain dominance in the personal-computer business (page 137). Windows will be built into a new operating system—the software that controls a computer's basic functions and runs applications software such as spreadsheets—that has been developed jointly by *IBM* and Microsoft. It will be sold with every new *IBM* personal computer except the most basic model—practically guaranteeing Microsoft's role as the key player in personal-computer software. "All the work I've been doing is finally seeing the light of day," says Gates.

More than just the story of a product, the *IBM*-Windows deal reveals the essence of William H. Gates III. At 31, the co-founder of Microsoft is typical in many ways of the young entrepreneurs who created the personal-computer industry in the 1970s. Competitors call him a technical genius. Gates still talks zealously about his "vision" of bringing computing power to "the masses." He even acts embarrassed when visitors note that since Microsoft went public a year ago, its stock has more than quadrupled, to about 90, making his 45% of the company worth roughly $1 billion.

But Gates's most notable characteristic is the one that makes him atypical: He has staying power. Over the past five years, while co-founder Steven P. Jobs was being forced out of Apple Computer Inc. and founder Mitchell D. Kapor was opting out at Lotus Development Corp., Gates was staying in control at Microsoft and turning it into a highflier. Whether by good planning or fast footwork, the intense bachelor who likes to drive his Jaguar a little too fast has become that rarest of entrepreneurs: one with the right blend of youthful energy, technical acumen, intellectual breadth, and business savvy to adjust as his company matures.

"Bill is very good at evaluating situations as they change," says Vern L. Raburn, a former Microsoft executive who is now chairman of software producer Symantec Corp. As Microsoft grew, for instance, Gates brought in professional managers to help run it. Adds Raburn: "He learned at a young age that you've got to give up power to get power."

AT THE CENTER. The results speak for themselves. Only a dozen years after his passion for computers led him to drop out of Harvard University, Gates has created a key company in the $35 billion personal-computer industry. Aside from the microprocessor, software is the most crucial part of a computer and is fast becoming the most profitable. And Microsoft is at the center of the personal-computer software business.

Windows, which uses graphics similar to those of Apple's Macintosh, will make *IBM PC*s much easier to use by simplifying the commands needed to operate them. It should boost the royalties Gates already gets from *IBM*. And it will do a lot more. Other software companies, which tend to create new products only for the best-selling computers, will write programs to run in concert with Windows. The resulting flood of software will make Windows *de rigueur* for the makers of *IBM* clones, who will have no choice but to offer it on their machines. Gates will be there to sell them the new operating system with Windows. The result: As early as next year, analysts say, Microsoft could displace Lotus as No. 1 in personal-computer software.

Of course, Gates has been a central figure in the microcomputer industry for years. The program that put Microsoft on the map and that still accounts for about 50% of its revenues is *MS-DOS*, the operating system for *IBM*'s original *PC*. Once *IBM* chose it, *MS-DOS* became an industry standard—just as Gates expects that Windows will. Compaq, Tandy, and all the clone makers followed *IBM*, and by last year *MS-DOS* was used on about 58% of the 7.1 million personal computers sold in the U. S.

Now Microsoft plans to make itself even more

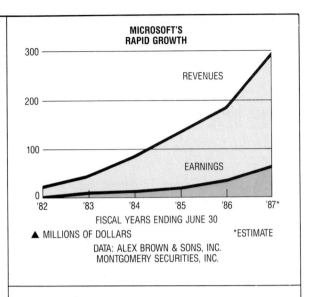

MICROSOFT'S
RAPID GROWTH

REVENUES

EARNINGS

FISCAL YEARS ENDING JUNE 30
▲ MILLIONS OF DOLLARS   *ESTIMATE
DATA: ALEX BROWN & SONS, INC.
MONTGOMERY SECURITIES, INC.

indispensable. It's writing a new operating system, called OS/2, for the three-year-old *IBM PC/AT*, plus another for the extremely powerful generation of new 32-bit personal computers, based on Intel Corp.'s new 80386 microchip, that *IBM* and others are just introducing. Both machines have lacked sophisticated enough software to take full advantage of the power of their chips—or to deliver the productivity that computer makers have promised. With the new operating systems, the machines will be able to perform several tasks at once—and handle the voluminous software instructions and graphics needed to make *PC*s nearly as easy to use as typewriters. The system for the *PC/AT* should be ready within nine months, the one for the 32-bit machine a year after that.

AVID READER. Despite its own huge software development budget, *IBM* wound up relying on Gates because he has what Intel Vice-President David L. House calls "an *IQ* that would peg the *IQ* meter." Gates's high school English teacher, Anne S. Stephens, recalls him memorizing a three-page soliloquy for a school play in one reading. He devours biographies of great scientists, businessmen, and politicians—to understand, he says, how they thought. At Microsoft, he focuses on technology, leaving management to President Jon A. Shirley, 48, hired from Tandy Corp. in 1983.

IBM'S NEW PC: HOMEGROWN AND HARDER TO CLONE

The new personal computers that International Business Machines Corp. has announced will no doubt prove to be a milestone for Bill Gates's Microsoft Corp. With these new machines, *IBM* has endorsed Gates's pet project, the software package called Windows, which presents information in an eye-catching graphic format. That endorsement should make Microsoft's programs among the most popular on the market. But the new *PCs* may be an even bigger milestone for *IBM*. They represent an aggressive attempt by the computer giant to regain its momentum in the personal-computer industry.

The company introduced four machines: two replacements for its *PC/AT* and one for its basic *PC*, plus a 32-bit machine that's as powerful as a small minicomputer. But as important as the computers themselves is *IBM*'s design approach. For the first time since the *PC* was hatched in an obscure laboratory in Florida six years ago, the company is focusing its full technological and marketing expertise on its personal computers.

In its rush to market with the original *PC* in 1981, *IBM* wound up with a product that was only about 20% its own design and 80% off-the-shelf parts. It was easy to clone. By contrast, about half the technology going into the new machines is being developed by *IBM*. On the 32-bit machine, the figure is 80%. The Entry Systems Div., the unit in charge of *PCs*, has called on its sister divisions for everything from chips to disk drives. "We're bringing high-end and intermediate systems technology to the *PC* business," says Edward J. Kfoury, *ESD* vice-president for development. The new *PCs* are dubbed "Personal Systems" to underscore their role as partners with *IBM* mainframes and midrange computers in corporate networks.

STEEPER PATH. *IBM* also is relying on its own semiconductor and manufacturing talents to distance itself from the competition. All the new machines use *IBM*-built chips that incorporate critical functions such as graphics. The basic electronics are constructed using a highly automated technique called surface-mounting. It requires a heavy investment in production equipment but delivers enormous savings when large volumes are manufactured. *IBM* has been perfecting its surface-mounting procedures for more than a year. Rival Compaq Computer Corp. started its first surface-mount line this winter.

The big news for the rest of the industry is what *IBM* didn't do: It didn't switch to totally proprietary hardware and software. That would have made it harder for customers to tailor the new *PCs* to their businesses, thus limiting *PC* sales. However, *IBM* did design a new way of sending graphic images to a screen and embedded that software in custom microchips. The machines' design also doubles the amount of software that will have to be written to make a clone 100% compatible with a new *PC*. Together, these two changes should slow down clone makers considerably—but it won't stop them. Says Dennis W. Andrews, an *ESD* product manager: "We're just making the path a little steeper."

By Geoff Lewis in New York

Even so, he's become an expert on legal issues, tax law, marketing and distribution, and accounting. He has also kept his ego in check, winning his employees' respect. "There are a lot of geniuses who can't affect the direction of the world," says House. "Bill can, because he's a shrewd businessman."

Gates developed a talent for business early. From a close-knit and prominent Seattle family, he grew up stimulated by bright people. His father, the first in his family to graduate from college, is a partner in Shidler McBroom Gates & Lucas, now Microsoft's law firm. His mother, a former schoolteacher, is a director of First Interstate Bank, chairwoman of United Way International, and a member of the University of Washington Board of Regents. Gates recalls that at the dinner table, he and his sisters, Kristianne and

Libby, heard lively discussions of his parents' work. "It was a rich environment in which to learn," he says. He still visits his parents' house, less than a mile from his own, for dinner a couple of Sundays a month.

'HOOKED.' Gates's parents enrolled him at Lakeside School, a private middle and high school known for being academically rigorous. There, at 14, he found his calling. Lakeside's Mothers Club put its rummage-sale proceeds for 1969 into a terminal linked by phone to a computer at a local computer company. Young "Trey," as his family called him, reflecting the "III" after his name, "became hooked on it," says his father, Bill Gates Jr. "Completely engrossed."

With three friends, Gates started the Lakeside Programming Group, and soon he and another member, Paul G. Allen, were sneaking back to the computer center in the middle of the night. During the day, they'd often skip gym class. Allen, who co-founded Microsoft and now runs a new software startup, still describes their experiences in metaphysical terms. "There's a certain clarity to [computing], a beauty to it. It's an art form," he says. "There was a period," concedes Gates, "when people thought we had gone overboard."

It was at Lakeside, where Gates once matter-of-factly told a teacher he'd be a millionaire some-day, that his flair for business took root. While his contemporaries were fascinated by computer technology, Gates also was fascinated by its practical uses. In his eighth-grade year, the Lakeside programmers started two commercial projects, whose profits paid for computing time. One developed a computerized payroll system for the school. The other used a computer to count the holes punched in cards by machines that monitor highway traffic.

Gates was temporarily kicked out of the group because he was two years younger than the others. But his friends soon found they couldn't do without him. When he came back it was on his terms: He headed the projects, and when the group created a company two years later to sell the traffic-counting system to municipalities, he was named president. The choice was obvious by then: He was the one group member who read business magazines.

Gates and Allen left Lakeside full of ambition. In 1973, when Gates enrolled at Harvard, Allen left the University of Washington and moved to Boston, too. There, the pair tried to think up new businesses involving computers. Opportunity knocked in the form of a cover story in *Popular Electronics* on a company called *MITS*, an Albuquerque-based maker of rockets and electronic kits. *MITS* sold a computer kit that used a new microprocessor from Intel and needed a computer language that hobbyists could use to program the machine. Gates and Allen thought they could write a condensed version of the language *BASIC*, used on large computers, that would fit the new machine's limited memory.

They beat a bunch of competitors to the task, partly because they had learned to write compact programs to hold down computing costs in high school. In June, 1975, they moved to Albuquerque and set up a partnership called Microsoft to produce the program for *MITS*. *MITS* ran into financial trouble and eventually folded. But Microsoft had found other customers in the fledgling computer industry. And in January, 1979, Gates and Allen moved their company to the Seattle area.

Enter *IBM*. It had begun to notice the mass-market potential of personal computers. Lacking its own machine and wanting to move quickly, it decided to buy most of the pieces from outside companies and approached Microsoft for an operating system. Gates didn't have one and suggested a competitor. But when *IBM* asked again, Gates saw dollar signs. He bought the rights to what he would turn into *MS-DOS* from a company called Seattle Computer Products Inc. and flew to *IBM*'s personal-computer headquarters in Boca Raton, Fla. There he bought a tie and negotiated a deal.

That contract catapulted Microsoft into the big leagues. From 1980 to 1981, its staff grew from 80 to 125 and its revenues doubled to $16 million. More important, Gates learned from *IBM*. For example, the bigger company seemed especially good at keeping development projects on schedule, something most startups can't do. It held regular meetings of new-product teams and set strict deadlines. Gates calls Microsoft's current development process about "one-third *IBM*'s and two-thirds Microsoft's."

PEPSI GENERATION. In most other ways, though, Microsoft is a 1,500-employee extension of Gates himself. Its median age is 31. Many employees share Gates's young-techie vocabulary. "Randomness" applies to any confused or haphazard situation. "Bandwidth" means the amount of information one can absorb. Things that go right are "radical," "cool," or, Gates's favorite, "super." Even Chief Financial Officer Francis J. Gaudette, at 51 Microsoft's oldest employee, is affected by the spirit. "I think young," he says. "I drink a lot of Pepsi."

The advantages of a youthful company are measurable. Microsoft people work long hours, and Gates sets the standard. He is chief strategist, oversees extensive product-development efforts, and meets regularly with his top executives, often on weekends. On weekdays he's at work from about 9:30 a.m. to midnight, though that time includes restaurant meals, often a hamburger, or talking with associates, which is "pretty relaxing stuff." Ann L. Winblad, a computer consultant and close friend, insists that after years of workaholism, Gates has learned to relax a little, even taking an occasional vacation. But, she adds, "there are parts of him that never leave the company behind." He still puts in "four or five hours on Sunday," testing new products, studying technical literature, and reading or writing memos.

The environment at Microsoft is equal parts family and West Coast informality. There are frequent picnics and parties, and every employee gets a free membership at a nearby health club. Except for scheduled meetings, programmers set their own hours. Even executives dress casually, some in jeans. Gates and Steven A. Ballmer, the vice-president for systems development who acts as liaison with *IBM*, don ties when visiting customers, but not when they are the hosts. Ballmer recalls one *IBM*er who couldn't remember a programmer's name and referred to him as "the guy without shoes." Informality works. Many Microsoft programmers earn less than they could elsewhere, though they do get stock options. Yet the company's annual turnover is less than 10%.

'OBVIOUS.' Microsoft also reflects Gates's perfectionism. His science teacher at Lakeside, William S. Dougall, says that "if a teacher was slow, he always seemed on the verge of saying, 'But that's obvious.'" At Microsoft, Gates willingly delegates authority, but he's fussy about how it's used. Vern Raburn resigned in 1982 as president of Microsoft's Consumer Products Group after Gates decided "he was not doing his best work." James C. Towne, now president of Photon Kinetics Inc., a Beaverton (Ore.) maker of fiber-optic equipment, was president of Microsoft for only a year before Gates fired him in 1983. Towne was a respected manager from Tektronix Inc., but he wasn't the technology enthusiast Gates wanted.

Still, Gates's down-to-earth manner keeps him on good terms with these people. He was best man at Raburn's wedding last May. And Towne says Gates handled his parting amicably, adding: "You can't help but respect him." The one big exception seems to be Kazuhiko Nishi, who handled Microsoft's sales in Japan until last year. The two haven't made up since they broke off their seven-year business relationship (page 140). "He's very stubborn," grouses Nishi.

Indeed, one side of Gates is abrupt and argumentative. He relies on what his father calls "hard-nosed conversational engagement" to make decisions. "It's a real part of the way he makes up his mind." When Gates starts work on a new product, he picks a team of about 10 people from engineering and marketing. It sets goals, divides up the work, then meets every couple of weeks to solve problems. And that's when Gates can be intimidating.

In one recent meeting, he swore at Charles Simonyi, Microsoft's top developer, and called his comments on a particular software feature "an extreme joke." He even offhandedly threatened to replace him. But ultimately, the decision went in favor of Simonyi. Says Jeffrey Harbors, who is in charge of developing applications software for Microsoft: "Bill has toughened us up. He used to just beat us up, and we went away feeling bad. You have to be able to take this abuse and fight back. If you back down, he loses respect. It's part of the game."

Although this approach sounds disruptive, it's hard to argue with results. With *IBM*'s business firmly in hand, Microsoft's revenues are expected to soar 52%, to more than $300 million, in the

WILL LOTUS OVERRUN MICROSOFT'S JAPANESE GARDEN?

Bill Gates's software empire has never been healthier. But there's one trouble spot. In Japan, Microsoft Corp. has run into stiff competition from archrival Lotus Development Corp. just as the $150 million market for personal-computer business software is ready to surge.

The battle is taking place at a bad time for Microsoft. Only a year ago, Gates cut his seven-year tie with longtime distributor and friend, Kazuhiko "Kay" Nishi. Nishi introduced Microsoft to Japan and boosted sales, but Gates became worried that Nishi, who has a well-known penchant for new projects, had stopped pushing Microsoft products hard enough. Under a severance agreement, the embittered Nishi kept exclusive marketing rights to Microsoft's premier application program, the Multiplan spreadsheet, for the last nine months of 1986—and did little to promote it. *ASCII* Corp., Nishi's publishing and distribution company, "had no interest in pushing Multiplan," says Masayoshi Son, president of retail distributor Softbank Corp.

BURGEONING MARKET. Microsoft is still far ahead in Japan. Its operating system, *MS-DOS*, is a virtual standard and will make up about 40% of the $23 million in revenues it expects from Japan this year. But Lotus could make it harder for Microsoft to increase its retail distribution and to sell more applications programs—a key part of its strategy. Good distribution will be crucial as the Japanese market for personal-computer business software triples to an estimated $450 million by 1992.

The Lotus threat is based on the success of the Japanese version of its 1-2-3 spreadsheet, introduced seven months ago. Industry sources esti-

fiscal year ending June 30, while net profits should increase by 80%, to $70 million. That would put it in a dead heat with Lotus as the largest microcomputer software company. At 41%, its pretax margins far exceed Lotus' 26% and the 27% of Ashton-Tate Co., the No. 3 producer of personal-computer software.

TOO TECHNICAL? The impending success of Windows also gives Microsoft a chance to increase its sales of applications software, the crucial market for long-term growth. Its first applications programs, a spreadsheet and word processor released in 1982 and 1983, were criticized as too technical. Gates added a marketing team to the development process, and by 1985 turned the emphasis from *IBM PC* programs, where Ashton-Tate and Lotus already dominated, to the popular Macintosh. The changes helped. Microsoft now sells about half of all Macintosh programs, according to market researcher InfoCorp. Excel, its spreadsheet program for the Macintosh, is considered by many to outperform even Lotus' 1-2-3.

The Windows deal means that Microsoft can concentrate again on selling applications software for *IBM PC*s. It is working on word processing software for these machines plus a data-base program, which manages records. Moreover, it is designing a version of Excel for the *PC*. "Excel is the first legitimate competitor to 1-2-3," concedes Edward Belove, Lotus' vice-president for *R&D*.

Ironically, Microsoft will get plenty of competition in this effort from *IBM*. The bigger company plans to be far more active in developing and selling highly profitable applications packages and is already offering volume discounts and a year's guarantee against defects in its programs. Matching those features will cost Microsoft and its rivals a bundle.

At least for now, Gates's victory with Windows seems to vindicate his product strategy: Decide where the future lies and bet everything on getting there first. Still, he has critics. Some claim that his vision is murky because he lacks a degree in computer science. "There are large gaps in his

mate that 1-2-3 is outselling Multiplan by 5 to 1 in retail channels. That's despite Multiplan's headstart, with 124,000 copies sold since 1983. Lotus is using the same marketing tactics that worked at home: mass-market promotion. Japanese distributors say Lotus has poured as much as $3 million into advertising.

To fight back, Microsoft has put marketing in the hands of Susumu "Sam" Furukawa, a onetime Nishi protégé. Furukawa, who was hired along with 18 other employees from *ASCII*, is heading a new Microsoft subsidiary that Gates established in May.

Competitors say that while Furukawa lacks Nishi's flamboyance, he does engender trust—an especially valued trait in Japan. He also fits the Microsoft personality profile. He got hooked on computers as an extension of a childhood hobby soldering model trains. After two years of college, he dropped out in 1978 to hang around Los Angeles and learn about computers at California State University. He returned to Japan eight months later to work for *ASCII*. "He's young and in love with the technology," says Scott D. Oki, Microsoft's executive vice-president. "He's a hacker."

JOIN THE CLUB. Furukawa's top priority is to "broaden our retail distribution." Last July he redesigned Multiplan's packaging to emphasize Microsoft's name, rather than *ASCII*'s. He also set up a retail card-membership system, a popular marketing device in Japan. Now 30,000 card-carrying customers can get support directly from the Japanese subsidiary. Furukawa, who oversees 46 employees, also says he's beefing up his retail sales team from 7 to 10. And he is increasing advertising—though he will spend only half as much as Lotus.

Some observers wonder if Furukawa knows enough about retailing. At *ASCII* he sold software the easy way—to Japan's powerful hardware makers, who in turn sold the programs through their own channels. Even detractors, however, feel that Furukawa was the best choice for the job. Now he just has to keep up with the swift pace Lotus is setting.

By Barbara Buell in Tokyo

knowledge," says an executive at one rival. Gates, who reads avidly on computer subjects, laughs off such criticism as "pretty random."

Robert Frankston, Lotus' chief scientist, also argues that Gates sometimes is "fixated on the neat technology of the week." Two years ago, Gates bet on Nishi's idea for a set of specifications that home computers makers would adopt to create a new mass market. It flopped.

NOT SCARED. Now Gates is toying with *CD ROM* technology, a technique for storing huge amounts of information on compact laser disks. Many software companies doubt that there's much of a market for this. But Microsoft is mounting a large research effort on it. In early March, it introduced its first product, a $300 program that combines word processing software with a dictionary, a thesaurus, a Zip Code directory, and Bartlett's *Familiar Quotations*. Gates thinks such products will reinvigorate the moribund home-computer market.

Perhaps the most intriguing question, asked by rivals and analysts alike, is whether Gates is taking on too much. So far, he has pulled it off. But as new technologies appear, notes Edward M. Esber, chairman of Ashton-Tate, "the paths keep multiplying."

Observers also question what will happen if Gates ever stumbles badly. He is extremely competitive and unaccustomed to losing. Last September, his *PR* firm staged a contest with editors of technical publications to prove that Microsoft's programming languages are the best in the business. Gates, who planned to compete, grew increasingly irascible the week before. Finally he told the agency to play down the contest—just in case he lost. The night before, he left a party early with a manual tucked under his arm and stayed up late to bone up on programming. The next day his mood was better: He'd won.

When pressed, Gates says he's looking forward to Microsoft's first major failure as a new, exciting challenge. "It doesn't scare me," he says. Of course, with *IBM*'s endorsement of Windows secure, there's not much to be scared of for the foreseeable future.

By Richard Brandt in Redmond, Wash.

DISCUSSION QUESTIONS

1. What characteristics and skills does the article ascribe to Gates, and how do they seem to have contributed to his leadership of Microsoft?
2. What qualities would you need to function well and be satisfied as a Gates subordinate?
3. What is Microsoft's corporate culture like, and how congruent with and supportive of its products and strategy does it appear to be?

CAN JACK WELCH REINVENT GE?

HE'S GETTING THE INDUSTRIAL GIANT READY FOR THE 21ST CENTURY

JUNE 30, 1986, PP. 62-67

In many ways, General Electric Co. is the quintessential industrial giant. Founded in 1878 to exploit the marvels of the day, Thomas A. Edison's applications of electricity, *GE* systematically built an empire of red brick and smokestacks ruled not by emperors but by cool and methodical chancellors. It grew into the most diverse of the nation's megacompanies, distributing light bulbs, plastics, and jet engines to the far corners of the earth. *GE* also became a model of management—a laboratory studied by business schools and raided by other companies seeking skilled executives. In retrospect, it all seems so natural, almost effortless.

If it ever was effortless, it certainly isn't now. Yesterday's marvels have become mundane, turned out in quantity by robots or by low-paid workers in developing nations. The hotbeds of innovation these days are small companies more akin to Edison's Menlo Park laboratories than to bureaucratic behemoths such as *GE*. As a result, the nation's third-largest company in terms of market value is undergoing the most wrenching change in its 108-year history. Chairman John Francis Welch Jr., a chemical engineer by training and a pugnacious achiever by nature, is trying to do nothing less than reinvent the big corporation. "Welch's *GE*," says Victor H. Vroom, a *GE* consultant and professor at the Yale School of Organization & Management, "is a model for the promise—and the problems—of creating the modern industrial company."

MASSIVE CUTS. Jack Welch puts it this way: "We want to be a company that is constantly renewing itself, shedding the past, adapting to change." In his book, that means concentrating on services and high-technology businesses. It also means keeping only those traditional businesses where *GE* can turn a respectable profit by dominating the market.

Welch has begun with the old-school manager's classic response to stagnating mature product lines and to more intense competition. Through massive personnel cuts and relentless divestitures of low-profit operations, he boosted earnings 54% from 1980 through 1985 despite revenue growth of only 13%. In 1980 *GE* earned about half its money from what Welch considers core manufacturing. Last year core manufacturing generated only a third of its $2.3 billion in earnings on total sales of $28.3 billion.

Welch's drastic changes have improved *GE*'s performance, but the company is not yet the superstar that he is striving to create (page 143). Profit margins have increased sharply, and *GE* has made huge productivity gains. Its stock has soared 38% in the past year, to just over 82, a record. During the Welch restructuring, however, sales have stagnated, and *GE*'s earnings growth and return on equity are well below those of the top 10% of U. S. companies.

Yet Welch's *GE* may be on the verge of cashing in on many of the moves he has made. And he recently launched two bold initiatives that will enable *GE* to push even faster into the high-tech and services sectors that he thinks will drive the economy of the 21st century. Within three business days in early June, *GE* wrote a check for $6.5 billion to buy *RCA* Corp. and another for an estimated $600 million to buy 80% of investment banker Kidder, Peabody & Co. More divestitures and drastic overhauling of the new prizes undoubtedly lie ahead. But Welch now has essentially shaped the company he wants. His task is to be as effective in generating growth from the *GE* of the future as he was at squeezing profits out of the *GE* of the past.

Moving into high tech and services, he has pared core businesses and bought RCA and Kidder Peabody

---

One thing is certain. The 5-ft. 8-in. man with the penetrating blue eyes will meet the challenge head-on, with the same combination of brute force, electrifying intelligence, and brimming self-confidence that has made him one of the most controversial occupants of America's executive suites.

At 50, Welch is a grayer version of the boy wonder who took over *GE* five years ago, but he hasn't slowed down. His 18-hour days still start with a jog at dawn through the wooded Connecticut countryside near his yellow-shuttered country ranch house, 20 mi. from *GE*'s Fairfield headquarters. On frequent long flights, he rarely takes a catnap while working from the battered "lucky" briefcase that accompanied him as he climbed his way up the hierarchy at *GE*. His first big break was the chance to run the company's young plastics business. Success there led to the top job in the consumer products division and a five-way horse race with other sector executives for the *CEO*'s chair.

NERVOUS STAFFERS. To watch him in that chair is to see a human dynamo in action. As Welch speaks, he reaches wildly for a pencil and fresh pad of white lined paper to make ragged sketches. His words tumble out, sentences abandoned midstream, showing traces of a stammer that has deviled him since childhood. The sketches resemble something a toddler might produce, but it doesn't matter: Welch is already six ideas past them.

HOW GE IS DOING: A REPORT CARD

The grades below are based on how General Electric's 1985 results rank in the BUSINESS WEEK 1000. Among these publicly traded companies with the highest market values, GE scores near the middle. But if Welch's strategy works, performance could improve sharply. Each grade is a composite of the variables in its category. If a company ranks in the top 10%, it gets an A. If it is in the 70%-90% range, it gets a B. Between 30% and 70%, it gets a C.

COMPANY: General Electric Co.
1985 SALES: $28.3 Billion
CURRENT MARKET VALUE: $37.3 Billion
MARKET VALUE RANK: 3

Category/Variable	1980	1985	Grade
PROFITABILITY & GROWTH			**C−**
Five-year annual sales growth	13.1%	2.1%	
Five-year annual earnings growth	19.2%	9.7%	
Profit margin	6.1%	8.3%	
EFFICIENCY			**C**
Sales per employee	$62,087	$93,043	
Profits per employee	$3,766	$7,684	
BALANCE SHEET			**B+**
Debt as percent of capital	22.4%	13.9%	
SHAREHOLDER VALUE			**B−**
Five-year annual return from dividends and stock appreciation	8.3%	23.8%*	
Five-year annual return on equity	18.5%	17.8%	

*As of May 30, 1986

DATA: STANDARD & POOR'S COMPUSTAT SERVICES INC.

Now a goodly portion of that energy will be focusing on his biggest new challenge—running *RCA* Corp. Already, many *RCA* staffers are getting nervous. "Morale is disastrous," says one executive. "Most of the corporate staff is going to be leaving." The reason: *RCA* is ripe for the same kind of treatment Welch administered at *GE*, where job cutting and removals of whole levels of management have reduced employment by a quarter in the last five years, to 300,000. *RCA* Chairman Thornton F. Bradshaw and President Robert R. Frederick have already done a good bit of

JACK WELCH'S BIGGEST DEALS

In the five years he's been in charge, Welch has radically transformed GE. His goals: Emphasize technology and services, and be first or second in all markets. So far Welch has sold 190 subsidiaries worth nearly $6 billion and spent $10 billion on 70 acquisitions. Here are his major deals.

ACQUISITIONS			DIVESTITURES		
Company	Principal business	Price (Millions)	Subsidiary	Principal business	Price (Millions)
INTERSIL 1981	Integrated circuits	$235	UTAH INTERNATIONAL 1984	Mining	$2,400
CALMA 1981	Computer graphics	$170	FAMILY FINANCIAL SERVICES 1984	Consumer lending	$600
EMPLOYERS REINSURANCE 1984	Financial services	$1,100	HOUSEWARE OPERATIONS 1984	Small appliances	$300
RCA 1986	Broadcasting, electronics	$6,500	AUSTRALIAN COAL HOLDINGS 1985	Mining	$213
KIDDER PEABODY 1986	Investment banking	$600	PATRICK PETROLEUM 1985	Oil production	$202

DATA: GENERAL ELECTRIC CO., FIRST BOSTON INC.

pruning by selling Hertz Corp. and most of *CIT Financial Corp.* and phasing out a costly videodisk venture. Even so, *RCA*'s nonbroadcasting operations—mainly defense and electronics—mustered puny operating profits of 4.5% of sales last year. By contrast, one of Welch's proudest achievements has been lifting his company's operating margin to nearly 15% last year from 12% the year before he took over.

For his part, Welch still isn't saying just what is in store for *RCA*. But he expects it to begin producing a profit for *GE* this year while diluting earnings per share by less than 5%. There clearly will be job cutbacks. Welch says that by the beginning of 1988 he wants the combined companies' corporate staff to be no larger than *GE*'s alone was last January—an implied reduction of about 19% overall. More detailed plans for the merger await the results of weekly meetings held since February by a committee of 17 top-level *GE* executives, each of whom has been required to bring a list of accomplishments and ideas since the previous session. Welch hopes to be ready to move by year-end.

'A CLEAN SHEET.' The thorniest problem is consumer electronics, where *GE* and *RCA* come to the table with diametrically opposed ideas. *RCA*, for instance, remains committed to manufacturing and assembling *TV* sets domestically. But *GE* decided last year to contract the work out to suppliers in the Far East. To arbitrate, Michael A. Carpenter, vice-president for business development and planning, has enlisted outside help: consultants from Telesis *USA* on manufacturing, Arthur D. Little on technologies, and Boston Consulting Group on marketing. "All options are open," says Carpenter. "We want to start with a clean sheet of paper and see if we can start a viable U. S. consumer business."

There may be more synergy in the defense business, where *GE* has been gaining rapidly. In jet engines, for instance, it has moved even with or slightly ahead of archrival Pratt & Whitney from a distant second five years ago. Add in *RCA*'s $1 billion in contracts annually, and *GE* climbs from the fourth-largest Pentagon contractor to third, behind McDonnell Douglas Corp. and General Dynamics Corp. In 1985, the combined companies would have had $7.2 billion in annual revenues from the military market—a safe haven from the foreign competition that ravaged *GE*'s consumer electronics business and threatened the small home appliances operation that it sold off to Black & Decker Inc. two years ago.

No wonder Carpenter says *GE* is "comfortable"—for now—with getting 20% of total revenues from defense. But *RCA* will get at least some new marching orders. "This merger puts pressure on *RCA* to learn to perform to budgets and strategic planning, which is where *GE* has always been a leader in the world," says Rear Admiral Stuart Platt, the Navy's advocate general for competition. What's more, Welch is unlikely to be content being No. 3 in any market. Acquisitions seem likely.

National Broadcasting Co., which Welch calls the "key asset" at *RCA*, appears to be exempt from major surgery. Under the patient guidance of Chief Executive Grant A. Tinker, the network stuck with slow-starting shows and posted steady gains before hitting it big last season with *The Cosby Show*. *NBC*, after years as an also-ran, finally made it to the top of the prime-time network rankings. Its operating earnings jumped 54% last year, to $333 million—half of *RCA*'s total earnings. Welch seems little concerned that *NBC*'s popularity might prove fickle. "What we bought was prime waterfront property," he says.

Welch, who is keeping oversight responsibility for the network to himself, will have to fill some key jobs quickly. Tinker has said he plans to step down soon. Bradshaw will remain only as a consultant. Frederick, who left *GE* four years ago in hopes of running his own company, is not expected to stay long. Frederick himself declines comment.

Integration of Kidder Peabody should be far easier. That task goes to one of Welch's protégés, Robert C. Wright, the president of General Electric Financial Services Inc. This mix of financial services businesses, mainly General Electric Credit Corp., earned $406 million last year, up from $142 million four years earlier. That makes financial services the second-biggest profit center after power systems, and its tax impact is even more impressive. Since its inception as a way to finance sales of *GE* products, *GE* Credit has moved aggressively into such things as leasing real estate and airplanes, claiming tax credits for depreciating the leased assets. With this kind of help, *GE*'s federal tax bill in recent years has ranged from zero to a minuscule $258 million.

GE's backlog of deferred taxes is so large that the tax reform bill pending in Congress, by cutting rates on that backlog, would provide a short-lived boost to earnings of an estimated 23% next year. But because the legislation reduces the incentive to exploit tax shelters, the financial group has already begun concentrating on more conventional activities by buying an insurance company and Kidder Peabody. *GE* executives, who hope to transform No. 15-ranked Kidder into one of the nation's largest investment banks, plan to become more involved in such things as leveraged buyouts and the creation of money market instruments secured by pools of auto loans and other asset-backed credits. "You'll see some interesting marriages," promises Vice-Chairman Lawrence A. Bossidy. Two already in process: the issuance of high-yield "junk" bonds and the combination of *GE* Credit's financial analysis with Kidder's research to advise ailing companies.

CONSTANT TURMOIL. Thus, for better or worse, his latest acquisitions are likely to prove the culmination of Jack Welch's response to the vision of the world he confronted when he took over *GE*. His vision: "A much smaller world, where winners and losers would be more clearly defined, with no place for also-rans." Early in his job, Welch sketched three circles containing the 15 businesses he thought *GE* should be in. Aside from a few miscellaneous operations that supported these manufacturing, service, or technology circles, the rest were marked for extinction.

He wasted no time making his vision a reality. Some 190 businesses, mostly in heavy industry, have already been sold, for a total of $6 billion. About 70 have been acquired, most in technology and services, for $10 billion. Some 100,000 jobs have been slashed. All this has put *GE* in a state of constant turmoil. And Welch's style has at times added to the friction. He doesn't pay much attention to hierarchies, preferring instead to get the news he wants directly from those involved, not their supervisors.

One former executive remembers being "in the box" with Welch, trying to get a project approved. "Jack will chase you around the room, throwing

'HE HATED LOSING— EVEN IN TOUCH FOOTBALL'

In postwar Salem, Mass., "The Pit" was an abandoned quarry where the sons of blue-collar families spent their afternoons playing baseball and basketball. "That was a scrappy place," recalls John F. Welch Jr., now the chairman and chief executive officer of General Electric Co. Friends recall it as the place where they first noticed the drive that would propel Welch throughout his life.

"He was a nice, regular guy but always very competitive, relentless, and argumentative," says Samuel E. Zoll, a friend who is now chief justice of the District Courts of Massachusetts. After all these years, Zoll still remembers how Welch chewed him out in midplay on the basketball court for letting a much bigger opponent score. "He never thought privacy was appropriate for such comments," Zoll says. No wonder Welch's high school magazine records his favorite saying as: "We're still pals?"

Welch's drive extended well beyond the basketball court. Salem was a town where most people had little education or money but a great deal of respect for both. Parents wanted their children to work hard and go to college. The Welches were no exceptions.

NO EGGHEAD. An only child, Jack Welch was born late in the lives of John Francis and Grace Welch. His father was a train conductor on the Boston & Maine. "There were tremendous support systems from our parents," Welch remembers, especially from his strong mother. "She told me I didn't have a speech impediment," he says, referring to his stammer, "just that my brain worked too fast." She backed him when he became bored with a factory job and quit.

After high school, Welch studied chemical engineering at the University of Massachusetts at Amherst. Classmates say Welch, who made the dean's list every year, was diligent but no egghead. They remember most his desire to win. "It was in his eyes. He was always looking one step ahead," says arguments and objections at you," he says. "Then you fight back until he lets you do what you want—and it's clear you'll do everything you can to make it work. It's a ritual. It's like signing up."

Such tactics have rankled some upper-level managers. A few even warn that Welch could drive away some key subordinates. Such criticism doesn't overly bother Welch: If there are occasional human sacrifices on the altar of change, so be it. Says Andrew C. Sigler, chairman of Champion International Corp., a *GE* director, and a friend of Welch: "Jack is horribly aware of the commotion *GE* has to go through. But his feelings are that if he lets up, it won't get done."

BEATING THE S&P 400. Welch can point to signs of progress. Since he took over, *GE*'s stockholders have fared a lot better than those of many other industrial giants. Each year since 1981, shareholders have been rewarded with average increases of 9% in dividends and 20% in stock price. In the same period companies in the Standard & Poor's index of 400 industrial companies showed average annual increases of 3% in dividends and 9% in price.

Welch has also maintained the strong balance sheet he inherited—and *GE*'s AAA bond rating. Even after buying *RCA* and Kidder Peabody, *GE* debt will rise from 14% to a still-conservative 32% of equity. Earnings per share should see a steady 10% or more increase annually, according to analyst Martin A. Sankey of First Boston Corp. And despite its recent rise, *GE*'s stock remains "grossly undervalued," says Sankey.

Before Wall Street gets more enthusiastic, however, Welch's leaner *GE* must show that it can achieve the stronger growth and stellar profitability that were the object of all the restructuring. Welch, in short, must show that he selected wisely in choosing the businesses he has kept and acquired. There are two prominent question marks in his future:

■ Can he convert the strong market positions he

William Mahoney, a Massachusetts businessman who was president of Welch's class. "He hated losing, even in touch football."

Friends say Welch was an accomplished, if not natural, athlete who always pushed himself to the limit. Robert C. Wright, president of *GE* Financial Services Inc. and a longtime associate, recalls Welch winning madcap ski races during sales promotions in *GE*'s plastics division, despite "looking like he was about to fall down any second." Welch still plays a competitive game of golf, sporting a 12 handicap.

In 1960, Welch took his doctorate in chemical engineering at the University of Illinois with a thesis on the role of condensation in nuclear steam supply systems. After graduation, he jumped at the chance to run a fledgling department for *GE*'s plastics division in Pittsfield, Mass. It was in Pittsfield that Welch and his wife Carolyn started to raise a family. They have been married for 27 years and have two sons and two daughters.

With one assistant, Welch shepherded a tough plastic called Noryl from the lab to a multimillion-dollar product used in car body parts and computer casings. The young engineer "was on fire," recalls Daniel W. Fox, the *GE* scientist who hired Welch. His flair was in marketing, where he turned the drab business upside down. He invited customers in to help design products and went all out on color print ads and glossy sales films. To sell plastics to the auto industry, he had comedians Bob and Ray do a radio ad in Detroit. "We saw him throw everything but the kitchen sink at the market," says William G. Simeral, an executive vice-president at Du Pont Co. who competed with Welch in those days and balefully watched *GE* overtake Du Pont in automotive plastics.

But there was no mistaking Welch's ultimate ambition. Recalls former Senior Vice-President Charles E. Reed, the division's general manager at the time: "Jack was always very sure of himself and wanted people to understand that he could operate with larger horizons." At 35, Welch was heading the division, and in two years he was group executive and a corporate vice-president. For a scrappy Salem boy who wouldn't tolerate boredom, the chairman's office was not far away.

By Marilyn A. Harris in Fairfield and Christopher Power in New York

seeks into healthy profits?

■ Can a management system shaken to its core and subjected to Welch's strong personality produce the innovations and new products needed to rejuvenate *GE*?

Welch has certainly put a distinctive stamp on management at *GE*. Under the former chairman, the patrician and reserved Reginald H. Jones, *GE* was a place where going through channels was a hallowed tradition. Welch cleared out the channels by, for one thing, eliminating sector chiefs and letting heads of businesses bring their funding requests directly to him. Many lieutenants relish reduced supervision. *GE* Financial's Wright, for example, negotiated the Kidder Peabody deal almost single-handed.

But other executives have a different perspective, attributable as much to management style as to management structure. Welch takes pleasure in giving and receiving a challenge—whether grilling a subordinate on the technical details of a project or presenting his views to the public. He once engaged a senior vice-president in a prolonged, emotional shouting match, embarrassing a roomful of managers. Then Welch thanked the subordinate for standing up to him. Welch calls this "constructive conflict." Such episodes, combined with extensive personnel cuts, mean that *GE* is no place for weaklings these days. "Every day is a tryout" for the new *GE* team, says one veteran.

As might be expected, such pressure doesn't always sit well with the troops. Those who are close enough to feel the heat from Welch but not close enough to share his confidence are most unhappy. Their complaint: Welch gets too closely involved with day-to-day operations, in one case ignoring three management layers to query a department manager about head counts.

'BETTER OPERATING GUY.' In part, *GE*'s structure, which hasn't had a slot for president or chief operating officer for more than 20 years, exacerbates the situation. But former employees blame the tension more on Welch's operational expertise—and need for control. "The main problem is he's a better operating guy than most of the people who run operations for him—and he knows it," says a former executive. Even some of Welch's

---

Welch's 'constructive conflict' and big personnel cuts make 'every day a tryout' for the new management

---

supporters wonder how innovative lower-level executives will be when subjected to what they see as the specter of constant oversight from the top man.

Welch's passion for hands-on management and technology can create problems. As sector head for the appliance group in 1978, he gave the go-ahead to develop a farfetched washing machine code-named L-7. The machine was to save energy by washing clothes by harmonic vibration, without spinning the tub. It was the great white hope for *GE*, which has never been a power in the laundry room. He maintained his interest in the product when he moved up to chief executive, and the four-year project created a machine "the size of a Titan booster," a former employee says.

The prototype cost some $15 million to $20 million and "did everything but wash clothes," says William E. Rothschild, a *GE* strategic planning veteran who is now a consultant. Rothschild and others blame Welch. The chairman's sheepish response: "I was new to the business, the case was persuasive and well-documented, and I supported it. It's not the only failure I've had."

Associates say that Welch has grown in the job. "He is more sophisticated and refined, with a broader perspective," says Bossidy. And these days Welch talks of building a spirit of sharing, though the words don't slide out quite naturally yet. "Diversity with unity is the key at *GE*," he says. He is optimistic about worldwide strategic alliances such as joint ventures. *GE* has more than

100 such arrangements, trading technology, distribution, and market presence around the world.

Some Welch subordinates also say they are more comfortable criticizing him these days. But the feeling is not universal. A group of officers were recently bothered by part of a statement of company values Welch had prepared. They felt one suggestion in it—that employees who weren't comfortable with the values should find work elsewhere—might not be received well. Before they could muster the confidence to confront Welch, however, they bought T-shirts inscribed with what *GE* staffers call the "meatball" logo and this message: "Subscribe to our values—or else!" Once confronted, Welch dropped the section.

APPLIANCE TURNAROUND. One standard Welch has not relaxed is his insistence that *GE* be No. 1 or No. 2 wherever it competes. This is a standard he has applied in restructuring the company and in allocating *GE*'s $21 billion in spending on plant, equipment, and research and development in the past five years. The favored candidates most often are high-technology businesses, such as medical equipment, but they also include plenty of the company's traditional businesses. *GE*'s track record with these core businesses may provide the best clues to whether the strategy will work.

Massive automation projects have achieved prompt results in some cases, most notably major home appliances. Roger W. Schipke, senior vice-president, recalls that when he took over as group executive in 1982, *GE*'s home appliance business "was an albatross around the company's neck." After a quarter in the red, the company made less than $10 million in the first half of 1982.

Schipke wasn't afraid to blaze new trails—especially with Welch behind him. The group executive asked for and got $1 billion over five years to automate Appliance Park in Louisville. The upshot: From 1981 to 1985, earnings nearly tripled, to $224 million. The turnaround—and the likelihood of massive continued funding by *GE*—is largely responsible for the current consolidation among rival makers, says Hans Werthen, chairman of Electrolux. His company recently acquired White Consolidated Industries Inc.

Heavy investment has also enabled *GE* to strengthen its position in railroad locomotives. After investing $350 million in its Erie (Pa.) locomotive plant, *GE* moved from a poor second in 1981 to nearly even with General Motors Corp. "Right now, they're a worthy competitor," says Peter K. Hoglund, general manager of *GM*'s Electro-Motive Div. It's not clear how profitable a competitor they are, however. *GE* recently won a prized order from China for 200 locomotives, but the company says the contract, for $200 million, was only a breakeven deal.

TURBINE TROUBLES. One core business is still in trouble: the power systems group, which includes turbines. A new man is in charge, and several plants have been closed. Even so, turbines aren't making money, concedes Vice-Chairman Bossidy, despite a recent major order, also from China. "But we'll stay," he vows. "The first thing any developing country does is put in an infrastructure—and that means power-generation systems."

The importance of turbines and locomotives runs deeper than a mere test of *GE*'s ability to rejuvenate stagnant businesses. Even pared back to their current size, the core businesses provide a

balance that could keep *GE* from being dragged down by an unforeseen shift in the economy.

Clearly, Jack Welch is undertaking one of the most massive jobs in American business. He must revive old businesses, create new ones, and blend the two into a cohesive structure. If he succeeds, *GE* will become a star performer—and retain its traditional position as a role model for American management.

By Marilyn A. Harris in Fairfield, with Zachary Schiller in Louisville, Russell Mitchell in Detroit, Christopher Power in New York, and bureau reports

DISCUSSION QUESTIONS

1. How, if at all, can an old company such as GE maintain the apparent freshness and vitality of a relatively new one such as Microsoft (discussed in the preceding article)?
2. How does John Welch appear to answer the challenge posed in question 1?
3. What characteristics of Welch does the article identify, and how do you suppose they affect his leadership effectiveness?

BIG TROUBLE AT ALLEGHENY

LAVISH PERKS, POOR INVESTMENTS—AND A BOARD THAT LET IT HAPPEN
AUGUST 11, 1986, PP. 56-61

In early 1985 a dummy corporation set up by Allegheny International Inc. purchased a magnificent Tudor home in one of Pittsburgh's best neighborhoods for $450,000. The bill for furniture, draperies, and crystal almost matched the purchase price, say former executives. Many employees were astonished by such spending in a year when *AI* lost a record $109 million. A senior executive told a colleague that one reason for the purchase was the lack of a decent hotel in Pittsburgh for entertaining directors and important clients.

The expense—less than $1 million—was not a huge sum for *AI*. The company manufactures Sunbeam and Oster appliances and had sales of $2.1 billion last year. But the fancy guesthouse is not an isolated case. It is typical of the extravagant

way of doing business at *AI* over the past five years. What's more, the extravagance continued even while stockholders watched the price of their shares tumble by as much as 70%.

AI provided its top executives with a lavish lifestyle and extraordinary benefits. Among the perks: a fleet of five jets (dubbed the "Allegheny Air Force" by insiders) and more than $30 million in personal loans available at 2% interest. Sons and daughters of senior executives were placed on the payroll—including one of the chairman's sons, who was appointed manager of a Manhattan hotel that *AI* owned. He was then allowed to live in the hotel's penthouse, which had been renovated with marble bathrooms, elaborate paneling, and other luxuries at a cost of more than $1 million.

Worst of all, Chairman Robert J. Buckley

steered the company into massive but highly risky real estate and oil and gas deals while telling shareholders little about the investments. Far afield from *AI*'s mainstream businesses, these investments were fraught with poor business judgments and even conflicts of interest that seemed to benefit company officers rather than *AI*'s owners—the shareholders. In one case, *AI* bought controlling interest in a troubled Florida condominium project in which Buckley and other top executives owned units (page 154). The purchase came after Buckley complained bitterly about repairs he needed. The huge risks in real estate and oil and gas ventures became clear only last year, when *AI* reported almost $100 million of pre-tax losses in those areas.

A three-month effort by a team of *BUSINESS WEEK* reporters and editors uncovered a pattern of questionable management practices at *AI*. Besides reviewing public documents, *BUSINESS WEEK* looked at some *AI* expense accounts and other internal documents and interviewed more than 30 former and present managers and executives, as well as past board members. Most requested anonymity.

BUSINESS WEEK repeatedly requested interviews with company executives and directors and submitted written questions. On July 30, *AI* said that no interviews would be granted. It said an earlier story "demonstrates an extremely negative bias to the company" (BW—May 19). *AI* also said some of the questions asked by *BUSINESS WEEK* touched on areas covered in a current Securities & Exchange Commission inquiry. The company's review has shown that the questions from *BUSINESS WEEK* are not justified, *AI* said. The company's auditor, Peat, Marwick, Mitchell & Co., also declined comment.

TIGHTENING THE SCREWS. The *AI* board, which former directors say has shown little independence, is under intense pressure from creditors and shareholders to clean house. *AI*'s banks recently forced it to sign a tough new loan agreement that gives lenders effective control over many strategic decisions. The *SEC* is looking into *AI*'s executive compensation, benefits, entertainment expenses, use of corporate aircraft, and certain real estate transactions. Several large shareholders are

THE ISSUES HAUNTING ALLEGHENY INTERNATIONAL

WAS SPENDING ON EXECUTIVE PERQUISITES TOO LAVISH?

As financial problems mounted, AI maintained a fleet of five corporate jets—including a $15 million Gulfstream III. Executives lived well and entertained grandly. Some say they even took pleasure trips overseas at company expense. AI spent $1 million to buy and furnish a splendid Tudor home in Pittsburgh and $500,000 on a resort condominium beside an exclusive golf course.

DID CONFLICTS OF INTEREST CLOUD EXECUTIVE JUDGMENT?

After Chairman Robert Buckley and other officers purchased condominiums in a troubled Florida project, AI bought a controlling interest—against the advice of its real estate unit. The company paid nearly $6 million for a Manhattan hotel; Buckley's son became its manager, though his qualifications were minimal.

WERE ACCOUNTING PROCEDURES PROPER?

Former executives charge that travel not related to business could be billed to the company, and executives might never be required to provide a business justification for the expense. The executives add that records on the use of company planes were sometimes kept deliberately vague.

DID SHAREHOLDERS GET ENOUGH INFORMATION?

Board member Alexander M. Haig Jr., former Secretary of State, receives consulting fees of $50,000 annually from the company. His contract was not mentioned in the company's proxy material. Last year, AI reported pre-tax losses of nearly $100 million in its energy and real estate businesses. Those losses came as a surprise to some shareholders, who complain that the company provided almost no information about the ventures.

WHERE WAS THE BOARD OF DIRECTORS?

AI's 14-person board includes prominent directors from outside the company. Yet even as financial results worsened, former directors say, Buckley encountered no significant resistance from his board. One problem may have been that four of the nine outside directors either have received or are receiving payments for work done for the company.

openly critical. And the New York Stock Exchange is threatening to delist *AI* if its financial condition fails to improve.

The behavior of *AI*'s management is all the more extraordinary in light of the company's financial results. Since 1981, when *AI* reported earnings of $81 million on sales of $1.6 billion, profits have fallen steadily, culminating in last year's loss. Meanwhile, shareholders' equity has plunged 81%, to $85.7 million. The common-stock dividend has been eliminated, and the company lost $1.8 million in the second quarter. *AI*'s shares recently traded at about 15, far below the high of 55 reached in 1981.

Management theory has it that strong outside directors are the best protection shareholders have. *AI*'s deterioration, though, has taken place despite a board that includes prestigious outsiders. Among them: Anthony J. F. O'Reilly, *CEO* of H. J. Heinz Co.; Alexander M. Haig Jr., the former Secretary of State; Richard M. Cyert, the president of Carnegie-Mellon University; Jean-Jacques Servan-Schreiber, the French author; Anthony J. A. Bryan, chairman of Copperweld Corp., and Mark H. McCormack, agent and investment adviser for well-known sports figures.

Not all the directors, however, can be considered completely independent overseers. One of the nine outside directors on the 14-man board is George T. Farrell, president of Mellon Bank. Mellon is the lead bank for the group of banks that has imposed the new loan agreement on *AI*. Three other outside directors have received money from the company beyond their normal directors' fees. A fourth, Spencer R. Stuart, founder of InveQuest Inc., a Dallas marketing and investment firm, received large commissions prior to becoming a director in 1984, former executives say.

AI's shareholders are increasingly restive. One of them, Horace J. DePodwin, the retired dean of Rutgers State University's Graduate School of Management, calls *AI* a textbook example of how even a star-studded board cannot be relied on to protect shareholders. DePodwin, now a professor of business policy at Rutgers, bought stock about two years ago. Since then, he has become disillusioned, and he recently fired off a letter to board members. "I respectfully suggest to the board that

Allegheny appears to be out of control," he wrote. "For the company to survive, an abrupt change is required in the extent of control exercised by the board, including control over corporate assets and management." Buckley met with DePodwin to answer the charges, but DePodwin says the answers were unsatisfactory.

A RISING STAR. To understand *AI*, you must first know its boss. The company is undeniably the creation of the ambitious 62-year-old Buckley. He grew up in New York, earned a law degree at Cornell University, and gained his first extensive business experience at General Electric Co. In nine years he rose to manager of union relations of the Schenectady (N. Y.) plant. He once said: "I went up in that company like my last name was Electric."

Buckley later ran Standard Steel, now partly owned by *AI*, and was president of Ingersoll Milling Machine Co. In 1972 he went to Allegheny Ludlum Industries Inc., a Pittsburgh-based specialty-steel producer looking for new blood. Three years later he was the boss. Already, Buckley had concluded that steel offered little future. He sold off the specialty-steel operations to its managers in 1980 and moved into consumer businesses by acquiring Wilkinson Sword Group Ltd. and Sunbeam Corp. By 1982 the rechristened Allegheny International had sales of $2.6 billion, almost three times the figure when Buckley became chairman. He predicted revenues would hit $5 billion as early as 1986.

ARTS PATRON. This success, combined with Buckley's considerable personal charm, helped him dominate his expanding empire, according to former executives. Those who dared to challenge the chairman risked quick dismissal. His sway extended to the board room. "Buckley ran it like his own show," recalls one former director. Key issues were discussed, says another former director, "but I didn't see the controversy I did on other boards."

Buckley, a music lover who once aspired to a career as an opera singer, became a prominent figure in the Pittsburgh arts scene. *AI* made large donations to the arts, especially the Pittsburgh Symphony Society, where Buckley was president. He planned an elaborate new corporate headquarters to crown a renewal of Pittsburgh's cultural district.

AI was also acquiring a reputation within Pittsburgh corporate circles for providing its top executives with a regal lifestyle. The company, which has operations worldwide, acquired a fleet of jets. Buckley once pointed out that he travels 330,000 mi. a year, mostly on a company Gulfstream III reserved for his use. *AI* held annual management meetings in such places as Boca Raton, Fla., and the Bahamas. They involved up to 100 executives and spouses flown in from around the world and sometimes cost hundreds of thousands of dollars. At one Florida gathering, an ice carving graced the banquet. It cost about $10,000, according to one key former executive.

While such perks are hardly unique, record-keeping at *AI* was often lax, and a culture began to emerge in which some top executives began to take extraordinary liberties. Two former executives told *BUSINESS WEEK* that they were allowed to take weekend vacations to Washington and London—charging everything to company accounts. These bills never appeared on their personal expense reports. Others say that corporate jets were sometimes used for such personal reasons as visiting vacation homes and taking families on

trips and that the nature of those flights was not always accurately recorded. According to one well-placed former executive, the "Allegheny Air Force" was pressed into service to ferry guests to the wedding of one of Buckley's children. *BUSINESS WEEK* could not determine whether Buckley reimbursed the company.

Three former *AI* officers say that they had serious questions about high expenses submitted by Christopher Lewinton, a London-based executive vice-president and board member who has since left the company. Lewinton declined to respond to *BUSINESS WEEK*'s questions. It is not clear whether the expenses were disallowed.

MORGAN'S CELLAR. In another case, an elaborate wine cellar was installed in Buckley's home by an *AI* subsidiary, now known as Bally Engineered Structures Inc. Three former executives say that the company paid bills for the purchase or shipment of wine for this cellar. According to one of these executives, more than $100,000 was spent to buy part of a wine collection that once belonged to J. P. Morgan. *BUSINESS WEEK* could not determine whether the company was reimbursed. Two former executives contend that the company paid for the wine cellar, but Buckley's son John, who works for Bally, says that his

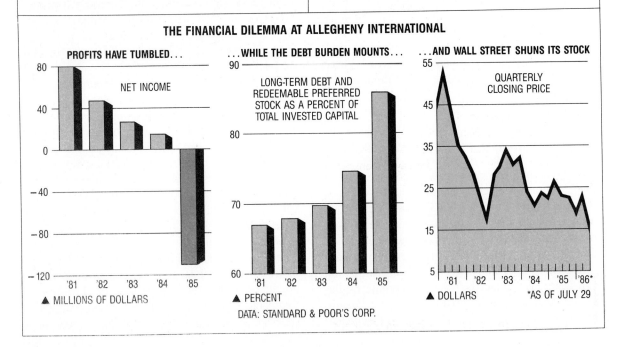

THE FINANCIAL DILEMMA AT ALLEGHENY INTERNATIONAL

PROFITS HAVE TUMBLED...
NET INCOME
▲ MILLIONS OF DOLLARS

...WHILE THE DEBT BURDEN MOUNTS...
LONG-TERM DEBT AND REDEEMABLE PREFERRED STOCK AS A PERCENT OF TOTAL INVESTED CAPITAL
▲ PERCENT
DATA: STANDARD & POOR'S CORP.

...AND WALL STREET SHUNS ITS STOCK
QUARTERLY CLOSING PRICE
▲ DOLLARS   *AS OF JULY 29

father repaid the company. *BUSINESS WEEK* has learned that the expense has been questioned by the *SEC*.

As *AI*'s financial condition worsened, some executives began to doubt the propriety of continued high living. "There is no question we were living way beyond our means," says one former officer. Raymond S. Fries, a former executive vice-president, says of the posh management meetings: "We could have had the same meetings in Pittsburgh without the enormous expense."

But *AI* didn't change its free-spending ways. Only a few months before buying the Tudor home in Pittsburgh, the company acquired a condominium in the resort country near Ligonier, Pa. The condominium is on the Rolling Rock estate, which is still controlled by the Mellon family, and backs onto what is one of the nation's most exclusive golf courses, Rolling Rock Club. Former executives say the total cost of this acquisition, including furnishings, came to roughly $500,000. Even though Buckley described the condominium's function as a place to entertain visiting dignitaries, it has been frequently used as a vacation retreat for Buckley and his family, the former executives say.

Such spendthrift habits help explain why overhead at *AI* is so high. Headquarters and other corporate expenses, for example, amounted to $50.7 million, or 2.5% of sales, last year. That's down from 3.2% of sales two years earlier. But William H. Miller of Legg Mason Wood Walker Inc., which owns a sizable block of *AI* stock, says expenses still are "grossly in excess of any reasonable amount that needs to be spent." Miller says that comparisons with similar companies show that *AI* should be spending half as much.

MARBLE BATHS. *SEC* documents suggest that the company is taking a closer look at expenses. *AI*'s 1986 proxy, sent to shareholders in March, revealed that the company is now counting personal airplane use as compensation and paying taxes on the imputed income for employees. Executives say at least one of the planes is up for sale.

Meanwhile, *AI* is straining to escape from a series of ill-fated real estate ventures. One of these, the Dover Hotel in midtown Manhattan, has raised apparent conflict-of-interest questions. *AI* originally purchased the hotel for $5.7 million in 1982, planning to convert it into a time-sharing residence. That plan proved to be unrealistic when *AI* belatedly learned what hefty sums it would have to pay rent-control tenants to move out. So the company began renovating the building for use as a hotel, starting with the penthouse, where it spent more than $1 million installing marble bathrooms and an elaborate rooftop greenhouse.

The first resident of the refurbished penthouse: Buckley's son Christopher. Even though former executives say that Christopher had no hotel experience, Buckley installed him as manager of the Dover. Christopher declined to comment. Despite *AI*'s financial pinch—and even with the investment of well over $10 million in the Dover providing scant income—Buckley rebuffed at least one potential buyer for the hotel. However, an agent working for *AI* says the hotel will be sold this fall, perhaps at a profit.

The company's elaborate new headquarters building is another example of Buckley's grand style. The building, which is going up in the midst of Pittsburgh's cultural district, is to be a 32-story granite tower that "will have a higher standard of quality than anything Pittsburgh is accustomed to," says an official of its developer, Lincoln Property Co. But *AI*, which is slashing its corporate staff to around 250 from 450 in 1984, needs far less space than it committed to at $26.50 per sq. ft. under the lease-back arrangement put in place to obtain financing.

AI has managed to sublease some of this space to Consolidated Natural Gas Co., but only by agreeing to charge *CNG* $6.50 a sq. ft. less than what *AI* is paying for the primary lease. As a result, *AI*'s spending on corporate office space could double, to some $5 million when it moves in. To add insult to injury, the new building will be called *CNG* Tower, not *AI* Tower, as originally planned.

AI's biggest real estate loss, however, came in Houston, where it owned a 34-story office building known as Phoenix Tower. Problems here started with the terms of the joint-venture deal, under which *AI* had to put up all of the cash while giving partner Albritton Development Co. half the equity. Construction didn't get under way until

HOW A LEAKY ROOF MAY COST ALLEGHENY DEARLY

I run a large company and am not a difficult man to get along with, but I promise you that if I take legal action I will not relent. If it takes $5 million, I will stop the project.... It would please me to do it for my friends, who are exasperated beyond belief.

That was the threat from Robert J. Buckley in a letter on company stationery to the manager of his Florida condominium when it needed repairs in 1981. Within a year, Allegheny International Inc., the company that Buckley heads, had bought controlling interest in the condominium project and a big chunk of another Florida real estate development. AI has yet to see a dollar of profit from the $16 million still sunk in the two projects.

The Florida forays were not AI's most costly gaffes in real estate. But the projects, where top executives also had financial stakes, provide striking evidence of how conflicts of interest tainted corporate decisions.

Buckley's problems involved a development called La Mer, a community of flat-topped concrete condominiums on a site featuring a 1,000-ft.

strip of seashore in Vero Beach. Buckley bought three units at La Mer and said that he "was instrumental in bringing a number of people into the property." Many of them were AI executives, including Vice-Chairman Clayton A. Sweeney, President Graemer K. Hilton, and Executive Vice-President Alan H. Anderson, all of whom have since left AI. Some AI executives invested as a group in still another unit.

Buckley was not a happy owner, as he recounted in a deposition taken last year as part of a lawsuit against the developer, Mackle Development Corp. Buckley told how one of his units had a leaky roof, a rusty stove, and a damaged bathtub. He said he had so little success in getting repairs that his wife "was getting sick, and I just took matters into my own hands." In early 1981, Buckley sent the manager the letter threatening legal action.

Shortly thereafter, AI's real estate unit was asked to study La Mer as an investment. In August, President Thomas P. Maletta issued a scathing report that advised steering clear. La Mer did not meet "specific standards we were looking for in terms of ROI [return on investment] and inter-

late 1982, after oil prices had already started plunging. To compound these problems, former executives say, AI passed up an opportunity to sell the building—when it was nearing completion in late 1983—at a price that would have enabled the company to recoup most of its original $80 million investment. Instead, AI allowed the building to stand vacant almost two years at a carrying cost of $1 million a month. AI finally sold the building to Sears, Roebuck & Co.'s Homart Development Co. late last year for $47 million, writing off more than $40 million. "They had a lot of opportunities to do better," says a veteran Houston real estate agent, "but they were asleep at the wheel." This debacle was the key reason that AI's

realty unit lost $62.3 million last year. But the losses may not be over. Despite the write-offs, AI disclosed that it has been forced to guarantee $114.5 million of debt incurred by the realty subsidiary.

AI also drilled a dry hole in the energy business, where it began investing in 1981. It pumped more than $30 million into an oil-and-gas-drilling venture sponsored by Houston-based Halbouty Energy Co. Though AI had virtually no oil and gas expertise, Buckley was enthusiastic, former executive Fries says, and the board went along. It was a decision they came to regret. As oil prices plunged last year, an appraisal found that reserves were far lower than estimated. AI was forced to take a

nal rate of return," Maletta said in a deposition. Nevertheless, that fall, *AI* bought controlling interest in La Mer.

Buckley testified that he played no significant role in the decision to proceed, attributing the idea to Maletta. Maletta's denial that he urged making the investment was corroborated in another deposition by *AI* General Counsel James T. Dougherty. Two former *AI* executives told *BUSINESS WEEK* that Buckley ordered the investment.

Eventually, *AI*, acting through its limited partnership that controlled La Mer, sued Mackle to force its removal as developer. *AI* achieved its goal last year, but only by paying Mackle $1.5 million to settle the suit. Not counting legal costs, *AI* has invested about $9 million in La Mer and a vacant piece of land next door.

GOOD ON PAPER. That vacant land indirectly got *AI* into trouble on the other side of the state. *AI*'s fellow investor in the land was Rodney L. Propps, who was planning a development called The Oaks near Sarasota. Propps envisioned a sprawling community of 900 spacious homes. Plans called for two golf courses, a dozen tennis courts, and an imposing clubhouse that featured a double-spiral staircase ascending to the grand ballroom. On the *AI* executives' visits to Florida, Propps quickly learned that they "enjoyed their junkets," as one of Propps's business associates puts it. Propps was soon obliging the *AI* brass with deep-sea fishing trips. In 1982, *AI* bought into the first phase of Propps's project, called Oaks I, as a partner. A partnership that included Maletta and *AI* Executive Vice-President Raymond S. Fries invested in Oaks I at the same time.

When the second phase of the project, Oaks II, came along, *AI* invested in that as well. But *AI* executives became unhappy with the progress of the development and managed last year to sell the company's interest to Propps for $9 million and get repayment of $25 million it had lent him. The transaction put *AI* in a position to make a profit from Oaks II, but there was a hitch. *AI* lent $7 million to Propps as part of the deal, and the loan is now tied up in the Chapter 11 bankruptcy proceeding initiated by Oaks II last year.

At the largely deserted Oaks II, the clubhouse—with its dining room tables still set for the next meal—is closed. The golf course is closed, too, its putting greens turning brown under the blistering sun. Oaks I, which is not in bankruptcy and is located just across the road, is in immaculate shape. But since Oaks II has most of the recreational facilities, the fortunes of investors in Oaks I depend heavily on whether the companion project can be rescued. Fries, who is no longer with *AI*, says he figures that the money the executives invested in Oaks I "is gone, and I have little hope of recovering even 50¢ on the dollar." *AI* seems to be in the same boat.

By William C. Symonds in Pittsburgh, with Pete Engardio in Sarasota

---

$32.2 million loss on the venture and stop investing in oil and gas.

SAFETY NET. This big energy loss, combined with the bloodbath in real estate, "came as a surprise to most people," says Gregory M. Drahuschak, a Butcher & Singer analyst. The reason: *AI*'s mention of these investments had been so brief in its reports that, analysts say, it was nearly impossible to fathom the risk being assumed.

Even while *AI*'s executives were sowing the seeds of their financial problems, their level of compensation was stirring discussion in Pittsburgh corporate circles. In 1984, when it earned a paltry $14.9 million, *AI* paid Buckley over $1 million in cash, more than the chiefs of two much larger Pittsburgh companies, Westinghouse Electric Corp.'s Douglas D. Danforth and *USX* Corp.'s David M. Roderick. Last year, *AI*'s heavy losses hit home, and Buckley's cash compensation plunged to $573,100, largely because he didn't earn a bonus. However, within the first three months of 1986, the board gave Buckley the chance to make up the difference by granting him the option to buy 140,000 shares of *AI* stock, more than 1% of the corporation's outstanding shares, at an average price of $17.88, close to the low for the decade.

Executive salaries at *AI* have been supplemented by millions of dollars loaned at a 2% interest rate. Although such programs are often used by companies to help executives acquire stock, $10.4 million of the $32.3 million in outstanding loans to *AI* executives was used for other things. "That is unusual as hell," says Jude Rich, president of Sibson & Co., a New Jersey-based compensation consultant.

Children of top executives also benefited from *AI*'s employment practices. Sharon Sweeney, the daughter of Clayton A. Sweeney, then vice-chairman, was hired as head of investor relations in 1985. Although bright, she brought little experience to the post at a time when major shareholders were already unhappy. Besides Christopher, two more of Buckley's sons are on the corporate payroll. Executives who worked with them say both are well qualified.

$10,000 A DAY. Where was the *AI* board while all this was happening? One possible explanation for its passivity and relative generosity is that a number of outside directors have financial ties to the company. Furthermore, *AI* has been inconsistent in letting shareholders know about these relationships. When Haig joined the board in 1983, for example, Buckley offered him an arrangement under which he is paid $50,000 for providing advice "in the area of safety and protection devices" no more than five days a year. The arrangement was first disclosed in a copy of the agreement attached to *AI*'s 1984 annual report filed with the *SEC*. There has been no mention of the arrangement in proxy materials mailed to shareholders. Meanwhile, a part-time employment agreement reached in 1983 with Lord Fanshawe, former head of Wilkinson Sword, was not mentioned in the proxy until this year. Whether or not such disclosures were legally required by the SEC, shareholders—in principle—should have been promptly and fully informed, Professor DePodwin says.

This year's proxy also disclosed that two consulting firms with which Director Mark H. McCormack is associated were paid $163,000 for work done for *AI* in 1985. Former executives say also that Director Stuart received substantial payments for helping set up some of *AI*'s real estate deals before he joined the board in 1984. Stuart couldn't be reached for comment.

How much the board knew of what was happening at *AI* is difficult to determine. Former board members say that the board did receive information on the oil and gas and real estate investments, though two directors say they cannot recall any board discussion of the company's highly questionable purchase of an interest in the Florida project in which Buckley owned condo units. Most boards do not typically review spending on travel and entertainment or use of executive jets. But the board did support Buckley's biggest gamble: the 1981 decision to pay $534 million for Sunbeam, far more than offered by rival bidder *IC* Industries Inc. The bid was based on an overly optimistic assumption by *AI* executives about future performance of the small-appliance business.

FAULTY PROJECTIONS. When these assumptions failed to materialize, the costs of servicing the heavy debt acquired in Buckley's restructuring began to cut deeply into earnings. Nevertheless, the board continued to support a management that was issuing wildly optimistic predictions. In early 1985, Graemer K. Hilton, then president of *AI*, said in a letter to shareholders that "the corporate restructuring is essentially complete," adding that we "anticipate an overall improvement in operating profit in 1985." Instead, operating earnings plunged from $63.7 million in 1984 to last year's loss of $57.5 million, and *AI* was forced to embark on a drastic program of selling assets to cut debt.

Buckley is now saying he plans to shrink the company to sales of $1.5 billion, focusing on its Sunbeam appliances and other consumer lines. But the margin for error is shrinking, too. In May officials of the New York Stock Exchange met with executives to discuss whether *AI*'s stock should be delisted. Among other things, *AI* no longer met the exchange's requirement that a company's tangible assets available for holders of common stock must exceed the company's liabilities by at least $8 million. *AI* had a deficit of $118.4 million at the end of last year.

Also hemming in *AI* is the new bank agreement, signed on Apr. 29, which commits the company to a strict schedule for repaying debt and places harsh restrictions on the payment of both common and preferred dividends. "The company is now backed into a damn near impossible corner," contends analyst Eric Billings, a Johnston, Lemon

& Co. analyst. Indeed, in a desperate bid to meet the terms imposed by creditors, Buckley is now selling off some of the consumer businesses that represent the company's greatest hope for the future.

Consider the case of Rowenta-Werke, a leading European producer of such appliances as toasters and irons that was half owned by *AI*. Buckley faced a deadline of June 29 for paying off $30 million of its bank credit. *AI* had launched a stock-rights offering in late May to raise money, but the issue had to be withdrawn within days because of shareholder complaints that it would only dilute the stock. With the company already forecasting a second-quarter loss, the only option was to sell assets. So he scrambled to sell the company's stake in Rowenta to Chicago Pacific Corp.

NO MERCY. The sale of Rowenta, which had sales of $265 million last year, was a crushing blow to Buckley's dream of making *AI* the world leader in small appliances. Even more ominous, however, was the financial loss. By mid-June, Buckley had signed a letter of intent to sell Rowenta to Chicago Pacific for at least $80 million, sources close to the deal say. But Chicago Pacific was well aware of *AI*'s situation and, days before the bank deadline, told Buckley that it would have to lower the price. To make matters worse, Rothmans Deutsch-land, which owned the other half of Rowenta, balked. As a result, for equal shares of Rowenta, Rothmans received $40 million and *AI* $34 million.

The outside directors are theoretically the shareholders' last line of defense. Yet Farrell, as president of Mellon Bank, is in a key position in the banking syndicate that is trying to lay claim to *AI*'s assets. At the same time, Farrell is responsible for preserving those assets for shareholders. Farrell declined to discuss the Rowenta deal.

The sad fact is that the Rowenta deal may not be the last time that Buckley accepts less than top dollar for *AI* assets. Come December, the company must reduce its debt load by an additional $150 million. After all of the mistakes at Allegheny International, it may be too late to hope that shareholder interests will come first.

By William C. Symonds in Pittsburgh, with bureau reports

DISCUSSION QUESTION

In discussions of the concept of organizational culture and leadership, the point is often made that leaders create a corporate culture, in part by role modeling. Discuss the values that might be conveyed to subordinates and embedded in Allegheny's culture by Chairman Robert Buckley's actions.

THE DOWNFALL OF A CEO

THE INSIDE STORY OF BILL BRICKER'S REIGN AT DIAMOND SHAMROCK

FEBRUARY 16, 1987, PP. 76-80, 84

When William H. Bricker stepped to the podium to answer questions from the press on Feb. 2, it sure seemed that he had some explaining to do. Diamond Shamrock Corp. had just announced that Bricker was stepping down as chief executive officer after launching the floundering company's third major restructuring in less than three years. Now it was time to sum up Bricker's decade at the top.

It was time to explain how a once-profitable chemical company with a modest oil operation and a solid future became a debt-ridden energy conglomerate with large, persistent losses. Time to explain why Diamond's shareholders missed out on Wall Street's most stunning rally in a generation (charts). And time to explain why, three times in two years, Bricker and his board of directors had rejected offers to buy the company. What's more, each successive offer was worth less than the one before. Even news of Bricker's resignation and the latest reorganization plan had failed to push the stock above the $15 a share that

DIAMOND'S BUMPY DECADE

1976

After a quick, seven-year ascent through the corporate ranks at Diamond Shamrock, Bricker, 44, becomes the company's chief executive. Diamond earns $140 million on sales of $1.4 billion; its stock ends the year at $34 a share.

1979

Bricker sets out to make Diamond a major energy company. He buys Falcon Seaboard, a coal producer, for $250 million and moves the corporate headquarters to Dallas from Cleveland.

1981

In a second expansion move, Bricker buys Amherst Coal Co. for $220 million. Diamond posts record earnings of $230 million on sales of $3.4 billion. Investors are impressed, and Diamond's stock nearly matches its all-time high of $40.

1982

The combination of a recession and lower prices clobbers energy companies. Even though Diamond's earnings fall 35%, to $150 million, the company spends $161 million to buy drilling rights in Alaska's Beaufort Sea. Shareholders suffer as Diamond's stock drops as low as $17.

1983

Bricker buys Natomas, a struggling oil company, for $1.5 billion. Diamond's drilling venture in the Beaufort Sea produces a dry hole and a big writedown. Diamond loses $60 million for the year.

1985

Bricker tentatively agrees to sell Diamond to Occidental Petroleum for Oxy stock worth $28 a share, then backs away. Diamond restructures. Bricker buys back stock and takes $891 million in write-offs, most because of energy prices and Natomas. Losses for the year total $605 million. Stock price at yearend: $14.

1986

Boone Pickens offers to acquire Diamond for limited partnership units valued at roughly $16 per share. For a second time, however, Bricker refuses to sell. Despite another round of buybacks, Diamond shares hover at $14.

1987

Pickens offers to buy 20% of Diamond's stock for $15 a share. Bricker announces a plan to split the company in two, launches another stock buyback, and resigns as CEO. Diamond's stock is unchanged at just under $15 on the news. Mesa offers $15 a share for all Diamond shares.

---

raider T. Boone Pickens Jr. was offering for 20% of Diamond's stock.

Bricker didn't flinch. "I am proud of the value we have delivered to shareholders," he said calmly. "I have completed my challenge. I have completed my assignment. If this doesn't make you proud as a professional manager, I don't know what would. If I stayed on for 20 years, I'm not sure I could top this."

It was a sadly familiar performance to people who watched Bill Bricker shoot up the ranks at Diamond, first by deftly managing its chemical business, later by serving an apprenticeship as president. Raymond F. Evans, Bricker's mentor and a predecessor as *CEO*, liked Bricker's canny instincts. Evans especially admired his affinity for the team spirit and participatory management that Diamond prized. But moving up that one rung on the corporate ladder in 1976 made all the difference. "He changed 180 degrees when he became *CEO*," Evans complains. "He just became a different guy. I guess his ego got him."

COMPLIANT BOARD. What Bricker wanted was a big-league energy company. And by the time he was done, Diamond had the trappings of the status he aspired to: a lavish 12,000-acre ranch on the Texas prairie, a $1 million box at the Dallas Cowboys' home stadium, and a fleet of airplanes to whisk him and his directors around the world. Bricker's compensation was lavish, too. In 1985, he earned $891,700 in cash compensation before taking pay cuts two years running. But Diamond's profits failed to measure up to Bricker's aspirations.

A three-month investigation by this magazine, including interviews with more than 40 former

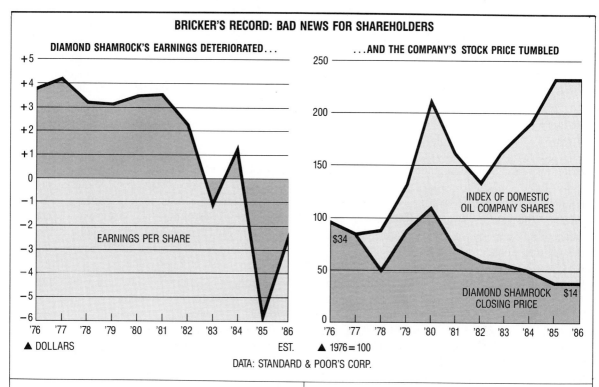

BRICKER'S RECORD: BAD NEWS FOR SHAREHOLDERS

DIAMOND SHAMROCK'S EARNINGS DETERIORATED...

EARNINGS PER SHARE

▲ DOLLARS   EST.

...AND THE COMPANY'S STOCK PRICE TUMBLED

INDEX OF DOMESTIC OIL COMPANY SHARES

DIAMOND SHAMROCK CLOSING PRICE $14

$34

▲ 1976 = 100

DATA: STANDARD & POOR'S CORP.

and current Diamond executives, reveals deep management problems. Under Bricker and a remarkably forgiving board, Diamond took unusual risks for its size. Write-offs associated with the purchase of Natomas Co. and with a dry hole in Alaska's Beaufort Sea cost some $800 million. By comparison, sales never topped $4.5 billion annually and now are only $2.5 billion. Bricker didn't sway from his goal, but his tactics for getting there became erratic. In 1978, for instance, he sold Diamond's gasoline service stations to Sigmor Corp. In 1983, he bought Sigmor back for $162 million. In the most recent restructuring, Sigmor's refineries and stations are being spun off from the exploration and production unit that will be the core of the new company.

In some cases, Bricker and other directors faced potential conflicts of interest involving Diamond and their personal investments. In one instance, Diamond purchased a stake in a prized bull partially owned by Bricker. In another, a 50%-owned Diamond unit invested in a biotechnology company partially owned by a Diamond director. In some of his dealings, Bricker's business judgment may have been influenced by friendship (page 162).

In the end, Bricker, 55, offered to step down in an effort to allay any concerns that he had become a big part of the problem at Diamond, one insider says. But whether his resignation or Diamond's new plan will lead to better results remains to be seen. After the breakup, each holder of 100 shares of the current Diamond will own 100 shares in a company with oil, natural gas, and coal production activities and 25 shares in a second company with refining and marketing operations. The latest moves are a more drastic version of a 1985 restructuring, in which Diamond spun off its oil-drilling and production operations in the Gulf of Mexico. The price of shares in both companies has dropped since then.

The centerpiece of the breakup is a $300 million investment in a new issue of Diamond convertible preferred stock by Prudential Insurance Co. The money will be used to buy back 20 million common shares, or about 18% of the common outstanding, at $17 a share. In return, Prudential gets an annual dividend amounting to 9.75%, three seats on Diamond's board, and veto power over any takeover bid.

Pickens couldn't seem to resist one last effort to

foul up the deal, however. On Feb. 4 he made Diamond an offer it seemed certain to refuse: $15 a share in cash for the company.

For Bricker, the world of raiders, takeover defenses, and risky oil ventures was a long way from the western Michigan farm where he spent his boyhood. He studied agriculture at Michigan State University, then sought broader horizons after getting a master's degree in horticulture. He landed a series of international assignments with chemical giant Bayer and still describes his days in Hong Kong and Egypt as the most rewarding of his career. When Bayer brought him back to headquarters in Germany, he recalls, he bridled under the regimentation.

AUTOCRATIC STYLE. In the mid-1960s, he joined Velsicol Chemical Corp. to head international sales. His work there caught the eye of Evans, whose grandfather had founded Diamond Alkali Co., which merged with Shamrock Oil & Gas Corp. in 1967. Bricker went to work for Diamond Shamrock at its Cleveland headquarters in 1969 and quickly set about bolstering its agricultural-chemical businesses.

Seven years later, Bricker, then 44, was a popular choice for chief executive. He got off to a strong start by buying new technology that made Diamond's plants more efficient. He also dumped several plastics businesses that were under pressure because of rising oil prices.

By late 1978, though, Bricker's autocratic style and bold ideas were alienating some of his former supporters. More important, he was getting Diamond into deals that would come back to haunt him. Bricker figured the outlook for energy prices meant that Diamond should plunge into production of oil, gas, and coal. So he proposed buying Falcon Seaboard Inc., a coal producer. But Evans and other directors opposed the deal—so strenuously that the board sent Bricker back to renegotiate. He got the price down to $250 million in stock, which the board accepted. Even then, however, Evans and at least one other director opposed the deal.

Evans eventually resigned when Bricker persuaded the board to move the company's headquarters from Cleveland to Dallas, to be closer to the oil patch. "I had the feeling from personal contact that he wasn't going to listen to anyone," Evans says. As old-timers on the board either resigned or retired, dissent became scarcer. Questions stopped bubbling up from management, as well. Many longtime executives concluded it was useless to fight Bricker and the flamboyant new culture he was creating at Diamond. Says one executive, now retired: "I look at group pictures from those days, and I can see in my face and my posture how little I fit in."

In 1982 oil prices sagged as inflation slowed sharply. Energy stocks took a pasting, and Diamond, whose earnings fell 35%, was especially hard hit. But Bricker was still stalking a big oil acquisition. That search led him to San Francisco-based Natomas, a $1.6 billion oil and gas producer. Its shares were selling at 15½—one-third of their price during the oil boom. Earnings were off, too, and Natomas had cut its dividend to conserve cash. Bricker's hostile tender offer caught Natomas' chairman, Dorman L. Commons, in a bad spot. Investors loved Diamond's offer of $23 in cash, and Commons couldn't find a more acceptable suitor that would be willing to pay more.

Six days later, Bricker and Commons met alone to resolve an impasse over Diamond's offer. Commons recounts in his 1985 book, *Tender Offer*, that Bricker asked for a counteroffer, and Commons responded with a proposal that seemed to him out of the question. Commons asked for 1.05 shares of Diamond—then trading at about 24—for each share of Natomas. Commons also proposed letting Natomas first spin off its American President Lines Ltd. and other shipping and real estate interests. Commons was incredulous when Bricker agreed. For his part, Bricker defends his negotiating skills, arguing that the final price was closer to his initial offer than to Commons' opener.

Analysts figured Bricker paid the equivalent of $12.50 a bbl. for Natomas' oil—or twice what reserves were fetching on the market those days. Diamond's stock dropped sharply in response to the announcement. It is now clear that Bricker paid too much—by a wide margin. Diamond has already logged a loss of some $600 million because it had to write down the value of Natomas properties in 1985. President Arthur Smith, of oil analysts John S. Herold Inc., recently called the Natomas purchase "one of the worst oil deals of the decade."

Diamond tried to fight back when Wall Street balked at the Natomas deal. The company ran a series of advertisements that pictured its executives as mavericks bucking "the conventional wisdom" of energy retrenchment. Featured prominently in the ads was Diamond's $161 million purchase in 1982 of leases in the Beaufort Sea off the North Slope of Alaska. It wasn't long before the first well, Mukluk I, turned out to be a dry hole—one of the most expensive the industry has ever seen. Bricker had to report his first annual loss, a $60 million deficit for 1983.

'PERFECT VISION.' Plenty of oil companies, of course, were taking heavy losses in those days from investments initiated under much more favorable economic assumptions. Still, "the investment Bricker was making was much larger in relation to the size of the corporation," says analyst Andrew Gray of Pershing Securities. "He was betting the ranch, and he lost it." Counters Bricker: "With hindsight, you can get perfect vision."

In fact, Mukluk was Bricker's last high-stakes roll. He began selling assets and cutting expenses in Diamond's first round of retrenchment during 1984.

Despite the financial pressures on the company, its layoffs and asset sales, Diamond's lavish executive perks seemed immune from the cost-cutting. One example: Riverside Farms, the company ranch outside of Hamilton, Tex. Bricker defends it as typical of the hunting camps favored by oil companies. But Riverside Farms is far more than that. The local tax assessor values the sprawling ranch and its spacious lodge at $9 million.

Besides raising Black Angus cattle to defray expenses and making pecan brittle for guests, Diamond used the ranch for corporate meetings and entertainment. Regular visitors included Sir Richard Musgrave, a professional shoot manager whom Diamond flew in regularly from Ireland to organize English-style pheasant hunts for customers and Diamond executives. Says Bricker: "If you're going to take time to entertain a customer, you try and do it in such a way that it's not an ordinary event."

In 1984, with earnings on a short-lived rebound, Diamond continued to entertain in style. During the Republican National Convention, company-chartered helicopters ferried guests to Riverside for a media reception honoring Nevada Senator Paul Laxalt. The company says that the reception was its contribution, as a corporation in the host city, to the convention.

As earnings fell, Diamond cut back its original fleet of five planes to three, including a 727 that is now up for sale. But the company at times augmented its own fleet with chartered planes. Diamond chartered a Boeing 707 to help fly directors and their wives to Indonesia with a side trip to Hong Kong in 1984. In other years, there were similar flights to Europe, Alaska, and Brazil. Diamond says that many multinational companies hold meetings overseas. Not all bring officers and spouses, however. "We go when we have something major in the offing," explains Bricker.

NO COMMENT. Bricker kept company planes on call for personal trips, too. Over a two-year period, Diamond's former manager of advertising, Donald Yeskoo, says he flew several times with Bricker from Dallas to Bricker's family ranch in Montana, often in the company of Mrs. Bricker and one of the couple's three sons. Diamond says that the board of directors requires Bricker for security reasons to use the corporate jet when traveling. It adds that the company routinely bills employees for services or reports them to the Internal Revenue Service as added compensation.

Bricker's Bear Creek Ranch in Montana brought him into a potential conflict of interest in 1982. Like Riverside Farms, Bear Creek raises Black Angus cattle, and Bricker bought a one-third interest in a bull called High Voltage. Later, Riverside Farms bought a third of the bull, too. Eventually, the animal was sold—at a profit for all parties—for $1.5 million. The transactions were all disclosed in Diamond's Securities & Exchange Commission filings. Diamond policy forbids employees to invest in oil wells, because of the potential conflict of interest. But Bricker says he had no conflict in the High Voltage dealings because he is not directly in charge of Riverside.

Another potential conflict at Diamond involved consultant John T. Kimbell, who is one of the

DID BRICKER GIVE A LITTLE TOO MUCH HELP TO A FRIEND?

Bill Bricker's management style was unusual in many ways, but nothing is more curious than his apparent eagerness to do deals with Vittoria de Nora, a 75-year-old Italian businessman. De Nora, an innovator of chemical production processes, first came into contact with Diamond Shamrock Corp. in the 1950s. By 1973, he owned 4% of the company's stock and sat on the board. But fellow directors asked him not to stand for reelection the next year because he was trying to do business with competitors.

Bricker and de Nora, however, are longtime friends, and the company's relationship with de Nora didn't end when he left the board. Two transactions are especially unusual: In one, Diamond sold a subsidiary to de Nora at what appears to be an attractive price. In another, Bricker involved Diamond in de Nora's efforts to sell a business.

In 1982, Diamond and de Nora set up a joint-venture called Eltech Systems Corp. to make chlorine production equipment. Two years later, however, Bricker staged an about-face: Diamond sold

its interest in Eltech to de Nora. A Diamond attorney explains that the decision to sell came because "the chemical industry was flat on its back."

Even so, de Nora got what looks like a bargain. He paid $108 million, or $13 million less than the value carried on Diamond's books. Eltech, what's more, had considerable potential. It earned $29 million on sales of $64 million in 1981. A former Diamond executive argues that the company, where Bricker is now an unpaid director, is a guaranteed moneymaker. "It is a near-monopoly," he says.

PRESSURE. The relationship between Bricker and de Nora also crops up in transactions involving Vertac Chemical Corp., a Memphis producer of agricultural chemicals. De Nora bought Vertac in 1980, after Bricker introduced him to the men who were selling it. But later Bricker seemed unusually interested in helping his friend sell out.

Vertac, in fact, may have sparked a conflict at *SDS* Biotech Corp., a joint venture between Diamond and Showa Denko, a Japanese company.

company's outside directors. In 1983, Kimbell extended a $300,000 loan to a new biotechnology company called Amtron Corp., received a stake in the company, and agreed to find venture capital, according to Amtron executives. Kimbell also became Amtron's chairman and president. Former research staffers at a Diamond Shamrock joint venture called *SDS* Biotech Corp. say the venture invested $300,000 in Amtron in mid-1984, even though staffers recommended against it. Amtron staffers say the money was used, among other things, to repay Kimbell's loan. Former *SDS* President Allan J. Tomlinson says he knows of no recommendation against the investment. The links between Kimbell and Amtron were disclosed in Diamond's *SEC* filings. Kimbell did not respond to written and telephone requests for comment.

For other Diamond directors, the question of

where loyalties lay was more subtle. As in many companies, the links among the board members constituted what Pickens scorns as a "good ol' boys club," instinctively protective of their station. *LTV* Corp. Chairman Raymond A. Hay is a Diamond board member, while Bricker is an *LTV* director. Diamond, which sold coal to *LTV*, is one of the creditors now seeking repayment under *LTV*'s Chapter 11 reorganization in bankruptcy court. Bricker was on the board of *AMF* Inc. until Irwin L. Jacobs took the company over, and former *AMF* Chairman W. Thomas York is still a Diamond board member.

What particularly irks at least one shareholder is how small a stake the officers and directors hold in the company. According to the latest *SEC* filings, they owned fewer than 75,000 shares outright, or less than one-tenth of one percent of total

Bricker wanted *SDS* to acquire Vertac, even though *SDS* managers say the price was too high. But one of the joint venture's officials says Bricker pushed the issue to the top, and that at a 1984 meeting Showa Denko's chairman rejected the purchase. The official says he was told that Bricker answered with an ultimatum: If *SDS* did not buy Vertac, then the joint venture was over.

Bricker remembers the meeting differently. He says that Vertac wasn't discussed. The company, by his account, was just one of a slate of *SDS* acquisitions he recommended. "Vertac was turned down," Bricker says, "and that was the end of it."

Diamond, however, soon bought out its Japanese partner—creating new problems. With cutbacks elsewhere, executives say they didn't want to confuse analysts and make them think Diamond was expanding in biotech. So Diamond used a shell corporation called Vanderbilt Development Corp. to hold the additional *SDS* interest.

Diamond executives immediately began trying to sell the business. Late in 1985, they found a buyer—Fermenta, a Swedish pharmaceutical company. But Fermenta, as it turns out, bought more than *SDS*. It acquired Vertac from de Nora at almost the same time. Diamond's 1985 annual report says only that Diamond and "its joint-venture partner" sold *SDS*.

These events raise troubling questions: Did Bricker jeopardize a relationship with Japanese partners and pull out of a joint venture just to help a friend? Was Diamond's sale of *SDS* somehow linked to Fermenta's purchase of Vertac from de Nora?

He involved Diamond in deals that may have benefited Vittoria de Nora

---

As for de Nora, his deal quickly soured. He took stock instead of cash and wound up owning 14% of Fermenta. But a scandal soon erupted. Fermenta's founder, Refaat El-Sayed, had falsified academic credentials, and there were bookkeeping improprieties at his company. Fermenta shares lost about 90% of their value, and the company was delisted by the Stockholm Stock Exchange in January.

When *BUSINESS WEEK* caught up with de Nora in Geneva, he declined an interview. "I have been retired for 10 years," he explained.

By Todd Mason in Dallas, with bureau reports

---

shares outstanding. At last report Bricker himself owned 35,700. Comments former director Fred S. Strauss, who says he still holds "in excess of" 100,000 shares: "I would rather have a company where the people on the firing line have their money at stake."

If the officers and directors held larger stakes, Strauss figures the shareholders would have come out better in the series of chances to sell the company. The first was in early 1985, when Bricker negotiated a tentative deal with Chairman Armand Hammer of Occidental Petroleum Corp. to have Oxy acquire Diamond. The deal involved a simple swap of one share of Occidental, then worth $28, for each share of Diamond, then worth $17. The companies announced that a deal was in the works.

NO REGRETS. Oxy's stock fell by 4½ points in

response to the deal: Investors feared that Diamond would sap Oxy's earnings. Bricker had failed to negotiate a "collar," or range, for an acceptable value of Oxy stock, so the Diamond directors scotched the deal the very afternoon it was announced. Recently, Oxy traded at about 32, some 17 points higher than Diamond stock. The deal still rankles Oxy executives, but they do not regret its demise. "Diamond Shamrock would have been a terrible drag on our stock," says one.

Diamond followed up the aborted deal with sizable stock buybacks, and Bricker jettisoned whole divisions to help finance them while furthering his strategy of becoming purely an energy company. Curiously, Bricker was also in the market to buy. In late 1986, only months after selling its chemical business, Diamond sent a team to Sweden to look into the purchase of Fermenta, a chemical company that had been shaken by disclosures of improper bookkeeping. Nothing came of the trip.

Meanwhile, Bricker had his hands full back home. In November, Pickens offered to buy Diamond for units in his Mesa Ltd. partnership. The offer was valued at $16 a share, compared with Diamond's $13.50 at the time. Diamond's board rejected the offer as inadequate. Pickens refused to go away, however. In January he came with another bid, this time for 20% of Diamond's shares at $15 a share. Diamond officers had no doubts that Pickens would wind up with an even larger stake and make life miserable for the company, even though anti-takeover provisions would kick in if he moved above 25%.

The board assembled in Dallas on Thursday, Jan. 29. Pickens' offer was due to expire in six days, and specialists from Diamond's investment banker, First Boston Corp., made a presentation on the breakup and the Prudential investment. According to one insider, Bricker asked the bankers to estimate how much his staying on would affect the value of the deal. The bankers told him the company would be worth more if he resigned. **FINAL DETAILS.** Bricker offered his resignation to the board. "My staying makes it easy for Boone to turn a proxy fight into a personal fight, and on that basis he could possibly win," one source quoted Bricker as saying. "I'm an easy target for him." The board assembled again over the weekend to iron out final details and accepted Bricker's resignation. Bricker declined to be interviewed by *BUSINESS WEEK* after he resigned.

Roger R. Hemminghaus, 50, who will head the refining and marketing spinoff, has long run those operations, which are profitable. Charles L. Blackburn, 59, a Shell Oil Co. executive who joined Diamond recently, is regarded as a no-nonsense manager who could shake up the unprofitable exploration operations.

With a heavy investment and three seats on the board of Blackburn's company, Prudential is unlikely to be as protective of the status quo as current Diamond board members are. But Pickens' latest offer increased the pressure on Diamond to sell its breakup to shareholders. Diamond's stock did not move after the deal was announced. If the estimates by Diamond's investment bankers are accurate, Bricker's departure may have at last created the shareholder value that eluded him for so long.

By Todd Mason in Dallas, with G. David Wallace in New York and bureau reports

DISCUSSION QUESTIONS
1. What aspects of leadership and decision-making styles are problematic in Bricker's tenure as CEO of Diamond Shamrock?
2. What ethical questions are raised about his actions as CEO?

HOW JIM TREYBIG WHIPPED TANDEM BACK INTO SHAPE

THE FOUNDER HAS REVAMPED PRODUCTS AND MARKETING, GAINING NEW RESPECTABILITY
FEBRUARY 23, 1987, PP. 124-126

Jim Treybig had a life plan. Fearing that a single career would get too boring, the plain-talking Texan set out to get rich by running his own business. After that, he figured, he'd get elected governor of Texas, then retire to dig up ruins in the Yucatán. Treybig, 46, still has plenty of time to get to Mexico. But after 20 years in California, he's been away too long to enter Texas politics. Besides, managing his company, 12-year-old Tandem Computers Inc., has proved to be anything but boring.

Tandem hit the minicomputer market like a shot with a design for almost faultlessly handling rapid-fire transactions, such as bank-account debits or airline reservations, as they happen. That technical wizardry sent the Cupertino (Calif.) company's revenues and profits doubling every year from 1976 to 1981. Vice-President Dennis L. McEvoy recalls: "We thought we could walk on water." Then reality set in. Tandem outgrew its lax cost controls, enduring four years of flat earnings.

Margins sagged. Its stock plummeted. "It was a tough adjustment for a company that has always been proud," Treybig says.

PERFECT TIMING. Realizing that Tandem was on a collision course with mediocrity, Treybig whipped it into fighting trim. In the past two years, the company has virtually replaced its line of products with a broader array, revamped its xenophobic marketing strategy by working with outside software companies, honed manufacturing efficiencies, and tightened financial controls.

The result: Profits shot up 113%, to $27 million, in the quarter ended Dec. 31 after rising 86%, to $68 million, in the year ended Sept. 30. Revenues jumped 23% last year, to $768 million, and the stock leapt in January to a five-year high of 58. No wonder analysts compare Tandem's new growth with the turnaround of Digital Equipment Corp. in 1985. John C. Levinson, an analyst at Goldman, Sachs & Co., expects earnings to jump 67% this year, to $2.40 per share. "Tandem has got its act together," he says, "and at a time when *IBM*'s at its weakest."

Tandem's efforts have also catapulted it to a new respectability in the market. Once relegated to selling systems mainly for isolated uses, such as networks of automated teller machines, Tandem is nosing its way into other areas, such as automated manufacturing operations. That's because its ma-chines can manage vast networks, expand capacity, and link up to other makers' hardware easily. It's also scoring more wins against chief rivals International Business Machines Corp. and *DEC*. "Tandem's gone from being a vendor of specialized offerings to where it can compete with most of the majors for most applications," says Loran R. Fite, a vice-president at Wells Fargo Bank, a Tandem customer.

Unlike Steven P. Jobs of Apple Computer Inc., M. Kenneth Oshman of Rolm Corp., and other Silicon Valley entrepreneurs of the 1970s, Treybig is still at the same company. Even rarer, so is most of his original management team, which has been reinforced with recruits from *IBM*, Burroughs, and Bechtel to help run sales, operations, and financial and strategic planning. "No heads rolled," says Chairman Thomas J. Perkins, the venture capitalist who bankrolled Tandem's start-up. "That's a measure of strength."

Not that it was easy. By mid-1984 it was clear that Tandem's narrow product line was limiting its appeal. Treybig sped work on both higher-powered and smaller, less-expensive systems. He also pushed through a raft of new storage devices and software. Last year the new products accounted for 75% of sales.

By then Treybig had also tackled marketing. Tandem had always thought that its fault-tolerant design was its best sales advantage. But surveys of customers showed that they were buying more for other features, such as Tandem's ability to track and update data between far-flung offices. So Treybig changed the sales pitch and beefed up what had been a skeletal headquarters group to focus on industries such as telecommunications and manufacturing. Before, "the sales crews were grabbing any customer they could find," says Gerald L. Peterson, marketing vice-president.

Treybig also realized that he needed to work with outside software publishers to reach new markets. It was a late discovery that *DEC* and others had made years before. But Treybig and Peterson followed suit. They set up a separate group of 100 specialists and three support centers around the country in late 1985 to do nothing but pamper software houses. In the past year, Tandem has tripled its software coterie to 225 companies,

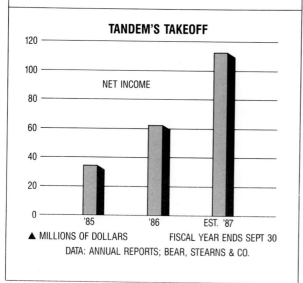

TANDEM'S TAKEOFF

NET INCOME

▲ MILLIONS OF DOLLARS   FISCAL YEAR ENDS SEPT 30
DATA: ANNUAL REPORTS; BEAR, STEARNS & CO.

many of them customers whose programs Tandem markets to others. "Tandem probably has the best third-party program in the industry," says Carol E. Muratore, an analyst at Morgan Stanley & Co. Adds Neal C. Hansen, president of Applied Communications Inc., a banking software house in Omaha: "It's a different company from two years ago."

Tandem has also established a special group to strike up joint ventures. Tapping Tandem's $240 million cash hoard, the group is investing in promising software vendors, for example.

THROUGH HOOPS. Customers have voted with their checkbooks. Allegheny Ludlum Corp. chose Tandem this year over *DEC* to automate the flow of data between its Pittsburgh headquarters and five steel mills. Financial Interchange Inc. of Houston, the largest regional banking system in the U. S., picked Tandem to replace an *IBM* mainframe to run the "Pulse" network of 4,000 *ATM*s from 1,800 financial institutions. Financial Interchange President Stan Paur calls that "one of the major marketing coups in this industry."

Tandem will need its renewed momentum to fight increasingly tough competition. Recent new products from *DEC* will challenge Tandem as the market for so-called on-line transaction processing heats up. Then there's Stratus Computer Inc., which makes fault-tolerant machines that *IBM* has resold since 1985. In January, Stratus introduced a system that offers more power than Tandem's for 75% of the price. Though Stratus lacks such nifty Tandem features as the ability to locate data easily anywhere on a worldwide network, "these are very strong offerings," says Kimball Brown, an analyst with Dataquest Inc., the market research firm. Tandem is planning a counterattack. It will bring out three new processors and software-programming tools this summer to solve shortcomings in its product line.

If Tandem jumped through hoops in the last two years, so did Treybig. Before the slide, his top managers say, he treated them as peers, relied on a consensus to make decisions, and seldom criticized products or strategy. But by the second year of flat earnings, Treybig was posting quarterly results on his door as a sign of his impatience. He also moved his office periodically to different de-partments to scrutinize operations. "Jim made the transition from team member to president," says Gerald D. Held, vice-president for new ventures.

That meant making tough decisions. By 1985, dozens of Tandem's 5,400 workers had bolted to competing startups, and morale was poor. But

> During the tough times, Treybig froze salaries and canceled Tandem's sales-incentive programs

Treybig froze salaries and canceled sales-incentive programs. "For what was supposed to be a very flexible environment, people got pretty brittle," recalls Anthony D. Turner, director of applied research.

With the good times back, so is the old Tandem spirit, thanks in large part to a worldwide electronic mail system and in-house *TV* network that Treybig uses to keep in touch with employees. All the previous trappings of company culture, such as swimming pools, paid sabbaticals, and Friday afternoon beer busts, are still around, too—and more ingrained than ever. When a newly hired New York manager eliminated his region's Friday get-togethers last year to cut costs, his boss in Cupertino persuaded him to reinstitute them.

The company's recent success has caused a few growing pains. It has faltered a few times in tying together its machines with customers' software, for instance. A slip-up in writing a piece of operating software recently delayed installation of a new reservations system at Western Air Lines Inc. for several months. Tandem has set up a small operation in Virginia to manage such jobs, and Held hints that Tandem may soon acquire a so-called system integrator that would help manage such projects.

Tandem could use the help. "The field has to deliver what seems a very firm commitment from Tandem top executives," says Mauro Weissman, president of Bedford Associates, the company that supplied Western's software. "We haven't seen that yet." With all he's been through in the past two years, Treybig should be able to overcome this latest challenge. But those ruins in the Yucatán might have to wait awhile.

By Jonathan B. Levine in Cupertino

DISCUSSION QUESTION
Leadership and corporate performance may have a chicken-and-egg relationship. Which comes first? Which causes the other? Is this article, what may have caused changes in Treybig's leadership style, and what may have caused changes in Tandem's performance?

CULTURE SHOCK AT XEROX

HOW DAVID KEARNS IS TRYING TO RESTORE ENTREPRENEURIAL VIGOR

JUNE 22, 1987, PP. 106, 108, 110

Over a recent dinner, David T. Kearns and his wife, Shirley, got to talking about quality. From her experience running the house to ordering from the L. L. Bean catalog, she doubted whether it was possible to get perfect products and service all the time. "She argued that you can't get 100% fault-free quality," recalls Kearns, Xerox Corp. chairman and chief executive. "But I think you can."

More than idle chitchat, the conversation struck at the heart of what Kearns has been trying to achieve at Xerox since becoming the company's third chief executive in 1982. He has focused on a simple theme: boosting the quality of Xerox products and service. To do that, Kearns is orchestrating major changes in the company and rattling its bureaucratic culture. He is trying to revive basic management techniques that Xerox seemed to forget in the 1970s: staying lean, delegating decision-making, and staying on top of the competition.

It also has meant an abrupt departure from the company's traditional product lines. His diversification into financial services, an area Xerox expects significant growth from in the future, amounted to a concession that, as Kearns puts it, "we could take our balance sheet and do better for our shareholders in another business." Businesses such as insurance, leasing, and mutual funds now account for half the company's profits.

NO TURNAROUND. His wife's doubting a 100% "defect-free" Xerox is not the only skepticism Kearns has encountered. Although he has halted a severe decline in Xerox' copier market share and made the move into financial services, there has been no dramatic turnaround. Xerox earned $465 million last year, well below its 1980 record, though revenues have risen by nearly 60%, to $12.9 billion. The company's return on equity is 9.5%, about half what it was in 1980, and long-term debt has doubled.

Even Kearns, 57, expresses dissatisfaction with the speed of his progress. "If someone dropped in here from Mars, like a T. Boone Pickens or a Larry Tisch, who was not constrained by the past, he would have been able to move faster," Kearns says. "When I look back, the most critical I can be of myself is for not moving fast enough."

To appreciate Kearns's challenge, you have to understand how Xerox evolved from an aggressive, rapidly growing, entrepreneurial concern to an impersonal, multibillion-dollar corporation. Under the guidance of founder Joseph C. Wilson, Xerox was the hot growth company of the 1960s and early 1970s. Wilson acquired exclusive world rights to inventor Chester F. Carlson's xerographic process and brought to the world a technology that changed the way people work.

By 1966, when Wilson handed the *CEO*'s baton to C. Peter McColough, the company dominated the copier market. But because of its tremendous growth, Xerox badly needed financial controls and clear lines of authority. McColough, a Harvard *MBA* who had managed the recruitment and training of Xerox' remarkable sales force, was up to the task. He promptly installed a modern management structure and recruited executives from big-name companies to fill key slots—and Xerox began to change.

McColough brought needed organizational reforms that at first produced good results, but they also made Xerox much too bureaucratic. "When I joined Xerox in 1960, everyone knew everyone else by their first name," says Don A. Kirkwood, a 21-year Xerox veteran who quit to start his own executive recruiting firm. "We ate, slept, and drank it. Then we helped to grow a bureaucracy.

You'd have a senior vice-president from corporate come in who people never heard of. They were indifferent to what he did and what he knew."

McColough acquired a slew of technology companies, many of which didn't pay off. There were long and costly product-development delays, and Xerox failed to capitalize on its scientists' innovations, from personal computers to data-communications networks. Both Eastman Kodak Co. and International Business Machines Corp. emerged as competitors, as did a number of Japanese companies.

SMUGTOWN, USA. Still, many of the decisions that ultimately got Xerox into trouble seemed right at the time. "It was a classic case of doing everything right," believes consultant Tom Peters. "They hired people from three of the best-managed companies, *IBM*, Ford, and General Electric. Only Procter & Gamble and *IBM* had better marketing groups. But there's nothing in the world that's harder to deal with than success." William F. Glavin, Xerox vice-chairman, agrees: "We were arrogant enough to think that no one could do anything better than we could. We didn't have anyone to learn from."

A "we-can-do-it-better" attitude pervaded the company. Top managers refused to believe the Japanese knew how to make quality copiers until long after losing significant market share to them. The company even treated vendors with disdain. "We were unwilling to ask a vendor for much help," says Wayland R. Hicks, now president of the company's business systems group. "We had the audacity to go to General Electric and tell them how to design electric motors for us."

Enter Kearns. Like Wilson, he is Rochester born and raised, with a business degree from the University of Rochester. A former sailor in the Navy, he joined Xerox in 1971 from *IBM*, became Xerox president in 1977, and saw the company's decline close up. He and fellow executives discovered as late as 1980 that the Japanese had a 40%-to-50% cost advantage over Xerox. "We did not understand the severity of the competition," he says. "I think that is an American problem that goes beyond Xerox."

When Kearns became *CEO* in 1982, he felt Xerox' culture impeded, rather than facilitated, the changes the company needed to compete. And as an insider, Kearns was bound by the company's traditions and its previous management.

CRASH PROGRAM. Nevertheless, he saw no choice but to try to make drastic changes. His toughest decision was eliminating 15,000 jobs in 1982-83. That went against the grain of what had long been a paternalistic company. For the jittery, fast-track executives who hung on to their jobs, the changes amounted to culture shock. They had gravitated to Xerox because the company moved its best people rapidly up the corporate ladder.

"People were getting their satisfaction not from the job they had," says Kearns, "but the job they were going to get." The result: Even some of Xerox' best managers had to confront the demoralizing prospect of staying in a single position for three to six years instead of 18 months. Xerox is trying to keep these managers challenged by regularly broadening their duties.

"When you roll these things up together, it's one helluva job," Kearns says. "It's just a lot tougher than I ever thought when I started down the track."

His progress in cutting the fat has been impressive. Xerox had 4.5 support staff for every manufacturing worker on the copier-assembly line in 1979-80. Now it's 1.5 to 1, with the most efficient plant as low as 0.7 to 1. For every services manager in the field, Xerox used to boast 13 technical representatives. Now it has one manager for every 18 reps.

'When I look back, the most critical I can be of myself is for not moving fast enough'

By creating small product-delivery teams, Xerox has reduced the labor needed to bring out a new machine by nearly 40% and cut almost 30% off the time it takes to get a new product to market. One of the latest copiers, the 1065, shipped in early February, took 51 months from design to market, compared with the 65 months it would have taken under the old system.

In the past the delays were partly a function of bigness. More people could say "no" to an idea or project than could say "yes" because authority became more centralized and removed from the troops in the trenches. One entire layer of corporate staff, for example, did little more than function as a watchdog. While they may have caught a mistake or two, they also made others in the corporation feel less significant.

"As the corporation grew larger, it was hard for people to have the same impact," says Hicks. "Nobody said: 'My job is to get a product into the market that will sell and make a profit for us.' No one really had that degree of accountability, and if he did, he didn't have the control of the resources or the authority to make it happen."

LESS IS MORE. Kearns has continued to challenge past practices. Take Xerox' use of huge numbers of vendors: In 1980, Xerox used to order parts and components from 5,000 vendors worldwide. When Kearns initially tried to get the numbers down, he ran into resistance.

"The purchasing people told us, 'You can't do that,'" he recalls. "'We need backup suppliers in case someone goes on strike or a plant goes down. You need to deal with more vendors—not less—to get competitive prices,'" Kearns says.

It wasn't true. Using fewer vendors gave Xerox more leverage to enforce tougher quality standards, get better prices, and forge more cooperative partnerships with them. Xerox now deals with fewer than 400 and hopes to trim this down to 250 companies over the next five years. The result: 99.2% of the parts arrive free from defects, compared with 92% four years ago.

A disciple of quality consultant-guru Phil Crosby, author of *Quality Is Free*, Kearns speaks passionately about moving the 99.2% figure to 100%, whether he's with his wife or a Xerox plant manager. He has elevated the issue of quality to a cause around which the company's cultural changes revolve.

The drive for quality helped Xerox save as much as $2 billion in the company's reprographics and information systems business, which has revenues of $10 billion. "Over the years, you grow up thinking that the greater quality you give a customer, the higher the price," Kearns says. "We now know that's not true. Quality drives costs down." That's so because getting it right the first time eliminates having to repair costly mistakes, which could also drive customers away.

SALES GAINS. These days, Xerox salesmen are more aggressive, too. The company enjoyed a 39.7% share of the market for the most expensive business copiers last year, up from 37.6% in 1982, according to Dataquest Inc., a research firm. Gains were even sharper in the market for the least expensive units, where Xerox' share jumped to 11.1% from 8.6%. Analysts expect Xerox to recapture ground this year in the mid-range segment, where it faces increasing competition and where its share fell to 24.1%, from 26.2% in 1982. Dataquest's numbers, however, tend to underestimate Xerox' strength because they measure market share by units instead of revenues, and Xerox tends to concentrate on more expensive copiers.

In Xerox' $2.4 billion office systems group, Kearns is narrowing the company's focus. Instead of being a general player in the personal computer market, Xerox is now emphasizing products that support what the company calls "document processing"—electronic publishing systems, electronic printers, networks, and software.

"In the past, Xerox was indecisive about what its role should be in office systems," comments Linda O'Keeffe, director of Dataquest's office systems group. "Their new approach builds on their installed base of word processors and plays to the public mental connection between Xerox and paper output."

The nagging question at Xerox is: Will it all come together—and when? The move to diversify into financial services with the 1984 acquisitions of property and casualty insurer Crum & Forster Inc. and investment banker Van Kampen Merritt Inc. finally seems to be paying off. First-quarter earnings from continuing operations jumped by 32%—mostly because of further gains in financial services. And last year the business, with 12,000 employees, accounted for nearly half of Xerox' net income. By contrast, the business products group, whose efficiency is vastly improved, employs

103,000. "Some of the excuses are going away," says Kearns, "and we're going to have to perform."

How would Joseph Wilson see it? "He took tremendous risks," considers Kearns. "He bet the company and his whole personal wealth. That's not really true of myself. I'm more of a professional manager than an entrepreneur. But if he's watching, I'd like to think he believes we came to the right judgments." More likely, Wilson would want to see a bit more evidence that Xerox has regained the magic that it once had.

By John A. Byrne in Stamford, Conn.

DISCUSSION QUESTIONS

1. Presumably, you have read a number of articles in this collection and gotten some sense of the often-expressed antipathy to bureaucracy. Is there an inexorable evolution toward bureaucracy as organizations grow? In what way does bureaucracy reportedly impede performance?
2. Does corporate success induce conceit? Discuss.
3. Is the reported succession of cultures at Xerox—entrepreneurial to bureaucratic to rejuvenation—a normal sequence? Discuss.
4. How is Kearns seeking to rejuvenate the entrepreneurial spirit at Xerox?

ROGER SMITH'S CAMPAIGN TO CHANGE THE GM CULTURE

APRIL 7, 1986, PP. 84-85

For nine consecutive nights in mid-January, thousands of Hughes Aircraft Co. employees and their families streamed into Disneyland. They were guests of General Motors Corp., Hughes's new parent, which rented the park for a $2.5 million party to welcome aboard the Hughes people.

The celebration illustrates the high value *GM* Chairman Roger B. Smith puts on his newest $5 billion high-tech acquisition. "The more I look at Hughes, the more I like it," Smith gloats. "I can't think of anything that pleases me more than how it's working out right now."

PASSE LEGACY. It will take more than a trip to the Magic Kingdom, however, to make Hughes a successful buy. Smith has been trying radically to reshape *GM*'s corporate culture and to digest an earlier high-tech acquisition, Electronic Data Systems. Now he faces the tough task of meshing the sharply different cultures of *GM* and Hughes. To exploit the marriage fully, Smith must move some of Hughes's technical expertise to *GM*'s auto divisions.

GM can use the help. Despite a four-year drive to reinvigorate the auto maker, many managers are still groping for a clear understanding of their new roles. Costs remain so high that the company's return on sales is the lowest in the industry. *GM*'s market share remains below its 1978 level. Earnings are expected to fall 15% this year. "*GM* will be around in the year 2000," says David O. Ulrich, a University of Michigan professor. "The question is, will it be competitive?"

It was one of Smith's predecessors, Alfred P. Sloan Jr., *GM*'s chairman from 1937 to 1956, who defined the modern corporation. But in recent years, Sloan's legacy at *GM* evolved into a bureaucracy that discouraged risk-taking and slowed decision-making.

Six chairmen later, Smith is dismantling that vaunted structure to create a more nimble outfit. When he became chairman in 1981, *GM*'s share of the U. S. car market was crumbling, and the company had just reported its first loss since 1921. Because of its high production costs, *GM* could not justify launching a new generation of domestic small cars to blunt Japan's market attack.

Smith moved decisively. He streamlined *GM*'s hierarchy and pushed decision-making many levels down into the ranks. In a 1984 reorganization, he created two super groups—Buick-Oldsmobile-Cadillac *(BOC)* and Chevrolet-Pontiac-*GM* of Canada *(CPC)*—to replace a decades-old structure of seven divisions and a major subsidiary. To lend a sense of direction, Smith has widely distributed "culture cards" that *GM* executives carry in their pockets to remind them of their new mission.

These moves, however, were just the beginning of a revolution that Smith is still trying to incite. To add technological clout, he bought *EDS* shortly after the car groups were reorganized. Last year he added Hughes Aircraft. And along the way, he launched Saturn Corp., an autonomous manufacturing operation aimed at competing with the Japanese in the small-car market.

Smith is counting on Saturn and his high-tech subsidiaries not only for their knowhow but also for the cultural changes they can bring to the core business. Saturn is combining the latest in factory- and office-automation technology with participatory management, which Smith says he wants "Saturn to sell by example" to the rest of *GM*.

TASSEL TABOO. That makes sense. But it's not as easy as it sounds. Even a hands-on manager like Smith must wait. "My fingers used to be longer before I chewed them off wanting to get my hands on Saturn," he admits. "Everybody says, 'Oh boy, the chairman of *GM*—what a pot of power.' But you'd better have people going with you instead of trying to drag them along."

Consider the problems Smith has encountered in trying to substitute the *EDS* emphasis on results for his veteran managers' faith in process and procedures. After *GM* transferred 10,000 data-processing workers and managers to *EDS* in 1984, Smith had a near-revolt on his hands. *GM* employees were angered over *EDS*'s rigid dress codes and rules of conduct that, among other things, forbade employees to wear tasseled shoes or drink alcohol over lunch. One *GM* manager characterizes *EDS*'s employee handbook as "something out of a 19th-century Presbyterian hymn book." Some 600 people quit; others filed for union elections with the United Auto Workers. Even today some *GM* managers confess to plotting ways to get around *EDS*'s systems.

To avoid similar problems with Hughes, Smith is pursuing a distinctly different strategy. For example, he wants to create close ties between Hughes and Delco Electronics, which makes semiconductors. But he has protected both units from culture shock by turning them into independent subsidiaries. "Hughes has a culture we don't want to disturb and a technology we want to tap," explains Donald J. Atwood, a *GM* executive vice-president.

Atwood is doing so through "fast-start" teams and project centers. There, engineers and scientists from *GM*, *EDS*, and Hughes try to apply Hughes's microelectronics and systems engineering to *GM*'s products.

This approach, of course, doesn't solve a deeper problem Smith faces in making *GM* a more dynamic, risk-oriented environment. Many *GM* managers caught in the car-group shuffle complain that they are uncertain about their new responsibilities and feel cut off from the support networks they had built up over the years. "You get bounced from one direction to another, and it's very confusing," says one *GM* manager. Thousands of managers and engineers have yet to receive permanent job assignments.

'DO IT YOURSELF.' One sign of Smith's struggle to remake *GM* is his growing reliance on consultants. A McKinsey & Co. study sparked the *GM* reorganization. Since then, managers have turned increasingly to McKinsey and others to find ways to apply the corporate strategy to their own operations. *BOC* alone figures it has worked with some 30 or 40 outsiders, notably United Research Co. "Our task is to accelerate the process," says Robert M. Isenhour, a *URC* senior vice-president. "We can help employees see how the new goals benefit both them and the organization and to adjust to their new roles."

There is another reason for the influx of consultants. After telling managers to make their own decisions, Smith steadfastly refuses to intervene. One senior executive calls the new regime "do-it-yourself management." In some cases, managers simply lack the expertise to get the job done in-house. Some of the results might have shocked Alfred Sloan. *BOC* worked out a decentralized model centered on four product groups, each of which is an integrated business. *CPC* chose a highly centralized scheme organized along functional lines but coupled with "matrix management" to provide open lines of communication between functions. Smith approved both.

Smith wins praise for such flexibility from *GM* insiders who had come to expect a more heavy-handed role from the chairman. "We didn't change—he changed," insists William E. Hoglund, *BOC* group vice-president. Instead of doing it all himself, "he is using us now."

Other Smith supporters, moreover, claim that the new culture has helped eliminate some inbred inefficiencies. When Chevrolet marketers requested specially equipped cars to penetrate the import-prone California market last year, engineers were able to turn them out in less than six months. In the old, hierarchical *GM* culture, the program would have taken 15 months. Last fall one group won increased allocations of *GM*'s intermediate cars quickly enough to capitalize on a surge in demand. So many levels of approval would have been required previously, company insiders say, that the brief upturn would have been over before the extra cars became available.

GM managers, often criticized for their preoccupation with short-term results, are now making more decisions based on long-term considerations. Two new automated plants are running at half of line-speed capacity—60 cars per hour—because of glitches in computer-integrated systems. Yet each plant employs a full complement of nearly 5,000 workers. "In the historical culture, we would be up there beating the daylights out of them for more production, and we would have gotten a new plant manager," says Hoglund. The possible result: product-quality problems. "Now they are getting encouragement and support" to get the problems worked out.

Concerned about the heightened tension among managers trying to cope with cultural changes, *CPC* Group Vice-President Robert F. Schultz urges his subordinates to stay away from their offices on weekends and to take their vacations. "We want them to be around and able to contribute," he says.

FAILURE LICENSE. In effect, Smith has granted his managers what the consultants call "permission to fail." He has also given them more authority—creating a variety of plum jobs. In the *BOC* group, for example, there are now four newly created product team leaders. Each runs the equivalent of a $10 billion company with all the functions of an independent business, from product design to manufacturing, finance to public rela-

tions. To a limited extent, each team markets its products to the *GM* divisions, which in turn sell to the public. "This has created new career paths and showed that it's O.K. to participate in the new, risk-taking culture," says *URC*'s Isenhour. "Those product team leaders got way ahead in their careers, and that sends a clear signal to the organization."

The problem is how deeply those signals reach. "At the top, the vision is pretty clear," says Ulrich. "The message may be down two or three levels, but they have another eight levels to go." To turn its core business around, to regain market share and profitability, Smith must convey his culture changes to the troops that make the company work. A trip to Disneyland is only a start.

By David E. Whiteside in Detroit

DISCUSSION QUESTIONS
1. Discuss Smith's observation on the limits of his power as a leader—the idea that you can't drag people along.
2. What problems did GM reportedly have with decentralized leadership and decision making?
3. What are some prominent features of the culture GM is seeking to create, and how do they differ from the company's traditions?

CHANGE AT *THE NEW YORKER* IS THE TALK OF THE TOWN

SI NEWHOUSE HAS TURNED THE BUSINESS SIDE INSIDE OUT— EDITORIAL COULD BE NEXT
MARCH 10, 1986, PP. 122, 126

Early last May, S. I. Newhouse and Steven T. Florio visited the Manhattan offices of *The New Yorker* at the invitation of legendary editor William Shawn. It was shortly before Newhouse consummated his $170 million purchase of the magazine's parent company, and the elaborately courteous Shawn took the properly awestruck pair on a tour of his domain.

Florio felt far less reverence for the business offices—an attitude that became apparent not long after, when he was named publisher of the 60-year-old magazine. In Florio's view, the magazine's circulation and ad-sales departments had grown inbred, clubby, and complacent. "I just blew it out of here with a fire hose," he says. The stream carried off many of New Yorker Magazine Inc.'s senior managers, including some who had been with the magazine for more than two decades.

FUNEREAL THOUGHTS. The weekly has been showing its age. Its circulation has been static, its ad pages have nose-dived, and it has been able to maintain revenue growth only by hiking ad prices, increasingly irritating its advertisers. In the view of many industry observers, The New Yorker's business practices had grown as fusty as its corridors. But Florio means to change all that. In his first nine months as publisher, he has instituted vigorous circulation promotions and begun an aggressive courtship of Madison Avenue.

Critics say that Florio's efforts threaten to destroy The New Yorker's hallowed position among U. S. magazines while placing it on a treadmill of high spending and low profits. In 1984, its last year as a public company, New Yorker Magazine

Inc. earned $10.3 million before taxes on revenues of $81 million, most of which came from the flagship magazine. Some competitors suspect that it is now breaking even at best. Others say that The New Yorker's thoughtful, often difficult copy is outdated in a world of glitz, brevity, and superficiality. "It's the only magazine of letters that has ever been commercially successful," says one publisher. "It could be that it has run its course."

Such funereal thoughts lead some observers to predict that Newhouse will make major changes. Many say he will fold his troubled Vanity Fair monthly and transfer its subscribers to The New Yorker. Newhouse is believed to have reincarnated Vanity Fair after being frustrated in earlier efforts to buy The New Yorker. "Si realizes he made a big mistake with Vanity Fair," a competitor says, "and now he can cover it up."

To the relief of The New Yorker's editors and writers—whose initial reaction to the acquisition bordered on open insurrection—Newhouse and Florio have thus far avoided any editorial interference. But rival publishers say that big editorial changes will have to come. They say The New Yorker's long series on topics such as geology and grain make too many demands on modern readers. "People's interests and alternatives have changed" while the magazine hasn't, says George J. Green, who was president of New Yorker Maga-

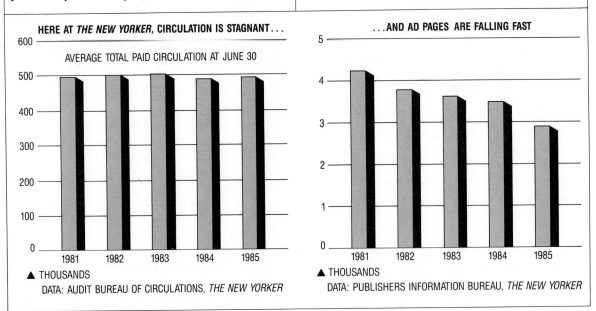

HERE AT *THE NEW YORKER*, CIRCULATION IS STAGNANT...

AVERAGE TOTAL PAID CIRCULATION AT JUNE 30

▲ THOUSANDS

DATA: AUDIT BUREAU OF CIRCULATIONS, *THE NEW YORKER*

...AND AD PAGES ARE FALLING FAST

▲ THOUSANDS

DATA: PUBLISHERS INFORMATION BUREAU, *THE NEW YORKER*

zine Inc. until 1984. "Take this week's issue and one from 20 years ago, and I challenge you to see what the differences are."

IRRITATED ADVERTISERS. No significant editorial changes are likely as long as the redoubtable, revered Shawn remains in charge. The choice of a

---

A host of magazines, from *Gourmet* to *Elle*, have loosened *The New Yorker*'s grip on affluent readers

---

successor to the 78-year-old editor, who is only the second in *The New Yorker*'s history, has been hot gossip for more than a decade.

Now it will be Newhouse's decision. He is said to be considering Robert A. Gottlieb, editor-in-chief of Alfred A. Knopf Inc., a Newhouse property; Robert B. Silvers, editor of *The New York Review of Books*; Tina Brown, editor of *Vanity Fair*; and George A. Plimpton. None of these choices sits well with the current staff, but insiders say that even a superb choice will cause trauma, especially if the successor is an outsider.

For now, Florio is concentrating on the magazine's business side. The 36-year-old carries good turnaround credentials. In his five years as publisher of *Gentlemen's Quarterly*, another magazine owned by Newhouse's Advance Publications Inc., he presided over a doubling of circulation to more than 600,000 and an increase in ad revenues to $25.9 million from $5.9 million. His goals for *The New Yorker* are more modest. He hopes to boost circulation this year by about 50,000 copies, to 550,000, and to increase advertising by about 100 pages.

Even such a small ad increase may be hard to pull off. For years, *The New Yorker* has been losing market share in such crucial categories as apparel, retail, automotive, and travel advertising. Ad executives say that's because a host of magazines, from *Gourmet* to *Elle,* have loosened *The New Yorker*'s grip on affluent readers. "Suddenly, *The New Yorker* has competition," says Leo E.

Scullin of Young & Rubicam Inc. "It doesn't stand out as much as it used to."

Late last year the magazine began a direct-mail solicitation to 2 million potential subscribers. It also tested a group of *TV* commercials based on stories that appeared in the magazine. The *TV* campaign, which has cost about $2 million so far, is now being launched nationwide. The ads are primarily intended to reach young agency media buyers, many of whom believe "the *New Yorker* reader is a 64-year-old member of a bird-watching club," Florio says.

In one of his most controversial decisions, Florio has also begun accepting ads the magazine previously rejected—horizontal half-pages, insert cards for readers to mail back to such direct-response advertisers as L. L. Bean Inc., and some racy ads of the sort that had always been banned by Shawn.

BILL ME LATER. Florio's moves win plaudits from agencies and advertisers. "I don't remember the last time I'd seen someone from *The New Yorker*," says Robert R. Giacomino, group media director at Grey Advertising Inc. "That's changing. They want to know what our needs are, which is different from saying, 'We are what we are, and you do business on our terms.' "

Many publishing executives, however, say that Florio is taking a huge risk—that you don't fool around with *The New Yorker*. Former managers say they avoided large circulation promotions because they wanted only devoted readers. Flashy ad campaigns may attract new subscribers who will be disappointed by the magazine and who won't renew. If *The New Yorker*'s stunning 75% renewal rate falls, the economics of the magazine could change. Says a former executive: "Maybe the whole reason *The New Yorker* was very profitable was that we didn't spend money on circulation."

One competitor who was a senior manager of the company estimates that *The New Yorker* is now spending an additional $3 million per year on circulation and promotion, an expense it will be saddled with permanently if the renewal rate deteriorates. At the same time, ad pages are still declining—by about 15% so far this year—and circulation revenue may be falling off because Florio has cut some subscription prices. He has also introduced credit for the first time—the "bill-me-later" subscription.

Some longtime advertisers are troubled by the changes. Tiffany & Co. has run ads in *The New Yorker* for 53 years. When one Tiffany ad in several publications gave an incorrect date for the sale of some jewels to Empress Eugénie, *The New Yorker* readers were the only ones to catch it. "I love that," says Suzanne McMillan, Tiffany's vice-president for marketing, who fears that new readers might pay less attention.

By Mark N. Vamos in New York

DISCUSSION QUESTION

The article notes the opinion that executives take a big risk when they "fool around" with the distinctive character of an enterprise. In the case of *The New Yorker,* what is risked? What unintended and unwanted results might flow from some of the changes described?

LETTING WORKERS HELP HANDLE WORKERS' GRIPES

SEPTEMBER 15, 1986, PP. 82, 86

General Electric Co.'s Appliance Park East plant in Columbia, Md., had poor labor relations from the day its doors opened in 1971. Employees made little use of *GE*'s complaint procedure because, management admits, they had no confidence in it. Although unions failed in four attempts to organize the plant's 2,300 workers, they usually garnered about 40% of the vote. "The workers were saying they didn't trust us," says Harvey S. Caras, a former manager of employee relations at the plant.

To solve that problem—and keep unions at bay in the bargain—Caras came up with a new vehicle for handling complaints: an appeals panel consisting of three hourly workers and two managers. In the panel's first four years it has issued about 80

decisions on everything from discipline to performance appraisals. While the panel may be only part of the reason, union activity at Appliance Park has dwindled. "We took away a major union issue," says Caras.

> Grievance panels that include peers may make employees more confident —and keep unions at bay

GE is the most prominent among a handful of major companies that have turned to peer-review panels as a way to keep unions out of plants that aren't already organized—half of *GE*'s plants aren't. Caras, now director of consulting services at Dallas-based Performance Systems Corp., has helped set up peer-review systems at 13 other *GE* plants and at 11 Borg-Warner Corp. automotive plants. In 1983, Control Data Corp. added peer review to its 24-year-old nonunion grievance system because, company executives concede, employees didn't trust the old system. Since 1984, employees discharged from Honda of America Mfg.'s plant in Marysville, Ohio, can appeal to a panel of six employees and one management representative.

Typically, peer review is simply added to a company's existing grievance process. At most nonunion companies with a complaint procedure, an employee tries to solve disputes first with his or her direct supervisor. If no agreement is reached, the employee can appeal to higher levels of management, including, in some companies, the chief executive officer. Peer review usually takes over after that process is exhausted.

BASIC TRAINING. At *GE*, three names are selected randomly by the aggrieved employee from a pool of hourly workers who have volunteered for peer-review duty. Each panel member goes through up to 12 hours of training in basic law and in peer-review guidelines. The panel, which usually includes the plant manager and an employee relations representative, hears the case and hands down a decision signed by all five members. *GE* says that management's position has been upheld in about 80% of the cases.

Both employees and management see benefits in peer review. "Something had to be done to get management to listen," says a worker who has served on a peer- review panel at Borg-Warner's Bellwood (Ill.) plant. "If you've got another peer listening to you, you think you can get a better shot." Some executives find that peer review puts managers on their toes. "Your supervisors do a better job because they don't want their people going up before a panel—it's embarrassing," says Robert F. Burnaska, a *GE* personnel relations consultant.

But the peer-review concept has some limitations, at least as it's been applied so far. The scope of virtually all existing peer panels is restricted. At *GE*, the panel cannot set pay or benefits or alter work rules—traditional union organizing issues. The Appliance Park system also excludes job evaluations and probationary terminations.

Peer review can turn into an empty promise if using it isn't encouraged. An internal *GE* report completed last January praised the peer-review concept but criticized the company's failure to promulgate it. "You [set up a peer review system], then you put it on the shelf and assume everyone will do it—but it needs maintenance," says Burnaska.

Some employees complain that peer review still gives the company the upper hand. Last year a Control Data systems analyst was fired for allegedly disclosing other employees' salaries to another employee. A peer review panel upheld the company. The fired employee questions the system's credibility because it doesn't permit the grievant to appear in person before the board. Instead, a written case is presented. He also says the system favors the company because it has staff with the time and knowledge to prepare cases. The personnel department helps employees prepare their cases. But the Control Data worker points out that the department took part in the decision to

fire him and therefore wasn't impartial. Control Data maintains that the system is fair, citing figures showing that employees win in more than a third of the cases.

> 'I don't think a worker should be put in the position of discharging another worker'

'NOTHING BEHIND IT.' Critics of peer review argue that the system pits employees against one another. "I don't think a worker should be put in the position of discharging another worker," says Hugh J. Smith, an international representative for the United Auto Workers, which tried unsuccessfully to organize Honda's Marysville plant. Smith adds that since Honda's review panels usually are convened several days after a discharge, the employee has little time to prepare for the hearing.

Some workers remain leery of peer review. Says one Control Data employee: "A union grievance system has power behind it. This has nothing behind it." But because companies can use the idea to supplant a traditional union function, use of it will probably grow.

By Jonathan Tasini in New York, with Patrick Houston in Minneapolis

DISCUSSION QUESTIONS

1. Although peer review can be considered a form of performance appraisal and appeals systems a form of grievance procedure, the GE program described in the article can also be seen as a more fundamental change in an organization's systems of communication and management. Discuss.

2. What objections can you raise to GE's use of appeals panels?

BUSINESS STARTS TAILORING ITSELF TO SUIT WORKING WOMEN

BENEFITS, PROMOTIONS, AND WORK RULES ARE CHANGING AS FEMALE EMPLOYEES FLOOD IN

OCTOBER 6, 1986, PP. 50-54

A few years ago, when the number of women at Merck & Co. approached one-third of all employees, the company decided to update its personnel policies. In 1980 the drugmaker helped to open a child-care center near its Rahway (N. J.) headquarters. In 1981 it began letting employees start work at any point from 7 a.m. to 9:30 a.m.—to give parents more flexibility. Two years later it started allowing some parents to work part-time or at home after maternity leave. In 1984, Merck funded a major study on how employees balance work and family life. And last year it created workshops and a counseling program to help parents cope with the double strain of job and family.

"Merck has recognized that lifestyles and family patterns have changed significantly over recent years," says Arthur F. Strohmer, executive director for human resources. "We believe the corporation can benefit from helping employees balance the demands of the family and the demands of the workplace."

PACESETTERS. It's a nascent movement, but the feminization of the work force is starting to transform the way employers treat employees. Companies are realizing that nearly half of all workers today are women, up from 33% only 20 years ago. It's also obvious that these female employees—80% of whom earn less than $19,000 a year, mainly in service jobs—have different needs than do male workers. Pacesetting companies such as American Telephone & Telegraph Co. and BankAmerica Corp. are tackling day-care shortages, putting in new or extended maternity and parental leave, and revamping fringe benefits. New promotion systems make it easier for women to raise children without ruining their careers. More companies pay women the same as men for so-called comparable jobs. Others are twisting the 40-hour workweek into multiple configurations. Nearly every change affects men, too, both husbands and fellow workers.

Like most major social changes, the reorientation of the workplace to women's needs is happening with distressing slowness: It may take decades for the majority of employers to change their view of women as second-class workers. But the explanations companies give for the newest experiments indicate that, ultimately, most employers will have little choice but to adapt. Adding to pressures from unions and women's groups is the primary motivation: self-interest. Two-thirds of the 15 million new entrants into the job market through 1995 will be women, according to the Bureau of Labor Statistics (charts), and in terms of sheer numbers, they will have more influence than ever before.

If labor shortages occur in the 1990s, as some economists predict, women will be in high demand, and only companies with the best policies will get the best workers. "What's driving companies is competition in the labor market," says Robert L. Shaughnessy, vice-president for personnel at *AT&T*. "As companies sell themselves to prospective employees, women will look at employers in a better light if they meet their needs."

Perhaps the most pressing problem for women workers is the acute shortage of day care (page

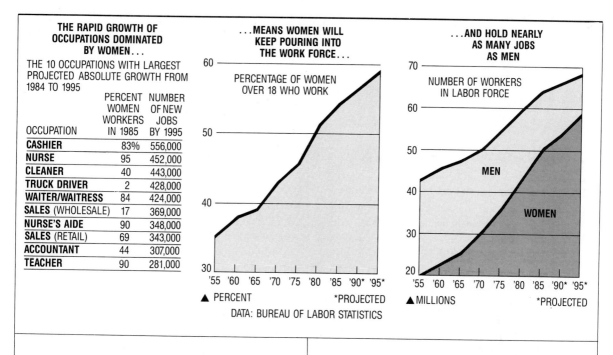

THE RAPID GROWTH OF OCCUPATIONS DOMINATED BY WOMEN...

THE 10 OCCUPATIONS WITH LARGEST PROJECTED ABSOLUTE GROWTH FROM 1984 TO 1995

OCCUPATION	PERCENT WOMEN WORKERS IN 1985	NUMBER OF NEW JOBS BY 1995
CASHIER	83%	556,000
NURSE	95	452,000
CLEANER	40	443,000
TRUCK DRIVER	2	428,000
WAITER/WAITRESS	84	424,000
SALES (WHOLESALE)	17	369,000
NURSE'S AIDE	90	348,000
SALES (RETAIL)	69	343,000
ACCOUNTANT	44	307,000
TEACHER	90	281,000

...MEANS WOMEN WILL KEEP POURING INTO THE WORK FORCE...

PERCENTAGE OF WOMEN OVER 18 WHO WORK

'55 '60 '65 '70 '75 '80 '85 '90* '95*
▲ PERCENT   *PROJECTED

...AND HOLD NEARLY AS MANY JOBS AS MEN

NUMBER OF WORKERS IN LABOR FORCE

MEN

WOMEN

'55 '60 '65 '70 '75 '80 '85 '90* '95*
▲ MILLIONS   *PROJECTED

DATA: BUREAU OF LABOR STATISTICS

181). Experts say that most parents who work must piece together two or three separate arrangements for child care. Although companies have barely touched the overall situation, they're beginning to try. The Conference Board estimates that 2,500 companies provided some form of child-care aid in 1985, up from 600 in 1982. About 150 have on-site centers.

Campbell Soup Co. started an on-site center at its Camden (N. J.) headquarters in 1983. "It's convenient and includes breakfast, so I don't have to cook in the morning," says Lisa A. Mooney, a credit specialist in Campbell's accounts-receivable department, who has a three-year-old girl and a two-year-old boy. "As much as I'd rather be home with them myself, I didn't have much choice. If we wanted to eat, I had to keep working." The center costs only about $40 a week per child. But there's room for only 130 kids, and 80 more are waiting to get in.

TRIAL RUN. Because on-site centers are costly and raise questions about a company's legal liability, most employers think it's better to stimulate the community supply of day care. In 1984, BofA put up $100,000 and gathered 23 participants, including other employers and foundations, that spent $700,000 on a pilot program in California to cre-

ate 1,000 new day-care slots by recruiting and training individuals to be child-care providers. BofA expects the project to continue in 1987 on a $1.1 million budget. Similarly, *AT&T* says it will start several experiments this year, from on-site centers to giving employees a building in which they can start their own facility.

International Business Machines Corp. went even further. In 1984 it spent $1 million to set up what may be the first nationwide corporate service for referring employees to community child care. With a budget estimated by outsiders to be $2 million a year, the service has referred 16,000 children. *IBM* also has given money to a nonprofit group that has trained 5,000 new providers to care for 13,000 children. "The [rising] number of women among our employees is leading us to consider things that didn't seem important before," says Jack Carter, *IBM*'s director of employee services.

Employers also are starting to look at problems that day care doesn't always handle. In 1985 companies such as Dayton Hudson Corp. and First Bank System Inc. in Minneapolis began contributing to a company called Chicken Soup, which cares for ill children so that their parents can work rather than stay at home. A nurse and a teacher are on duty from 6 a.m. to 6 p.m. In 1983,

CHILD CARE: THE PRIVATE SECTOR CAN'T DO IT ALONE

In the 15 years since President Richard Nixon vetoed a bill providing for a national day-care system, the American family has been through an economic and cultural wringer. Fewer than one in 10 households now resemble the white-picket-fence world where father's income lets mother stay home with the kids. Yet parents seeking child care must rely on the social policies and institutions of a simpler era and on the workings of the market. All have failed to meet the need.

The result is a child-care crisis for the middle class as well as for the poor. More than half of all mothers now work, mainly because they must. The relatives and neighbor ladies who used to baby-sit are probably out working, too. Despite the urgent need for more child care, what has emerged is an ad hoc, fragmented, inadequate network that bewilders parents with services that too often range from minimal to dangerous or bad. The once-private matter of child care has become a public policy issue that demands action.

DESPERATION. The extent of the problem is impossible to quantify. About 10 million children under age 6 have working mothers, and the number is growing. An estimated 15% are looked after in licensed child-care centers. "Family day-care homes," largely unlicensed, where a woman tends children in her home for a fee, take care of another 40%. The rest are with baby-sitters or relatives or in part-time preschool and other programs that may be exempt from licensing.

Some of these are competently operated. But many providers lack professional training, and most are paid low wages. Even in licensed facilities, staff turnover is high and quality may be indifferent. Out of desperation, many parents patch together inconvenient, stress-producing, or part-time arrangements that leave them dissatisfied.

No one is suggesting a uniform, monolithic federal program. For one thing, it would cost tens of billions of dollars. For another, in the past 15 years a considerable infrastructure has been assembled: for-profit centers and chains, home-based care services, non-profit facilities, community resource and referral services, and employer-sponsored day care (page 178). Such diversity is a strength. But the private sector is not meeting the sheer size of the need or coordinating the various services. It can't assure quality care or serve the growing numbers of poor children.

To do that, "government has to get more resources in the system," says Representative George Miller (D-Calif.), chairman of the House Select Committee on Children, Youth & Families. Few families can afford $8,000 a year or more for in-home care, or the $5,000 that education specialists say buys the best infant care outside the home, or $2,500 for full-time preschool at a licensed group facility. More women are heading households, and the average woman earns $9,300. More than half of all working, married women have husbands earning $20,000 or less.

Even affluent parents are often faced with inconvenience or compromise. Alfred J. Kahn, professor of social work at Columbia University, sees an absolute shortage of care for infants and toddlers, as well as for school-age kids, more of whom are fending for themselves after 3 p.m. Facilities for ill children or those with special problems are practically nonexistent. Although some day-care chains have room for 20% more children, Kahn says, "no one can afford to pay."

When care is affordable, compromises often must be made. At North West Child Development Council 3M Co. gave money to a Minneapolis *YMCA* so it could expand the hours of a summer center for school children. Says Cheryl Ann Smith, a secretary at 3M: "I dropped off my 11-year-old daughter in the morning. My husband picked her up at five, and we didn't have to worry all day. It made life so much easier and cost half the price of private day care."

Maternity leave is another issue where some movement is visible. No more than 40% of working women have any form of maternity leave—including those who use sick and vacation leave.

Inc., a private, nonprofit agency that runs 17 day-care centers in North Carolina, parents pay $40 to $50 a week for infant group care. North West's one-to-seven caretaker ratio meets state standards but is twice what child development experts say is optimal. Susan H. Law, the agency's executive director, has lobbied for tighter standards. But, says Law, "if you make it one-to-four, nobody could afford to put their kid in there—even if you pay minimum wage." And with higher liability-insurance costs, more centers must cut budgets or raise fees.

Corporations run up against the same cost constraints. "In the long run," says Dana E. Friedman, senior research associate at the Conference Board's Work & Family Information Center, "corporations cannot shoulder the full responsibility for employees' child-care needs. This is truly an area for partnership between the public and private sectors." Employers, she suggests, could buy into a system lubricated with government funds.

A FEW SOLUTIONS. Some of the problems could be addressed with relative ease. As a start, public schools could stay open a few hours longer, providing supervised play for children until their parents came home from work. Volunteers, older students, and retirees could help. But even such schemes call for some public support; much child care can never pay for itself.

No child-care system can erase the dual responsibility working parents face, either. But most developed countries have found ways to soften the conflict between raising a family and supporting it. France, Belgium, Italy, Canada, Israel, and the Scandinavian countries, among others, subsidize child care. More than 100 countries provide job-protected maternity leave with some wage replacement (table). A few offer longer parental leaves and flexible scheduling, with no loss of seniority or benefits. Some provide a family stipend to spend on child care or support women who stay home.

FOUR COUNTRIES THAT MANDATE LEAVES FOR PARENTS

Only the basic benefit is described. In most countries—and more than 100 offer such benefits—leaves are extendable for multiple or complicated births, and the employee is guaranteed the same or a comparable job upon return to work. The U.S. has no parental leave policy.

CANADA 15 weeks for mothers at 60% of pay, with national social insurance picking up the tab. Two additional weeks at no pay

FRANCE 16 weeks for mothers at full pay, but only up to a maximum covered by social security. Six months at up to 100% of maximum for third or subsequent child. Unpaid parental leave of up to two years for both mothers and fathers*

SWEDEN 40 weeks for mothers or fathers at full pay, 90% covered by social insurance and 10% by employer, 12 additional weeks at preset flat rate. Or, a combination of partial leave and cash. Additional unpaid leave until child reaches 18 months

WEST GERMANY 14 weeks for mothers at full pay, with social insurance paying up to the average wage and the employer the rest. Subsequently, up to 10 weeks' leave with social insurance only, plus another 10 months at a reduced rate

*Extra unpaid leave only for employees of companies with 100 or more workers

DATA: SHEILA B. KAMERMAN, SCHOOL OF SOCIAL WORK, COLUMBIA UNIVERSITY

The U.S. has a precedent: During World War II, child care centers were set up to help bring women into the factories. But it has no policy. There is no mandated maternity leave, outside the requirement that employers treat pregnancy no differently from any other "disability." But such benefits don't cover 60% of working women. Edward Zigler, a Yale University child development expert, abhors the result: infants as young as three weeks in child care.

Although most large corporations provide some sort of leave, many don't guarantee that a woman will get her job back if she's off more than six to eight weeks. But according to Catalyst, a New York women's organization, about 35% of 400 major companies it surveyed have increased the length of paid maternity leave in the past five years.

DEMOGRAPHICS. There's no common approach. Lotus Development Corp. in 1985 began offering up to four weeks of paid time off to adoptive parents—men or women. Three years ago, BofA

A parental leave bill is pending in the House. It would provide up to 18 weeks of unpaid leave for mothers or fathers within two years of the birth or adoption of a child (BW—May 19). That would help parents with the costly, guilt-ridden, risky problem of outside baby care. But the bill has been bitterly opposed by business groups as too expensive and as leading toward mandated paid leave. Passage may not be in the cards this term.

Still, interest in child-care issues now spans the political spectrum. Representative Nancy L. Johnson (R-Conn.) has introduced a bill that would provide child-care vouchers for poor families—if states relax standards for family day-care homes. This has pleased some conservatives, who argue that licensing and regulation itself chokes off supply. But this approach, also taken by a number of states lately, worries longtime child-care advocates. At a time when child abuse scandals seem to indicate too little accountability, reducing standards "is not the way for this country to take care of its children," argues Columbia's Kahn.

One legislative priority for child-care activists is expanding the child and dependent care tax credit to provide more help to lower-income families. Activists also urge beefing up block grants to states. These funds are used to contract services for the poor at private day-care centers or to give vouchers to families to purchase care. Representative Miller wants to add $300 million per year to the $2.7 billion alloted this year—little more than the $2.5 billion spent six years ago.

This sort of aid to the poor would seem wise public policy. Affordable child care, for one thing, could be a stepping stone out of welfare dependency. A successful Massachusetts program, in fact, has tied workfare to child care. What's more, if we don't meet the needs of poor children, they can grow up into teens and adults with expensive problems. Society should not regard child care as a luxury.

By Elizabeth Ehrlich

began to reimburse some adoption expenses up to $2,000. In 1981, Hewlett-Packard Co. said employees could combine sick leave and annual leave and use it for maternity leave. "I left July 1 on the regular maternity leave," says Gorete Araujo, a production worker in *HP*'s Cupertino (Calif.)

plant. "After that was used up, I took about two more weeks of sick leave and vacation leave I had saved."

Business is fighting proposed federal legislation requiring up to 18 weeks of unpaid maternity leave for both men and women, but blue-ribbon

---

BankAmerica has rebuilt its career ladders so more female tellers can become vice-presidents

---

panels supported by big companies are calling for even better benefits. One group, which includes top executives from International Paper Co. and Warner Communications Inc., is proposing six months of unpaid leave. The pressure is demographics: By 1995, 80% of women aged 25 to 44 will be working, up from 50% in 1970. And 90% of them will be mothers.

Besides trying to make life easier for women workers, companies are concerned with the productivity lost when employees deal with family problems at work. A recent study by John P. Fernandez, a manager of personnel services at *AT&T*, found that 77% of women and 73% of men handle family issues on the job. One tactic for preventing this is to give parents more flexibility. A 1979 pilot program that let federal workers vary their hours was made permanent last year. Employees can pick their starting and quitting times within a range of two hours. Or they can work longer hours one day and shorter hours the next. Up to 500,000 employees do this each year.

Companies have been trying similar experiments: SmithKline Beckman Corp. and Transamerica Occidental Life Insurance Co. have had flexible work schedules since the mid-1970s. *IBM* and Merck started programs in 1981 that require employees to be at work during core business hours—usually 10 a.m. to 3 p.m.—but permit flexibility during the rest of the day.

In 1983, Shaklee Corp. began to let employees negotiate with their supervisor to reduce their workweek—with a commensurate cut in pay—while retaining seniority status and most benefits. A written agreement spells out how many hours per week the employee will work and how long the arrangement will last. In recent years, Control Data, Merck, and Continental Illinois National Bank have put computer terminals in some employees' homes so they can work while caring for their kids. This year, First Bank in Minneapolis began letting some employees use sick leave to stay home with an ill child.

But flexibility is often granted grudgingly—and there are usually drawbacks. Flexible work provisions in a new contract reached in July between the state of Massachusetts and the Service Employees International Union let Rhonda L. Black, a state social worker in Boston, share her job with another mother. "I wanted to spend time at home with my daughter after she was born," Black says. But she adds: "I'm only getting $11,000, and we [she and the other worker] share medical and dental benefits. They also made it clear they were going out of their way for me."

Because maternity leave often disrupts women's careers, some employers are beginning to change seniority and promotion systems. Most career ladders are designed for people who don't take time off, so women who leave to bear children lose their places in the promotion track and lose seniority needed for advancement. This often makes it tough to move up from pink-collar jobs.

PROTECTING INVESTMENT. Around 1980, when BofA saw that too few women were being promoted from teller, it took a close look at the roadblocks between entry-level and mid-level positions. After this review, the company began to base seniority on cumulative service rather than consecutive employment. This means that women, who comprise 72% of the bank's work force, can have children and still advance. "We invest so much in training, and we wanted to reduce the turnover of women to protect our investment," says Robert N. Beck, BofA's executive vice-president for human resources. In 1980, 7.2% of the bank's vice-presidents were women; today 22% of them are.

But even the most active employers have only scratched the surface: Most new female employees still land jobs such as secretary, teacher, nurse, or clerk. Although some have scored highly visible advances in law and medicine, this movement has been limited primarily to higher-paid professions that are out of reach for most female workers. Almost half of all women still work in job categories that are 80% or more female. And 70% of all men still hold jobs in fields that are at least 80% male.

Many women's groups believe that it is as important to raise the pay of traditionally female jobs as it is to get women into "male" jobs. This is beginning to happen: Northwestern Bell Telephone Co. recently devised a job evaluation system with the Communications Workers of America that reflects comparable worth—the idea that women should be paid the same as men for comparable jobs as well as for the same jobs (BW—Apr. 28). Control Data and *IBM* have quietly been raising the pay of some women who in statistical studies looked as if they were earning less than company norms. And in the past several years a few cities and 12 states have begun to implement comparable-worth programs.

FLEXIBILITY. But it's unclear when women as a group will start to make real progress on pay. Although the average female worker has 12.65 years of schooling, while males have 12.57, women's pay for full-time work averages only $15,600 a year—compared with $24,200 for men. Many economists believe labor shortages will force companies to push up women's wages faster than men's. But some predict the wage spread will actually increase: "More low-paid women entering the economy will keep the gap from closing in the next 10 years," says George P. Sape of Organization Resources Counselors, a management consultant firm. "It may even widen in the next five."

In the meantime, employers are tailoring health, life, and retirement insurance to the changing work force. Instead of offering the same benefits to everybody, an increasing number of companies are offering flexible packages that let employees choose what they need. A single mother might pick child care and high medical coverage, while an older man might choose to rely on his spouse's medical plan and boost his take-home pay. More than 500 companies have such plans, compared with less than 100 in 1983. New England Medical

Center's new system permits workers to pick a mix of benefits. They can even take extra health insurance as wages.

For all that's beginning to happen, it may be years before women enjoy a role equal to that of men in the economy. Overcoming the tradition that a woman's primary place is at home with the kids is made more complicated by the cost and extra effort employers must exert to do it. But leading companies have started the process—and the work place may never be the same.

By Aaron Bernstein in New York

DISCUSSION QUESTIONS

1. Identify all those human resources policies and programs mentioned in the article that seem to you to be responsive to the needs of women in the workforce.

2. How can self-interest increase the responsiveness of corporations to the needs of women at work?

3. What are any arguments you can raise, pro and con, for any one of the policies described in the article, and, on balance, what is your position on adopting the policy?

THE DISPOSABLE EMPLOYEE IS BECOMING A FACT OF CORPORATE LIFE

ECONOMISTS SAY SO-CALLED CONTINGENT WORKERS MAKE UP 25% OF THE LABOR FORCE

DECEMBER 15, 1986, PP. 52-53, 56

The relationship between companies and their employees has changed dramatically in the 1980s, most notably because of the wage, benefit, and work-rule concessions that many workers have been forced to make. But while cutbacks have grabbed the headlines, a potentially more significant change has been taking place. To augment their cost-cutting—and in a few cases to neutralize unions—companies have started creating pools of "contingent" workers to replace regular employees working traditional 40-hour weeks.

Economists believe that the ranks of contingent employees—those who work at home, for outside contractors, or involuntarily work part-time— have doubled since 1980, to nearly 17% of all workers (chart, page 187). If employees who choose to work part-time are included, there are 25 million contingent employees, accounting for 25% of the work force, calculates Audrey Freedman, a Conference Board economist. The use of such employees—most of them women—is cutting labor costs and making business more competitive. But these people are considered "dispensable" by employers, says Kathleen E. Christensen, a professor at the City University of New York. She adds, "We're creating a second-class tier in the labor force."

DOUBLE BIND. That's not true for all contingent workers. Professionals such as highly skilled software consultants, for example, can find high-paying part-time jobs. And admittedly imprecise surveys by the Bureau of Labor Statistics show that the number of those who choose to work part-time totals several million.

But for many other employees, contingent work is more an affliction than a blessing. According to *BLS* surveys, 3.8 million part-timers would like to find full-time work but can't. This puts them at a double disadvantage: Government figures show that part-timers earn an average of $4.17 an hour, vs. $7.05 for full-time workers. Moreover, some 70% of part-timers have no employer-provided retirement plan, and 42% have no health insurance coverage, according to the Employee Benefits Research Institute in Washington. Congress has noticed. Next year it may consider legislation that would mandate minimum fringe benefits for part-time workers.

You can find a precedent for contingent work

in Japan. There, a small number of "core" workers hold well-paid, lifetime jobs. But at least 75% of workers have much less cushy arrangements, including 8% who work part-time and are subject to frequent layoffs. James W. Walker, a vice-president at management consultants Towers, Perrin, Forster & Crosby, says the new U. S. trend is more an outgrowth of cost-cutting than a conscious effort to copy the Japanese. But he adds: "We're moving toward the Japanese system."

Contingent work is growing most rapidly in the service sector, where many jobs are low-skilled or can be done far from a central facility. Part-timers have accounted for 40% of the retail industry's job growth over the past 12 years, according to the *BLS*, and in 1985 made up more than one-third of all retail employees. Airlines are another example. Spurred by competition stemming from deregulation, carriers have been replacing regular—often unionized—workers with lower-paid part-timers who do everything from baggage handling to taking reservations. Since 1983 the number of airline part-timers has more than doubled to 49,000, or 12% of all employees.

COMPUTER COMMUTERS. More and more workers are being trapped in such jobs. Divorcee Linda Macki Williams supports her two children by working 30 hours a week at three part-time jobs, each paying about $5 an hour. The 38-year-old college graduate does clerical work for a church, works in a nursing home, and writes obituaries for a small newspaper in the Milwaukee suburb where she lives. None of the jobs provides medical insurance, and recently she learned that she may need open-heart surgery. "I need a full-time job that pays benefits, but they're hard to find," she says. "Meanwhile, the nursing home wants me almost like I'm on call, even though I tell them I have other jobs."

The contingent work force is most dramatically evident in the number of people who work at home—up four times since 1980, to 8.9 million. At J. C. Penney Co., two dozen telephone order-takers in three cities work at home. Pacific Bell has about 100 workers ranging from budget analysts to engineers who "telecommute" via home computers to jobs in California. Gil Gordon, a consultant in Monmouth Junction, N. J., estimates

PETE REFORMAT: LESS PAY FOR THE SAME SWEAT AT THE MILL

Peter Reformat has been on both sides of the fence. As a pipe fitter with 10 years' seniority at *USX* Corp.'s Gary Works steel plant, he earned $13 an hour plus ample benefits. But then the company attacked high union labor costs by contracting out the work that Reformat did.

"I got laid off about two years ago—and went right back to work in the Gary Works for a small company that paid me $5 an hour and no benefits," says the 30-year-old member of the United Steelworkers.

Many steelworkers have been forced to follow Reformat's path in recent years as steelmakers have struggled to survive. Subcontractors employ the equivalent of 7.5% of the industry's work force, up from 3% in the mid-1970s, according to a study by PaineWebber Inc. Among companies opting to use subcontractors, *USX* has been the most aggressive. The study estimates that the company has lowered the number of in-house hours needed to produce a ton of steel from 10 to about 4 since 1982—and that subcontracting accounted for one-third of the improvement. Subcontracting is a key issue in the current 18-week work stoppage at *USX*.

Since his initial layoff, Reformat has landed a better job with another *USX* subcontractor. This one is unionized and pays more—though he's currently working construction while on layoff during the *USX* shutdown. But even when the dispute ends, he'll still be a contingent worker. He'll be back in the Gary Works, but *USX* will have much more flexibility to dismiss his employer—and thus lay him off—than it had when Reformat was a *USX* employee. For starters, it won't have to pay him the two years of supplemental unemployment benefits—up to 85% of normal pay—that it would have owed him as a *USW* member. That's exactly what management likes about turning core workers into contingent ones.

CAROLYN HOBBS: 'I'M FORTUNATE TO HAVE FOUND THIS JOB'

Home may be a sweatshop for many women workers, but not for Carlynn E. Hobbs of San Jose, Calif. A so-called independent contractor for a Seattle insurance company that uses home-based workers, Hobbs for three years has calculated insurance policy premiums in her living room.

The pay—$6 an hour and no benefits—is 30% below what she earned at an office job doing similar work in the late 1970s. But she says it isn't easy to find home-based jobs as interesting as insurance-rating, which she likens to solving puz-

zles. Moreover, setting her own hours—and doing as little or as much work as she chooses—lets Hobbs tailor her schedule to the needs of her sons, ages 9 and 11. She sets her own pace as she works three to four hours a day, averaging 25 hours a week.

Hobbs first tried to get homework when she saw an ad for it in 1979. She didn't get that job, and it wasn't until 1983 that her fortunes changed. Now she supplements the income of her husband, who works as an engineer in Silicon Valley and has been laid off twice in the past five years because of the volatility of the industry. She's lucky in another respect, too: Unlike many workers in the insurance industry, she doesn't have a quota to meet. The company relies on the industriousness of its home workers rather than riding them to produce. Says Hobbs: "I'm fortunate to have found this job."

that more than 300 companies are testing such arrangements. Sometimes homework can be a good deal: The Penney workers receive the same pay and benefits as their on-premises counterparts. So do Pacific Bell's home workers. But often, the trade-off for working at home is substantial.

Some enterprising employers are even dispensing with their work forces altogether and opting for employee leasing. An outgrowth of the temporary help formula perfected by agencies such as Kelly Services and Manpower Temporary Services, which place about 700,000 workers a year, leasing works like this: A company technically dismisses its workers. They then are hired by an outside company whose only function is to pay them and administer their benefits—using money provided by the original employer.

LOOPHOLE. Because they "employ" so many people, leasing companies can get cheaper group rates on benefits. They also let professionals such as doctors sidestep a federal law requiring that small-business employees be covered by the same pension plans as the owners.

Now the idea is spreading to major employers: Hospital Corp. of America plans to use up to 120 leased workers at a 60-bed psychiatric facility it

will build in California. "This is going to grow in the health care industry," predicts Douglas Lewis, *HCA*'s vice-president for acquisitions and development.

The use of contingent workers is also on the rise in manufacturing. For decades, International Business Machines Corp. has used part-timers and subcontractors to help avoid layoffs of permanent staff. Other companies are catching on. Employees of subcontractors—called business services by the *BLS*—have doubled since 1980, to 4.4 million.

Apple Computer Inc., which laid off 20% of its work force last year, hires temporaries to staff 5% to 10% of its remaining payroll of 5,000. "If we bring someone on board full-time, there is an implied obligation that the job won't disappear," says Michael Ahearn, Apple's manager of staffing. "But that can happen in an industry as volatile as ours."

BEARING THE BRUNT. Since the late 1970s, Motorola Inc. has had three classes among its 90,000 employees. About 30%—those with at least 10 years of seniority—are guaranteed a job. An additional 40% are regular employees but don't have absolute assurances against layoffs. The rest have six-month contracts that Motorola can terminate

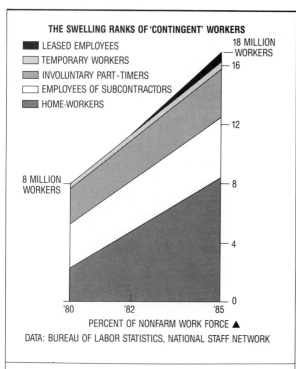

THE SWELLING RANKS OF 'CONTINGENT' WORKERS

- ■ LEASED EMPLOYEES
- ■ TEMPORARY WORKERS
- ■ INVOLUNTARY PART-TIMERS
- □ EMPLOYEES OF SUBCONTRACTORS
- ■ HOME-WORKERS

18 MILLION WORKERS
16
12
8
4
0

8 MILLION WORKERS

'80   '82   '85

PERCENT OF NONFARM WORK FORCE ▲

DATA: BUREAU OF LABOR STATISTICS, NATIONAL STAFF NETWORK

A large contingent work force could end up as a mixed blessing for everyone. It may be good for getting low-skilled work done cheaply. But employers often don't train contingent workers for higher-skilled jobs. Ultimately, this could reduce the skill level of the U. S. work force and make

> Some 70% of part-timers have no employer-provided retirement plan, and 42% have no health insurance

U. S. companies "less internationally competitive," warns Paul Osterman, a professor at Boston University. In addition, employers—or taxpayers—may soon be asked to cough up some of the money that companies are saving with contingent workers. Next year, Senator Edward M. Kennedy (D-Mass.), a labor ally and the incoming chairman of the Senate Labor & Human Resources Committee, is expected to resume his long-standing campaign to increase the basic benefits that employers are required to provide by law.

Meanwhile, Japan's experience is showing that the contingent work force idea isn't all it might seem. That country's weakening economy is causing employers to take the virtually unheard-of step of laying off core workers. And contingent work has essentially turned the majority of Japanese workers who don't enjoy the job security and high wages of core workers into an inferior class of citizens. The U. S. is likely to face similar problems as it develops its own version of a contingent labor force.

By Michael A. Pollock in Washington and Aaron Bernstein in New York

on 24 hours' notice. Casey Koziol, vice-president for personnel administration, says most contract workers are motivated by the lure of regular employment status.

In autos, outside suppliers make it easier for the Big Three to extend job guarantees to their workers. "In some cases it's impossible to get costs down to the wage levels of outside companies," says Stan Surma, Ford Motor Co.'s chief labor negotiator. "So we're outsourcing." When demand drops, suppliers—and their employees—bear much of the brunt. Subcontracted work already accounts for 70% of the value of each car that Chrysler Corp. makes. Of course, before a company can rely more on suppliers, it first has to cut its own work force. General Motors Corp.'s effort to do that was the focus of a recent strike at its Delco Electronics Corp. subsidiary that nearly halted *GM*'s auto production. United Auto Workers leaders say that subcontracting will be a major point of contention in next year's negotiations for new contracts at *GM* and Ford.

DISCUSSION QUESTION

Why would employers favor the use of a "contingent workforce," and what are its implications for management and society?

IBM'S FANCY FOOTWORK TO SIDESTEP LAYOFFS

WITH COMPUTERS IN A SLUMP, IT'S JUGGLING JOBS AND SHIFTING WORKERS AROUND TO SPARE THEM THE AX

JULY 7, 1986, PP. 54-55

More than 50 years ago, International Business Machines Corp. Chairman Thomas J. Watson Sr. said that the company shouldn't lay off employees—and *IBM* has respected his wish ever since. It goes to what most companies would consider extreme lengths to maintain full employment. But the computer industry slowdown is putting this to the test. The No. 1 computer maker expects flat earnings for the second year in a row, and it will have to do some maneuvering to preserve its no-layoff reputation. "We haven't had a full-employment problem like this since the early 1970s," says Walton E. Burdick, vice-president for personnel.

To avoid layoffs, *IBM* has severely restricted hiring and plans to hold its domestic work force to 242,000—the same as 1985. Overtime is being slashed from the usual 5% or so of total hours to 1% to 2%—the equivalent of eliminating more than 1,000 jobs. Employees have been asked to use leftover vacation, essentially creating work for some 2,300 workers who might otherwise be idled. The number of students hired this summer—usually 7,000—will be slashed. Some temporary workers, who normally number about 4,000, are not being rehired after their agreements expire. And *IBM* is pulling back some work from its 35,000 subcontractors. The result of all this: Regular *IBM* employees keep their jobs, while some students, temporaries, and workers at subcontractors lose theirs.

MOVING THE WORK. Most other U. S. companies would resort to mass layoffs to slash the payroll. But *IBM* circumvents the usual route through what it calls "resources balancing"—or moving work to people and people to work. This system helps shape IBM's strategic planning at nearly every level, from when and where to build a plant to how to manufacture a new product.

Moreover, by keeping its workers happy, it helps keep unions out.

Such balancing demands a lot from employees. Because *IBM*'s high-tech products change rapidly, it's constantly phasing out old jobs and creating new ones. So the company continually educates, retrains, and redeploys workers. In 1985, *IBM* spent $550 million educating workers—from training secretaries to be technicians to teaching engineers how to keep up in a fast-changing field. In all, some 10,000 employees were trained for new jobs. About 7,300 changed locations, at a cost to the company of $60,000 each. Nearly half of these relocations were for balancing; the remainder were for promotions or other reasons.

A good example of how balancing works occurred at *IBM*'s Burlington (Vt.) semiconductor plant. In 1982 a recession and low-priced 64K memory chips from Japan were biting deeply into sales. To make matters worse, *IBM* was allowing its other plants to begin buying chips from outside suppliers. Instead of resorting to mass layoffs, Burlington's managers decided to step up research and development so that the plant could switch to a 256K chip. They also set out to retrain workers and reorganize Burlington's 7,761 jobs to boost productivity and make the new chip price-competitive.

The plant managers' scheme was a complicated one. First, manufacturing jobs had to be cut because sales had fallen. Long-term, however, manufacturing would grow if demand returned. As this happened, the managers wanted to boost productivity by reducing the 74% of the work force not in manufacturing.

JOB SCOUTS. To slim down manufacturing in the short run, Burlington cut overtime from 10% to zero and encouraged workers to take unpaid leaves of absence under standard *IBM* policy. It made room in the lab for manufacturing workers by speeding up research and by not rehiring most of the 100-odd students who worked there. Temps were not rehired, and some subcontracted work was brought in-house.

But the tough part came in 1983, when the plant set out to pare its nonmanufacturing staff. This took a full-scale campaign. A team was formed to scout for openings at other *IBM* sites. Corporate permission was granted for a costly early-retirement program. And because the new chip's sales had picked up, management requested volunteers to go to manufacturing, where pay and status are lower. Volunteers could return to non-manufacturing after a year, and clerical workers were offered training to make the switch to production.

By 1985 no one had lost a job, and the plant had gained 235 new positions as demand rose. All told, more than 400 people changed jobs from 1982 to 1984. Seventy-six nonmanufacturing workers voluntarily moved to manufacturing. A third of those chose to remain after their one-year commitment expired.

Keith Weaver was one of the latter. He had spent 17 years in manufacturing, operating a machine that aligns the light rays used to help etch a chip wafer. In 1980 he was promoted from manufacturing to engineering. Three years later, Weaver volunteered to go back to his old job and decided to remain there. "I wasn't happy doing engineering," says the 41-year-old technician. "You don't see results right away." Weaver took no pay cut, but he's two salary grades lower now, so he has a lower pay cap.

'I'VE BEEN MOVED.' Some 100 nonmanufacturing employees transferred temporarily to different *IBM* plants. Thomas Sissel spent two years at *IBM*'s computer storage component plant in San Jose, Calif., where he taught other engineers to handle the photolithography process used in Burlington. "No one pushed me, I didn't lose any money, and I was paid a per diem so we could keep our house here in Burlington," says Sissel, who's 41 and has a wife and two children. But there were sacrifices: "When we got back, I found that I was behind some."

To get workers to switch jobs, Burlington man-agers met with supervisors in a local movie house to explain the plan. Supervisors then met with their 20 or so employees, discussing decisions to move in detail with individuals. "There's a little sell there, but no coercion," says Fred A. Couse, then Burlington's personnel manager.

Because changing jobs is a way of life at *IBM*, employees joke that its initials stand for "I've Been Moved." "Employees have to understand their role," says Ursula F. Fairbairn, *IBM*'s director of personnel resources. "That's part of how they protect their jobs—by being flexible." But *IBM* does meet resistance. Partly because of the rise in two-career families, "there was a rapid decline in the willingness of employees to move in the 1970s and early 1980s," says personnel vice-president Burdick. *IBM* started paying a bigger share of relocation expenses and cut the number of workers it moves from 5% to 3%.

Even if some regular employees have to switch jobs more than they'd like, they're better off than outsiders. When times are tough, the jobs of temporaries and students—who sometimes account for 5% to 6% of the work force—can disappear quickly. Most vulnerable are employees of *IBM* subcontractors. *IBM* contends that even if it wanted to let its employees do all the subcontracted work possible, it lacks the capacity to make more than 5% of the $10 billion worth of goods it buys from outside. But that could account for thousands of workers.

In fiscal 1984, Tandon Corp., in Chatsworth, Calif., sold $232 million worth of disk drives to *IBM*, accounting for 58% of its $401 million in sales. Last year it shipped disk drives worth $91 million to *IBM*, and sales slumped to $286 million. *IBM* didn't cause all of the falloff, but layoffs and attrition reduced Tandon's 4,645-person work force by 32%. Seagate Technology, based in Scotts Valley, Calif., laid off 28% of its 900 employees in 1984 after *IBM* cut back on its purchases of disk drives.

BEARING THE BURDEN. The link between such job losses and *IBM*'s full-employment efforts is fuzzy, but, as at Burlington, job preservation can be a factor. Says Scott C. Holt, Seagate's former vice-president for sales and marketing: "*IBM* is concerned about its impact on us, but sometimes it uses its vendors for some part of the market fluctuations and makes small companies go through tremendous ups and downs."

Burdick is careful to point out that *IBM* doesn't give its employees an ironclad promise of a lifetime job. But he's pretty sure that the company will make it through this bout, just as it did in previous deep slumps in 1961 and again in 1971. Assuming he's right, most U. S. workers probably will wish that their companies were more like *IBM*.

By Aaron Bernstein in Burlington, Vt., with Scott Ticer in Los Angeles and Jonathan B. Levine in San Francisco

DISCUSSION QUESTIONS

1. How does IBM attempt to avoid layoffs, and what are the implications of its policy of providing permanent jobs?
2. Should IBM-like human resources management policies be used in as many firms as possible, or would a "disposable employee" policy better serve society and the economy? Discuss.

SEXUAL HARASSMENT: COMPANIES COULD BE LIABLE

MARCH 31, 1986, P. 35

As Mechelle Vinson tells it, she had little choice. For four years, she says, her boss at a branch of Capital City Federal Savings & Loan Assn. in Washington threatened her job and her life if she didn't succumb to his sexual advances. Vinson says she reluctantly gave in but decided to quit in 1978 after consulting a lawyer. Then Vinson, who had received a series of raises and promotions over the years, stunned top Capital City officials by charging the thrift with sexual harassment.

This isn't any ordinary sexual harassment case. It's the first one the U. S. Supreme Court has decided to hear, and it has broad implications for all employers and employees. The court will decide whether companies are liable for sexual advances by one employee toward another even if senior management isn't aware of the behavior.

'SCARLET WOMAN.' The oral argument scheduled for Mar. 25 comes as claims of sexual harassment are on the rise. Harassment was charged in 6,342 job-discrimination cases filed in fiscal 1984, up from 5,110 claims in fiscal 1982, according to the Equal Employment Opportunity Commission. Federal courts in the past six years have heard about 300 sexual harassment cases. And that figure may seriously understate the problem. "It's astonishing how few women act after they've been subject to this kind of behavior," says Sarah E. Burns, assistant director of a sex-discrimination clinic at Georgetown University. The 31-year-old Vinson, now a nursing student, says she filed suit because "I had to go on with something I knew was right."

Her case is one of a new wave of discrimination suits that charge "environmental" sexual harassment. Early complaints were simple "quid pro quo" claims in which employees alleged explicit threats of job loss unless they granted sexual favors. Vinson's case goes a step further, contending that she and other female employees worked in an atmosphere that was pervaded by sexual aggression on the part of her supervisor, ranging from fondling to indecent exposure.

At her trial, the bank—which denies any wrongdoing or responsibility—introduced testimony about her dress and behavior and suggested that she encouraged the advances. The testimony led the trial judge to conclude that any relationship between Vinson and her boss was consensual. "It's the classic 'Scarlet Woman' defense," says Vinson's lawyer, Patricia J. Barry. The U. S. Court of Appeals in Washington overturned the trial court ruling and ordered the lower court to accept the notion of environmental sexual harassment.

Because of its potentially sweeping effects, the case has drawn heavyweight support to both sides. The Reagan Administration and employers are siding with the *S&L*, now known as Meritor Savings Bank. Employers fear that a decision in Vinson's favor will make it nearly impossible for them to protect against liability. "An employer can't correct a problem unless it knows of a problem," says Stephen A. Bokat, who directs the U. S. Chamber of Commerce's litigation center. The Chamber wants the court to relieve employers of any liability unless employees first give management a chance to correct the alleged misconduct.

VIGILANT. Barry calls that idea "ridiculous." In Vinson's case, she says, "any complaint would have had to go through her supervisor, the very person who was sexually harassing her and threatening her life." Vinson is seeking a new trial, which she hopes will result in an award of back pay, unspecified amounts of actual and punitive damages, and legal costs. She is backed by women's groups, organized labor, and 29 members of Congress. They fear that the court will reject altogether the theory that sexual harassment is a form of sex discrimination, thus destroying the legal basis for future lawsuits.

If Vinson wins, some labor lawyers predict, employers will have to be much more vigilant about policing morals in the workplace—since an office affair that turns sour could result in a sexual harassment claim. Joanne L. Hustead, a lawyer associated with the Women's Legal Defense Fund, doubts that things will go that far. She says that employers who have a written policy against sexual harassment—and train supervisors and subordinates to abide by it—needn't worry. But everyone agrees that a victory for Vinson when the court rules later this year would pose significant liability problems for employers. The only question is how much.

By Paula Dwyer in Washington

DISCUSSION QUESTIONS

1. What distinguishes the new wave of sexual harassment cases from the earlier complaints?
2. Why is the Vinson case of such importance to employers?
3. What should employers do to cope with "environmental" sexual harassment?

HOW A&P FATTENS PROFITS BY SHARING THEM

ITS INNOVATIVE PLAN GIVES WORKERS A BONUS FOR RAISING PRODUCTIVITY—AND THAT'S HELPING TO REVIVE THE CHAIN

DECEMBER 22, 1986, P. 44

In the late 1970s, rivals called Great Atlantic & Pacific Tea Co. the worst-run supermarket chain in the business. Shoppers were deserting A&P in droves. Managers doubled as baggers, and worker morale reached an all-time low. By 1982, after four straight years of losses, A&P had shrunk to 1,016 stores from 3,468 in 1974.

But then A&P found an important resource: its employees. In an experimental arrangement negotiated with the United Food & Commercial Workers (UFCW) at 60 stores in the Philadelphia area, workers took a 25% pay cut in exchange for an unusual promise: If a store's employees could keep labor costs at 10% of sales—by working more efficiently or by boosting store traffic—they'd get a cash bonus equal to 1% of the store's sales. They'd get a 0.5% bonus at 11% of sales or 1.5% at 9.5% of sales. It was a gamble in the low-margin supermarket business, but it worked.

VESTED INTEREST. In the four years since then, the bonus approach has spread to 281 stores, including 47 this month in Baltimore and Washington, D. C. A&P Chairman James Wood says the novel arrangement accounts for a big chunk of the company's 81% increase in operating profits since 1984, leading to a doubling of A&P's stock price, to $24. Wood wants to extend the plan to A&P's 850 U. S. stores, many of which have been renamed Super Fresh to distance them from A&P's lackluster image.

Employees are happy, too. Combined with the company's turnaround, the bonus deal has boosted their wages. Philadelphia A&P workers now earn $10.40 an hour in base wages plus an average of 85¢ an hour in one-time bonuses. The average food store wage in the city is $10.60. "It has been very successful," says Wendell W. Young III, president of *UFCW* Local 1357 in Philadelphia and an originator of the idea.

So far, some 230 *A&P* stores on the bonus plan have cut labor costs to no more than 11% of sales. *A&P* won't say how many are below 10%. But the company's overall labor costs have been cut from 13% to 11% of store sales vs. an industry average of 12%. Just as important, says Wood, is the effect of the bonus incentive on per-store sales, which have jumped 24% since 1984, to $7 million a year. With a vested interest in improving the way their stores are run, workers have made useful suggestions in bimonthly meetings with store managers and at the regional level.

In Richmond, Va., employees suggested that the pathway between the checkout lanes and store shelves be widened, because in peak times the checkout lines stretched into the aisles, and customers would leave rather than fight the crowd. In one black and Italian neighborhood in Philadelphia, employees suggested adding large sections of popular ethnic food. Previously, all *A&P* stores had to carry the same items. "You'd be amazed at the willingness of people to participate when they can say anything without fear of reprisal," says Thomas R. McNutt, president of *UFCW* Local 400 in Landover, Md.

The concept of linking bonuses to labor costs—a form of profit-sharing—stemmed from the predicament of *A&P*'s Philadelphia stores. After the company closed all 81 stores there in 1981, the *UFCW*'s Young gathered $5,000 pledges from each of 600 workers to bid for store leases. Ultimately, they bought six stores, which still are employee-owned. The British-born Wood, who felt that *A&P*'s woes stemmed from a lack of "the motivation you find at a family business," then thrashed out the bonus plan with Young—and reopened 60 stores. "The idea of people getting a piece of what they are trying to achieve has always appealed to me enormously," he says.

MIXED FEELINGS. *A&P*'s rivals said Wood was crazy to offer 1% bonuses in a business where profit margins aren't much larger. But the dividends from the Philadelphia experiment have silenced them. "It's an interesting approach that we might try sometime," says a Kroger Co. executive. And Wood, who was brought in by Germany's Tengelmann Group after it purchased 51% of *A&P* in 1980, hasn't sat still. In 1983 he agreed to buy 63 money-losing Kohl's food stores from Batus Inc. on condition that the unions would accept the bonus incentive. Threatened with closure, they agreed to the plan, and Kohl's earned $2 million in 1985.

UFCW leaders have mixed feelings about the *A&P* system. Although it has worked well, it also involves putting part of wages at risk, something workers ordinarily don't volunteer to do. Nor does the *UFCW* want the idea to spread to highly profitable chains such as Giant Food Inc., which the union argues can pay higher wages because Giant's per-store sales are more than twice *A&P*'s. "If I took the plan to Giant, the workers would be on strike in a heartbeat," contends the *UFCW*'s McNutt.

But intense competition and mergers in the retail food business have spread labor concessions to many chains. If that continues, the *A&P* profit-sharing model may one day be an industry standard.

By Christopher S. Eklund in Philadelphia

DISCUSSION QUESTIONS

1. Evaluate the A&P plan in light of motivation theories you have studied, such as expectancy theory, goal setting, and so on.
2. What pros and cons do you see in the bonus plan?

THE AIDS EPIDEMIC AND BUSINESS

A FRIGHTENING DISEASE POSES DELICATE QUESTIONS FOR EMPLOYERS

MARCH 23, 1987, PP. 122-128, 130, 132

Kyle always makes sure he laughs when his colleagues make crude jokes about *AIDS*. That way, he hopes, they won't realize he has the disease. Since he was diagnosed as having acquired immune deficiency syndrome in December, the once ambitious 24-year-old employee of a Florida financial services firm has led an uncertain—and secret—life. To Kyle, there is one thing almost as bad as having the deadly illness: losing his job. And he has little doubt that would be the outcome. "They're so naive about this that they'll fire me on the spot," says Kyle, who asks that his real name not be printed. "They believe you can catch *AIDS* through the air or from handling the same sheet of paper."

So far, Kyle has toughed it out. He fabricates excuses to explain his many medical appointments and puts in overtime to cover his absences. Even if he doesn't get fired when his employer learns of his disease, he probably would not find work a pleasant place to be once his secret got out. Although a Mar. 3 ruling by the U. S. Supreme Court now makes dismissal less likely, workers who have fought and reversed dismissal through the courts often have found reinstatement to be a hollow victory. One *AIDS* sufferer recently returned to work to find anonymous notes on his desk carrying such messages as "Don't use our water fountains." Rather than face fearful co-workers, many employees with *AIDS* simply disappear from their jobs and eventually join the growing ranks of unemployed *AIDS* patients who are already straining social services in some cities.

No one knows for sure how many Kyles there are. But statistics make it plain that almost every major employer in the U. S. will soon have to grapple with *AIDS* among its workers. By 1991, the Centers for Disease Control in Atlanta estimates, nearly 100,000 people will be living with the disease. In addition, as many as 10 million people by then may be carrying the virus even though they show no symptoms. Current research indicates that at least half of them will eventually develop the disease, which destroys the body's immune system, leaving it prey to a host of lethal infections.

Some companies are already acutely aware of *AIDS*. San Francisco-based Pacific Telesis Group has been averaging 40 to 50 employees absent with *AIDS* in its 75,000 statewide work force; last year 20 PacTel employees died of *AIDS*-related illnesses. But to most, the disease still seems remote. So far, 39% of *AIDS* cases in the U. S. have been in New York and San Francisco. And the disease continues to be concentrated among homosexual and bisexual males (66%) and intravenous drug users (17%). As a result, many companies do not believe it will become a problem for them. Ford Motor Co. is not atypical when it says it has no reason to believe any of its 382,000 employees worldwide has *AIDS*.

Yet the steady spread of *AIDS* has already carried it into all 50 states and most countries of the world. It now has a toehold in the heterosexual

> 'They are so naive about this that they'll fire me on the spot. They believe you can catch AIDS through the air or from handling the same sheet of paper'
>
> KYLE, AIDS patient

population, especially among minority groups, and is spreading. No drug has been found that can cure the disease, but treatments are improving. That means that *AIDS* patients will be living—and working—longer, making it more difficult for companies to ignore the epidemic. "The consequences of *AIDS* for the corporation have not been realized yet," says Gary M. Rankila, a Minneapolis attorney and gay-rights activist.

NO-POLICY POLICY. According to current projections, productivity lost because of illness and premature deaths caused by *AIDS* could cost U. S. industry more than $55 billion in 1991. So far, a handful of companies, including Syntex, BankAmerica, *AT&T*, Eaton, Transamerica, and Pacific Telesis, have adopted specialized personnel policies to handle the problem *AIDS* poses in the workplace. Others have decided to treat *AIDS* just like any other fatal disease. Control Data Corp. is typical of these companies. It conducted a study that predicts that, at most, 104 of its 34,000 employees will die of *AIDS* in the next five years—fewer than will die of other major killers. And it believes the best way to handle the situation is to treat it the usual way. "We wouldn't have a policy on *AIDS* any more than we'd have a policy on heart attacks," says Bob Jones, director of the company's health services department.

Other executives, such as Albert Bowers, president of Syntex Corp., believe they should play a broader role. "Some executives feel we shouldn't get involved in such a 'messy business' as this," says Bowers, who unstintingly lobbies other chief executives to educate their employees and support community efforts to halt the spread of the disease. "But people who don't realize the magnitude of this disease are being ostriches." William J. Schneider, corporate medical director for Morgan Guaranty Trust Co. in New York, agrees: "We need to take a much more aggressive stand to help curb the spread of the disease."

One executive who has declared war on *AIDS* is Robert D. Haas, chief executive of San Francisco's Levi Strauss & Co. "*AIDS* is not somebody else's problem," insists Haas, who first became aware of the crisis in 1983 when a group of gay employees wanted to run an information program at Levi Strauss but feared the reaction of other workers. Haas and members of senior management helped staff a booth and distribute materials, and he now urges other executives to do the same. "It's a social disease, not a homosexual disease," he says. "With good education you can promote a work environment free of disruption and fear."

LOTS TO LEARN. Companies trying to alleviate the fear are finding that misconceptions about the disease die hard. "In spite of all the information pouring out, there are a lot of people who are completely ignorant," declares Brian V. Beaudin, director of human resource services for the Con-

---

'I had to do an unpopular thing: Suggest AIDS is a community-wide problem we business leaders need to take seriously. It's part of our professional lives'

ROBERT D. HASS, CEO, Levi Strauss & Co.

---

necticut Business & Industry Assn. For example, despite efforts by blood banks to refute the idea that giving blood can be dangerous, one woman at a recent seminar on *AIDS* at a law firm in Los Angeles asked: "Can you get the virus by donating blood?"

Stephen Wroblewski, who is the *AIDS* coordinator in the Massachusetts Public Health Dept., says employers and employees alike have a lot to learn about *AIDS*. At sessions with employees, he says, "we talk to people who won't share pens, who are afraid of going into restrooms used by employees with *AIDS*, or who are afraid of sharing water fountains." As for employers, many are still unrealistic, he says. They "still think people with *AIDS* will come and tell them they have it."

Yet many *AIDS* patients resign rather than face the often unpleasant outcome of telling their managers they have the disease. Take Walter, a former computer programmer in Atlanta. His managers have not forbidden his return, but "they don't really want me to come back," he says. "They said it'd be real ugly." But not all *AIDS* sufferers can give up their financial security—and risk their medical benefits—so easily. Companies that handle the situation carelessly often find themselves in court for trampling on their employees' civil rights.

PHONE THREATS. Paul Cronan, an employee of New England Telephone & Telegraph Co., told his supervisor he was infected with the virus. The supervisor allegedly told some of his co-workers. And some of them left threatening telephone messages for him. Cronan sued in 1985, charging that the phone company violated his privacy.

Frequently, a case like that is enough to make an employer change its policy. After the case was settled out of court last October, Cronan was reassigned to the company's Needham (Mass.) facility. Because "fear was rampant among our employees," says New England Telephone spokeswoman Ellen Boyd, the company held educational sessions for employees and is now "looking at an *AIDS* education policy."

Employers who solved the problem of *AIDS* in their workplace by firing those with the disease— and sometimes even those who they believed might get the disease—are finding that this option no longer works. The Justice Dept. muddied the issue last June with a memorandum stating that acting on an irrational fear of contagion was not prohibited by federal law and thus not discriminatory. That led to a surge of dismissals, particularly in small companies. "Employers thought, 'Now we can fire anyone with *AIDS*,'" notes Mauro A. Montoya, legal services coordinator for the Washington (D. C.)-based Whitman-Walker Clinic.

But more *AIDS* patients are fighting for their rights. Last year, the New York City Human Rights Commission received 314 complaints of *AIDS*-related discrimination. San Francisco's Human Rights Commission handled 65. Los Angeles deputy city attorney David I. Schulman had 140 such complaints cross his desk.

AIDS activists are finding that the law is increasingly on their side. Already, 21 states and several cities have legislation or court rulings that make *AIDS* a "protected handicap," a distinction that prohibits employers from firing people simply for having the disease. And many attorneys believe that the Mar. 3 Supreme Court ruling in *School Board of Nassau County vs. Arline* effectively negates the Justice Dept. opinion.

In that case, Gene H. Arline, a Florida schoolteacher, suffered from recurring bouts of tuberculosis but claimed she was not contagious. She argued that her firing by the school district violated Section 504 of the Rehabilitation Act of 1973, which prohibits discrimination based on a handicap. The high court agreed, extending the act's protection to those with transmissible diseases. The opinion bars employers from deciding what constitutes a contagious disease.

Testing prospective employees to determine if they have antibodies against the *AIDS* virus—

> 'The consensus is, AIDS discrimination is contrary to the law. I've had about 75 cases. All settled out of court'
>
> GARY M. RANKILA, attorney

which means they have been exposed to *AIDS* but are not necessarily actively infected—is also extremely controversial. Proposals to require such antibody tests as a public health measure were quashed at a meeting held by the Centers for Disease Control in early March. There was a strong consensus that such testing violated the public's right to confidentiality, especially because a positive test does not necessarily mean the person will develop *AIDS*. And to many companies, such testing looks like a sure way to attract discrimination lawsuits. "That witch-hunt mentality is wrong," says San Francisco attorney Victor Schachter, who counsels corporations on employment issues. "We advise against testing."

DROPOUTS. Nonetheless, some companies are using the tests. Dallas-based Enserch Corp., for one, screens food-service employees even though a spokesman admits there is no medical evidence that *AIDS* can be transmitted through food or casual contact. Some experts charge that companies are surreptitiously testing employees' blood samples that were taken for other reasons. Others believe some employers are illegally using such common employment application questions as "Are you married?" in an attempt to screen out potential *AIDS* patients.

The most controversial use of *AIDS* testing is by insurance companies. So far, insurers have been prohibited from excluding coverage of *AIDS* in their policies. But as payouts in medical benefits

VOLUNTEERS, HOME CARE, AND MONEY: HOW SAN FRANCISCO HAS MOBILIZED

The hammers are still pounding at the 15-bed Coming Home hospice in San Francisco. There, volunteers are converting a former Catholic convent into the nation's first residential care facility for *AIDS* patients in the terminal stage of illness. For $140 per day, Coming Home will look after patients who would otherwise live out their remaining weeks in hospitals charging up to 10 times as much.

Projects like Coming Home, a nonprofit facility financed through community fund-raising, have earned San Francisco what U. S. Surgeon General C. Everett Koop called a "pioneering role" in caring for *AIDS* sufferers. And they have made this city a model for public health experts now girding to combat the *AIDS* epidemic in other communities.

IMPRESSIVE RESULTS. At the core of San Francisco's *AIDS* effort is a close-knit fraternity of health care professionals, volunteers, researchers, and service organizations. They marshal support for people with the disease and get them out of the hospital as quickly as possible after bouts of illness. The network has yielded impressive results: In San Francisco a typical *AIDS* patient runs up about $40,000 in medical expenses between diagnosis and death, compared with a bill as high as $140,000 in other parts of the nation.

The gay community is behind the city's rapid mobilization against the disease. In contrast to such urban centers as New York, where intravenous drug users account for 30% or more of all *AIDS* cases, in San Francisco more than 95% of *AIDS* patients have been homosexual men. They are predominantly young, well-educated, and employed. And they wield political clout. Ever since

the disease took hold in the city, they have been a force for action by the municipal government. "It was clear in 1981 that we had something unusual and explosive on our hands and had to act," says San Francisco Mayor Dianne Feinstein.

As a result, the city of San Francisco will spend $11 million in *AIDS*-related education, research, care, and other services this year—more than $15 per resident. Those dollars help support such activities as the San Francisco *AIDS* Foundation, a clearinghouse of information that has become a national resource.

Business has not only supported the *AIDS* Foundation financially, it has also led the nation in forging progressive corporate policies. Last year, Levi Strauss, BankAmerica, Pacific Telesis, Wells Fargo, Chevron, Mervyn's Department Stores, and *AT&T* pitched in to make a videotape, *An Epidemic of Fear*. The *AIDS* Foundation has since sold some 650 "*AIDS* in the workplace" kits, which include that videotape.

City funds also finance the *AIDS* program at San Francisco General Hospital, which treats more than one-third of the city's *AIDS* sufferers. Led by University of California at San Francisco hematologist Paul Volberding, clinicians provide both care and research aimed at treating *AIDS* sufferers outside of the hospital. Patients are released into a network of organized home health care that provides complete daily assistance for as little as $90 per day. Coming Home will fill any gaps between such home care and hospitalization by providing closer medical supervision in a home-like environment.

A pool of volunteers is indispensable to the city's success in coping with the epidemic. Last

and life insurance for *AIDS* sufferers mount, insurers are trying to protect themselves from risk. And many, including Aetna, John Hancock, and Metropolitan, require the *AIDS* antibody test as a prerequisite for some types of individual health and life insurance policies.

The insurers' use of the test draws angry charges of discrimination from gay activists. And some cities and states, including California, Wisconsin, and the District of Columbia, have banned testing. The insurance companies retaliated by dropping out of those markets. In the nation's

year approximately 450 volunteers organized by the Shanti Project, a volunteer organization, provided 110,000 hours of emotional and practical support for 80% of San Francisco's *AIDS* patients. They offer everything from housecleaning to transportation and visits for the homebound. "In San Francisco if you have a fire you call the Fire Dept., but if you have *AIDS* you call Shanti," says one patient. "Its resources are invaluable."

OVERWHELMED. Can the system that works so well in San Francisco be transplanted? The Robert Wood Johnson Foundation is betting that it can with $17.2 million in grants for similar programs in 10 cities including New York, Seattle, Atlanta, and Miami.

But even San Francisco's system can be overwhelmed by the swelling number of patients. More than 2,800 people have been diagnosed with *AIDS* in the city so far, and more than 1,700 have died. At least 50% of the estimated 80,000 to 150,000 gay and bisexual men are believed to be infected. By 1991, experts predict, the city will have 18,000 people with *AIDS*. "I have real concerns as to where we are going to care for these people," says Volberding. Already, absenteeism and turnover, a warning of burnout, are on the rise among his staff. Moreover, it is getting harder to find volunteers, and the hospitals are overflowing. In *SF* General's *AIDS* ward, patients wait to be treated in the hallways: The hospital has just 20 beds reserved for *AIDS*.

Volberding is convinced that soon the city—and the nation—must forge a new system to meet the crisis. During a packed gathering at the annual meeting of the American Association for the Advancement of Science in February, he called for federal planning and advocated the establishment of national regional hospitals that specialize in treating *AIDS*. He warned: "The San Francisco model works for now but not in the future."

By Joan O'C. Hamilton in San Francisco

capital, which has the strictest law, an estimated 80% of the 600 insurance companies in business there no longer write policies. Others have replaced the antibody test with a more accurate test that pinpoints those with active *AIDS* infections by analyzing the disease-fighting white blood cells

that are affected by *AIDS*. "The category of people who have a poor T-cell count are rejected as a class," says David E. Gooding, executive vice-president for individual insurance at Transamerica Occidental Life Insurance Co.

'LOADED DICE.' Gays charge that discrimination by the insurance companies goes much further than the use of the sometimes imprecise antibody test. They accuse the insurance companies of what might be called "lavender lining"—denying policies to men who live in postal Zip Code districts known to have a high percentage of gays. In addition, Mark S. Senak, a lawyer at the Gay Men's Health Crisis in New York, charges that insurers are refusing to pay health care claims of *AIDS* patients by invalidating policies on technicalities. He cites one client who was denied compensation because he failed to mention on his application that he had once been treated by an acupuncturist. "Insurers by far have been the worst corporate citizens" in the *AIDS* crisis, says Senak.

The insurers deny any discrimination. However, they claim they face an impossible burden of claims unless they screen out high-risk applicants. The American Council of Life Insurance contends that those who test positive for *AIDS* antibodies have a 20 times greater chance of dying within five years than those who do not. Moreover, a 1985 survey of 325 life insurance companies found that health benefits claims were heavily concentrated in the first and second year after the policies were issued. "If you know something insurers don't, it's a problem," says James C. Hickman, an actuary and the dean of the University of Wisconsin Business School. "The system doesn't work with loaded dice."

But attorney Benjamin Schatz of the National Gay Rights Advocates' *AIDS* Civil Rights Project says he spends a lot of time on insurance discrimination cases. Working out of a small office decorated with posters advertising condoms in San Francisco's Castro district, Harvard-trained Schatz says he gets 30 inquiries each week from people around the nation who feel they've been victimized. One of his current suits is against Great Republic Insurance Co., of Santa Barbara, Calif., on behalf of a healthy gay client. Great

BANK OF AMERICA'S BLUEPRINT FOR A POLICY ON AIDS

In 1983, Bank of America made what Nancy L. Merritt now calls a "compassionate mistake." An employee diagnosed with AIDS had recovered from his initial sickness and wanted to return to work. His manager, fearing the reaction of co-workers, called a meeting to explain his illness. "She didn't realize she was violating his privacy," says Merritt, vice-president and director of equal opportunity programs. Two pregnant women refused to work with him. After talking to public health and medical experts, the company invited the AIDS patient to return—and the women resigned. "We took our stand," says Merritt. "It is not a contagion issue. And the employee can come back and work as long as he or she is able."

That incident became the basis of one of the first and most sweeping corporate policies for dealing with AIDS. Developed with the input of benefits specialists, human resources experts, the corporate health department, and company attorneys, it has since become a blueprint for other companies grappling with the issue of AIDS in the workplace. Here Merritt discusses that policy.

AIDS raises a myriad of questions in the workplace: How do you manage an employee with AIDS? How should managers separate the attitudes of employees from the realities of the disease? How do you balance the needs of business and ethical issues? And such questions will become more and more pressing as the tragic AIDS epidemic continues.

A goal of any employer is to provide a safe work environment for all workers. With AIDS that should be simple: It is not a casually contagious disease, and there is little risk of transmission in the workplace. But given the irrational fear that AIDS often inspires, the best way to avoid a difficult and disruptive situation is to prepare and educate both management and employees before the first employee gets AIDS.

The first thing to keep in mind is that an employee's health condition is personal and confidential. A company must take reasonable precautions to protect such information. At Bank of America, employees are not required to tell their managers that they have AIDS or other life-threatening illnesses. But they are assured they can work with the human resources department to facilitate benefits and discuss other illness-related concerns.

TALKING AND READING. We have taken pains to make sure that our human resources department is well-informed about AIDS. Managers are encouraged to contact that department if they or members of their staff need information about any life-threatening illness, not just AIDS. That department is ready to answer any questions managers may have about an AIDS-related situation or about the contagious nature of an illness.

We also ask that managers contact human resources personnel before they make any demands of an employee—such as asking a worker to obtain a physician's statement regarding ability to continue work or assessing whether that person's continued presence poses a threat to the employee,

Republic sent a letter to agents in 1985 telling them to ask additional questions of single men "in occupations that do not require physical exertion," specifically citing occupations including antique dealers, interior decorators, consultants, and florists. James Pritchett, president of Great Republic, denies discrimination but says the company has discontinued the policy.

Whether or not insurers are discriminating, the fact remains that it is nearly impossible for someone to get medical or life insurance coverage after being diagnosed with the disease. So some companies are helping employees with AIDS retain their benefits for as long as possible. "I don't want an employee quitting out of panic," says Nancy L. Merritt, vice-president and director of equal opportunity programs at Bank of America. "He's going to need our benefits."

co-workers, or customers. In all cases, Bank of America reserves the right to require an examination by a medical doctor appointed by the company. Providing a supportive work environment for people with life-threatening illnesses not only helps them financially, it can even prolong their lives.

As long as employees with *AIDS* are able to meet acceptable performance standards—and their condition is not a threat to themselves or others—they should be treated like other employees. If warranted, we make reasonable accommodations for the employee—flexible work hours, for example—so long as these do not hamper the business needs of the work unit.

The fact remains, however, that some employees will be uncomfortable with a co-worker's life-threatening illness. Although managers must be sensitive to these concerns, special consideration is not usually given beyond normal transfer requests. Apprehension is usually based on a lack of information. Since we published our policy, we have not had any requests for a transfer based on fear of a co-worker's illness.

An employee who becomes sick with *AIDS* should be encouraged to seek assistance from established community support groups for medical treatment and counseling. Bank of America has a worldwide directory of *AIDS* resources and services that we make available to our employees. Sometimes we assist employees in getting help such as grief counseling or advice on how to talk to or treat a co-worker with *AIDS*. Nobody is comfortable with issues of death and dying—not managers, not co-workers, and not people with a life-threatening illness.

Bank of America believes that companies can also play an important role in the benefits arena for people with *AIDS*. It is clear that the best and most cost-effective way to treat a person with *AIDS* is through "case management" programs that provide for home or hospice care. However, such flexible benefits coverage is a fairly recent development, and many insurance companies still do not reimburse these expenses. We have been pleased with the outcome of working with third-party insurers to provide this flexibility.

Education is critical. If you look at the numbers coming out of public health departments, we seem to be at the edge of the forest looking in. Prevention is currently the only way to stop the spread of this disease. And large companies are well-positioned to provide this education.

It is important to make educational materials available to all employees in a systematic way through newsletters, informal sessions at lunchtime, and other vehicles. The key is to make sure that all educational efforts are appropriate to the company's culture. You don't want to send out frantic alerts to employees. In some companies, holding mandatory sessions might cause alarm. Our strategy is to make information available and handle more specific needs as they arise.

We also believe the bank's role in education extends into the community. We see an exponential benefit of having well-informed employees. Many of our branch managers, for example, sit on school boards or are active in the local chambers of commerce. They can carry the message even further. It goes without saying that it's critical to have management support for these programs. Fortunately, our board and top management committee's main concern was "Are we doing enough?"

HOPEFUL. For employees with *AIDS* who don't work for companies that have adopted special policies to cover the disease, some relief is on the way. A provision of the 1986 Budget Reconciliation Act requires companies with more than 20 workers to offer employees group insurance rates for 18 months after they leave the company, whether they leave voluntarily or not. Although rates can still be expensive, the bill is a boon for *AIDS* patients who might otherwise be unable to get coverage.

Nick Latham, 43, a management consultant in San Francisco for New York consulting firm Towers, Perrin, Forster & Crosby Inc., continues to work. He was diagnosed with *AIDS* last October and is now taking the experimental drug *AZT*, the first shown to prolong the lives of patients with *AIDS*. He is hopeful about the future: "So much of society's attention is now based on death and how many people are dying of *AIDS*," Latham observes. "I think we should be focusing on how many people will be living with *AIDS*. That is the much more powerful issue." And one that corporations can no longer avoid.

By Joan O'C. Hamilton in San Francisco, with Julie

Flynn in Los Angeles, Patrick Houston in Minneapolis, Reginald Rhein Jr. in Washington, and bureau reports

DISCUSSION QUESTIONS

1. What are some of the corporate policies concerning AIDS that are discussed in the article?
2. What legal issues does AIDS pose for management?

AIDS RESEARCH: WHERE THE BATTLE STANDS

SOME DRUGS ARE PROMISING, AND THERE HAS BEEN PROGRESS TOWARD A VACCINE

No four-letter word inspires more fear or carries a greater social stigma than *AIDS*. Despite five years of intense research, the disease is shrouded in rumor and misinformation. But the fear isn't unfounded. *AIDS* kills, and there is still neither a drug to cure it nor a vaccine to prevent it. "*AIDS* has been a moving target," admits June E. Osborn, dean of the University of Michigan School of Public Health.

Yet an intense research effort is making headway. During the past two years scientists have collected more data on the nature of *AIDS* than they have during 40 years of research on polio. Moreover, the tools of molecular biology that they're using, such as the ability to decode *DNA* and produce treatments based on the body's own defenses, barely existed a decade ago. It is frighteningly true that had *AIDS* struck in the early 1970s, medical science would have been as helpless as it was 400 years ago when a syphilis epidemic left 10 million dead in Europe.

Just three years after the first cases were identified in 1981, two teams of American and French researchers independently discovered the *AIDS* virus, sparking hope that it could eventually be beaten. "Within a year, we could see the different strains of the virus, as well as how it had evolved," says L. Patrick Gage, vice-president for exploratory research at Hoffmann-La Roche Inc. in Nutley, N. J. "That gave us a clear target for developing therapeutics."

SISTER DRUGS. Numerous laboratories and more than two dozen biotechnology and drug companies, including Genentech Inc. and Chiron Corp., are racing to beat *AIDS* with the same weapon that defeated polio: a protective vaccine. *AIDS*, however, is proving to be a far more difficult problem. Its genetic structure, for example, varies considerably from one strain to another, and an effective vaccine would have to protect against all the strains. Even so, French researchers in Zaire are already testing the first vaccine. Whether it is effective will not be known until April.

There is also no definitive word on drugs that either permanently shut down the reproductive machinery of the virus or that rally the body's defenses into squelching it (table, page 201). At the top of the list are the very few drugs that might either kill the virus or stop it from spreading from one cell to the next. Two sister compounds, *AZT* and *DDC*, seem to hold special promise.

Burroughs Wellcome Co.'s drug *AZT* was the first to win widespread approval as a treatment for *AIDS*. It was cleared in England and France in early March, and the Food & Drug Administration is soon expected to make it widely available to patients with *AIDS* and the early form of the disease called *AIDS*-related complex *(ARC)*. Although the drug does not cure the disease and has serious side effects, it does prolong the lives of many who take it, especially if they suffer from *ARC*. It also stops the virus from reproducing in the brain, possibly preventing some of the brain

THE MOST PROMISING DRUGS IN THE WAR ON AIDS

DRUG/DEVELOPER	
AZT **Burroughs Wellcome**	The first drug shown to prolong the lives of AIDS patients, especially those in the early stages of the disease. The drug blocks the virus' ability to reproduce but causes anemia so severe that frequent blood transfusions are necessary. Already approved in Britain and France, full-scale U.S. approval is imminent.
DDC **Hoffmann-La Roche**	A sister drug to AZT that appears extremely promising in laboratory experiments. Has been tested on only nine patients so far, but some researchers believe it may prove to be more potent and less toxic than AZT.
AL721 **Praxis Pharmaceuticals**	Developed to treat the symptoms of drug withdrawal, it is in very early stages of testing against AIDS. Trials with eight patients with AIDS-related swelling of the lymph nodes have been encouraging.
GRANULOCYTE-MONOCYTE COLONY-STIMULATING FACTOR Genetics Institute	Animal tests with the substance have been encouraging, but results from the first human tests probably won't be available until late spring.
ALPHA INTERFERON **Biogen/Schering-Plough** **Hoffmann-La Roche/Genentech**	Has proven to be an effective treatment of Kaposi's sarcoma, an AIDS-linked skin cancer. It is now being tested against AIDS in combination with AZT.
INTERLEUKIN-2 **Hoffman-La Roche/Immunex Cetus**	Tests with IL-2 alone have been disappointing but limited. Researchers, however, speculate that it may be more effective in combination with other drugs. Tests with AZT are planned.
CYCLOSPORINE **Sandoz**	A highly toxic drug used to prevent rejection of organ transplants. Last year, French researchers reported that it can control AIDS in early stages. Larger tests are under way in the U.S. and Europe. No results have been reported.

DATA: BW

damage now commonly associated with *AIDS*.

AZT's close relative, *DDC*, has just been put into early clinical tests. "We're at the same point with it as we were with *AZT* a year and a half ago," says Samuel Broder, the National Cancer Institute researcher who has tested it on nine patients so far. But Broder and others are optimistic: Laboratory studies suggest that *DDC* may be more effective and less toxic than *AZT*.

SYNERGISM. Researchers also hope to find more effective ways to use those drugs in combination with new gene-spliced ones that boost the body's immune defenses, such as interleukin-2. Scientists in San Francisco recently began testing *AZT* together with acyclovir, used to treat herpes. In laboratory experiments the two seem to work synergistically to kill the virus.

Against the backdrop of a frantic search for cures, other researchers are getting a firm handle on exactly who stands the greatest chance of contracting the disease. The consensus: *AIDS* remains unusually hard to get. Although the virus is found in a variety of body fluids, including saliva, tears, urine, and vaginal secretions, it is in the greatest concentrations in blood and semen. To date, only those two body fluids have been conclusively shown to transmit it.

Outside the body the virus is fragile, easily killed by sunlight, common household cleaners, and even hand soap. Unlike the flu or hepatitis A viruses, it can't be spread through contaminated food or water because it prefers to infect immune-system cells not usually found in the mouth or throat.

Some studies indicate that a woman who has frequent sex with a carrier of the virus has a 33%-to-50% chance of becoming infected—roughly the same as for catching syphilis or gonorrhea. But

BW/HARRIS EXECUTIVE POLL: THE CORPORATE RESPONSE TO AIDS IS SLOW

Corporate America is beginning to respond to the AIDS crisis, though most companies have not adopted a special policy for dealing with its victims. Nearly a third of all executives polled said their companies have had employees who contracted the disease. Most of those surveyed, all of whom are involved in personnel and benefits, don't believe that their companies' top management would favor mandatory testing for AIDS of all job applicants.

Q Does your company have in place a specially tailored policy for dealing with employees who have AIDS?

A Has in place 10%
Doesn't have in place 89%
Not sure 1%

Q How long has this policy been in place?

A 3 years or more 6%
2 years or less 92%
Not sure 2%

Q You say your company doesn't have such a policy in place. Do you think it should, or are your existing general policies adequate?

A Think it should 16%
Existing policies adequate 74%
Not sure 10%

Q How would you rate the level of concern shown by your company's top management over the problem of AIDS in the workplace?

A Great concern 14%
Some concern 50%
Not much concern at all 31%
Not sure 5%

Q To the best of your knowledge, have any employees died from or contracted AIDS?

A Have died from or contracted AIDS 29%
Have not 63%
Not sure 8%

Q How would you rate the concern among your employees about working with people who have AIDS?

A Very high 9%
High 21%
Not very high 35%
Not high at all 21%
Not sure 14%

Q If a co-worker objected to working with an employee who has AIDS, would you move the employee who has AIDS, move the co-worker, or insist that the existing work situation not be changed?

A Move the employee with AIDS 8%
Move the co-worker 14%
Insist that the existing situation not change . 29%
Not sure 46%
None of the above 3%

Q Has your company launched a formal educational campaign about AIDS?

A Has launched 15%
Has not launched 85%

Q You say your company hasn't launched an educational campaign. Are you considering doing so?

A Are considering 22%
Aren't considering 72%
Not sure 6%

Q Do you think that companies should limit any AIDS educational campaign to the facts about getting AIDS in the workplace, or should companies tell employees specifically how to avoid getting the disease?

A Limit it to workplace risk 35%
Tell workers how to avoid
getting AIDS 45%
Not sure 17%
None of the above 3%

Q Many insurance companies have argued that they should be permitted to require people applying for insurance to take blood tests for the presence of AIDS antibodies. Has your company considered instituting such a test for prospective new employees?

A Has considered 9%
Has not considered 87%
Not sure 4%

Q If you had to say, do you think the management of your company would favor or oppose a policy of requiring a test for AIDS for all job applicants?

A Would favor 23%
Would oppose 62%
Not sure 15%

Poll of 600 senior human resources, benefits, and personnel executives at companies drawn from the BUSINESS WEEK 1000. Survey was conducted Mar. 4–10 by Louis Harris & Associates Inc. for BUSINESS WEEK. *Edited by Stuart Jackson*

epidemiologists in Tennessee found that even after four years of steady sexual contact, infected spouses pass the virus to their partners only about 20% of the time. The chances are smaller for one act of intercourse.

Indeed, the idea that *AIDS* is rapidly becoming a major, undiscriminating threat to Americans is the subject of considerable speculation. The estimate by the Centers for Disease Control in Atlanta that up to 1.5 million Americans already carry the virus cannot be verified without much wider testing. And that estimate is as high as the number obtained from studies on applicants to the military—the largest single group for which reliable blood test results exist. "The prevalence of *AIDS* is unknown," admits James W. Curran, head of the *AIDS* program at *CDC*. "And there is a lot of variability by age, sex, geography, and sexual orientation."

Nor does *AIDS* seem to be sweeping wholesale into the heterosexual population, even though the number of heterosexual cases is increasing. Experts estimate that by 1991 about 5% of *AIDS* cases will be heterosexuals who do not use intravenous drugs and who have not received a blood transfusion. About 3.7% of the cases reported to date have been such individuals. But roughly half of those have been people from central Africa or countries such as Haiti who may have contracted the disease before moving to the U. S. In New York City, the percentage of *AIDS* cases who are heterosexuals outside those risk groups has stayed constant at 2% since 1982.

Intravenous drug use is the main way *AIDS* is spread to heterosexuals and, through infected mothers, to children. For a non-*IV* drug user who is straight, monogamous with a similar partner, and hasn't received a blood transfusion, the chances of developing the disease are still only about one in a million. "Heterosexual transmission is still slow and likely to stay slow," says Paul Volberding, director of the *AIDS* program at San Francisco General Hospital.

NEW UNDERCLASS. Even so, the disease is creating a new group of *AIDS* victims within the nation's ghettos. Often destitute, homeless, and more likely to use intravenous drugs or work as prostitutes, these victims now make up about two-thirds of the heterosexual cases reported to date. Black and Hispanic women are up to 15 times more likely to become infected than white women. And women within the *AIDS* underclass are also the mothers of about 70% of the children who have contracted the disease. By 1991 some 3,000 children may have it—an eightfold increase from 1986.

Those statistics bear a striking resemblance to the incidence of *AIDS* in central Africa, where the annual rate of infection is one adult in 1,000. Although it also appears to be spread through the frequent use of prostitutes, as well as dirty medical needles, cultural factors may also contribute to the wider incidence of heterosexual *AIDS* in Africa. Ceremonial mutilation of women's genitals is widely practiced. And those women bleed more readily during vaginal intercourse—providing the virus with the blood it prefers for infection.

Around the world, however, anal intercourse is the practice that puts most people at risk. It often produces tiny tears within the wall of the rectum, giving the *AIDS* virus an easy portal into the body. Anal sex may be risky for another reason. Last January researchers at the National Institutes of Health discovered that the *AIDS* virus may prefer to infect and multiply in cells in the rectum and colon rather than certain other types of body cells.

Just as sobering is the firm evidence that the risk of developing *AIDS* may actually increase, rather than decrease, with the passage of time after exposure. An ongoing *CDC* study of 6,700 homosexual and bisexual men in San Francisco found that 4% of those infected developed the disease within three years. That figure, however, jumped to 36% within seven years. "We thought *AIDS* would be like cancer—if you lasted five years your chances of beating it would be much better," says biologist Jay A. Levy at the University of California at San Francisco. "Now it's beginning to look like five years is the median."

PREVENTION IS KEY. But some researchers suspect that factors other than exposure to the virus play a role in determining who develops the disease. These co-factors include infections with other viruses such as hepatitis B, anemia, poor diet, lack of sleep, the use of certain recreational drugs, stress, or even a genetic flaw in the body's immune system.

Although dramatic new therapies and vaccines are being readied to help fight *AIDS*, public health experts continue to emphasize that prevention, not treatment, is the key to curbing the disease's pernicious spread. They recommend that all people, whether they consider themselves at risk or not, limit their number of sexual partners. Condoms are also a highly effective, if not foolproof, tool for preventing *AIDS* transmission.

That these measures work is more than just speculative. Last year, largely because of educational efforts in San Francisco, the annual rate of new infections among the gay men being tracked in the *CDC* study dropped to 7%, from a high of 20% in 1984. The message from that effort underscores a British *AIDS* educational slogan: No one needs to die from ignorance.

By Sana Siwolop in New York, with Scott Ticer in Atlanta, Reginald Rhein Jr. in Washington, Lois Therrien in Boston, Christopher S. Eklund in Philadelphia, David Hunter in Paris, Mark Maremont in London, and bureau reports

AFFIRMATIVE ACTION: AFTER THE DEBATE, OPPORTUNITY

APRIL 13, 1987, P. 37

The great affirmative action debate of the 1980s is over. After years of controversy within the Reagan Administration, among employer groups, and between the civil rights and conservative movements, the Supreme Court has effectively settled the matter for private industry. The issue no longer is whether companies should embrace preferential hiring and promotion plans for women and minorities, but how they can use the plans effectively.

The court's Mar. 25 decision ended a nightmare that has been plaguing companies since the Reagan Administration began trying to rein in affirmative action. Employers found themselves caught between women and minorities, who threatened to sue if there was no affirmative action plan, and white male workers, who might go to court alleging reverse discrimination.

The Supreme Court ruled 6-3 that the public transportation agency of Santa Clara County, Calif., was justified in giving a road dispatcher's job to Diane Joyce, who scored two points less than a man on a test but was found to be otherwise well-qualified by a panel of supervisors. The county's promotion plan passed muster because it met a three-pronged test set by the justices: It was flexible, temporary, and designed to gradually correct the imbalance in the overwhelmingly white, male work force. "It truly was a model plan," says Stephen A. Bokat, general counsel for the U. S. Chamber of Commerce, which had sided with earlier Administration efforts to fight affirmative action.

NEW SAFEGUARDS. The ruling is the best indication to date that the Supreme Court will permit employers to do as much as they can on their own, without waiting for a court order and despite continued Justice Dept. arguments to the contrary. The Administration's view remains that affirmative action plans are permissible only if they help individual victims of discrimination. But the county agency had never admitted, nor had anyone ever alleged, that it discriminated against women and minorities. Lack of such evidence clearly did not bother a majority of the high court.

Now companies are armed with new safeguards against employees prone to sue because they were passed over for a job or a promotion. They can update their affirmative action plans, many of which have been moldering since the Reagan Justice Dept. began its anti-affirmative action crusade. The court is not saying an employer must have a plan, nor is it removing a boss's discretion to hire the most qualified person for a job. In fact, it cautions that any plan must not "unnecessarily trammel" the rights of workers who won't benefit from affirmative action.

With the key legal issues settled, companies can view affirmative action as an opportunity rather than a burden. A diverse work force is in their best interest. Personnel administrators say a variety of backgrounds often produces a multitude of ideas on how to solve problems, develop products, or market services.

But perhaps the best reason for affirmative action is found in demographics. The Labor Dept. says the U. S. will face a serious labor shortage by the late 1990s as the "baby bust" of the late 1960s and '70s reduces the number of entrants into the job market.

SUBTLE BARRIERS. Employers will need growing numbers of highly skilled workers to compete in a high-tech economy. Companies will have to tap women, minorities, and immigrants to fill those jobs. Those groups will account for more than 80% of the growth in the labor force for the rest of the century.

Women and minorities need affirmative action, too. Efforts since the early 1970s have succeeded in broadening employment opportunites. Still, women and minorities frequently encounter subtle but very real barriers as they try to climb the corporate ladder.

The Supreme Court appears to have ended a decade of confusion over affirmative action. Employers can now safely follow the example set by Santa Clara County and step up their efforts to recruit, train, and promote the people who are going to help forge America's economic future.

By Paula Dwyer

DISCUSSION QUESTION
What does the Joyce decision imply for management's approach to affirmative action?

PART 5

CONTROLLING

Many of the important developments in the practice of controlling have occurred in recent years in the areas of production and operations management and management information systems. Accordingly, the selected articles in this part emphasize these topics.

The first two articles focus on management information systems. The first describes how the Shop 'n Save supermarket chain uses computers to provide prompt and detailed information on inventories, sales, delivery schedules, product turnover, employee work schedules, and more. These information systems provide abundant information for tight control of all of these variables and are credited with helping management improve its profit margins. The second article shows how the information systems can be extended to customers and suppliers through electronic data exchange (EDI). In other words, there is no need to confine the new information technology to intracompany operations; it can be and has been expanded to include intercompany relations in several industries. A third article describes new high-level career opportunities for managers in information systems.

Articles in the next section focus on production and operations management. The first article identifies the lack of quality in manufacturing as a key to the weakened international competitiveness of American industry. The article offers extended discussion of quality problems and progress in coping with them. The two remaining articles describe technological innovations that are helping to increase efficiency in manufacturing: computer simulation of manufacturing processes and the expanded use of robots.

AT TODAY'S SUPERMARKET, THE COMPUTER IS DOING IT ALL

IT HAS MOVED BEYOND THE CHECKOUT TO TRACK EVERYTHING FROM PILFERAGE TO PROFIT

AUGUST 11, 1986, PP. 64-65

Ronald K. Springer isn't one to get nostalgic. When he started in the grocery business 25 years ago, one of his chores was to take home piles of invoices and figure his store's gross profit on truckloads of food. Today, as manager of the Super Shop 'n Save in South Portland, Me., Springer oversees a market that beeps and whirs as computers do everything from figuring those dreaded invoices to setting up work schedules for checkout clerks. "I don't think the old days were simpler," he says. "They were more difficult."

More than half of the nation's supermarkets are equipped with scanners, those computerized checkout machines that read the bar code on a box of Wheaties. At least one in four uses a central computer to help run the business. But now, food stores such as Springer's are going beyond that, becoming what might be called "electronic supermarkets" permeated by computers. Says Timothy M. Hammond, senior vice-president of the Food Marketing Institute, a grocers' trade group: "Within the last couple of years, the industry has moved to phase two—using the mound of scanning data to influence management."

"Phase two" is rewriting the rules of the trade, both for small outfits such as Gromer Super Markets Inc. in Elgin, Ill., and for giants such as Safeway Stores Inc. Data of unprecedented precision, on everything from pilferage to profit per item, are giving the best supermarket managers a competitive advantage that some analysts say could double profit margins, which today average only 1.2%. It's even having a major impact on foodmakers such as Campbell Soup Co. The numbers, for instance, can help tell a manufacturer that better packaging will sell more of his products.

The new system is working well at Hannaford Brothers, the Scarborough (Me.) owner of Shop 'n Save stores. In 1980, Hannaford posted a respectable 1% profit margin, then the industry average. Since that time, by using computers in all phases of its business, Hannaford has boosted margins steadily, to 1.8% in the first quarter of this year. "I would characterize what's happening as a revolution," says Hugh C. Smith, a product management specialist at Hannaford.

With data flowing from stores and warehouses to an *IBM* 4381 mainframe at headquarters, Hannaford calculates virtually every cost involved in getting its goods from manufacturer to consumer—including shipping expenses, warehouse handling requirements, bulkiness of display, energy needs at the store, and the time canned corn spends on the shelf before it's bought. Hannaford crunches these data for each of its more than 17,000 products and each of its 65 stores.

'EYE-OPENER.' The resulting richness of detail is staggering. "We can call up a report on the direct profit contribution of pickle Brand X at store Z during some seven-week period," says James J. Jermann, Hannaford's vice-president for merchandising. Armed with such information, retail buyers and marketers can for the first time make truly informed decisions on, say, which brands of gherkins to carry and how to price them. That's a far cry from the not-so-distant days when a gro-

USING INFORMATION TO MAKE SUPER-MARKETS MORE EFFICIENT

STEP 1: Raw data flow from stores and warehouses to a mainframe computer, usually at chain headquarters. Included are sales records from checkout stands, data on product delivery schedules, employee work schedules, energy use, and the amount of time products spend in chain warehouses before they're shipped to stores.

STEP 2: The numbers are crunched to help make better decisions about what products to sell, how to display them, and how to make their storage and delivery more efficient. Headquarters can determine which brands of soap make the most money, for example, and cut back on the least profitable ones. Or it can use computer-projected cost estimates to gauge how profitable a new brand of soap might be. The numbers might also suggest whether products should be delivered directly to stores or go to a central warehouse first.

STEP 3: Headquarters sends its recommendations back to the store and to warehouse managers and their assistants. Sometimes called "Plan-a-Grams," these instructions include detailed schematics of every shelf, showing the store manager where to display each of the up to 17,000 products sold in large supermarkets. The plan may even recommend prices for these goods.

STEP 4: Headquarters also gives or sells the numbers generated in Step 1 to manufacturers, which may subsequently modify their products. For instance, the numbers may tell a soap maker that its products would sell better if they were packaged differently.

DATA: BW

cer's only guide to profit contribution was the markup percentage on a given item, which often ignored variable costs such as transportation.

"Computerized profit calculations have been a real eye-opener for the retailer," says John R. Phipps of Touche Ross & Co. As the accounting firm's director for food industry consulting, Phipps is the guru of what the industry calls direct product profitability *(DPP)* analysis (table). The concept was born in the early 1960s, but it wasn't until the cost of mainframe computing power fell in the 1980s that *DPP* caught on.

Retailers have always known that certain items must be priced as "loss leaders," carried primarily to bring shoppers into the store. But Phipps says that "*DPP* is showing that about 20% of the items in a typical grocery store actually lose money, which means that the more of those you sell, the more you lose." In these cases, *DPP* analysis serves two novel functions: It identifies exactly which products hemorrhage profit, and it offers clues about how to stop the bleeding.

UNEXPECTED WINNER. The results are often surprising. House brands, once considered big money-makers because of their low initial cost, turn out to be skimpy performers compared with better-advertised name brands that move faster. Paper products are also a drag on profit, given their bulk and small price. Stores must sell toilet paper, but *DPP* numbers suggest limiting variety and avoiding costly promotions.

One of the supermarket's unexpected winners, according to *DPP*, is the freezer section. It has traditionally been perceived as too energy-intensive to reap big returns. But frozen meals actually outperform the average grocery item almost two to one because of their large markups. Once enough frozen items have been sold to cover energy costs, profits soar. Soft drinks, dairy goods, snack foods, magazines, and other products delivered directly to stores by manufacturers also make more money than previously thought, because store employees aren't used to stock them.

The wealth of detail compiled by *DPP* often helps retailers and manufacturers streamline their operations. At Hannaford and other chains, *DPP* is translated into "Plan-a-Grams"—printouts that show store managers, shelf by shelf, exactly where to place their stock to maximize profit. A decision on whether to display three rows of Skippy peanut butter rather than two has never been trivial from a profit standpoint. But with Plan-a-Grams, that decision can be based on more than instinct.

NEW SOPHISTICATION. *DPP* information also helps Procter & Gamble Co., Campbell Soup, and other manufacturers design more efficient containers and shipping methods. *DPP* studies have shown that stores prefer to stock lighter-weight packages of detergent, so manufacturers have set out to limit the air and water content in their packages. "We get calls every week from manufacturers interested in our *DPP* findings," says Hannaford's Smith. Hannaford and an increasing number of other chains sell access to their scanning data and cooperate with manufacturers running *DPP* experiments. Some, such as Safeway, staff a separate office to design and run such tests for manufacturers they deal with.

Hoping to build on the industry's new sophistication, automation consultants, market researchers, and hardware and software producers are promoting an expanding array of scanning spinoffs. Set to debut later this year in some markets is the "electronic shelf," which will offer shoppers cost and nutrition information at the touch of an electronic display—and let retailers constantly revise prices at the touch of their own buttons. Assuming that consumers don't mind having their privacy invaded, new identification cards tied to scanners will let stores track individual families' purchases and target them with coupons and ads. In the long run, scanning and *DPP* analysis will not be limited to supermarkets. Drug chains, convenience stores, and even department stores already are planning their own versions of the system.

The move toward *DPP* analysis could also transform the staff back at the headquarters of the new electronic supermarket. Managers who know computers are already in increasing demand. "Retailing has always had an image problem with *MBA*s," says Walter J. Salmon, an expert in the field at Harvard business school. "If in fact *DPP* leads to reorganizations in favor of sophisticated product managers, *MBA*s will be more attracted to the food industry."

Even so, store managers don't seem to see automation as a threat to their authority or their intuition. Ron Springer says he needs help to manage his 250 employees and 17,000 products: "Bring it on. Bring it on."

By Gary Geipel in Scarborough, Me.

DISCUSSION QUESTION
How does the use of computers described in the article facilitate control?

AN ELECTRONIC PIPELINE THAT'S CHANGING THE WAY AMERICA DOES BUSINESS
ELECTRONIC DATA INTERCHANGE IS LINKING COMPANIES, CUSTOMERS, AND SUPPLIERS
AUGUST 3, 1987, PP. 80, 82

Wal-Mart Stores Inc. can lose a bundle in sales if it runs out of popular garments at the height of a season. In most cases, new orders simply can't be whipped up and delivered fast enough to meet seasonal demand. But Seminole Manufacturing Co. is doing something about that. By setting up a new electronic information pipeline, it has cut its delivery time of men's polyester slacks to Wal-Mart by 50%, to 22 days. Now the discount chain is better-stocked in the 64 size and color combinations of Seminole's slacks, and pants sales are up 31% over nine months.

To get those results, Wal-Mart and Seminole have started using a technique called electronic data interchange *(EDI)*, and they're not alone. After years of unfulfilled promise, *EDI* is spreading from a few hardcore industries—groceries, transport, and pharmaceuticals, mostly—to dozens of others, from the chemical sector to electronics. "It's a basic way of changing the way America does business," says Audrey L. Mandela, a market researcher at Yankee Group in Boston. She predicts that the $35 million business of selling *EDI* communications services and software will grow 60% a year through 1990.

ONE FORMAT FITS ALL. In a nutshell, *EDI* allows specially formatted documents, such as purchase orders, to be sent from one company's computer to another's. This seemingly simply step leads to a

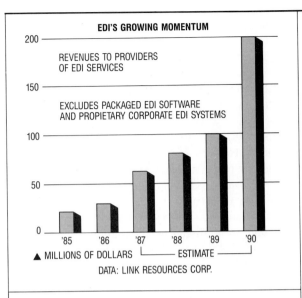

EDI'S GROWING MOMENTUM

REVENUES TO PROVIDERS OF EDI SERVICES

EXCLUDES PACKAGED EDI SOFTWARE AND PROPIETARY CORPORATE EDI SYSTEMS

▲ MILLIONS OF DOLLARS — ESTIMATE —

DATA: LINK RESOURCES CORP.

host of advantages. It lets companies use fewer data-entry employees, thus eliminating human error and avoiding delays of days or weeks. It can lower inventory levels, eliminate lost invoices, and improve customer service, since suppliers can respond faster to customer needs. Another plus: Salespeople, no longer relegated to logging routine orders, can spend more time selling.

With all those pluses, why has *EDI* taken so long to take off? One reason has been lack of standards. Since *EDI* was conceived in the late 1960s, most systems have been proprietary, and few used the same computer formats for the same kinds of documents. Only the largest companies could afford such custom-made systems. In the past 18 months, though, "a lot of disparate industries have gotten together and agreed on [document-format] standards," says Mark A. Winther, a market researcher at Link/*IDC* Resources Corp. "That's why there's a groundswell—people don't have to reinvent the wheel."

Daniel S. Codman, a co-founder of *APL* Group Inc., a Wilton (Conn.) maker of *EDI* software, adds that interest has also been fueled by the "acceptance of personal computers as a universal business tool and the availability of affordable *EDI* software." Before, only a company with a mainframe and $50,000 software could afford to test the waters, he contends. Now *APL*'s *PC*-based packages run $1,650 to $6,000.

In businesses such as the $55 billion textile industry, which has suffered as retailers doubled their purchases of cheap Asian apparel over the past five years, adopting *EDI* has become a way to get an edge over foreign rivals. Led by textile magnate Roger Milliken, 220 top retail and clothing executives convened earlier this year to back industry-standard formats for purchase orders, shipping documents, and other forms. Their hope: to beat Asian rivals by making it easier for retailers to deal with U. S. suppliers. "This is the beginning of a revolution in our industry," boasts Milliken, chairman of Milliken & Co.

The idea is to move information faster from the retailer's cash register to the textile maker's factory floor. Sales data, new orders, shipment information, inventory receipts, and invoices will all flow smoothly up and down the line. In one five-month test at four J. C. Penney Co. stores, sales of the retailer's Stafford brand suits jumped 59% after it linked up with Lanier Clothes, an Atlanta apparel supplier. That's because the quick turnaround made possible by *EDI* let the stores replenish supplies of popular suits fast enough to meet that season's demand. And although it had more sizes on hand, Penney cut inventories 20%.

In other industries, *EDI* already is so pervasive that it would be impossible to do business without it. Among auto-parts makers, for example, the widespread adoption of *EDI* for everything from invoicing to change-of-design orders over the past three to four years has been dramatic. "It allows us to put our products on the same schedule as a customer," says Subhash S. Valanju, director of information systems at Rockwell International Corp.'s Automotive Operations in Troy, Mich. Now, instead of going to warehouses, the items go "from our dock to their dock," he adds. "Without it, just-in-time [inventory control] would not have been practical."

Increasingly, the winners in all this are such companies as McDonnell Douglas, *GE* Information Services, Sterling Software, and Control Data. They provide networks and electronic mailboxes through which customers can send and receive documents. *GEIS*, for example, which started up its *EDI* service only 16 months ago and hopes to turn a profit on it next year, now has more than

1,000 customers and is gaining more than 100 a month. "Developing critical mass is essential for this to take off," says Steven P. Korn, *EDI* marketing manager at *GEIS*, a division of General Electric Co.

TOUGH SELL. Large banks also are figuring out how to cash in on *EDI*. In April, many of them adopted what is known as the corporate trade exchange *(CTX)* standard, based on the new *EDI* standards set forth by the American National Standards Institute. Once banks and their customers are tied into an *EDI* loop, *CTX* will make it possible to transfer money from a merchant's account to a supplier's account electronically, eliminating massive amounts of paperwork and making it easier for businesses to balance their books.

For all the benefits that *EDI* promises, it may still take a while to attain critical mass. Many analysts had predicted much faster growth for *EDI*, but "they were naive about how long it takes companies to decide to use something like this," says Yankee Group's Mandela. A two-year cycle is not uncommon, points out Link's Winther.

Richard C. Norris, of Arthur D. Little Inc., says the decision to adopt *EDI* is like choosing to learn Chinese: "It's not something where you turn on the switch. It's a long, hard slog" because a company must integrate its own computer systems before it can gain the greatest benefits from *EDI*. "A lot of companies are finding they are not as automated as they think," Norris says. But the effort should be worth it. "*EDI*," he adds, "will have a profound effect on how businesses relate to one another."

By Catherine L. Harris in New York and Dean Foust in Atlanta, with Matt Rothman in Pittsburgh

DISCUSSION QUESTIONS

1. What is EDI, and how does it work?
2. How does EDI facilitate management control?

MANAGEMENT'S NEWEST STAR

MEET THE CHIEF INFORMATION OFFICER
OCTOBER 13, 1986, PP. 160-164, 170, 172

Something had to be done—and Laurance T. Burden did it. An internal study at Firestone Tire & Rubber Co. had just found the tire maker's manufacturing process woefully out of date. One conclusion: plant managers often guessed how much rubber they needed to fill an order, wasting time and money if they were wrong.

Guessing wasn't good enough for Burden, Firestone's vice-president for information services. After the 1982 study, Burden and the vice-president for U. S. tire operations designed a computer system to track every step in building a tire, from having the right amount of rubber on hand to checking the treads. The system, now running at two Firestone plants, has helped boost productivity by 15% and saved millions. Burden plans to install it in Firestone's other five plants by 1988.

There's a new breed of manager surfacing in the executive suite. As countless chief executives come to grasp the importance of information to their businesses, they're seeking people like Burden and assigning them a high-stakes mission: figuring out how to fashion a confusing array of often-incompatible computer and communications equipment into a cudgel that can clobber the competition. Some members of this new information elite sit behind such recognizable nameplates as senior vice-president, vice-president for information services, or information resources manager. Others are beginning to get a higher-sounding title to reflect their new status: chief information officer, or *CIO.*

However it's listed in the company directory, the job requires executives equipped to straddle the historic gulf between the nontechnical people in the boardroom and the traditional directors of management information systems *(MIS)* down on the data-processing floor, who often lack a broad sense of their company's overall business mission. Much more than just cheerleaders for new technology, CIOs look for ways to harness the power of new information technologies to slash costs, boost productivity, create new products, improve sales and marketing, and help set a company's strategic direction. The concept is still evolving, and today's CIOs are as different as the corporate cultures that spawn them. But most perform three basic functions:

■ They oversee all the company's technology, including data processing, office systems, and telecommunications.

■ They report directly to a high-ranking executive such as the chief executive officer or chairman.

■ They concentrate on long-term strategy and planning while leaving the day-to-day operations of the computer room to subordinates (table, page 215).

"The job calls for a Renaissance man," says Eugene F. Bedell, vice-president for information services at First Boston Corp. in New York. "You have to provide technical leadership while you also talk strategy." Adds Leon Jackson, an Arthur D. Little Inc. consultant: "You have be part missionary, part salesman, and part consensus-builder."

NEW GUARD. Typical of the new guard is Max D. Hopper, a senior vice-president of American Airlines Inc., who just returned to the airline after a 3½-year stint as executive vice-president at Bank of America. Hopper, 50, is in charge of about 4,000 people and a budget of $400 million, including the airline's computer expenditures. But he is also responsible for selling American's Sabre computerized reservations system to other airlines, making it a marketing tool instead of just another data base. Such sales contributed 6% of American's revenues last year—and 28% of profits. "Our technology is a key aspect of our ability to expand," says the jovial Hopper, who meets with Chairman Robert L. Crandall for an hour or two each week. "Without it we wouldn't keep growing the way we have and offering the services we do."

So far, most chief information officers are in America's biggest corporations. In a recent survey of 120 of the nation's 500 largest service and industrial companies, the Big Eight accounting firm of Arthur Andersen & Co. found that 40% have one. While other surveys have produced lower estimates, the experts agree on one thing: CIOs are likely to proliferate in the next few years, especially in banking, financial services, airlines, and insurance—the most information-dependent businesses. "Once the CEO recognizes that he's got to do something to harness the strategic use of information, he's not going to do it himself," says Melvyn E. Bergstein, an Andersen managing director. "He's going to change the organization."

There are some who worry about the trend. Big corporations do not create new executive titles every day, and the growing presence of the CIO moniker causes Thomas J. Peters, co-author of *In Search of Excellence*, to fret that some companies are adding them in "fad-like fashion" by pinning a higher salary and fancier title on the MIS director. Those who disagree argue that even if the title itself evaporates, Corporate America has recognized the crucial role of computers and information. Companies will need senior-level people, they say, to handle the CIO job (page 220).

'SNOW-PROOF.' The advent of the CIO mirrors what happened when senior accountants blossomed into chief financial officers in the 1960s. "The accountant kept track of what we spent," says Eleanor M. Luce, director of management information systems for MCI Inc. in Rye Brook, N. Y. "Then we said we're going to have a CFO to worry about the financial health of the company."

Most of the people filling the new CIO jobs aren't computer types. Fewer than half have extensive technical experience, according to a recent survey by John Diebold & Associates, a consulting firm. They should speak enough computerese to be "snow-proof" with subordinates who watch over the equipment, says Professor James C. Wetherbe, director of the University of Minnesota's Management Information Systems Research Center. But the CIO's job, which brings a heftier salary, larger staff, and broader responsibilities than the old information-services manager, "is not for the classic computer jock or machine-room honcho," says Michael A. Weiner, a Diebold vice-president. "Chief information officers will know technology but must know business. They're more

WHAT A CHIEF INFORMATION OFFICER DOES

The CIO must be a strong communicator. Straddling two camps, he must explain to managers how they can make the best use of technology while making the technical side understand what management wants. Michael Simmons of Fidelity Investments acted in such a go-between role in coming up with a way to offer clients hourly pricing of mutual funds.

To get across his ideas on using technology for competitive advantage, the CIO must have access to top management. Thomas J. English, director of corporate information resources management at Federal-Mogul Corp., sits on the auto-parts maker's executive council. Jack L. Hancock, executive vice-president of Wells Fargo Bank, huddles often with the bank chairman.

The CIO concentrates on long-term strategy—and leaves the running of computer systems to technical experts. When Pennwalt Corp. bought the Turco-Purex division of Purex Industries Inc. last year, Robert M. Rubin played a key role as Pennwalt's director of information systems by figuring out how the two companies could mesh their computer operations.

The CIO has ultimate responsibility for selecting, buying, and deploying all the company's technology, including equipment and staff used in data processing, office automation, and telecommunications. At Security Pacific National Bank in Los Angeles, for example, Executive Vice-President John P. Singleton controls a budget of $300 million and a staff of 4,000.

---

interested in what works than how it works."

GOOD TRAINING. That's not to say that managers who grew up on the technical side can't make the transition into a *CIO*'s shoes. Many are doing so. Robert C. Forney, 40, director of information systems at Akron-based GenCorp Inc., is studying for an *MBA* at Kent State University to supplement his undergraduate degree in computer science and build his credibility with line managers at the diversified manufacturer. Robert M. Rubin, who ran the marketing department at Sun Co. for four years before joining Pennwalt Corp. as director of information systems in 1984, suggests that experience in line management is an even better recipe for success. "Running a profit-and-loss cen-

ter is the best training a future *CIO* can get," he says. "You start to understand what businessmen do."

As their roles expand, the first priority of most *CIO*s is to squeeze the most out of their company's computer budget, holding down costs while mak-

---

> ### The CIO post 'is not for the classic computer jock or machine-room honcho

---

ing more effective use of what the company already has. When John M. Hammitt became vice-president for information management at Pillsbury Co. in 1983, one of his first acts was to put all computer spending on hold for a year while he reassessed what the company really needed (page 216). He used the time to develop a strategic, company-wide blueprint for technology use.

Hammitt hasn't been the only one reassessing his resources. From 1982 to 1984 corporations raised their computer spending by an average of about 18% a year, estimates International Data Corp., a Framingham (Mass.) market research firm. That binge left many senior managements feeling that their information-processing budgets were out of control. As a result, many corporations have started a period of digestion that has helped cause the computer industry's most prolonged slump in recent memory. The rate of annual spending growth has skidded to 9% in the past two years.

SCORING POINTS. Now *CIO*s are looking to use what they have in more strategic ways. They want to cut operating costs for line managers and make an impact on the company's bottom line. At Air Products & Chemicals Inc., workers who helped produce natural gas at 80 U. S. plants once had to read meters, write reports on the condition of the equipment, keep inventory, and then mail everything to headquarters in Allentown, Pa. But Peter W. C. Mather, vice-president for management information services at the $1.8 billion company, saw a way to save time by having computers take over many of those tasks. Mather spearheaded the

AN INFORMATION GURU WHO'S DEMYSTIFYING HIGH TECH

"I have written no more than six computer programs in my life."

It's an odd boast for someone who is Pillsbury Co.'s vice-president for information management. But John M. Hammitt isn't a traditional computer manager: He doesn't even have a computer in his office. "I don't require the tool day to day," he explains. "I deal with people."

If Hammitt breaks the high-tech mold, that's the way he wants it. A University of Chicago *MBA* who cooks Middle Eastern and Indian meals in his spare time, "John can sit with senior management and explain technology and not be perceived as a technocrat," says Thomas Morin, a fellow Minneapolis chief information officer at Medtronic Inc., a maker of medical devices.

'COACHES AND LEADERS.' Hammitt, 42, left Morton Thiokol Inc. three years ago to step into his newly created position at Pillsbury. He also stepped into a mess: Pillsbury's information systems had "suffered a decade of negligence" while the company grew through a series of acquisitions in the 1970s, says Professor James C. Wetherbe, director of the University of Minnesota's Management Information Systems Research Center.

Hammitt's first move was to stop all new spending for a year to reassess the company's technology. Now, armed with a comprehensive blueprint, the $5.8 billion purveyor of Poppin' Fresh dough, Green Giant corn, and Burger King hamburgers is updating its systems. Spending is back on the upswing at $90 million for the year that ends next May, up 20% from the year earlier. Hammitt expects outlays to grow at that rate until 1989, with an influx of hardware, software, and staff.

More important than the technology, Hammitt says, are staffing changes he has made. He replaced technically oriented managers of information systems with executives who have broader backgrounds. "They're more coaches and leaders than technicians," Hammitt says. He has also recruited entry-level staffers from *MBA* programs and boosted computer staffs by 50% in Burger King and the U.S. consumer-foods group. He presses his 650 subordinates to understand the business needs of their units and to avoid computer jargon in communicating with line managers. "It's a mind-set change on our part," Hammitt says.

The result is that managers and systems staffs have jointly improved their gathering and use of information. Managers now know months earlier than they used to how a new product is selling—or how much a coupon is being used in different regions. "Because we've got better information," Hammitt says, "we're able to respond to the market more quickly."

CLOSE MONITORING. Hammitt is now moving to improve customer service. To fill orders from distributors and grocery stores on time, the company is installing systems that monitor manufacturing and distribution in the foods group. By using computers that track inventory, costs, and efficiency, Pillsbury is also upgrading distribution of food and supplies to Burger King franchisees. For senior managers, the company is installing equipment to chart trends and business performance.

Hammitt is betting that within five years these moves will pay for themselves three or four times over. Meantime, the initial success of the new systems has turned once-skeptical line managers into enthusiastic promoters. Says Roger L. Headrick, Pillsbury's chief financial officer: "Now they want to know how they can do more—and how they can do it faster."

By Mary J. Pitzer in Minneapolis

creation of a $30 million system that ties computers in the plants into a central computer at headquarters.

By controlling production levels, watching for and adjusting patterns of energy consumption in the plants, and even alerting engineers when the equipment needs upgrading, the system has increased the energy efficiency of the company's gas production by 14%, saving $25 million a year. By cutting operating costs, "information services has been recognized as a viable profession at Air Products," Mather says.

As *CIO*s win points with such projects, their chief executives are handing them operations that range far afield of the data processing floor. Edward A. Schefer, vice-president for information management at General Foods Corp., also supervises the company's critical function of market research. As vice-president for corporate administration at Aetna Life & Casualty Co., Irwin J. Sitkin oversees everything from computer systems to the print shop, mail room, and corporate art gallery (page 219). And Darwin A. John, an engineer by training who started out with Scott Paper Co. as *MIS* director in 1979, now serves as chief planning development officer as well as chief information officer. His goal: to "posture information as part of overall strategy."

For many *CIO*s, showing management how computers can help create new products is an increasingly important part of the job. In 1985, brokers for Boston's Fidelity Investments wanted to be first to come up with a way to guarantee customers the price of a select mutual fund at the hour they bought or sold it, rather than the price at the day's close. That way, customers who acted quickly on news affecting the market would not suffer full-day declines.

BIOLOGY TEACHER. They turned to Michael Simmons, a former high school biology teacher and International Business Machines Corp. systems engineer who functions as Fidelity's chief information officer. One of 15 presidents of Fidelity's parent company, *FMR* Corp., Simmons came up with a way for Fidelity's computers to take a feed of proprietary data from another brokerage house, pull out those trades that affected the price of stocks and bonds in Fidelity's 32 select funds, and

let Fidelity become the only U. S. seller of mutual funds to offer hourly pricing. No longer does management regard the computer operation "as some kind of giant calculator," says Simmons. He reports directly to Chairman Edward C. Johnson III.

*CIO*s are enjoying their most dramatic impact by honing the way their companies sell and market products. The group sales force at Northwestern National Life Insurance Co. has been isolated from headquarters in Minneapolis because 435 salespeople and support staff have used stand-alone personal computers in 25 regional offices. But David W. Haskin, a senior vice-president for corporate resources whose previous job experience was in personnel and general management, is currently having those offices connected to the company's *IBM* 3090 mainframe with midsize computers. That way salespeople can find out rates and deliver proposals immediately instead of waiting two weeks. The "gut feeling" of R. Michael Conley, Northwestern's vice-president for group sales, is that Haskin's move will spark sales.

Ross C. Ahntholz has a similar goal at Olin Corp., the Stamford (Conn.)-based chemical maker. He installed an *IBM PC/AT* at one facility where a major customer stores bulk chemicals delivered by Olin. The customer used to have to call Olin when something went wrong there—if, for instance, the temperature was dropping enough to affect the quality of the product. Now the computer monitors the process and automatically alerts Olin's headquarters of problems. Olin often responds before the customer even knows that there is a problem.

By next year, Ahntholz, who started his business career in marketing and sales before coming to Olin as director of information services in 1980, hopes to give customers access to a system showing where Olin's tank cars are at any given time and when they're likely to arrive at the customer's door. "Traditionally, we have been storekeepers of data and information," Ahntholz says. "The role is changing from storekeeping to facilitating change with technology."

The impetus to launch such change often starts in the executive suite, where chief information officers are fast becoming high-ranking advisers to

THE TECHNOCRAT AS STRATEGIC PLANNER

For as long as computers have been around, banks have relied on them to manage the flow of financial transactions. But when Carl E. Reichardt took over as chairman of Wells Fargo Bank in 1983, he decided that his bank's information systems could be used to far greater advantage. To help fashion computers into true strategic weapons, he soon turned to Jack L. Hancock, a senior vice-president in charge of computer systems who had been at the San Francisco-based bank only 10 months.

Reichardt gave Hancock more than computers: He put him in charge of corporate strategic planning and personnel and later named him executive vice-president. By integrating the three jobs, Hancock says, the bank turned information from "a byproduct of some computer" into a tool for creating "strategic alternatives that management could choose from."

The wisdom of this decision showed up in May, when Wells Fargo bought Crocker National Bank from Midland Bank *PLC* for $1.1 billion and moved up from 12th to 10th on the list of the nation's largest banks. Hancock, one of five top Wells Fargo executives who had begun planning the purchase two years earlier, culled reams of data on Crocker from computerized financial statements, commercial data bases, Federal Reserve Bank reports, and a variety of other sources.

His staff then set up computer models of how the 613 branches, 1,190 automatic teller machines, and 26,000 employees of the two banks could best be melded. The staff also outlined the ways Crocker could help strengthen Wells Fargo's position against competitors in each region of California. All this information helped Reichardt hone his bargaining position before his final offer to Midland in February.

It also helped Wells Fargo move quickly once the deal was done. Within a month after the merger, Hancock's staff completed a layout of the two banks' combined data and voice networks. Within three months, it linked all the automated teller machines. On the day the merger became final, Wells Fargo fired 1,640 excess employees, including most of Crocker's middle and senior managers.

Hancock, 56, also has a major day-to-day role at Wells Fargo. He believes that decentralizing computer operations and getting critical information resources to the bank's business units are the best ways to boost efficiency. Now the bank's line business managers, most of whom had little previous technical experience, manage their own computer systems.

'REAL INNOVATION.' One result: Wells Fargo's commercial lending division recently rolled out highly sophisticated artificial-intelligence software to help determine loan applicants' creditworthiness accurately and quickly. "That's how you get real innovations in the use of information—by getting users involved," says David R. Vincent, a Santa Clara (Calif.)-based consultant who has studied Wells Fargo.

Such successes help explain the close relationship between Reichardt and Hancock, a lanky, self-effacing Southerner who helped launch the U. S. Army's computer operations in the 1950s and was a major general in charge of its noncombat computer operations when he retired in 1978. Reichardt can often be found in Hancock's office at the end of the day, chewing over recent events or strategy. Says Herbert Z. Halbrecht, the executive recruiter who brought Hancock to Wells Fargo: "Jack's true title is *consigliere* to the chairman." These days, that's what being chief information officer is all about.

By Jonathan B. Levine in San Francisco

senior management. At Aetna, Sitkin sits on the management committee. At Wells Fargo Bank, Executive Vice-President Jack L. Hancock, who is responsible for computer systems, strategic planning, and personnel, talks often with the bank's chairman. This kind of access allows Hancock to play a leading role in the most important decisions affecting his company, as he did in helping chart Wells Fargo's acquisition of Crocker National Bank earlier this year (box).

A COMPUTER EXPERT WITH A PIPELINE TO THE TOP

When the Conference Board decided a year ago that the nation's top information executives were getting important enough to merit their own council, the man it tapped as chairman was Irwin J. Sitkin. That was hardly surprising. Sitkin, 56, is considered one of the foremost information gurus in the insurance industry, which is itself one of the most information-intensive businesses in the world.

As vice-president for corporate administration at Aetna Life & Casualty Co., the tall, trim, soft-spoken Sitkin has thrown his mantle over more corporate operations than most other chief information officers in the U. S. And he is closer to the seat of power than many of them. "He really is a senior executive of his company," says George Newman, a senior research associate at the Conference Board. "He can be a role model for others."

Sitkin supervises much more than Aetna's $280 million computer operation: The mail room, print shop, travel department, telecommunications, facilities management, real estate, personnel, and training also report to him. His grasp even extends to Aetna's new electrical co-generation plant and its art gallery, a 1983 Sitkin inspiration that holds six shows a year.

Sitkin says his broad charter makes sense because all the operations are information-related in some way—the print shop because it handles electronic publishing, the travel department because it relies so heavily on computers, the mail room because it supervises electronic mail, and the art gallery because that's a form of information, too. With an information executive in charge, "the opportunities for synergism are tremendous," he says.

WATERMELONS. His wide-ranging responsibilities give Sitkin a pipeline to the top. He reports to President William O. Bailey and is a member of Aetna's top-level corporate management committee, where he "helps senior management determine what our priorities ought to be," Bailey says. He also attends board meetings, though not as a member.

Like many of his peers, Sitkin almost stumbled into his *CIO* job. He started with a *BS* in agricultural economics from Cornell University, but the closest he ever got to agriculture was as a watermelon inspector for a railroad. After leaving the Air Force in 1954, he joined Aetna for two reasons: "what the job was called—*IBM* supervisory clerk trainee No. 2—and the idea of working with *IBM* equipment." Within a year, he and two other employees had created what he says was the first computer program for the property-casualty business, plus a new 500-employee department called machine accounting. "It opened new vistas," he recalls.

Nowadays, Sitkin also wields strong influence on Aetna's planning and marketing. At a recent management committee meeting, the president of Aetna's reinsurance subsidiary was outlining his forecast for the year when Sitkin urged him to discuss his new "expert system" for structuring truckers' liability reinsurance coverage. Sitkin then sought feedback from another division president who had received an expert systems proposal. A spirited discussion ensued on the potential for expert systems—a topic that probably wouldn't have come up without Sitkin. "I'm not making the big decisions in the company," he says. "But I influence them."

By Resa W. King in Hartford

Having the ear of the chief executive or chairman is one of the keys to success as a *CIO*. That has certainly been the case at Enron Corp., the $10 billion Houston energy concern that used to be called *HNG*/InterNorth Inc. Chairman Kenneth L. Lay recognized that information systems had become more important to Enron since deregulation and increased competition rocked the natural gas industry. So he named J. Ronald Knorpp chief information officer in 1985 and made it clear

WILL CHIEF INFORMATION OFFICERS GO THE WAY OF THE HULA HOOP?

Not long after the Arab oil embargo pushed petroleum prices skyward, U. S. companies decided that transportation costs had to be watched and controlled. Up sprouted a bumper crop of corporate transportation czars. When manufacturing efficiency became the shibboleth at the start of the 1980s, many companies rushed to put a senior executive in charge. The same happened with strategic planning. And quality.

But it's a fact of life in the American corporation: Fads fade "faster than the fashions in Paris," says James J. O'Toole, a management professor at the University of Southern California's business school. Strategic planners fell out of favor when companies realized that executives and line managers were supposed to play that role. Over the years many other in-vogue titles have disappeared—or ended up quietly slipping into the corporate woodwork under the domain of such executives as the chief financial officer and the executive vice-president. Will chief information officers be next? Not right away.

WARNING SIGNS. It's true that there are some early warning signs of faddishness. Trade groups such as the Chicago-based Society for Information Management are pushing for the spread of the *CIO* title. And computer publications and management journals are publishing articles with headlines such as *Chief Information Officer: Does Your Company Need One?*

Some critics think that companies are prematurely answering yes. "It's likely that a lot will treat the whole issue in fad-like fashion by hoisting the *CIO*'s flag next to the chairman's and putting some lower-level management-information-systems guy in the job," warns Thomas J. Peters, co-author of *In Search of Excellence*. Adds Duncan B. Sutherland, a Houston-based office automation consultant with *CRS* Sirrine Inc.: "Too many companies are looking at it as a panacea."

Still, there are some big differences between *CIO* positions and top-level jobs that have come and gone over the past two decades. It's crucial for many companies to have someone who translates between the data processing department and the executive suite. And most members of the current generation of senior managers won't be computer-literate anytime soon.

This means that the rising star of the *CIO* is likely to keep ascending, at least until a next generation of executives—ones who know their way around an electronic spreadsheet—gets to the top. By then, using computers as a competitive weapon should be even more important than it is

that the job was at the same level as the chief financial officer and chief legal officer. When Knorpp gave a presentation to 30 line managers, Lay was there. "The typical *MIS* director couldn't begin to ask the chairman to attend his meeting," Knorpp says. "Because I'm working for the chairman, this is his charge, and everyone knows it."

Not all of Knorpp's counterparts at other companies face such smooth sailing. Some run smack into fellow managers who fear the idea of one person controlling the flow of data in a big corporation. When Pennwalt's Rubin arrived at the company, a vice-president told him: "You seem like a really nice guy, but we'll have nothing to do with you because we don't need central guidance." After Rubin upgraded computer systems throughout the company, the same fellow "said he'd like to chat with me," Rubin recalls. "Within six months we were working well together."

'SHOW-ME ATTITUDE.' Other *CIO*s bump up against line managers who feel that an information czar represents another layer of management separating them from the chief executive. "It isn't always easy to persuade line bosses that somebody

today. So chief executives may still be inclined to delegate this role to a trusted peer.

FROM THE TOP. Chief executives who create the position should guard against letting a *CIO* amass a huge centralized staff at the expense of having experts down in the trenches, consultants and executive recruiters agree. Peters and others suggest, too, that it's best to look for *CIO* candidates among the top performers in sales, marketing, operations, and finance—and then teach them what they need to know about technology. The alternative—trying to turn technically oriented staffers into businessmen—will turn the *CIO* position into "a glorified *MIS* director's job," says David R. Vincent, president of Information Group Inc., a consulting firm based in Santa Clara, Calif.

Perhaps most important is support from the chief executive. In fact, many experts believe the *CIO*'s job will be effective only in companies where the idea comes from the top. "If it isn't something the *CEO* feels he needs, it will not succeed," says Michael A. Weiner, a vice-president at consultants John Diebold & Associates.

When will it be clear that *CIO*s are here to stay? Once the job becomes a stepping-stone to chief executive, says Peters. "If you're really serious about having a *CIO* and give the job to one of the three aspirants to the *CEO*'s throne, you're making a statement that the job is important," he adds. "Otherwise, it's just a parking place."

By Gordon Bock in New York

working a computer knows what is best for the operation," says Firestone's Burden, who gained substantial credibility after he installed a point-of-sale network of sales terminals at the company's 1,500 retail automotive centers to improve the control of parts and inventory. "Middle management has a show-me attitude and a skepticism that is understandable. You really have to make the case."

GenCorp's Forney found the same thing when he moved up from manager of computer services to director of information systems at his company, which makes everything from tires to tennis balls. "Some view it as interference, an extra level of approval, or somebody looking over their shoulder," he says.

Getting involved in the affairs of line managers is a sea change from the way information managers acted in the past. The old-line technocrats weren't concerned with holding down line costs while they performed such back-office tasks as calculating the payroll and balancing the books in the glass-enclosed, air-conditioned computer rooms known as "glass houses." Because those functions weren't seen as strategically important, information managers reported to the chief financial officer. "We were more in tune with the computer industry than with the businesses we were supporting," notes Thomas J. English, director of information resource management at Federal-Mogul Corp., a Southfield (Mich.) maker of automobile parts.

Computers haven't ceased doing the corporate grunt work, of course, and such old-style information executives still exist. But more and more, they are becoming just one among the many managers reporting to *CIO*s, whose functions and responsibilities are getting broader. That has led to some jealousy because the old-line contingent is less than thrilled with being relegated to nuts-and-bolts work in the computer room while chief information officers with better business credentials whiz by on their way to high-visibility jobs with salaries of $250,000 and up.

FORCED OUT. The threat of trouble can be real. In one case, an *MIS* director of a Los Angeles-area real-estate developer was forced out when a new *CIO* judged him to be someone "who did not understand management's needs for information." In general, though, *MIS* directors aren't in danger of becoming extinct. "While the chief information officer is the captain of the ship, there's a need for a person in charge of the engine room," says A. D. Little's Jackson.

The trend toward *CIO*s hasn't hit most of Corporate America yet. Many chief executives, having long confined computer technology to the backwaters of the back office, are still not convinced that computers can be used to gain a competitive advantage.

But when just one rival makes that happen, they often feel driven to catch up. "People resist change," says the University of Minnesota's Wetherbe. "But that is being preempted by fear for survival." So it's a safe bet that there'll be more chief information officers on the scene in years ahead. Whether they'll be as influential as Firestone's Laurance Burden depends on what kind of information—and results—they deliver.

By Gordon Bock in New York, with Kimberley Carpenter in Philadelphia, Jo Ellen Davis in Houston, and bureau reports

DISCUSSION QUESTIONS

1. What is a CIO, and what does one do?
2. What skills and preparation would help you obtain a CIO position?

THE PUSH FOR QUALITY

TO BEAT IMPORTS, THE U.S. MUST IMPROVE ITS PRODUCTS.
THAT MEANS A WHOLE NEW APPROACH TO MANUFACTURING

JUNE 8, 1987, PP. 130-136

Quality. Remember it? American manufacturing has slumped a long way from the glory days of the 1950s and '60s, when "Made in the U. S. A." proudly stood for the best that industry could turn out. But the prince of quality has since turned pauper. While the Japanese were developing remarkably higher standards for a whole host of products, from consumer electronics to cars and machine tools, many U. S. managers were smugly dozing at the switch. Now, aside from aerospace and agriculture, there are few markets left where the U. S. carries its own weight in international trade. For American industry, the message is simple: Get better or get beat.

Across the U. S., alarm gongs are clanging, and more and more managements are scrambling to make fundamental adjustments that will ensure better quality in their products and services. When you're losing markets to higher-quality foreign goods, "it's easy to get religion," says George E. P. Box, director of research for the Quality & Productivity Improvement Center (QPIC) at the University of Wisconsin. For the first time in years, quality experts are cautiously optimistic. "We're making progress, but there's a lot to go yet," says Richard A. Freund, who spent 35 years in quality control at Eastman Kodak Co. before launching Quality Planning Services in 1983.

Clearly, the drive to improve quality is blossoming into something far more substantial than the blizzard of buzzwords in the late 1970s. That was when quality circles erupted on the industrial scene—a fad that soon faded when it became clear that they could never provide the quick fix that many companies were hoping for. This time around executives are being more realistic. Managing for quality means nothing less than a sweeping overhaul in corporate culture, a radical shift in management philosophy, and a permanent commitment at all levels of the organization to seek continuous improvements.

What finally sank in to U. S. industry is the tremendous cost of ignoring quality. In most traditional factories that cost is probably the biggest item on their list of expenses, and it is always bigger than gross profit. But because the cost of quality is rarely broken out in gory detail, management has no idea of its true dimensions. When quality audits are performed, they invariably uncover huge "hidden plants" staffed and equipped just to find and fix defective products.

The typical factory invests a staggering 20% to 25% of its operating budget in finding and fixing mistakes. As many as one-quarter of all factory hands don't produce anything—they just rework things that were not done right the first time. Add in the expense of repairing or replacing the flawed products that slip out of the factory and into the market, and the total burden of "unquality" can mount to a punishing 30% or more of production costs.

UNDER THE GUN. No wonder many experts rank poor quality as the No. 1 drag on U. S. productivity and competitiveness—and the chief opportunity to trim prices and enhance profits. But the last thing managers under the gun of foreign competition want to hear is that they should spend more money to raise quality. But those executives couldn't be more wrong, says Myron Tribus. The former director of the Advanced Engineering Study Center at Massachusetts Institute of Technology declares that the "first principle" of management-by-quality is this: "Quality is never your problem. It is the solution to your problem."

Tribus, who last year left *MIT* to head the American Quality & Productivity Institute *(AQPI)*, pins the blame for America's quality downfall squarely on Frederick W. Taylor. The inventor of time-and-motion studies, Taylor laid down the principles of "scientific management" at the turn of the century. Today the end result of blindly following his mechanistic, heirarchical methods is that U. S. factories have become riddled with creeping inefficiency.

Compare similar products from the U. S. and Japan, and the amount of labor needed to turn out the products is higher in the U. S.—and the ratio worsens as the products get more complicated (chart, page 225). This extra labor not only hikes the product's cost but also increases the risk of human error, since blue-collar workers in Tayloresque factories are still treated as mindless cogs in the machinery of production. "We hire workers for their hands, and we forget about their heads," says Ronald D. Snee, manager of quality systems for product engineering at Du Pont Co. To compete in international markets, "we need both," because the people down in the pits are the ones who really understand what's wrong with the system.

Fixing the manufacturing system, not its products, is now seen as the primary key to better quality. The approach is based on a timeworn notion: An ounce of prevention is worth a pound of cure. The objective is to spot the cause of product defects, so the problem can be tackled at the source rather than after the fact. "Learning to remove the causes of variation," says Tribus, "is the first step in improving a process."

The latest technique for doing that is called statistical process control, or *SPC*. Basically, it gauges the performance of the manufacturing process by carefully monitoring changes in whatever is being produced. The goal is to detect potential problems before they result in off-quality products, then pinpoint the reason for the deviation and adjust the process to make it more stable. The difficulty is that manufacturing all but the most simple products involves dozens, maybe hundreds or thousands, of separate operations, and each is

THE MAN WHO TAUGHT JAPAN HOW TO MANAGE FOR QUALITY

For most of the 60 years that J. M. Juran has been preaching the virtues of quality, he has been, by choice, a loner. And until a decade ago, the blunt-talking Romanian immigrant was more widely acclaimed in Japan than in the U. S. "He taught us that the most important thing to upgrading quality is not technology, but quality management," says Junji Noguchi, executive director of the Japanese Union of Scientists & Engineers *(JUSE)*. Most U. S. companies took that lesson to heart only recently.

When Juran turned 75 in 1980, he decided to end his one-man show. To ensure that his mission will be carried on, he set up the Juran Institute Inc. in Wilton, Conn. Although he would never admit it, his one regret may be that in 1969 he turned down a request from *JUSE* to use his name on an award to recognize the cream among winners of its coveted Deming Prize, named after W. Edwards Deming, a rival consultant. But in 1981, Juran did accept Japan's Second Class Order of the Sacred Treasure—an extraordinary honor for a consultant. Boasts Juran: "I'm the first person to get it for quality."

affected by multiple variables. Only sophisticated statistical analyses can sift through such a vast maze of intertwining relationships to isolate those that lead to deficient quality.

TOTAL CONTROL. The Japanese picked up on *SPC* quickly because they have been honing statistical quality methods for 30 years, ever since quality guru W. Edwards Deming crossed the Pacific in the 1950s. The Japanese Union of Scientists & Engineers, scratching for ways to enhance the image of Japanese goods and spur exports, invited Deming to present a series of lectures on statistical methods for improving quality control on the factory floor. Later, *JUSE* also asked J. M. Juran, another quality pioneer, to teach Japanese executives the secrets of managing for quality. Juran contends that quality improvement must be a formal part of the business plan and of each manager's annual performance review—an approach often called total quality control, or *TQC*. While few U. S. companies paid much heed to Deming and Juran, the Japanese avidly embraced their ideas, and *JUSE* credits the pair for the minor miracle that Japan pulled off in the 1970s.

A few U. S. companies have a tradition of quality-consciousness, and they are sparking the current revival by applying the new *SPC* techniques just as vigorously as the Japanese. *AT&T*, Corning Glass, Du Pont, Ford, Hewlett-Packard, *IBM*, Kodak, and Westinghouse are frequently cited as the leaders. Each can relate impressive case histories of the power of management by quality.

Take the joint venture that Hewlett-Packard Co. set up in Japan with Yokogawa Electric Corp. For a decade, recalls Craig A. Walter, *HP*'s corporate quality director, *YHP* struggled along, always at the bottom of *HP*'s operations in product quality and profitability. In 1975, Kenzo Sasaoka took over as general manager and decided that *TQC* was the way to turn the place around. Sasaoka installed a pilot program on one line in 1976 and, notes Walter, "immediately reduced the defect rate by several orders of magnitude."

Gradually the statistical quality approach was expanded into all levels of manufacturing, plus research and development, administration, and even sales. And in 1982 *YHP* won the Deming Prize, Japan's most coveted industrial award. A greater reward for *HP* was the unit's jump from dead last to the head of the profitability list. And *YHP* stayed there for five years running until last year, when the strength of the yen pushed it down a notch.

Comparing 1985 with 1975, *YHP*'s manufacturing costs plummeted 42% and product defects shrunk 79%. Meanwhile, revenues per employee climbed 120%, market share shot up 193%, and profits soared 244%. Equally important, notes Walter, applying *TQC* to the *R&D* process trimmed the time it takes to get new products to market by a third. "Since half of *HP*'s sales this year come from products new in the past three years," he adds, "you can see why reducing those cycles is so important."

RUDE MESSAGE. Whole industries are now taking up the quality challenge. Detroit and Silicon Valley, both of which suffered severe market share losses due to inferior quality, are heavily committed, as are the textile, steel, and major-appliance industries. The auto makers were rudely roused in 1980 by the discovery that the quality of Japanese cars had pulled ahead by a wide margin and that U. S. drivers were not buying imports just because they cost less. So the Big Three launched crash catch-up efforts that have narrowed the gap significantly, although it still hasn't been closed.

Similarly, the U. S. semiconductor companies paid dearly for allowing Japanese rivals to wrest the lead in quality. That crucial wedge was exploited by Japan's chipmakers in attacking the U. S. market for computer-memory chips in the late 1970s. Today the Japanese dominate memory chip sales, both in the U. S. and worldwide. While U. S. producers say their quality is now competitive with Japan's, the bulk of the memory business seems lost forever.

For the remnants of America's once-prosperous steel and textile industries, quality is nothing less than survival. "Of all the industries that are responding to the quality need, the steel industry

THE JAPANESE EDGE IN MANUFACTURING

As products become more complex the Japanese are more efficient

Product	Manufacturing steps	Labor index*
AUTOMOBILE	1,200	1.98
FORK LIFT TRUCK	900	1.82
AUTO ENGINE	250	1.62
AUTOMATIC TRANSMISSION	200	1.41
COLOR TV	80	1.15
STEEL SHEET	17	1.0

*The ratio of hours of labor, U.S. vs. Japan

DATA: BOSTON CONSULTING GROUP

WHEN *CONSUMER REPORTS* TALKS, BUYERS LISTEN—AND SO DO COMPANIES

Whether they're buying automobiles or life insurance, drain cleaner or refrigerators—or practically anything else—millions of shoppers won't plunk down their money until they consult *Consumer Reports*. For 51 years the publication of Consumers Union has been a fiercely independent arbiter of quality goods and an ardent advocate of consumer rights. It has published *CU*'s ratings of thousands of products and services without ever losing a libel suit. And today, its monthly circulation is at an all-time high of 3.8 million.

A 90-member technical team puts products through their paces at *CU*'s headquarters in Mount Vernon, N. Y. When they can, they use the same tests industry uses. They check the laundering power of washing machines, for example, by washing pre-soiled fabric swatches and measuring their brightness with optical instruments. If no standard tests exist, *Consumer Reports* invents them. To rate facial tissues, *CU*'s technical team built a "sneeze machine" that squirts a controlled spray of water and air through a tissue mounted on embroidery hoops.

OPEN BOOK. *CU* describes its tests in detail when it rates products. But those explanations don't always placate the manufacturer whose product comes in last. If a company isn't happy with its

was probably under the most pressure to deliver in the short term or be eliminated," says Peter J. Trepanier, vice-president for quality for Armco Inc. At his company's Middletown (Ohio) Works, more stress on *SPC* and greater worker responsibility have yielded a 25% improvement in manufacturing costs, saving $2.5 million a month. Since Inland Steel Co. hired a platoon of consultants from Nippon Steel Corp. in 1985, the company has slashed its reject rate of flat-rolled steel in half. And Bethlehem Steel Corp.'s shipments to Ford Motor Co. now get turned back only 1% of the time, compared with 8% in the early 1980s.

To win back customers in the apparel market, America's import-battered textile companies are mounting a just-in-time delivery campaign that hinges on guaranteed quality. Swift Textiles Inc. each morning ships just enough denim for a day's production at the nearby Levi Strauss & Co. plant in Valdosta, Ga. With Swift certifying the quality of the denim, Levi has closed its warehouse and quality-testing lab. "The system will not allow us any mistakes," says Swift Vice-President Donald L. Massey. The gamble seems to be paying off. To fill new orders, Swift recently announced a $52.3 million, three-year expansion that will boost denim capacity 50% and add 300 jobs.

To avoid having to play catch-up, the major-appliance makers decided to slam the door before Japanese competitors could get their toes in the U. S. market. They beefed up quality and reliability with a range of new products that seem to have left little maneuvering room for newcomers.

A PUSHOVER. Other companies would do well to heed the example of the appliance industry, warns Armand V. Feigenbaum, president of General Systems Co. and another guiding light in the push for quality. That's because offshore producers now regard virtually every U. S. market as a pushover for better-quality products. The attitude of foreign executives, he says, is that "you can't help but succeed in the U. S. market today." Moreover, pressures from overseas will only intensify, adds Du Pont's Snee. "The Pacific Rim countries are now doing to the Japanese what the Japanese are doing to us," he explains, and this is bound to spur the Japanese to still higher levels of quality.

Improved quality doesn't come quickly, nor is it painless. It takes at least a couple of years just to get into the swing of things and train managers

rating, *CU* responds with an invitation to visit its labs.

Many companies have made changes in their products after getting a bad rating from *CU*. Although Whirlpool Corp. chafed at criticism that its washing-machine design made repair too difficult, on its new models the cabinet pops off to allow access to key parts.

In its April, 1973, issue, *Consumer Reports* rejected an entire category of products—microwave ovens—because doors on all 14 models tested were leaking radiation. Since then, ovenmakers have changed their designs. Today, "there's very little leakage around those doors," says *CU* technical director R. David Pittle.

MEDIA PUSH. While *Consumer Reports* remains *CU*'s major endeavor, the organization is branching out. In the last two years it has launched a travel newsletter, produced six home videocassettes, spruced up its *Penny Power* children's maga-zine, and formed a book-publishing company. Since January, *CU* has been selling dealer's-cost listings for most auto models and options. Its media push also includes a thrice-weekly syndicated newspaper column, plus radio and television spots. All this has helped *CU*'s bottom line. Last year it earned $3.4 million.

The prosperity has not diluted *CU*'s activism. Founded by labor unionists in the 1930s, it was among the first organizations to urge consumers to boycott goods made in Nazi Germany. Now *Consumer Reports* is alarmed that many Americans are slipping into poverty. So it is kicking off a three-part series on the working poor. But will the outspoken judge of what's good comment on how well U. S. manufacturers stack up against the Japanese? No way, say Pittle. "Our purpose is to provide an objective evaluation of a product—regardless of who made it."

By Mimi Bluestone in Mount Vernon

and then workers to be comfortable with statistical analysis tools. The process has to start at the very top and filter down, because without solid evidence of support from the executive suite, workers quickly tag the program as yet another management sham. "Quality is not evangelism, suggestion boxes, or sloganism—it's a way of life," declares Feigenbaum, who was manager of quality control at General Electric Co. before he founded his Pittsfield (Mass.) consulting company in 1969.

The most resistance usually comes from the middle-manager and supervisory levels. For many of these people, management by quality seems a threat to their authority—if not their jobs. Shop-floor workers are usually eager to assume responsibility for the quality of their work. But for middle managers, says Box of Wisconsin's *QPIC*, "it's a different game from the one that they learned." They must function less like bosses and more like football coaches, relying on powers of persuasion rather than "do-this" directives.

HP's Walter admits that despite clear signals from President John Young that quality is a top priority, the quality thrust hasn't gone without hitches. "Even with *HP*, some people are risk-takers and pioneers, and not others." At Ford, too, some middle managers are still struggling to accept the idea that costs really do head down when quality perks up. But Ford's quality gains have already produced telling evidence: Last year its fattened profits exceeded those of General Motors Corp.

The core of the revolution in quality can be captured in a phrase: customer satisfaction. But it has a surprising twist. Every person on a production line is the customer of the preceding operation, so each worker's goal is to make sure that the quality of his or her work meets the expectations of the next person. When that happens throughout the manufacturing, sales, and distribution chain, the satisfaction of the ultimate customer, the buyer, should be assured. Says Walter of *HP*: "It's been revolutionary for some people to think that they have a customer."

That is especially true for operations "upstream" from the factory—product design, in particular. A high wall has always stood between design and manufacturing, with designers essentially ignorant of how their creations are translated into finished products and not in the least eager to

AMERICA'S QUEST CAN'T BE HALF-HEARTED

It's a shocking statistic. As many as one-quarter of American factory workers don't produce anything; they simply fix other workers' mistakes. Is it any wonder that foreign manufacturers have stolen the march on U. S. companies in the battle for worldwide market share? As the costs to individual companies and the economy escalate, executives are coming to the realization that a weaker dollar, lower wages, and protectionism won't solve America's competitiveness problem. Making better products will.

American products once set the standard, but no more. Present-day American consumers are hooked on foreign-made products, and even rising import prices can't choke off their demand. The reason is that Japanese cars, German machine tools, and a host of other foreign products are simply superior in quality to their U. S.-made substitutes.

Quality, of course, has a different meaning for different people. To some, it is fancy features and flashy styling. To others, it is a clean and simple look. But at its most basic, quality means that something works well and is durable. Everything else is extra. And these days, foreign producers are outdoing U. S. makers on the basics—and frequently on the frills. Some American manufacturers, it's true, have succeeded in lowering defect rates and warranty claims in recent years, but that's not enough. Foreign makers keep setting new, far tougher standards for performance, reliability, and durability.

How did this happen? America led Europe and Japan into the post-World War II era, helping to rebuild their industries. The Japanese, frustrated by their early failures, took lessons in management from American experts. The U. S. economy grew to dominate the postwar world, and it is that very dominance that eventually bred complacency and a sense of invincibility. "We got fat and sloppy," says economist Lester C. Thurow of Massachusetts Institute of Technology.

To be fair, certain elements of quality were never of paramount concern to Americans. The nation grew with the discovery and the exploitation of new frontiers—first geographic, then technological. Once they'd exhausted something, Americans wanted to move on. This frontier mentality formed the basis of post-World War II consumerism. People wanted convenience, disposability, trendiness. By contrast, the Japanese had few

find out. Well-manicured designers toss their ideas over the wall, and leave the nitty-gritty details to the dirty-fingernail types in the factory.

LEAPFROGGING. But tearing down that wall is a crucial step in the drive to boost quality. Juran and other experts assert that no more than 20% of quality defects can be traced to the production line. The other 80% is locked in during the design phase or by purchasing policies that value low price over the quality of purchased parts and materials. To attack those areas, companies are developing new computer systems that are "smart" enough to analyze the quality of a product while it still exists only on a computer screen. "The goal is to design out the cause of quality problems at the very start," says A. Blanton Godfrey, head of quality theory at *AT&T* Bell Laboratories.

Such automated-quality systems could help the U. S. stop playing catch-up and do a little leapfrogging. "There's no question that we could do better than the Japanese," asserts Box. Because the Japanese still rely mainly on paperwork and manual methods to implement quality control, just-in-time, and related schemes, he argues that U. S. factories could "jump ahead" by exploiting their lead in computer-based management. "I saw what this country can do" during World War II, adds Box, "and I still believe we can do anything we put our minds to."

By Otis Port in New York,
with bureau reports

natural resources and, after the war, no place to go. At first, the products of their reviving industries were ridiculed as low-cost, low-tech junk. But within a couple of decades products made in Japan came to reflect what its culture had long revered: economy of design and ease of operation—the perfect marriage of form and function.

HARD SLOG. Now, U. S. industry, humbled by the example of others, is trying to boost quality. Dozens of quality gurus are hiring on at companies to start the process. Sometimes, it works. The company redesigns the product, adopts the latest statistical control methods, and gives workers a measure of control and a sense of pride in their craft. Other times, the gimmicky hardware is snapped up and the rhetoric resounds, but the message is mixed. To save costs, a research budget is slashed. To boost productivity, schedules are speeded up. "Employees are pretty clear on reading signals," says quality expert David A. Garvin of Harvard business school. "Even when managers say they want quality, the signal coming through loudest may be 'get the goods out the door.' "

Improving quality requires nothing less than an upheaval in corporate culture. Engineers, designers, marketers, administrators, and the production workers on the line have to work together to ensure quality, and they all have to know that they are critical to the process. Financial incentives and psychic rewards can smooth the way. But if the process is half-hearted or poorly planned, quality will become simply another fashionable word in the executive's lexicon or yet another trendy promotion vehicle for new goods. And a product with fancy features and high-tech glitz, like today's gold-plated military hardware, may well turn out to be less reliable than its simpler counterpart.

Providing the appearance of quality is easy. Truly improving quality is a long, hard slog, and it frequently carries a steep up-front cost. Unwilling to spend money to save money, some executives are resisting quality-enhancing measures just as they resisted energy-conservation measures in the 1970s. But the initial investment in equipment and training is well worth making. Eventually, the savings from not having to make repairs or to pay off warranties or to settle liability suits far exceed the costs of a quality program. And the biggest returns by far come when productivity, market share, and profits rise. That may be cold comfort to executives fixated on next quarter's bottom line. But managers, and the stock market that judges them, had better start acting as though quality pays, because that's the clear lesson of the worldwide competitive battle of the 1980s.

By Karen Pennar

DISCUSSION QUESTIONS

1. What role does quality play in the competitiveness-productivity problem of U.S. industry?
2. What is the argument that scientific management is the cause of quality problems?
3. What is statistical process control?
4. Why does American management seem so much slower in adjusting to the ideas of Juran and Deming than Japanese management?
5. Is the quality difference a reflection of differences in the attitudes of American and Japanese workers?

THIS VIDEO 'GAME' IS SAVING MANUFACTURERS MILLIONS

COMPUTER SIMULATION, NOW FAR MORE THAN A TESTING TOOL, REMAKES THE FACTORY FLOOR

AUGUST 17, 1987, PP. 82, 84

You pass by the factory manager's office, and what do you see? He and his top engineers are huddled around a computer screen where cute little symbols are threading their way through mazes. Are these well-paid professionals playing video games on company time?

Look again: The screen display is a recreation of the factory floor, replete with machine tools, robots, flexible manufacturing cells, and materials-handling vehicles. The goal of this game is to exploit those resources in the most efficient way and turn out the highest-quality, lowest-cost product. Welcome to the era of manufacturing simulation.

While the exercise may have make-believe overtones, the payoff can be real. That's what the engineers at Northern Research & Engineering Corp., a consulting subsidiary of Ingersoll-Rand Co., learned when they designed a complicated line for making ball bearings. They figured they would need 77 machine tools performing 16 different processes. But when they fed the information into a computer and simulated the line in operation, they quickly realized the plan could be improved. They were able to eliminate four machines, saving $750,000 for their client, Torrington Co. With computer simulation, says Northern Research senior engineer James M. Hanson, savings of several million dollars are "not unusual."

Computer simulations of real-world systems aren't new. They have been used to analyze air-traffic control and telephone switching systems. Pilots learn to handle new aircraft by flying simulated planes. And the military has long used computer models to play war.

ECONOMIC APPEAL. What is new is that simulation is moving into manufacturing in a big way. Even small companies are turning to it in order to solve everyday problems and help make major strategic decisions. "Actually, the little job shops need it most," says F. Hank Grant, president of Factrol Inc., a West Lafayette (Ind.) supplier of simulation software. "For starters, it would do wonders for their ability to handle just-in-time scheduling," which more and more major manufacturers are imposing on vendors.

Driving the trend are some increasingly attractive economics. While large computers are still required for the toughest jobs, today's personal computers can run simulation programs that just a decade ago "would have taken a mainframe to its knees for several hours," says Samuel M. MacMillan, who heads the effort to use simulation for decision-making at Electronic Data Systems Corp., a subsidiary of General Motors Corp. And these days the software can cost as little as a few hundred dollars, although $10,000 to $100,000 is more typical.

This new affordability comes none too soon. Simulation will prove vital in bolstering U. S. competitiveness, declares W. David Kelton IV, associate professor of management science at the University of Minnesota. Moreover, modern manufacturing systems are getting too intricate to analyze with pencil and paper. As factories move closer to the goal of computer-integrated manufacturing *(CIM)*, in which computers orchestrate all phases of a manufacturing operation, "the process becomes so complex that no one person can collect all the whereases and wherefores in his head," says Christopher V. Kuhner, manager of *CIM* engineering at Digital Equipment Corp.

Perhaps no company knows better than *GM* how hard it can be to put modern manufacturing technology to work. When the auto giant's engineers conceived a high-tech production system for a new engine called the Series 60, they planned to use automatic guided vehicles *(AGVs)* to transport parts and materials. They figured on using two *AGV* loops to keep the line supplied with parts—one for the guts of the engine and another for "trim" such as belts and hoses.

MAJOR FLAW. Then *GM*'s *EDS* subsidiary built a computer model of the system. It worked fine at the low volumes predicted for the first year or so. But when *EDS* cranked up the model to simulate the higher outputs that *GM* expected in later years, the engineers uncovered a major flaw: The system's computer couldn't handle the hectic flow of *AGV* traffic. They had to develop a new control logic.

Simulation can also point the way to substantial savings in existing factories. Polaroid Corp. used it to study three production lines where traditional inventory buffers are still located at strategic intervals. The buffers assure that if one section of the line hits a snag, the whole line won't shut down. But they tie up both capital and floor space. Simulation showed how the buffers could be reduced by as much as 25%. The company also uses simulation to analyze capital investment decisions and staffing policies. Overall, says William T. Cousins, head of Polaroid's management-science staff, the savings have been so great that simulation is generating close to an incredible 150% return on investment.

Yet many line managers still balk at the idea. They resist a computer model, says Polaroid's Cousins, because they think of design as "something they can do on the back of an envelope." Randall P. Sadowski, vice-president of Systems Modeling Corp., a supplier of simulation software in State College, Pa., agrees: "Managers just haven't believed that the computer can reflect their manufacturing system properly."

NEW WRINKLE. Now, though, the holdouts are being won over by the latest wrinkle in the technology: animated graphics. In the past, simulation was performed mainly by mathematical experts, and all too often only they believed the results because the answers arrived in difficult-to-decipher printouts. But with graphics displays, the

simulation plays out on the screen step by step, for all to see. "Animation gives managers confidence" in the results, says Alan B. Pritsker, founder of Pritsker & Associates Inc. and one of the fathers of manufacturing simulation. Even

---

Even small companies can put the technology to use solving everyday problems

---

though the only real change is to make the computer's number-crunching operations visible, for many seeing is believing.

To encourage more companies to try simulation, software producers have developed special user-friendly packages that minimize the programming required. In many cases, this software allows someone with no programming expertise to construct a computer model by choosing from a menu of icons and English commands. But because these programs must sacrifice flexibility to gain ease of use, they tend to be tailored for particular applications, such as materials-handling systems.

That limitation is not expected to hurt sales, however. Outlays for simulation software are projected to more than triple between 1986 and 1990—to $60 million, by one estimate. Pioneers from the early and mid-1970s, such as Pritsker and Wolverine Software Corp. in Annandale, Va., suddenly are beset by some two dozen ambitious upstarts. Some of them are concentrating on software for small computers. "The metaphor I keep using," says Kenneth R. Laugherty, president of Micro Analysis & Design in Boulder, Colo., "is that we have to do with simulation what VisiCalc did with spreadsheet analysis."

Meanwhile, the power of the latest mainframes and minicomputers is setting the stage for quantum jumps in simulation techniques. Van B. Norman, who in 1982 co-founded Auto-Simulations Inc. in Bountiful, Utah, predicts that factories will soon be running software that combines simulation with "on-line" troubleshooting, based on so-called expert systems. When such software senses that something has gone wrong, the expert system automatically directs the simulation model to evaluate possible responses. Within minutes, it will lay out the shop manager's course of action. By itself, explains Wolverine President James O. Henriksen, a simulation can answer only the questions put to it. But with an expert system's help, the production manager will be able to ask the right questions.

Factrol, spun off by Pritsker in early 1986 to apply simulation technology to on-line control, has signed up 30 major companies in just 18 months—and that's without a full-blown expert system in the software. Even without one, the program is "smart" enough to keep a constant eye on the computer that runs the factory control program and to continually update its model. This helps factory managers quickly close any production gaps between what they predicted and what is actually happening.

OVERCONFIDENT? Some simulation experts worry that the glitter of the new simulation packages may make some users overconfident. The seeing-is-believing syndrome could lead a manager to think that one or two simulation runs can provide all the answers. But any single run means very little. Since each represents just one of many possible scenarios, numerous runs must be made to obtain statistically valid results. "Watching cartoons on a screen," says Wolverine's Henriksen, "is no substitute for good statistical work."

But within five years, says MacMillan of *EDS*, simulation programs will include expert systems steeped in statistical knowhow. These systems will watch over the simulation, warn the user when the results are not reliable, and help interpret the findings.

Properly applied, simulation seems set to become a powerful addition to industry's tool chest. "It can make an enormous contribution to American productivity," says Stephen D. Roberts, professor of industrial engineering at Purdue University. It can also do the same for Europe and Japan, of course—and sales of simulation software are picking up overseas. So U. S. manufacturers who do not wring what they can out of this new technology may soon find themselves falling behind not only their more nimble domestic competitors but also their offshore rivals.

By William G. Wild Jr. and Otis Port in New York, with bureau reports

DISCUSSION QUESTION
Why is simulation important, and how might it enhance competitiveness?

BOLDLY GOING WHERE NO ROBOT HAS GONE BEFORE

'STEEL-COLLAR' WORKERS ARE BREAKING OUT OF DETROIT AND MAKING EVERYTHING FROM CANDY TO UNDERWEAR

DECEMBER 22, 1986, P. 45

Robots are starting to show up in some rather unexpected places. In a custom upholstery factory, one slices carpeting to fit the inside of vans. A novelties company has a robot that stretches balloons flat so they can be printed with "Happy New Year" and other festive slogans. In Smithfield, R. I., yet another holds class rings in position while they are engraved by a laser at Laser Fare Ltd.

"Robots are becoming lighter, faster, stronger, and more intelligent—and that's going to open up more applications," says Thomas G. Gunn, an automation consultant at Arthur Young & Co. Not long ago most steel-collar workers were confined to automotive plants. But today's sophisticated models are being snapped up by a variety of companies, from candy makers and pharmaceutical houses to underwear manufacturers and plastics molders. These companies are now buying one or two robots, says Brian R. Carlisle, president of Adept Technology Inc., which specializes in small, facile robots. But soon such companies will follow the electronics industry, which has begun to order systems that employ 15 to 20 robots.

MOTOWN SLOWDOWN. Even so, it will take a lot of growth before the industry recovers from the devastating cutbacks at General Motors Corp. (BW—Aug. 25). This year roughly 45% of all robots sold in the U.S.—a market estimated at a bit less than $600 million—went to Detroit. In fact, *GM* alone represents 35% of total robot sales.

GMF Robotics Corp. is taking the brunt of the pain. A joint venture of *GM* and Japan's Fanuc Ltd., *GMF* depended on General Motors for 75% of its revenues. Although Chrysler Corp. and Ford Motor Co. continue to move forward with robot purchases and several new Japanese auto plants are being built in the U.S., "it would be impossible to offset the impact of the *GM* cutbacks," asserts Laura C. Conigliaro, an automation analyst at Prudential-Bache Securities Inc. She figures the *GM* slump will drag down robot sales by more than 15% next year—a big comedown from the 20% and higher annual gains of the early 1980s.

But David C. Penning sharply disagrees. He watches the robot business for market researcher Dataquest Inc. and believes that U.S. sales will be up by 8% to 10% next year. "Robots are spreading fast beyond Detroit," explains Penning. By 1991 automotive sales will have dipped to second place, he predicts, after the electronics industry. And the catch-all of "other" applications will have climbed to 23% of shipments.

Indeed, some suppliers that don't rely heavily on *GM* are doing quite well. Asea Robotics Inc., the New Berlin (Wis.) unit of Sweden's Asea conglomerate, is "riding high," says President Bjorn Weichbrodt. Cincinnati Milacron Inc.'s robot division will also be in the black for 1986, notes George T. Rehfeldt, group vice-president, although he expects a sales drop in 1987. Both will continue to push nonautomotive sales and are beefing up their ability to integrate robots into complete automation systems—and then help put them to work. "We are selling a solution instead of just a machine," says Rehfeldt.

While most robot makers are struggling to position themselves in the new markets, Adept Technology has become the industry's bright new star. Adept is cruising nicely through the slowdown. Sales this year are soaring more than 75% and should come in at around $25 million. For 1987, the San Jose (Calif.) company, founded in 1983 by expatriates from robot pioneer Unimation Inc., expects revenues to hit $40 million.

Rather than target a particular industry, such as autos or electronics, Adept concentrates on basic operations common to many industries: the handling and assembly of small parts, such as electronic components, motors, and appliances. To move its robots quickly to market, Adept sells many machines to so-called systems integrators, which in turn sell finished systems to users.

QUALITY OR BUST. Other successful robot makers are blazing similar trails. Pittsburgh's American Cimflex Corp. specializes in robots that dispense fluids. Electronics companies use them to glue the new breed of surface-mount chips to printed circuit boards. Unlike Adept, however, Cimflex also provides in-house systems-integration services. Such services are often essential to sell automation to the many new, smaller customers. "We have to make the customer feel pretty cozy that we'll take responsibility" and make sure the entire system will work, says Timothy J. Bublick, national sales director for DeVilbiss Co., a unit of Champion Spark Plug Co.

Robot makers are also paying more attention to quality. Charles C. Frost, chairman of Frost Inc., a small but heavily automated machine shop in Walker, Mich., says many companies shy away from robots because of faulty equipment and poor field support. Last January, Robert J. Piccirilli, Chrysler's director of manufacturing engineering, warned that quality laggards would be scratched off Chrysler's vendor list. "We performed a simple 50-hour test run, and not one of the robots we tested performed without a problem," he said. His remarks sent a chill through the industry—but produced results. Piccirilli says quality has since improved.

Whether 1987 turns out to be the first downturn in the industry's history or just a temporary slowdown, Roger E. Gower, president of Intelledex Inc., a Corvallis (Ore.) builder of small assembly robots, remains optimistic. "Next year will be tough," Gower says, "but we'll see the start of an upturn, especially among companies new to robotics."

By Russell Mitchell in Detroit, with Richard Brandt in San Francisco, Zachary Schiller in Cleveland, and James E. Ellis in Chicago.

DISCUSSION QUESTION
Which factors would support and which would suppress growth in robotics applications?

PART 6

MANAGEMENT TOPICS FOR SPECIAL EMPHASIS

Two topics command special emphasis in contemporary management because of their rising importance to the conduct of successful and worthwhile enterprises: international management and ethics and social responsibility. The first five articles deal with international management. McDonald's worldwide successes, reported in the first article, provide a marvelous case for analyzing how a company with a distinctive culture of its own manages to adapt to the extremely varied cultures of countries in which it operates. Subsequent articles explore additional issues such as the ongoing tensions in South Africa and the potential lessons to be learned from Japanese and Korean management.

The final group of five articles explores issues of ethics and social responsibility. Topics include how to help future managers learn more about ethics, balancing shareholder financial interests with divestment in South Africa, corporate responsibility to disclose hazards related to product designs, the uneven vigor of the Occupational Safety and Health Administration, and the prospect of homicide charges against corporate officials in some cases of employee death caused by criminal negligence of management.

International Management

McWORLD?

McDONALD'S CAN MAKE A BIG MAC ANYWHERE. BUT
DUPLICATING ITS CULTURE ABROAD WON'T BE SO EASY

OCTOBER 13, 1986, PP. 78-82, 86

It's lunchtime on the Boulevard St. Germain, in the heart of Paris' Latin Quarter. Students in cashmere sweaters cluster around tables at a neighborhood bistro, quietly conversing or reading *Liberation*, the trendy Paris daily. A bow-tied professorial type in tweeds settles into a chair beneath a marble bust of Voltaire.

Don't let the reading-room atmosphere fool you—downstairs it's fast-food business as usual. Burgers sizzle, Quarter Pounders and Filet-O-Fish sandwiches slide down stainless steel ramps, and electronic cash registers beep. Welcome to McDonald's France.

France isn't the only country outside the U. S. to have a Big Mac attack. In Japan, kimono-clad women visiting a Shinto shrine stop afterward at "Makudonarudo" for a "biggu makku" and a shake. When West German Chancellor Helmut Kohl held a party for 1,000 children recently, he served up 3,000 McDonald's hamburgers. Thai teenagers now save their bahts (worth 4¢ each) for weeks so that they can be part of the latest fad: hanging out at a McDonald's.

IRON CURTAIN. From Switzerland to Singapore, Malaysia to Mexico, the Big Mac is fast becoming as ubiquitous as Coca-Cola. Last year, McDonald's Corp. opened a record 220 restaurants outside the U. S., nearly 40% of all new McDonald's locations. Five years ago only 28% of openings were abroad. The company now rings up a fifth of its $11 billion in sales from branches in 42 countries. And it has no plans to slow down: It is negotiating to move into Hungary and Yugoslavia, which would make it among the first food companies to crack Eastern Europe.

Anyone who thinks this blazing success is due solely to the popularity of hamburgers and fries, though, doesn't understand McDonald's. The company is exporting the management skills that spurred its growth in the U. S.—not just its fast-food products. The key to this success is a unique ability to marry the advantages of bigness—purchasing and marketing might and rigorous operating controls—with the freewheeling, entrepreneurial style of its franchisees and suppliers. These "partners" tend to be hard-driving, creative business people who put their own money on the line. In the U. S., it costs a franchisee upwards of $250,000 to open a single store. These entrepreneurs help McDonald's act smaller and younger than it is.

While foreign rivals are clobbering many U. S. companies, McDonald's management recipe is in hot demand around the world. By making the most of this, McDonald's is proving that a major U. S. corporation can grow without restructuring, stock buybacks, or megadeals. Pretty heady stuff for a company that many on Wall Street came to view several years ago as burned out.

McDonald's is still expanding steadily in the U. S., of course. On average, it opens a store every day of the year. There is a steady stream of new products, such as the McD. L. T., and new restaurant concepts, such as McSnack, a takeout-only store.

Still, with 7,000 stores in the U. S., there aren't that many prime sites left. Moreover, the $48.5 billion domestic fast-food market is mature, growing at a real rate of only 1% per year. And competition from Burger King Corp., Wendy's International Inc., and a spate of new entries is intense. As a result, foreign expansion is the real

FROM SINGAPORE TO SAO PAULO, A NETWORK OF TRUE BELIEVERS

As chief executive of a small wine-exporting company in the French village of Annonay, near Lyon, Michel Antolinos often faced a dilemma at lunchtime. The local brasserie served meals only from noon to 1 p.m. If he showed up at 11:50, he was too early. If he arrived at 12:50, he was too late. So when a McDonald's emissary arrived in Lyon seven years ago to recruit the city's first McDonald's franchisee, Antolinos abandoned his Bordeaux and Beaujolais for milk shakes and Big Macs.

Antolinos is one of scores of international franchisees and venture partners who have bought into the quintessential American business dream. And he is one of the major reasons why McDonald's push abroad has been so successful. The company has a simple approach: Carefully select local partners and give them a large helping of freedom to develop local appeal.

Antolinos has become a firm believer in the basic McDonald's philosophy—squeaky-clean food operations and friendly service. But above that, he considers himself a true entrepreneur because all three of his outlets in the commercial center of Lyon bear his personal touch.

MOZART AND BRAHMS. A nonsmoker, Antolinos bans all Gitanes and Gauloises from his restaurants, which are decorated with lots of green plants and natural-finish wood. Health-conscious, he instructs his cooks to go easy on the salt. The music piped in his restaurants is Mozart and Brahms. "We've created a sophisticated, refined atmosphere," he says.

Antolinos' autonomy has its limits, however. McDonald's requires him and other overseas operators to adhere to the same rigid operating rules that make the burgers and fries so consistent in U. S. outlets.

"McDonald's sells only a [management] system, not products," maintains Robert Kwan, the 36-year-old managing director of McDonald's Restaurants Singapore Pte. Ltd. McDonald's brings each foreign operator to one of its four Hamburger Universities. And company consultants provide a steady flow of advice on topics ranging from promotional campaigns to employee training.

"It's the perfect partnership," says Kwan, whose flagship outlet in the heart of Singapore's bustling tourist district set McDonald's world volume record in 1982, ringing up more than $5 million in sales. "We're 100% locally operated, like all international franchises. The message that comes out from Chicago is 'What can we do for you?' rather than 'What did you do and why?' "

The McDonald's strategy makes for something different from just another American multinational—key to McDonald's future growth (chart, page 241).

GUNG-HO. McDonald's is off to a good start, but it faces tough challenges. Other chains, notably Kentucky Fried Chicken Corp.—No. 2 in locations outside the U. S., with 1,773—are also looking overseas for opportunities. The network of loyal suppliers that keep McDonald's standards high in the U. S. has been difficult to clone. In addition, McDonald's has found that the cost of doing business is higher overseas—so that profits aren't nearly as good as they are stateside. While international operations contributed 24% of corporate revenues last year, they accounted for 18% of operating income and an even smaller percentage of net profit.

The biggest challenge in foreign markets, though, is more fundamental. McDonald's strategy hinges on its ability to infuse every store with its gung-ho culture and standardized procedures. That's routine in the U. S., where the company hands out one franchise at a time and the average

al in foreign markets. McDonald's is more a loose federation of like-minded people in the same business.

Gregory Ryan, the company's joint-venture partner in São Paulo, Brazil, maintains that one of the company's strengths is what he terms the "cross-pollination" of knowhow from one international base to another. There are regular pow-wows among McDonald's foreign operators.

Ryan, for example, has spent time at McDonald's operations in both West Germany and Britain to study innovative store designs—and he recently played host to the head of McDonald's Hong Kong operation. The sessions allow the international partners to share information and trade ideas and to nurture a "family feeling." Germany, Britain, and Japan already have their own Hamburger Universities, "and we'll have ours, with an exchange program of professors with these other institutions," Ryan says proudly.

On these trips, Ryan meets people who have been carefully screened by McDonald's. The company seeks out true believers—not restaurateurs but people who demonstrate an entrepreneurial flair and share the company's values. This allows McDonald's to export successfully not only its management system but also its distinctive culture. After all, it is the shared values—including its dedication to quality and sense of family—that bond McDonald's far-flung partners together.

Consider Norman Sinclair, who holds a McDonald's franchise in Perth, Australia. He quit his job as a British Leyland auto mechanic in 1978, sold his house, and used the proceeds to make an offer to McDonald's. He quickly discovered, however, that a McDonald's franchise cannot be bought with money alone.

The company put Sinclair to the test. "After passing the interview panel, you work five days in a local McDonald's store," he says. "If you get through that, you volunteer for 800 hours of unpaid service. You don't get to that stage without committing yourself. If it's below your dignity to mop floors, clean toilets, and roll your sleeves up, then you're not going to succeed: Your attitude is wrong."

PLAYING IN PERTH. Sinclair had the right stuff. He moved into the McDonald's parking lot in a trailer. In four months he had his first McDonald's restaurant—at Toowoomba in Queensland. Twelve months later he moved to head up larger branches in Brisbane. In 1982 he was asked to help lead McDonald's charge into western Australia, an area dominated by Burger King Corp.'s Happy Jack's outlets.

Sinclair espouses the company's cultural values much the way Ray A. Kroc used to. "Your biggest challenge and your fiercest competition is yourself," he maintains. "When you are a McDonald's manager, you have an enormous responsibility to live up to their standards. Never lose sight of the fact that you won't be in business making a profit unless you give value." A little trite, perhaps. But it's the clear message that seems to play in Perth as well as it does in Peoria.

By Madlyn Resener in Lyon, Cheryl Debes in Singapore, Graham Lloyd in Perth, and Rik Turner in São Paulo

franchisee has two or three stores. In many foreign markets, though, McDonald's must enlist large partners who have a key role in learning and transplanting the organization's values. So far, McDonald's has attracted and trained effective partners (page 238). But this could become more difficult as the company's international base expands.

These obstacles do not seem to worry the superconfident but unlikely team that runs McDonald's. Don't look for the slick Ivy Leaguer with an international patina at McDonald's headquarters in Oak Brook, a Chicago suburb. The company's top executive group, referred to internally as the "barbershop," sets the tone. "We have three chairs in a row," says Edward H. Rensi, 42, president of U. S. operations. "We have a give and take" with each other and everyone else in the company.

In the head chair: Chairman and Chief Executive Fred L. Turner, 54, plain-spoken and press-shy. A former door-to-door salesman, he began working for McDonald's founder Ray A. Kroc at

23—at the grill. President Michael R. Quinlan, Turner's 41-year-old heir apparent, joined at 18 as a part-time mailroom clerk. Rensi dropped out of college in 1966 and went to work at a McDonald's in Ohio.

Formal education counts for little at McDonald's: Fewer than half of its corporate officers graduated from college, and the company doesn't employ a single Harvard *MBA*. Executives emphasize strong traditional values—loyalty, dedication, and service—in keeping with McDonald's family-like culture. To commemorate Kroc's birthday, executives will spend a day working in a McDonald's store in early October.

'ROBOTS.' So intent is McDonald's on fostering a family feeling that it employs one executive, James S. Kuhn, dedicated to "making the company feel small." His title: vice-president for individuality. Kuhn drums up excitement by developing a spate of awards, meetings, and conventions. A convention favorite is "Dunk the *CEO*." Quinlan got a pie in the face at one meeting. "It's hokey, it's corny, but it shows people the bosses are human," says Kuhn. "People say, 'Look at Quinlan with pie on his face. He must be an O. K. guy.'"

Kuhn admits that keeping this culture going will be tougher now that McDonald's is taking on the world. To help spread the gospel, the company is putting together a videotape on Kroc for foreign joint-venture partners. International partners and their employees are now regulars at many meetings and conventions. Indeed, a few years ago a group of Canadian franchisees invited the joint-venture partner from Hong Kong to dress up as a Canadian Indian and join them at a major McDonald's powwow.

Within this environment, however, there are unusually rigid procedures for operations. So rule-bound is McDonald's that one sociologist recently claimed jobs in its restaurants are unfit for young people. "These are breeding grounds for robots working for yesterday's assembly lines, not tomorrow's high-tech posts," contends Professor Amitai Etzioni of George Washington University.

The rules are meticulously detailed in phone-book-like operating manuals. These cover everything from how often the bathrooms must be cleaned to the temperature of grease used to fry potatoes. Some cultures, such as Japan's, have embraced these regulations to the letter—even more so than many of McDonald's domestic disciples.

McDonald's demands product and service quality, and the strict procedures assure consistency. Yet such rules stand in contrast to the entrepreneurial spirit the company somehow instills in each of its franchisees. Some management consultants call it "tight-loose" management: Operating procedures are tight, but McDonald's culture permits a loose approach to individual creativity. That encourages different marketing methods tailored for local markets—and even a few menu modifications.

In Brazil, for example, McDonald's sells a soft drink made from the guaraná, an Amazonian berry. And patrons of McDonald's in Malaysia, Singapore, and Thailand have savored milk shakes flavored with durian, a foul-smelling Southeast Asian fruit considered locally to be an aphrodisiac.

TRICKLE-UP. While teenagers in Brooklyn aren't likely to sip durian milk shakes anytime soon, most of the company's major product breakthroughs—from the McD. L. T. to the Egg McMuffin—stem from franchisee experimentation. Kuhn says that's because all over the world, McDonald's hires "compulsive achievers"—and doesn't "kick their ass if they come to us with weird ideas."

For the most part, though, McDonald's serves up Big Macs as usual—and they sell like crazy. "If I wanted to do something with shark's fin, I would fail miserably," says Daniel Y. C. Ng, managing director of McDonald's Restaurants (Hong Kong) Ltd. "People know we don't know how to make shark's fin here."

Beyond local product additions, foreign partners can help steer the company away from potentially expensive pitfalls. In Japan, for example, Den Fujita, president of McDonald's Co. (Japan) Ltd., avoided the suburban locations typical in the U. S. and stressed urban sites that consumers could get to without a car. "We don't just sit here and take everything given to us from the U. S.," Fujita says. "We have to make improvements to get better operations."

The affiliation with local entrepreneurs also can help McDonald's blend in with the national landscape. Even if the joint-venture partner is an American, McDonald's usually hires a local corporate staff. "We try to come on like a local company, not 'Big Mac Yankee dog,'" says Quinlan.

McDonald's, of course, is a U. S. institution. As such, it exports part of the American lifestyle. That makes it a target, too. Days after the U. S. bombed Libya, for example, a mob gathered in front of a Barcelona McDonald's to protest. Quinlan, who was visiting the company's Spanish operations, was trapped in the restaurant as the angry mob swelled. "I shut down the store and got the hell out of there," he recalls. That night, the restaurant was firebombed.

The company structures its franchise and joint partnerships abroad in a way that harnesses entrepreneurial energy. "McDonald's has succeeded because it has aligned its own interests with the franchisees," says John F. Love, author of *McDonald's: Behind the Arches* (page 18). "Ray Kroc's idea was very simple: 'I succeed if my franchisees succeed.' It's the trickle-up theory."

SLOW START. Likewise, if the franchisee fails, so does McDonald's. The risk abroad is far greater—especially since the company often must award the rights to large territories or entire countries. In 1972, for example, McDonald's reached an agreement with American businessman Raymond Dayan to develop restaurants in Paris. But the company later claimed that Dayan didn't meet McDonald's cleanliness standards and tried to cancel. After a bitter four-year court battle, McDonald's won back its name. At the time, that left it with only one remaining restaurant in France.

Industry analysts say only McDonald's and Kentucky Fried Chicken are making meaningful profits on their foreign restaurants. The payoff is slow, too: *KFC* doesn't expect to make a profit in new countries for three to five years, says Chairman Richard P. Mayer. In some cases, it takes McDonald's 10 years. Even then, net margins may not be what they are in the U. S. because of increased costs for real estate and importing some supplies.

More than one experienced operator has been dashed on the rocks of foreign shores. This summer, Wendy's International sold its 16 money-losing outlets in England to a division of Whitbread & Co. Even McDonald's tried several times to break into Australia before succeeding in 1971.

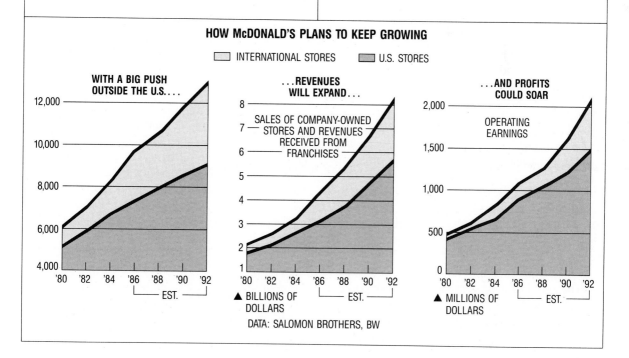

HOW McDONALD'S PLANS TO KEEP GROWING

INTERNATIONAL STORES   U.S. STORES

WITH A BIG PUSH OUTSIDE THE U.S....

...REVENUES WILL EXPAND...
SALES OF COMPANY-OWNED STORES AND REVENUES RECEIVED FROM FRANCHISES
▲ BILLIONS OF DOLLARS

...AND PROFITS COULD SOAR
OPERATING EARNINGS
▲ MILLIONS OF DOLLARS

EST.

DATA: SALOMON BROTHERS, BW

BAG THOSE FRIES, SQUIRT THAT KETCHUP, FRY THAT FISH

To find out how a McDonald's restaurant works, Correspondent Kathleen Deveny spent a lunch hour behind the counter. Her report:

On my way down Chicago's Magnificent Mile, past Tiffany's and Gucci, to the McDonald's restaurant, I keep thinking back to the Tastee Treet in Minneapolis. That was my first job, making ice cream cones and flipping burgers for the high school students who swarmed into the converted gas station during the short summers.

McDonald's is nothing like Tastee Treet. Here every job is broken down into the smallest of steps, and the whole process is automated. The videotape that introduces new employees to French fries, for example, starts with boxes of frozen fries rolling off a delivery truck. Stack them in the freezer six boxes high. Leave one inch between the stacks, two inches between the stacks and the wall. Cooking and bagging the fries is explained in even greater detail: 19 steps.

OUT OF SYNC. Anyone could do this, I think. But McDonald's restaurants operate like Swiss watches, and the minute I step behind the counter I am a loose part in the works. By noon the place is mobbed. I keep thinking of the McDonald's commercial that shows former Raiders Coach John Madden diagramming the precision moves of a McDonald's crew in action. I imagine a diagram of my own jerky movements, zigzagging wildly behind the counter because I keep forgetting the order.

I bag French fries for a few minutes, but I'm much too slow. Worse, I can't seem to keep my station clean enough. Failing at French fries is a fluke, I tell myself.

Condiment detail sounds made to order. First comes the mustard, one shot of the gun, five perfect drops centered on the bun. Next, the ketchup: One big shot. Quite a difference from Tastee Treet, where I used to measure out the ketchup by writing my boyfriend's initials on each hamburger bun.

I try to speed up. Now a quarter ounce of onions and two pickles—three, if they're small. Cover them with a slice of cheese, slap on the burger. Another slice of cheese.

I am happy with the tidy piles I am making, but the grillman is not as pleased. I move too slowly, and he could cook the patties and dress the buns a lot faster without my help.

Disheartened, I move on to Filet-O-Fish. I put six frozen fish patties into the fryer basket and drop them into the hot grease. When the red light flashes, I put the buns in to steam. After a few minutes, the square patties are done. I line them up in neat rows and center the cheese on each. I try to move faster, but my co-workers are playing at 45 rpm, and I'm stuck at 33 1/3.

Debbie, the crew member who rescued my French fries earlier, comes back to see how I'm doing. It's my last chance to shine. I pull out more cooked fish, slap on the cheese, burn my hands on the buns, and pinch my finger in the tartar sauce gun. "You're doing O. K.," she somehow says. That's all I wanted to hear. The regimented work is wearing on my nerves. The strict rules, which go so far as to prescribe what color nail polish to wear, are bringing out the rebel in me. I can't wait to get back to my cluttered office, where it smells like paper and stale coffee and the only noise is the gentle hum of my personal computer.

The reasons for these misadventures abroad are as varied as the cultures the fast-food chains hope to conquer. Winning government approval to enter a new country can take years. Once approval is won, restaurant sites must be chosen—and given the quality of demographic data in some countries, that can be about as scientific as a game of darts. In underdeveloped nations, the chains must introduce the concept of fast food. Although there are few U. S. competitors, newcomers must wrest business from a host of small restaurants in each country. In Singapore, street vendors sell roughly $1 billion a year of noodles, chili crab, and Chinese vegetables in open-air stalls—local versions of the Golden Arches.

Even in cultures accustomed to heat-lamp cuisine, government control of broadcasting systems can mean relearning the marketing techniques a company has fine-tuned at home. "In the U. S., we have a system in place, but overseas you have to start from scratch," says Gilbert N. Stemmerman, vice-president in charge of International Dairy Queen Inc.'s 581 overseas locations.

PERFECT BUNS. Although it reduces company profits, McDonald's prefers to rely on joint-venture partners to ease its way into new countries. The company does operate wholly owned subsidiaries in some countries—Canada, West Germany, and Australia, for example. But even these have considerable autonomy. And the partners, often local business people, usually get a 50% interest in the business. "They drive us with new ideas and more stability," says Jack M. Greenberg, chief financial officer. "They are more aggressive and more innovative because their stake is greater."

So far, the greatest overseas challenge for McDonald's has been duplicating its impressive supply system for everything from potatoes to plastic straws. In the U. S., suppliers are fiercely loyal. They have to be: Their fortunes are closely linked to Big Mac's. Overseas, McDonald's has found that suppliers are far less willing to invest in equipment capable of meeting McDonald's specifications.

Although Quinlan says he would like to use local suppliers only, the company has not yet managed this in many markets. In Britain, one coffee supplier even claimed that the specifications were too high for consumers, who would never appreciate the extra money McDonald's would be spending.

The most difficult item to procure in Britain, however, turned out to be the lowly hamburger bun. After quality problems at two local bakeries, McDonald's put up its own money to build a plant with two partners—something it has never resorted to in the U. S. "British industry had no confidence that McDonald's would succeed in England," says Robert E. Rhea, chairman of McDonald's Hamburgers Ltd.

SPUD FARMS. More often, supplies meeting McDonald's exacting standards are unavailable. "McDonald's maintains very rigid specifications for all the raw products we use, which is the key to consistency," says Robert Kwan, managing director of McDonald's Restaurants Singapore Pte. Ltd.

McDonald's has perhaps gone to the greatest lengths to procure raw materials for one of its best-liked products: the golden French fry. In Thailand, that has meant helping farmers cultivate Idaho Russet potatoes.

Although McDonald's opened its first restaurant outside the U. S. in Canada in 1967, "international expansion is just starting to pay off," says Charles S. Glovsky, an analyst with Alex. Brown & Sons Inc. Japan, Canada, and Germany—the company's largest markets after the U. S.—are now steady profit producers, according to Hugh S. Zurkuhlen, a Salomon Brothers analyst. Australia and Britain just moved into the black. And as McDonald's builds up a large base in new markets and is able to spread marketing and administrative costs, margins should widen dramatically, says Zurkuhlen.

McDonald's can afford to take a long-term view of its foreign push. The chain collects 11.5% of all the revenue its franchisees take in, and it operates 2,000 company-owned restaurants. Analysts estimate the company could earn $480 million this year, up about 11% from 1985, and it consistently posts a return on equity of more than 20%. Moreover, McDonald's has proven that American fast food is more than a fad in foreign markets. "The fact that [because] it's U. S., it's magic . . . that wore off a long time ago in Singapore," says Kwan. "The key now is the total experience of coming to McDonald's."

FRESH FLOWERS. At home, of course, McDonald's will continue to grow—even though pessimists have predicted a fast-food glut for decades. This hasn't fazed McDonald's. It has expanded steadily and now has 18% of the market.

All the domestic opportunities haven't disappeared, either. Future gains will come mostly from broadening the menu and adding new, specialized restaurants. Promising locations include smaller towns, hospitals, office buildings, college campuses, and Navy bases. Ambiance will vary accordingly. A new store in the posh Crocker Center office tower in Los Angeles, for example, features fresh flowers on every table and strolling musicians two days a week.

The real future at McDonald's, however, depends on attracting new customers in far-flung locales—such as Istanbul, where the chain will open in October. So far, the company's executives have done that remarkably well. And they've scored an even greater coup: exporting a unique management style that melds economies of scale and entrepreneurial enthusiasm. No small achievement for a "barbershop" in Oak Brook, Ill.

By Kathleen Deveny in Oak Brook, with John E. Pluenneke in Bonn, Dori Jones Yang in Hong Kong, *Mark Maremont in London, Robert Black in Toronto, and bureau reports*

DISCUSSION QUESTIONS

1. What conditions make successful performance in foreign markets so important for McDonald's?
2. McDonald's seems to have it both ways: its decentralized franchise system fosters entrepreneurship; its centralized systems of purchasing, control, and marketing foster efficiency. If this combination of adaptive diversity and rigid standardization (these loose-tight properties) explains its success overseas, can it be approximated in other industries outside of fast foods? Discuss.
3. What do you think accounts for McDonald's success abroad?

ALL ROADS LEAD OUT OF SOUTH AFRICA

IBM AND GM MAKE THEIR MOVE, AND OTHER COMPANIES RUSH TO FOLLOW

NOVEMBER 3, 1986, PP. 24-25

If there were ever any serious question that U. S. business was set to flee South Africa, General Motors Corp. and International Business Machines Corp. have answered it. Within 24 hours, the two American giants announced their plans to leave, and Honeywell Inc. and Warner Communications Inc. followed a day later. Many other companies will undoubtedly do the same.

Their decisions effectively spell the end of the long-standing argument that U. S. corporations might be the agents of social change in a segregated society. With the government in Pretoria apparently committed to defying criticism from the West, a U. S. sanctions law on the books, and unrelenting divestment pressure, that idea, however genuine, has simply lost its underpinnings. "The snowball," says an executive of a U. S. company with South African operations, "is growing very fast."

That doesn't mean that all commercial ties are ending—and for that reason, the pressure on even those companies that have pulled out won't end either. Foreign business is moving "away from direct investment and wholly owned subsidiaries toward licensing agreements and independent distributorships," says David Hauck, senior analyst at the Investor Responsibility Research Center in Washington. "It's a way of getting off the blacklist" and stemming losses without cutting off all trade links. Indeed, most recent departures of U. S. companies have involved the sale of units to local management, along with arrangements to supply parts and technical knowhow.

Those continuing relationships are already drawing fire from anti-apartheid activists in the U. S. They are gearing up for a new phase of lobbying that will be far more technical, specific—and difficult to make effective. "We're carefully reviewing the growing numbers of withdrawals to assess how the products of those companies are used in South Africa," says Timothy H. Smith, executive director of the Interfaith Center on Corporate Responsibility. Smith cites the case of Motorola Inc., whose radios are still sold to the South African government through a local company, although the company pulled out its assets in 1985. Adds Cecelie Counts of TransAfrica, a Washington-based anti-apartheid group: "We want to sever the link between American expertise and the apartheid system."

'NAIVE.' The quickened pace of the flight is beginning to isolate the few U. S. companies still trying to do business in the midst of apartheid (table). "Our official position is to stick around," says an executive of a U. S. subsidiary in Johannesburg. "But it is naive to think that there is one American company that doesn't have a contingency plan for leaving." He says his company is carrying on an "ongoing courtship" with four South African companies interested in buying the Americans out.

Already, more than 70 companies, joined last month by Coca-Cola, Procter & Gamble, and Baxter Travenol Laboratories, have left or announced departure dates in the past 18 months. Yet many large companies with South African units insist that the recent exits will not affect them. A Hewlett-Packard Co. spokesman insists that "it is HP's intention to stay and continue our own anti-apartheid efforts." But others are showing signs of uneasiness. Dresser Industries Inc., for example, appears to be winding down its operations from 800 employees to "several hundred." Xerox Corp., which employs 790 people in South Africa, said that it was "exploring alternatives," and a spokesman for SmithKline/Beckman Corp. admitted that patience "with the pace of change is running out."

The discomfort level for companies with South African ties has been rising for some time, so while no one was surprised, the suddenness of the IBM and GM moves raised some questions. Some say companies are rushing to beat the effects of the U. S. sanctions bill that will bar new investment in South Africa, along with bans that include new loans and computer sales to the government. "It was never the intention to make these [rules] disinvestment provisions," says a Capitol Hill staffer. "But now it seems that is what's happening."

URGENCY. For example, GM and IBM will inject money into South Africa under local employee-buyout arrangements. GM will pay off local debts so that the new owners won't have an unmanageable burden. And IBM will lend its employees the money to buy the local company. Both companies will be paid in future years from future profits. They were worried that such moves would not have been possible once parts of the sanctions law take effect in mid-November. Robert A. White, GM's managing director in South Africa, says GM pushed up the sale date by six weeks as a result. "It gave us a sense of urgency," he says.

A recent change in the Sullivan Code, the rules U. S. companies voluntarily follow to help offset the effects of apartheid in the workplace, added to the pressure. After the Sullivan committee took a tougher line in rating companies in October, many U. S. companies, even some of the best performers, dropped several notches. IBM was one of a dozen American companies that fell from the top category. Many U. S. pension and mutual funds automatically sell any holdings in the stock of U. S. companies whose South African units don't make the top Sullivan grade.

THE DOZEN BIGGEST U.S. COMPANIES STILL IN SOUTH AFRICA

	Number of employees (1985)
MOBIL	3,182
USG	2,631
GOODYEAR	2,471
CALTEX	2,186
RJR NABISCO	2,084
ALLEGHENY INTERNATIONAL	2,025
JOHNSON & JOHNSON	1,389
UNITED TECHNOLOGIES	1,261
COLGATE-PALMOLIVE	1,234
NORTON	1,228
3M	1,174
AMERICAN CYANAMID	1,167

DATA: INVESTOR RESPONSIBILITY RESEARCH CENTER (AS OF OCT. 22)

U. S. companies are also becoming the target of South African resentment—by blacks and whites alike. A *GM* survey of white consumers, its principal market, showed that whites saw the company as being against the South African government and too political. For that and other reasons, *GM*'s share of the South African car market dropped to just over 5%, from 12% five years ago. "Our brand image ranks above our company image," says *GM*'s White. And *IBM*'s managing director told dealers that "we perceive anti-American sentiment growing in the South African market."

Among blacks, the alienation is worse. Nearly all black leaders—excepting Zulu chief Mangosuthu Gatsha Buthelezi but including Nobel prizewinner Archbishop Desmond Tutu—have supported disinvestment for a long time. One American multinational executive says that black protesters have threatened his company's black employees with violence and that a company bus was hijacked.

The immediate impact of disinvestment on the business left behind will be slight. *GM* South African Ltd., for example, will continue to buy components and designs from *GM*'s Adam Opel subsidiary in West Germany and a Japanese company, Isuzu Motors Ltd., in which *GM* owns a major stake. Licensing agreements will still make money for *GM*. And the carmaker says it might even repurchase the company if conditions improve. *IBM* equipment will continue to be imported by South Africa. While the sale of the sales-and-service unit is being worked out, the company will be run by a trust including an *IBM* executive on the board.

Nor will the exit of U. S. companies lead to a full-scale retreat of European investors. But there is growing concern about divestment pressure on them from the U. S. John R. Wilson, executive chairman of Royal Dutch/Shell Group in South Africa, told local management this summer that "Shell's position is not comfortable. The threat of disinvestment is real." Still, European companies will be slower to act than American firms because their stakes in South Africa are so much larger. In 1985, U. S. direct investment in South Africa totaled about $2.5 billion. By contrast, British companies have a total investment of about $8.5 billion, or 45% of all foreign investment. And West Germany is South Africa's second-largest trading partner, after the U. S.—though those numbers predate the imposition of sanctions by the U. S. and the European Community.

LINKS. No one argues that even a total withdrawal of U. S. capital from South Africa would be enough to force Pretoria to change. Yet the effects can't be dismissed, especially if apartheid opponents in the U. S. succeed in forcing American companies to deny South Africa access to U. S. technology. Unlike Rhodesia, where sanctions were widely regarded as having failed, South Africa is an industrialized nation and thus more dependent on its links with the West.

South Africa's political hardliners could of course prove willing to sacrifice the country's industrial strength and wealth of natural resources on the altar of a political system that ultimately isn't viable. If that happens, a recent report issued by the U. S. Consulate in Johannesburg could turn out to be prescient. It warned that South Africa was on its way to becoming "just another African country: chronic debtor, import-starved . . . a repressive regime unable to manage its own domestic constituency in any positive way." U. S. companies aren't waiting around to find out if that's right.

By Elizabeth Weiner in New York and Steve Mufson in Johannesburg, with bureau reports

DISCUSSION QUESTIONS

1. Should a company operating overseas adapt to the laws of its host country, perhaps seeking to change them from within, or not? Discuss.
2. Should U.S. companies refuse to operate in countries with dictatorships? In countries with various shortfalls in democracy and civil liberties? Where should lines be drawn? Discuss.

YOU DON'T HAVE TO BE A GIANT TO SCORE BIG OVERSEAS

TWO MID-SIZE U.S. COMPANIES ARE FINDING THAT
THE GREATEST TRADE BARRIER IS PSYCHOLOGICAL.

APRIL 13, 1987, PP. 62-63

America's swollen trade deficit of $170 billion last year is vivid evidence of the daunting challenges that await U. S. companies trying to compete overseas. The foreign arena has proved particularly hostile for small and mid-size companies. The Commerce Dept. estimates that about 80% of manufactured U. S. exports are generated by only 250 companies.

But the performance of smaller companies is crucial to the future of the economy. Michael R. Czinkota, a deputy assistant secretary of Commerce, points out in a recent study for the National Center for Export-Import Studies at Georgetown University that shifts in the worldwide marketplace inevitably take their toll on corporations. "It is therefore imperative to encourage small and medium-size U. S. businesses to participate in that market, so that they can become the large corporations of the future," he writes.

The good news is that smaller companies can do well overseas. Witness Molex Inc. and Loctite Corp. Says Loctite Chairman Kenneth W. Butterworth: "The problem really lies in the mind. That is the greatest trade barrier in America." Here's how Loctite and Molex surmounted that barrier.

MOLEX: FAR-FLUNG BUT CLOSE-KNIT

The squat, ugly building tucked away in the nondescript Chicago suburb of Lisle hardly looks like the headquarters of a successful multinational. But what seems like just another stodgy midwestern company is a fast mover abroad. Since 1979, Molex Inc. has logged more overseas sales than domestic. Foreign business accounted for nearly 64% of the $292 million worth of electronic connectors it sold last year.

Since the weaker dollar is magnifying the value of the sales it rings up in foreign currencies, Molex is expected to show a particularly impressive performance for the year ending in June. Analyst James P. Hickey of William Blair & Co. projects a 20% improvement over last year's earnings of $32 million.

Molex makes some 2,500 varieties of connectors used in such applications as linking the wires in an automobile or the circuit boards in computers and videorecorders. It had little choice but to go abroad: In the early 1970s, its customers were setting sail to take advantage of cheaper labor. Today, Molex has 38 factories overseas.

Still, Molex remains very much a family business. Chairman John H. Krehbiel's family owns nearly half the common stock. And it was Krehbiel's younger son, Fred, who pioneered Molex's foreign expansion. In 1965, Fred had just left his job as an executive at the Chicago White Sox after Bill Veeck sold the club. His elder brother, John Jr., was already in line to be president, so Fred volunteered to go overseas. "There wasn't much else for me to do around the company," he says.

One of the first problems Fred tackled was a four-year-old joint venture with a Japanese company, Showa Musen Kogyo. Molex had set up the venture with a loophole that permitted *SMK* to copy and sell Molex products. Though it might have been easier to pull out, by 1973 Fred obtained full ownership for Molex.

Today, Molex's five Japanese plants do more than supply local manufacturers. Miniaturization techniques developed for portable Japanese electronic products are now used throughout Molex. The company also learned about quality control and Japan's more efficient just-in-time inventory management.

Molex's other foreign operations have provided valuable lessons, too. One is staying close to customers so the company can better determine their needs. For example, Molex moved to Singapore in 1978 after General Electric Co. moved its television manufacturing there. When *GE* stopped making *TV*s in Singapore last year, Molex had plenty of business left—from the scores of multinationals that had set up shop in the meantime.

'FAMILY DAY.' Molex has also insisted on keeping its plants small, so that managers can keep in close touch with operations. And it insists on local management. "If I were Japanese, I wouldn't want to work for an American," says John. "We can't expect Americans to understand those local cultures."

At times, the Krehbiels have learned that lesson the hard way. When Molex held a dinner for Japanese workers and their spouses, both wives and female employees stayed home to take care of the children. Now, Molex has a "family day" instead, and everyone comes.

A more thorny problem in the early days was allocating sales commissions. Domestic sales personnel, whose commissions were tied only to domestic deliveries, would sometimes try to talk a customer with a foreign operation out of buying a product from Molex overseas, and Molex would lose the sale altogether. Today, commissions go to the person involved in the sale, no matter where the delivery takes place. Clearly, there are difficulties in building foreign sales. But for Molex, at least, the costs of overcoming them were time and money well spent.

By Kenneth Dreyfack in Lisle

MOLEX INC.

1986 revenue: **$292** million
Foreign sales: **63%**

Five-year sales growth*

Domestic **17%**	Foreign **23%**

* Annual rate

DATA: MOLEX INC.

LOCTITE: HOME IS WHERE THE CUSTOMERS ARE

Baosheng Xu spends most of his time these days in training at Loctite Corp.'s Newington (Conn.) headquarters. About a year from now he will return to his native China as general manager of a Loctite plant to be built in Shandong Province. There he will blend Loctite adhesives and sealants for sale to auto makers, machinery manufacturers, and other customers.

Baosheng, 34, has 10 years of experience in Chinese industry, and he personifies the Loctite approach to foreign markets: Look local. "I have the language," Baosheng explains, "I know the system, and—most important—I know where to get things done."

The results of Loctite's approach are impressive. For the fiscal year that ended last June, 47% of its $267 million in sales came from overseas. Loctite's 14% jump in profits, to $23.2 million, was largely the result of strong performance in foreign operations. With the help of a weaker dollar and the acquisition of a large French distributor, it expects to get 60% of its 1987 sales from overseas.

Loctite is probably best-known for Super-Glue, but its biggest moneymakers are industrial applications for anaerobic adhesives, which form a tight bond in the absence of air. The adhesives are popular for use with bolts and other airtight applications. Loctite has pushed hard overseas almost since its founding in the 1950s, and today the

LOCTITE CORP.

1986 revenue: **$267** million
Foreign sales: **47%**

Five-year sales growth*

Domestic: **4%**   Foreign: **7%**

* Annual rate

DATA: LOCTITE CORP.

company does business in 80 countries, with factories in Ireland and Brazil. Expansion is taking it into several countries in the Far East and Latin America.

MOSTLY LOCAL. Loctite's international scope is a source of pride to its bushy-browed, Australian-born chairman and chief executive officer, Kenneth W. Butterworth. "Out of 3,000 people in the company worldwide, probably 55% to 60% are not Americans," he says. In fact, Loctite has only two or three Americans working outside the U. S. Five of its six top executives have lived and worked in at least three other countries.

Operating comfortably abroad is important to Loctite because it works closely with its customers. For instance, Theodore F. Patlovich, the senior vice-president who heads Loctite's International Group, personally headed the team that traveled to a government factory in China to address a serious leakage problem with internal-combustion engines. The team helped assemble 300 engines, using adhesives that form gaskets and hold bolts in place. After some 2,000 hours of tests and field trials, the Loctite team virtually eliminated the leakage. Result: After five years of negotiations, Loctite has a 50-50 joint venture with the Chinese.

The Chinese experience also illustrates Loctite's staying power. "One of the things that really disturbs me about foreign companies, especially Americans', is the lack of persistence and patience," says Patlovich. "Americans cannot go to China, Japan, or Korea one time and walk away with an agreement. It takes a tremendous amount of work."

For all its efforts to look local, Loctite will buck tradition when necessary. In Japan, engineers may lose face working in sales, but Loctite insists on it.

"Once they are out in the field, they come to like talking about assembly lines with Toyota people and electronics problems with Hitachi people," explains Akira Machii, president of Loctite (Japan). "After all, they are fellow engineers."

Loctite dominates the industrial market in Japan. Says an official at rival Toagosei: "Loctite set and showed us the goal for industrial adhesives: high-performance adhesives that help promote automation and productivity." That achievement is now paying dividends closer to home. When Nissan Motor Co. and Honda Motor Co. built plants in Mexico and California, they specified Loctite products. The company hopes for similar good fortune at the new Toyota Motor Co. plant in Kentucky—demonstrating yet another advantage of having happy customers all over the world.

By Resa A. King in Newington

DISCUSSION QUESTIONS

1. How can managers in overseas assignments, such as those from Molex and Loctite, improve management in the U.S.?
2. What are some of the experiences of these companies that reveal the importance of cultural differences in management?

THE DIFFERENCE JAPANESE MANGEMENT MAKES

JULY 14, 1986, PP. 47-50

Four years ago, General Motors Corp.'s auto-assembly plant in Fremont, Calif., was the model of America in decline. The absentee rate hovered at 20%. There were usually 5,000 or so grievances outstanding, an average of about one for every employee. Wildcat strikes interrupted production, and labor and management feuded like the Hatfields and the McCoys. In 1982, *GM* shut Fremont's doors and later turned it over to Toyota Motor Corp. as part of a joint venture called New United Motor Mfg. Inc. *(NUMMI)*.

At Fremont today, 18 months after the first Chevrolet Nova rolled off the line, it looks as if the frog has turned into a prince. Adding little new technology, *NUMMI*'s Japanese bosses set up a typical Toyota production system, with just-in-time delivery and a flexible assembly line run by teams of workers in charge of their own jobs. They hired back most of the former United Auto Workers members who wanted work—even their militant leaders. *NUMMI* makes a single auto, while *GM* built several models. But its 2,500 employees can assemble 240,000 cars a year, roughly equal to what it took 5,000 or more people to produce under *GM*. There are only two grievances outstanding, and absenteeism is running under 2%.

Japan is transplanting its distinctive manufacturing and labor practices to the U. S. Japanese companies have had some of the advantages startups usually enjoy, such as younger, less expensive labor and tax breaks from states and cities. But otherwise, they are competing on a level playing field, using American workers and paying American costs. "We have the same members, the same building, the same technology—just different management and a different production system," says Joel D. Smith, a *UAW* representative at *NUMMI*.

HUNDREDS OF IDEAS. Three Japanese auto-assembly plants—Toyota in Fremont, Honda in Marysville, Ohio, and Nissan in Smyrna, Tenn.— seem to prove that Japanese companies can make products of nearly the same quality as they make in Japan, at nearly the same cost. The three now produce 560,000 vehicles a year in the U. S.—up from nothing in 1982. New U. S. plants have been announced by Toyota, Mazda, SubaruIsuzu, and Mitsubishi. As the output of Japan's transplants approaches 1.6 million vehicles by 1990, they will become a major force in the U. S. market, selling almost as many units as Japanese imports (chart, page 252).

The Japanese are starting to make their presence felt in other industries. Nippon Kokan took a 50% stake in National Steel Corp. in 1984 and has steadily boosted its role in managing the company. Three of National's top six officers, including the newly designated president, are now from Nippon Kokan, and they've begun to implement hundreds of ideas to cut costs and improve quality. "They want to use the same practices here that they have in Japan," says Harry E. Lester, a United Steelworkers negotiator. Altogether, four of the nation's seven largest steelmakers have sold equity stakes to Japanese companies or formed joint ventures with them.

In many of the most basic manufacturing sectors—from ball bearings to industrial filters to machine tools—the Japanese are buying companies and forming joint ventures. Although there are some horror stories, the newcomers often run factories better than the U.S. owners did. For example, two plants that Firestone Tire & Rubber Co. sold in the early 1980s are being run by the Japanese. *ATR* Wire & Cable Co., a consortium of three Japanese companies, bought Firestone's troubled steel-cord and bead-wire plant in Danville, Ky., in 1981. Tokyo-based Bridgestone Corp. took over Firestone's truck-tire plant in LaVergne, Tenn. Both companies have taken dramatic strides in improving labor relations and productivity.

But the biggest Japanese investments so far have been in autos, and that's where the results seem clearest. The Nova that *NUMMI* builds has fewer options than most Detroit cars and is simpler to produce than the cars and trucks *GM* made in Fremont. Even so, *NUMMI* is clearly more productive than other U. S. car plants: The company says its cost of production is "comparable" to Toyota's cost in Japan. Integrated Automotive Resources Inc., a Wayne (Pa.) consulting firm, estimates that the Nova takes about 21 man-hours to assemble, while *GM*'s most comparable model, the Chevrolet Cavalier, takes 38.

MUTUAL TRUST. At Honda of America Mfg. Co. and Nissan Motor Mfg. *USA*, results have been similar. Honda says it makes Accords in Marysville at roughly the same cost as its parent, Honda Motor Co., does in Japan. "The quality of our cars is almost the same as in Japan," says Honda of America's President Shoichiro Irimajiri. Nissan *USA* President Marvin T. Runyon says the productivity level at his plant, which makes subcompacts and pickup trucks, is 90% of the level the parent company enjoys in Japan.

While Detroit tends to concentrate on high tech to fight off imports, a key element of the Japanese transplants' success is their adroit handling of American workers. The Japanese approach to production, emphasizing flexible teams, just-in-time deliveries, and attention to quality, demands extremely high employee loyalty, which is a sharp departure from the traditional adversary relationship in most U. S. factories. Workers given responsiblity for running the production line will care about and catch mistakes, but only if they trust management. The trust must be mutual, too, because the just-in-time delivery system, which depends on a steady stream of components, is easy to sabotage.

To cultivate loyalty in the U. S., Japanese management has learned how to translate Japanese methods to fit the American values of equality and individualism. Japanese managers elicit cooperation by presenting themselves as equals. At Nissan *USA*, Honda, and *NUMMI*, there are no privileged parking lots for executives. Honda's top executives eat in the employee cafeteria—there are no private dining rooms for big shots. Everybody there wears white overalls with his or her first name sewn on them. Employees are called "associates." Honda President Irimajiri has no office. He sits in the same room with a hundred other white-collar workers.

Because Japanese managers make personal sacrifices, they've probably done more to win over even hard-bitten *UAW* members than formal corporate concessions would do. "When *GM* was here, we hated each other," says Tony De Jesus, president of the new *UAW* local at *NUMMI*. As president of the old *GM* local, he led a wildcat strike in 1978. "It's true we were partly to blame. There were a lot of drugs and a lot of absenteeism. But we were a reflection of the *SOB*s we worked for. Now management's given us a voice and more responsibility and listens to us." Says a *NUMMI* executive: "The difference between now and under *GM* is like night and day."

Minimizing layoffs has helped to develop worker loyalty. At *ATR* in Danville, business conditions were so rough last fall that workers feared a major cutback. But *ATR* management built up inventory, shifted workers to housecleaning chores, and moved production from a Japanese factory to Danville to avoid layoffs. Now, says a frustrated *UAW* organizer, "we can't persuade the *ATR* people of the need for a stronger union. The company never lays people off."

WORKING SMARTER. Most of the ways that Japanese managers nurture American loyalty cost relatively little. But Japanese methods seem to produce more results than the confrontational approach still taken by many U. S. employers. "The Japanese philosophy is to make people an important item, as opposed to the typical U. S. philosophy that workers are just an extension of machines," says D. William Childs, *NUMMI*'s general manager of human resources.

This emphasis on cooperative labor relations partly explains the transplants' improved productivity. At *NUMMI* there are no industrial engineers telling workers what to do. Employees help decide how their jobs will be set up—and they often find faster ways to do things. For example, in the old *GM* plant at Fremont, the person who installed windows on right front doors had to walk from his toolbox to each car three times as it moved along the assembly line. Now, by rearranging the equipment, the worker goes to the car just once and follows along as it passes. So the job now requires 11 steps rather than 23.

Japanese methods have increased flexibility, too. In Detroit, some factories have 100 or more job classifications. While the production-line workers with harder tasks are trying to finish their jobs, other people may run out of work. Because everyone does several jobs under the Japanese team system, work is spread more evenly. This also makes other team members pick up the slack if someone goofs off—and builds peer-pressure discipline into the line.

The result is a company that's light on its feet. Honda operates with only several hours' supply of most components on hand. Combined with workers who can change jobs easily, this allows it to shift production quickly to another model as needed. The company can also retool rapidly for new models, changing door or fender shapes in a matter of minutes. "When we started making the new

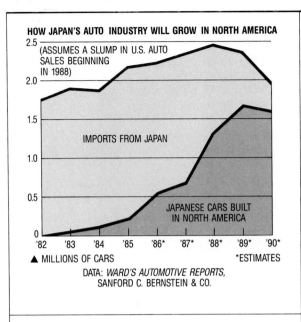

HOW JAPAN'S AUTO INDUSTRY WILL GROW IN NORTH AMERICA

(ASSUMES A SLUMP IN U.S. AUTO SALES BEGINNING IN 1988)

IMPORTS FROM JAPAN

JAPANESE CARS BUILT IN NORTH AMERICA

▲ MILLIONS OF CARS   *ESTIMATES

DATA: *WARD'S AUTOMOTIVE REPORTS,* SANFORD C. BERNSTEIN & CO.

Accord on Sept. 17, 1985, we changed over our line on a shift change," says plant manager Scott Whitlock. In Detroit, this can still take weeks or even months.

BIGGER BONUS. Will the success of Japanese transplants endure? Some worker goodwill is likely to fade over time. Fremont's transformation came in part because the former *GM* employees went jobless for two years, which made them more willing to accept new working conditions. Now workers may have jobs, but they are working harder than ever before. The speed of the assembly lines at *NUMMI* is already starting to generate friction among employees. And at *ATR* in Danville, employees rotate shifts, working seven days straight with four days off—with no overtime pay.

If past is prologue, however, Japanese managers will respond adroitly to labor problems with carefully calculated steps to appease workers. One reason the *UAW* hasn't gotten very far in organizing Honda is that the company changed its profit-sharing formula in February so that workers will get quadruple the old $500 bonus. It also set up a grievance system for the first time, providing a response to complaints within two days.

Although Japanese companies operating in the U. S. face the same conditions as American ones, they buy many more of their parts overseas.

NUMMI, Nissan, and Honda all say that about half of the value of each vehicle they produce is made in the U. S. But this can be deceptive. *NUMMI* imports 60% to 70% of its components from Japan. This means the domestic content of the Chevy Nova comes out at 50%, but mainly because it includes such items as labor and transportation costs.

Honda and Nissan say they want to boost their domestic content to more than 60%. This would create more American jobs, but it may not help U. S. auto-parts companies. To preserve quality, the Japanese auto makers have already urged more than 40 of their suppliers from Japan to come to the U. S. At Honda's annual "vendor appreciation day" in Stouffer's Dublin Hotel near Columbus, Ohio, last April, 5 of the 16 vendor awards went to Japanese auto suppliers with U. S. operations. "Even if we knock 'em dead, we won't get the same percentage of business as we do with our domestic customers," says James S. Reid Jr., chairman of Standard Products Co., a supplier of rubber and plastic parts to Detroit that has yet to win business with a Japanese car company.

The growth of Japanese companies in the U. S. also presents labor with a dilemma. Although unions are delighted that their workers have jobs, they must now decide whether to cooperate Japanese-style. The *UAW* has gone along with *GM*'s Saturn project, which puts union members on an equal footing with management from the board of directors on down. The union has signed similar, though less radical, deals at *NUMMI*, at *GM*'s Van Nuys (Calif.) plant, at Mazda, and at dozens of lesser plants. In addition to the *UAW*, rubber workers, steelworkers, and electrical workers are coming face to face with Japanese management. In several cases they have signed pacts giving away hard-earned gains.

HIGH-TECH PANACEA. U. S. management is divided, too. Primarily under the pressure of imports, American companies have begun experimenting with so-called Japanese ideas—many of which actually originated in the U. S. in the 1930s. Variations of the just-in-time approach and the team system are being tried at a range of major companies, including Ford, *GM*, General Electric, Goodyear, and Weyerhaeuser. The goal is fewer strict job categories and more flexibility. But the most common approach is to spend heavily on new technology as a competitive panacea (BW—June 16).

The arrival of Japanese manufacturers on U. S. soil will intensify the pressure on both management and unions to make crucial choices, not only about how to respond to the Japanese but also about how to relate to each other. As a domestic Japanese presence makes itself felt in sector after sector, neither U. S. labor nor management can argue that Japan outcompetes them only because Japanese workers live in tiny houses and skip vacations. And there will be nowhere to hide: Even if the protectionist gates are slammed shut, the Japanese will already be inside.

By Aaron Bernstein in Fremont, with Dan Cook in Marysville, Pete Engardio in Smyrna, and Gregory L. Miles in Pittsburgh.

DISCUSSION QUESTIONS

1. What improvements have occurred under Japanese management? Why?
2. It is often suggested that American management practices must be adapted to foreign cultures to succeed. Are Japanese management practices more universal?
3. How does Japanese management differ in the use of human resources? Of what significance are these differences for organizational effectiveness?

KOREA'S NEWEST EXPORT: MANAGEMENT STYLE

ITS U.S. PLANTS ARE RUN BY EGALITARIANS WHO TAKE PRIDE IN BEING MORE FLEXIBLE THAN THE JAPANESE

JANUARY 19, 1987, P. 66

Hai Min Lee sits in the employee cafeteria at Samsung International Inc.'s northwestern New Jersey television assembly plant and eats brown rice from a plastic container. Wearing a blue Samsung uniform, the president leaves the immaculate, glass-enclosed lunchroom with its mountain view to go to his Spartan office, which overlooks the parking lot.

Lee's unassuming air is characteristic of the egalitarian management style South Korean companies have been quietly exporting to their U. S. subsidiaries since the early 1980s. Names such as Lucky-Goldstar, Samsung, Hyundai, and Daewoo, which once appeared only on foreign-made *TV*s, microwave ovens, and refrigerators, now are appearing on the doors of U. S. factories.

The Koreans, who have displayed a Japanese-like knack for exporting products to the U. S., are mimicking another Japanese strategy: building a stateside manufacturing base. Korean companies have invested only $200 million in U. S. plants,

compared with $2.6 billion spent by the Japanese. But the Korean investment could swell to $5 billion in the next decade, says the Korea Economic Institute of America.

Lucky-Goldstar Group was the first large Korean company to put down U. S. roots: It opened a *TV* and microwave plant in Huntsville, Ala., four years ago. Samsung followed in mid-1984.

GOOD LISTENERS. Don't confuse these immigrants with the Japanese, though. Yes, Koreans also espouse teamwork, employee participation, minimal hierarchies, and the corporation-as-family idea. But they tend to tailor their practices to the American style. "The Koreans are more flexible than we are," admits Shinichi Nishikawa, spokesman for Hitachi America Ltd. Adds Thomas G. Dimmick, a Samsung manager: "The Japanese are from a homogeneous society, so they are less accepting of anything that is not Japanese. Korea is a land of division, so the people are willing to listen and not get their feet stuck in concrete."

Koreans have yet to be as efficient as the Japanese in operating U. S. plants. The average American worker at a Korean-run plant produced $94,000 in goods in 1984, well above the $87,000 produced in comparable plants owned by U. S. companies. But that's far from the $155,000 produced by American workers at Japanese-run plants, according to the U. S. Bureau of Economic Analysis.

Management experts predict the gap will close. One reason: Korean managers work 70 to 80 hours a week, compared with 60 to 70 hours for Japanese and 50 for Americans. Another: "Most Korean managers were educated in the U. S., so they understand American thought processes," says Y. S. Chang, head of the Asian Management Center at Boston University.

The Korean formula appeals to Americans. "I used to work at an *RCA* plant, and they took the employees for granted," says Myrtel Sanders, a Samsung worker. "You can voice your opinion here. I once spoke up to a manager. I would have been fired anywhere else, but it was O. K. There's no union here either, but we get all the benefits we need." Korean management techniques are also getting attention from U. S. manufacturers. *USX* Corp. recently brought Pohang Iron & Steel Ltd. into a $300 million joint venture at the company's Pittsburg (Calif.) steel plant.

Like the Japanese, Korean managers encourage face-to-face meetings between management and workers. "It's strange that Americans make decisions by writing memos," says Won Lim, personnel director at Goldstar Electronics International. "We prefer the consensus style." Adds Lee: "The person who knows the factory process best should not be left out."

At Samsung, managers and workers exchange ideas freely on the plant floor or in the lunchroom. At monthly meetings workers celebrate birthdays and managers check on employees' personal needs. "If a worker is buying a house or getting a divorce, we get the company lawyer," says Lee, who had worked with Samsung for 17 years before moving to the U. S. two years ago.

The meetings also serve as gripe sessions, from which changes often emerge. For example, workers suggested raising the height of the belt carrying *TV*s through production stages so they wouldn't have to bend over and strain their backs. In another session, workers asked that music be piped into the austere plant to relieve boredom. The notion of worker participation is reinforced by Samsung's "power and free" assembly line. Workers can adjust the line's speed.

NO SINGING. Samsung's Korean managers know when to adapt their style to Americans. Instead of sitting in open office areas, as is the custom in Korea, Samsung managers are separated by lightly tinted glass. Samsung's U. S. employees don't sing a company song or take exercise breaks. But there are Korean touches. Employees address Lee as President Lee and Dimmick as Manager Tom.

The Koreans have a long way to go before their American workers measure up to the labor pool in Korea, where wages are one-sixth as high as the $6-and-up hourly scale in the U. S. And Lee admits it's sometimes an uphill fight to instill the post-Confucian work ethic. "If a Korean worker has a good idea or thinks of a way to eliminate a step from the assembly line, he says so," he explains. "Even if Americans have a good idea, they follow instructions. Koreans will do what's best for the company because the company is part of themselves." That concept will likely remain foreign to Samsung's U. S. workers.

By Laurie Baum in Ledgewood, N. J.

DISCUSSION QUESTIONS
1. What is a key difference between Korean and Japanese management?
2. At this writing, domestic Korean labor relations are reportedly facing riotous conditions, with enormous losses due to strikes. Management is reportedly rigid and autocratic. If these reports are accurate, what explains the very different picture of harmony and productivity in U.S. Korean plants described in the article?

HARVARD'S $30 MILLION WINDFALL FOR ETHICS 101

NOW COMES THE REAL PROBLEM: WHAT TO DO WITH THE GIFT

APRIL 13, 1987, P. 40

It could be called a case of throwing money at a problem that money helped produce. At least, that's what some skeptics made of outgoing Security & Exchange Commission Chairman John S. R. Shad's giant gift to the Harvard business school to fund a teaching program in ethics for *MBA*s.

The Mar. 30 gift of $30 million is intended, Shad says, to teach students that "ethics pays." To prove his point, the former E. F. Hutton & Co. vice-chairman is ponying up $20 million personally. Fellow Harvard alumni are expected to kick in the rest.

The impetus for all this generosity is the rash of insider-trading prosecutions. Many have touched Harvard deeply: Former Kidder, Peabody & Co. Managing Director Martin A. Siegel, who pleaded guilty to two felony counts of securities law violations, got his *MBA* at the school. Another, second-year student Randall D. Cecola, got the boot after he pleaded guilty to insider trading at Lazard Frères & Co.

DEFLATING. Still, the enormity of the gift, which exceeds the annual budgets of virtually every graduate business school in the country, shocked educators. "I've been trying to raise money for ethics at $100,000 a crack, and it's hard business," grouses Dean John W. Rosenblum of the University of Virginia's Darden Business School. "It's a little deflating to hear that a university which hasn't decided what to do in ethics gets $30 million." Adds Donald P. Jacobs, dean of Northwestern University's J. L. Kellogg School of Management: "I honestly don't know what I'd do with [all that money]."

Jacobs isn't alone in his puzzlement. Harvard itself may be overwhelmed by the gift. School officials vaguely say the grant will support research projects, faculty development, and awards to ethical business leaders. They don't elaborate. Harvard also doesn't require its students to study ethics—and maintains the grant won't change its policy. Moreover, the school's only *MBA* ethics teachers, Kenneth E. Goodpaster and Barbara Ley Toffler, were recently denied tenure. Adds a Harvard junior professor: "They still have to sell this to 100 tenured faculty who think the whole discipline is garbage."

That apparently is not the thinking at all graduate business schools. Some, like the Darden School, offer established programs in business ethics. Darden boasts three faculty members who teach a mandatory ethics course for first-year students. And its 18-year-old Center for the Study of Applied Ethics creates teaching materials, tracks scholarship in business ethics, and sponsors seminars in the subject for executives.

OBSESSION. Educators, though, are divided on how ethics should be taught. Some believe ethics should be part of every course, while others think it should be taught in separate classes by people trained in philosophy and business. They also question whether students can be taught to act ethically if they haven't already developed standards on their own. "You can't take morally disabled people and recreate them," says H. J. Zoffer, dean of the University of Pittsburgh's business school.

Harvard, however, certainly has the dollars to make a go of it. The students may be another matter—they refused to vote on an ethics code for the school in 1985. Says one Harvard teacher: "*MBA*s aren't interested in ethics. They're obsessed with getting jobs and competing with each other."

By John A. Byrne in New York, with Alex Beam in Boston

DISCUSSION QUESTION
Can ethics be taught? If so, how should it be taught?

WHY DIVESTING ISN'T ALWAYS THAT EASY

WHEN MULTIBILLION-DOLLAR PENSION FUNDS MUST SHED MAINSTAY SECURITIES, THE CHOICES BECOME COMPLICATED

MARCH 17, 1986, PP. 71-72

Roland M. Machold, New Jersey's investment director, is no fan of apartheid. Convinced that South Africa is a risky bet, he's kept securities of companies that do more than 5% of their business there out of the state's $13 billion pension funds. But now Machold is grappling with an August, 1984, law requiring him to sell all securities of companies with South African ties by 1987. "It's a terrible idea from a financial point of view," he says.

Machold has begun liquidating $3.5 billion worth of stocks, bonds, and commercial paper issued by companies with South African business. He's taken $6 million in losses, mainly from selling long-term bonds early, and run up $5 million in extra transaction costs. Another nagging worry: Somebody might sue him, claiming that in complying with state law he violated his fiduciary duty.

NO CHALLENGES. New Jersey's divestment effort is the biggest to date—and the most strict. But Machold's concerns are shared by more and more money managers, as pressure to divest comes to some of the largest public funds. Money managers for church groups, individuals, and small college endowments have been very successful at tailoring investments to social or political aims. "But it's not clear that they would have done as well managing a fund 10 times as large," concedes Jamie Heard, deputy director of the Investor Responsibility Research Center, a prime source on companies' involvement in South Africa.

So far no one has challenged divestment laws as conflicting with a fiduciary's duty to maximize gains for beneficiaries. New Jersey's Attorney General presumes that the law itself is ample protection. But New York City Assistant Comptroller Steven J. Matthews has prepared for a five-year limited divestiture of the city employees' $9.3 billion pension funds by getting lots of legal advice. As the only such plan to proceed without a law on the books, "We have to be extra careful to be litigation-proof," Matthews says.

Not everyone sees it as a problem. "Investments can be made that alter the human condition and still are prudent investments," argues Henry E. Parker. A former treasurer of Connecticut, Parker worked for and administered a 1982 law partly divesting the state's public pension fund. The law, which rejected nonsigners of the Sullivan Principles and some others, has been widely copied. The statute seems not to have hurt Connecticut's public retirees. Their fund, now $3.9 billion, has returned an average of 12.7% a year since mid-1980.

Of course, Connecticut's portfolio still includes plenty of companies that do business in South Africa. Total divestment brings more headaches. It means eliminating nearly all industrial equipment, chemical, drug, international oil, and major bank stocks, according to a 1984 study by Wilshire Associates. The universe of acceptable high-grade bonds and commercial paper would contract. Under a strict reading of New Jersey's law, banks now out of South Africa—but still with loans there—would be *verboten*. So might subcontractors of companies operating there. "We have a long road ahead of us to figure out who the hell we can invest with," Machold sighs.

Boston Co.'s F. Corning Kenly manages $40 million in South Africa-free funds. He thinks the problem is mostly in the minds—and techniques—of "fundamentalist" money managers.

Since they evaluate companies by qualitative criteria such as strategy and business mix, political restrictions botch up the process. Kenly, a technician, picks stocks by computer screening of market performance and other quantitative measures. Checking for South African connections "is just another screening to eliminate unwanted securities," he says.

HOTLY CONTESTED. The choices remaining, though, may look a lot different from the sorts of companies big, conservative institutions tend to embrace. Only about 350 U. S. companies operate in South Africa, but among them are 150 of the companies making up the Standard & Poor's 500-stock index—and 40% of its capitalization. That's a worry for New Jersey, where big holdings in big companies—such as a $300 million chunk of International Business Machines Corp.—are long-term mainstays. There's no one obvious substitute for *IBM*. Switching into a host of smaller companies can mean racking up additional research and transaction costs. And Machold thinks skipping blue-chip stocks could cost up to $25 million per year.

These still are hotly contested arguments. In a study for the Africa Fund, a nonprofit educational organization, Theodore A. Brown constructed a portfolio of the 124 largest South Africa-free companies, averaging $1.5 billion each in market value. Over five years, it outperformed, with slightly higher risk, a set of 124 comparable, nonrestricted stocks. In Michigan, consultants think divestment of the state's $12 billion pension fund would bring extra transaction costs of only $23 million over five years, since over that length of time many stocks would be routinely traded. The state may stretch out the process further, with large Michigan companies like General Motors Corp. among the last to go.

By Elizabeth Ehrlich in New York

DISCUSSION QUESTION

How do you reconcile the obligation of a financial manager to maximize gains for beneficiaries with prohibitions against investing in South Africa?

A NUCLEAR CLOUD HANGS OVER GE'S REPUTATION

UTILITIES SAY IT KNOWINGLY SOLD FLAWED PLANT DESIGNS
JUNE 15, 1987, P. 32

The serendipitous discovery of misplaced documents at a federal courthouse in Cincinnati has put General Electric Co. in the hot seat. The highly sensitive papers, which were supposed to be sealed, were left on a table in the court clerk's office, where a Cleveland newspaper reporter spotted them on May 28. They were written in 1975 and detail the pressure *GE*'s nuclear division had been under during the energy crisis to come up with a winning reactor design. Bowing to competitive forces, *GE* was risking its reputation by selling power plant designs that either hadn't been tested or contained potential flaws, according to memos written by a number of the division's engineers. For more than 10 years, *GE* zealously guarded these papers from public disclosure.

Now that the memos are out, government officials and a group of nuclear power plant owners are wondering whether *GE* should be held responsible for cost overruns worth billions. And consumer groups are demanding that at least one *GE*-designed plant be shut down. At the very least, says Nuclear Regulatory Commissioner James Asselstine, "this is likely to raise once again questions about the adequacy of *GE*'s design" for nuclear facilities.

GE calls the documents "ancient history" and claims they demonstrate *GE*'s concern for quality. But with utilities under pressure not to pass along cost overruns, *GE* may soon face huge claims from those who bought its boiling-water reactor designs, known as the Mark series. At least 22 reactors could be involved.

FALSE ASSURANCES? The documents were

among court papers filed in connection with a three-year-old lawsuit being tried in Cincinnati. Three Ohio utilities, which jointly owned the failed Zimmer nuclear project near Cincinnati, are suing *GE* for fraud. Zimmer, a *GE*-designed nuclear power plant, was converted to a coal-fired plant in 1984 because of design flaws and cost overruns. Zimmer's owners charge *GE* knowingly sold them a flawed design and seek damages that could reach $1 billion. *GE* wouldn't comment on the suit.

The memos concern an internal study called the Reed Report. Prepared in 1975 at *GE*'s nuclear division in San Jose, the 1,000-page report discussed the technical aspects of the Mark III, a new reactor system the company was about to market. Questions were raised in the memos about potential design problems. Wrote one engineer: "If [*GE*'s Nuclear Engineering Div.] is to nurture a quality image in the nuclear power industry in the next decade, it will have to be done through the medium of product service rather than product quality . . . since the product itself can't do so." The company later assured customers who had heard of the Reed Report that any problems had been resolved.

However, *GE* engineers who helped prepare the Reed Report say problems weren't being addressed. "If *GE* knew a problem existed with an earlier Mark series design, then they told the customer. But they didn't tell them about potential problems that existed with designs on the drawing board," says Dale G. Bridenbaugh, a 23-year veteran of *GE*'s nuclear program who resigned in 1976.

ANTINUKE AMMO. This is not the first time *GE* has had to defend its power-plant designs. *GE* is also being sued by the Nebraska Public Power District over the design of a nuclear plant, and the company faces another suit in Washington brought by the Washington Public Power Supply System over design flaws.

The issue will come to a head as electric utilities seek rate hikes from state regulators. Hearings on Perry I, a *GE*-designed nuclear facility managed by the Cleveland Electric Illuminating Co., are under way to determine if $800 million in redesign and retrofitting costs should be passed on to ratepayers. Already, *CEI* is under pressure from those involved in the hearings to look to recover some of those costs from *GE*.

The *GE* papers may also embolden antinuclear groups. Licensed only last year, Perry I is meeting stiff resistance. Critics want it shut down until the *GE* material is publicly examined. But the real issue, says J. Lee Bailey, a *CEI* spokesman, "isn't a safety issue. We spent $800 million making it safe. The key question is: Who will pay?"

Over the years, *GE* has refused to allow the Reed Report to be copied, showing it only to a few customers. Last year, after long negotiations, it let two *NRC* engineers read, but not keep, the study. But even tighter security surrounded the memos, a sort of freewheeling commentary on the Reed Report that details serious doubts engineers had about *GE*'s nuclear products. Even within the company, some of those who did know about them thought they had been destroyed long ago. Their resurrection in Cincinnati could prove costly indeed to General Electric and the reputation for quality it has been working hard to improve.

By Dan Cook in Cleveland,
with Bill Sloat in Cincinnati,
Russell Mitchell in Stamford,
and Barbara Starr in Washington

DISCUSSION QUESTIONS

1. Discuss GE's handling of the Reed Report and the memos commenting upon it.
2. One source in the article says, ". . .they [GE] didn't tell them [customers] about potential problems that existed with designs on the drawing board." What should be the obligations of a company to disclose such information? How should the magnitude and severity of the health and safety consequence of a design defect bear upon setting standards for disclosure? Suggest and defend some ethical guidelines for thinking through what a company ought to disclose about designs of its products that contain potential harm.

OSHA AWAKENS FROM ITS SIX-YEAR SLUMBER

IN THE PAST 16 MONTHS THE REGULATOR HAS LEVIED FINES OF $9 MILLION

AUGUST 10, 1987, P. 27

Last May, Occidental Petroleum Corp. Chairman Armand Hammer told stockholders that *IBP* Inc., Oxy's meatpacking subsidiary, was set to turn in "a record performance." Hammer was right—but not in the sense he intended. On July 21 the Occupational Safety & Health Administration jolted *IBP* with its largest proposed fine ever, $2.6 million, for doctoring accident and illness records.

IBP is not alone. After six sleepy years under the Reagan Administration, *OSHA* is abandoning what critics called a hands-off approach to workplace health and safety violations. Labor Secretary William E. Brock III has the agency flexing its muscles again.

NEW BALL GAME. A week after *IBP*, *OSHA* added General Dynamics and Uretek, a fabric-coating company, to its growing hit list. It announced a $615,000 penalty against General Dynamics Corp. for record-keeping violations and slapped a $480,000 fine on Uretek Inc. for health and safety infractions. *IBP* and *GD* say they will contest the fines, and Uretek is expected to do the same.

Secretary Brock is undeterred. According to agency insiders, more big fines are on the way. "The whole ball game has changed," says Patrick R. Tyson, *OSHA*'s chief from 1985 to 1986.

The agency's newfound vigor isn't limited to enforcement. In August an *OSHA* task force plans to unveil a new approach to standard-setting. Instead of issuing detailed rules for specific chemicals, which can take years, it will prescribe handling procedures for broad classes of substances. *OSHA* has issued only 16 standards since its creation in 1971, and many already are outdated. Supporters hope that the new strategy can break a notorious regulatory logjam.

Brock, who assumed his post in 1985 after the resignation of regulation foe Raymond J. Donovan, last year tapped John A. Pendergrass to lead the charge. Pendergrass, 61, a low-key former 3M Co. industrial hygienist, doesn't want to return to the contentious relations with employers that prevailed during the Carter Administration, but he has no qualms about going after flagrant violators. "We want employers to accept their responsibility, as they would in any other area of business," he says.

The enforcement push began in April, 1986, when *OSHA* fined Union Carbide Corp. $1.4 million for alleged bookkeeping, safety, and health violations. The company, without admitting wrongdoing, settled that case and a smaller one on July 24 by agreeing to pay $408,500 and make sweeping health and safety improvements. In the past 16 months, total fines have skyrocketed to $9 million, up from a paltry $14,166 in 1981.

Even so, many skeptics, conscious of the Reagan Administration's antiregulatory stance, wonder whether the agency's activism will last. Says Margaret Seminario, safety and occupational-health director for the *AFL-CIO*: "The program has been so weakened over the years, we're really waiting to see."

SCORING POINTS? Industry representatives are increasingly nervous. Some business executives think that the agency is trying to polish its tarnished image with headline-grabbing cases. Says Richard Boggs, whose firm, Organization Resources Counselors, advises companies on regulatory compliance: "A few [big cases] to get attention is fine, but after 18 months of doing this, you've got to question *OSHA*'s priorities."

Are Brock and Pendergrass coming on like the Untouchables just to score political points? *OSHA* officials deny it. *OSHA* Deputy Assistant Secretary

Frank White attributes the new activism to what he calls "a coming of age." He adds: "We're trying to have the maximum influence with limited resources."

"Limited" is right. After years of tight budgets, the agency has enough inspectors to visit only 4% of U. S. workplaces. Still, says former *OSHA* chief Tyson, "the price of poker has gone up." And executives who once might have ignored *OSHA* will think twice before taking that gamble.

By Hazel Bradford in Washington

DISCUSSION QUESTION

Discuss the desirability of society's allowing OSHA's efforts to rise and fall with the political preferences of elected administrations.

A DEATH AT WORK CAN PUT A BOSS IN JAIL

A TEXAS HOMICIDE CONVICTION MAY SPUR SIMILAR PROSECUTIONS

MARCH 2, 1987, PP. 37-38

Kenneth Oden, the 36-year-old prosecutor of Travis County, Tex., is not antibusiness. But he's making local companies nervous just the same. On Feb. 13, Oden won what may be a landmark conviction when an Austin employer pleaded no contest to criminally negligent homicide in the deaths of two employees. The case is sending a strong message to companies nationwide: If a worker is injured or killed on the job because of management negligence, corporate executives may find themselves with criminal records. Most people think "corporations are different from people in that they don't have a heart to feel or a butt to kick," Oden drawls softly. "Well, I think there is going to be some more butt-kicking."

After a 15-month legal battle, an Austin judge sentenced Joseph Tantillo, president of Sabine Consolidated Inc., a construction company, to six months in jail. Although Tantillo's previously clean record earned him probation and no jail time, legal experts believe this is the first time a corporate executive has been sentenced to a jail term for causing the death or injury of an employee through negligence. In addition, the Texas court ruled that federal labor laws did not preempt the state from filing criminal negligence charges. Tantillo is appealing. Charges against two other Sabine managers were dropped.

Corporate executives have been held criminally responsible before for injuries or death in the workplace. In 1985 three Illinois executives were convicted of murdering an employee who died after inhaling cyanide fumes. The decision is being appealed. The Texas decision, however, marks a departure by focusing on negligence. "Our theory wasn't that [he] intentionally killed the men," says Oden, "but that [he] showed a disregard for basic safety measures in the face of obvious risks to the employees."

Negligence, say *AFL-CIO* officials, is the key factor in the vast majority of health and safety violations. They argue that most injuries and deaths occur at companies such as Sabine where untrained workers, unaware of health threats, are exposed to chemicals or unsafe working conditions by managers or executives trying to cut corners.

ANGRY PROSECUTOR. In the Sabine case, two workers, Benjamin Eaton, 40, and Juan Rodriguez, 32, were working at the bottom of a 27-ft. trench on Sept. 10, 1985, when the walls buckled, trapping them beneath tons of earth. Both men smothered. The state alleged that the soil was unstable and that the trench should have been shored up by proper safety devices or its walls sloped less sharply to prevent a cave-in.

The incident might never have gone beyond a civil suit or a small fine if Oden hadn't become incensed by the poor working conditions at the site. Moreover, Oden and other local prosecutors are increasingly policing work sites as enforcement by the Occupational Safety & Health Administration has fallen off as a result of budget cutbacks. Searching for an innovative legal approach, Oden dusted off a 13-year-old Texas corporate liability statute that had never been used to prosecute an individual executive for this kind of offense.

The Sabine conviction will only intensify growing demands from public health activists to bring criminal charges against corporate executives whose companies violate health and safety standards. "Traditionally, corporations have been dealt with in civil courts, which is not a deterrent," says Russell Mokhiber, an attorney with the Corporate Accountability Research Group in Washington.

Whether the Sabine decision will lead to a host of similar cases nationwide depends, of course, on whether it survives likely appeals to state and federal courts. But in the meantime, Oden says he will press on. Other prosecutors may well follow.

By Jonathan Tasini in New York

DISCUSSION QUESTIONS
1. Should corporate executives be tried for the death or injury of an employee through negligently hazardous conditions at work?
2. Given that OSHA visits only a tiny percentage of workplaces and has not established adequate safety and health standards, will the courts be an alternative source of regulation? How much and by what methods should society protect the health and safety of workers? Discuss.